THE ENTREPRENEUR'S HANDBOOK

THE
ENTREPRENEUR'S
HANDBOOK
1

Joseph Mancuso

Head, Management Engineering Department
Worcester Polytechnic Institute

ARTECH AH HOUSE

Preface

In my opinion, a handbook should contain all the information needed on one topic. Just as The Microwave Engineers' Handbook offers all the curves, constants and information for its field, the entrepreneur's handbook is intended to be equally complete. The intent of this carefully selected grouping of readings is to provide a convenient single source of solutions for starting, financing, and managing a technical firm. While it is not perfect, from my knowledge it is the best presently available.

While working as a consultant to several hundred managers of technical firms (including many entrepreneurs) I recognized the need for such a handbook. Rather than attempting the colossal chore of writing the answer to everyone's problems, which I'm not even sure I could do in one lifetime, I've elected to conveniently package the best solutions already written by the experts. No single author is an expert in everything. However, specific experts within certain disciplines do exist. The result is a blend of contrasting views by experts in each field which I call The Entrepreneur's Handbook.

In 1973, I began the process of helping entrepreneurs solve day to day problems by publishing an easy-reader-book entitled "Fun 'n' Guts — the entrepreneur's philosophy," (Addison-Wesley). While this book intertwines telling it like it is and humor, it is intended to provide an equal balance of both reading pleasure and assistance in doing the job. This follow-up work, The Entrepreneur's Handbook, is offered to provide assistance only. While pleasure reading is enjoyable, the trade-offs in assistance are an undesirable by-product. The need for other views and solutions to operating problems is staggering. Consequently, I have published this immense two-volume reader in an attempt to make a serious dent in the operating needs of managers of technical enterprises.

The organization of these two volumes is chronological. The concept of an entrepreneur's life cycle, where one passes through phases which correspond to the successive phases of business growth, is totally my concept, as expressed in "Fun 'n' Guts." I have carried over this concept to this two-volume work. Depending upon where you are right now in your life cycle curve, may I suggest you jump in and begin reading at this point rather than at the beginning.

Whether or not every manager will benefit from reading each of the two volumes was not a criteria used to organize this book. Should everyone purchase both volumes of the two volume sequence? Depending upon an individual's needs, he may only need one of these two volumes. This choice depends not on the material in the handbook, but more on your position on the entrepreneur's life cycle. If you are in the venture financing stage, why not begin by reading that chapter first? Other chapters may provide value, too, but none are as likely to be as immediately helpful as your current need. However, having the material in a ready-access mode by your desk may eventually encourage you to "read ahead." When this happens, and I know the premium on your time, you may begin an active rather than a reactive program. If this occurs, you've warmed my heart and made it all worthwhile.

In any case, we both agree you have a tough assignment. So I offer you good luck and good reading.

Each manager need not read every article, and the articles each manager elects to read will be put into practice in differing manners. Collecting information, making decisions and accomplishing results is still the irreplaceable task of a manager. This handbook only offers a source of information and purposely makes little attempt to assist a manager in the other aspects of his role. But decisions are only as good as the information they are based upon, so, while not a complete how-to-do-it-kit, this handbook does offer a wide variety of insightful input information.

While this handbook is designed primarily for entrepreneurs, it will also be valuable to managers of small companies or divisions of larger companies. The issues of managing are strikingly similar. After all, what is the difference between the tasks of a manager of a small company and an entrepreneur? Not much, in my opinion. One is an internal entrepreneur while the other is an external entrepreneur. The greater differences between these two jobs is based upon the risk and reward structure, not day-to-day work. So, one handbook should be equally valuable for both.

What is vitally different about this handbook is the subject matter. This handbook will provide little value for entrepreneurs who operate gas stations, dry cleaners or restaurants. The selections of readings are focused on the problems of managing a significant manufacturing enterprise. In addition, the greatest value will be directed toward enterprises with a significant base of technology. To my knowledge, this is the first and only such collection of readings.

Starting, financing and managing a technical firm requires certain unique skills. The other competing texts on managing offer general solutions, while this book was compiled specifically for managers in technologically-based enterprises. In my opinion, the skills needed to succeed at this task are complex and difficult to master. They are certainly different from the skills needed by managers of non-technical enterprises.

Acknowledgement

Ted Saad and Bill Bazzy, grand and glorious entrepreneurs in their own right, had the foresight to encourage this manuscript in its embryonic stage. They saw the need, and provided invaluable assistance in pulling together the loose idea to make this a handbook. If each could slow down his business activities long enough to breathe easy, either or both of these men could have written any or all of these articles. They are successful both as entrepreneurs and managers of technological firms. In addition, Mike Miskin and Derwin Hyde at Artech House provided valuable inputs into the article selection and placement. Thanks, Mike, Derwin, Billy, and you, too, Rosemarie.

Mr. Jack Howell at Addison-Wesley deserves a smiling nod for his contribution to "Fun 'n' Guts — the entrepreneur's philosophy." An internal entrepreneur within a medium-sized company saw a need and nurtured my desire to help other entrepreneurs.

Students at Worcester Polytechnic Institute in Massachusetts were the real authors of this handbook. While studying within a management engineering curriculum, they put this dual academic training to practice. Without their inputs, I'd still be searching and evaluating articles for the handbook. Thank you, Don Gorsuch, Ron Bolin, Mike Murray, Dave Gerth, Dean Stratouly, and all the other students in my course in Small Business Policy (MG-3990). Oops, I almost forgot Mrs. Mary Eaton and Mrs. Gretchen Schwamb, the departmental secretaries in Management Engineering at WPI. Without their help, this handbook would be nothing more than illegible chicken scratches.

Numerous entrepreneurs, managers of technical firms, and academicians all provided advice on the selection of articles. Each group provided invaluable inputs. The authors of each of these articles (as well as the publishing journals) are the meaningful contributors to this handbook. Thank goodness each recognized a problem and invested the time to become expert and finally completed the loop by publishing a super solution.

Someday I'd hope to meet each author individually. After you read over the material, I'm sure you will feel the same way. While I don't agree with every position of every author, I certainly value their views. The selection criteria was more concerned with evidence offered to support an opinion than the value of the opinion per se.

My wife and two daughters never asked "why" when Daddy was working at his desk at the basement. They unselfishly accepted the notion that helping entrepreneurs is more noble than Daddy rolling on the floor playing with the children. Let's hope they were right and let's all say thanks to my girls. And, by the way, don't forget to thank your family for their sacrifices, too. They deserve it without exception.

While I've accepted and valued all these inputs, the final selection and organization rested with me. The inadequacy is mine, and mine alone. The buck starts and stops here.

Dedication

With uneasy expectations that these two volumes will be your silent source for solutions, I dedicate this work to the teachers who taught me.

Fred Adler, Reavis & McGrath
Alan Barrett, B.T. U. Engineering
Roger Carlson, C-O Manufacturing
Tony Chapporone, A crook
Peter Clapp, Free lance
Bill Constantine, Gurnard Manufacturing
My Dad
Bob Dentler, Boston University
Dom Emello, Vector Sales
John Engelsted, O.S. Walker Co.
Joe Ferriera, Boston University
Bill Grogan, WPI
The Heaps, Hancock Paint Co.
Paul Hines, New England Instrument
Bob Lalli, Vector Sales
Ted Levitt, Harvard Business School
Matt Lorber, Printer Technology, Inc.
Bob Meyer, Aerosol Techniques, Inc.
Peter Ottowitz, Glamour Care, Inc.
Gordon Paul, University of Massachusetts
George Perraudin, Lanewood Labs
Marcel Plante, Steinerts Music Store
Jack Reynolds, Free lance
Richard Riggs, Riggs Investment Co.
Ted Saad, Sage Labs
Al Schwieger, WPI
Art Snyder, Bank of the Commonwealth
Ray Stata, Analog Devices
Hank Taunsend, M.C.A.
Bernie Triber, Lanewood Labs
Frank Tucker, Harvard Business School
Cliff Tuttle, Aerovox Capacitor Corp.

Table of Contents

4-8 Kelley, Albert J., "Venture Capital" from his book published by the Management Institute School of Management, Boston College, Chestnut Hill, Boston, MA, 1971.

This article defines what a venture capitalist is and outlines the techniques he employs to achieve his goals and the degree of risk associated with this type of investment. What motivates people to pool their resources in high-risk ventures? What are the sources of financing? Professor Kelley is Dean of the School of Management at Boston College and a world-recognized expert on venture capital.

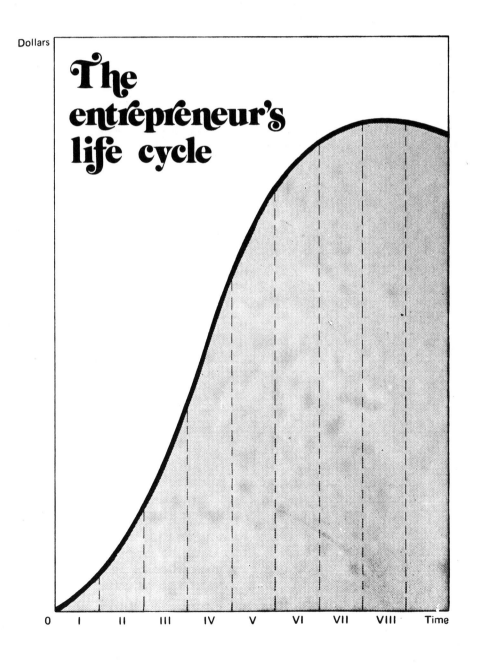

CHAPTER I

WHO IS THE ENTREPRENEUR?

An entrepreneur is someone who creates an on-going business enterprise from nothing. A "technical entrepreneur" accomplishes this objective by utilizing technology to build an enterprise. What attributes characterize a technical entrepreneur? What environmental factors and experiences have influenced his personality development, needs for achievement and motivational drives — his willingness to gamble in order to create a new business enterprise? These are difficult questions. However, information has become available in the last two decades from a group of people who have been systematically investigating entrepreneurs and now their importance in the economic success of the country is becoming better understood. By reading through these two volumes, an entrepreneur can gain insight and understanding of the characteristics common to entrepreneurs. This information can be valuable before and during the entrepreneurial experience and these readings can provide data points for entrepreneurs already submerged in the process to study.

An entrepreneur is an innovator capable of combining varied ingredients to produce and market a product or service. He is able to put together the people, the financing and the production and marketing resources for a newly-created firm. But foremost, he is the one who recognizes potentially profitable opportunities, he is the one who conceptualizes the venture strategy, and he is willing to become the driving force which successfully moves the idea from the laboratory to the marketplace. A technical entrepreneur does all this in the complex world of technology. This added feature makes this process even more difficult; the problems of comprehending technology alone can be staggering.

Based upon my research, I have concluded that a technical entrepreneur is usually the first child in a family having a self-employed father whose fatherly guidance results in the entrepreneur's high need for achievement. Formal education may be pursued to the extent that a Master's degree is obtained, but entrepreneurial tendencies emerge early during formal schooling. He has lots of energy and is willing to drive hard to make his chosen course of action work.

Moderate risks are taken but only against realistic and achievable odds. One preliminary study on personal values indicated that entrepreneurs rate higher than average in aesthetic, theoretical, leadership and need for recognition and achievement, and lower in practical-mindedness, conformity and need for support.[1]

At the time of starting his first business, the successful entrepreneur is typically in his thirties and he is married to an exceptionally supportive wife, and he has saved a little seed money according to my research. He has developed a probing curiosity about technological advancements, business affairs and people. An entrepreneur possesses keen insight into himself and his environment. Although he has family responsibilities, the successful entrepreneur is still willing to make the personal sacrifices required in starting the new business. So are the other members of his family, or, if they are not, divorce and family tragedy are the outcome of choosing between career and family.

The Forbes article, "The Incurables," offers insight into an interesting group of successful entrepreneurs. The work of great Americans such as Fairchild and Lear are discussed. These men are symbolic of the free enterprise system in America. This article can be contrasted to the more scholarly work of John Hornaday and John Aboud as they offer results of research into the characteristics of entrepreneurs. By using psychological tests on a group of 60 entrepreneurs they conclude scales of achievement, support, independence and leadership are good predictors of entrepreneurial drives.

A comparison with the article above is offered by Herb Wainer and Irwin Rubin as they report on "The Motivation of Research and Development Entrepreneurs." These last two studies were conducted during the past few years and they present an interesting contrast in opinion. The need for power and achievement of 51 entrepreneurs in technology based companies was the focus of the research by Wainer and Rubin.

All entrepreneurs, especially the technical types, are extremely task oriented. Given a choice between doing and thinking, they choose doing. In the interview with Dr. David McClelland he describes this drive as the person's need for

1

achievement. He characterizes high need achievers as preferring to personally be responsible for solving problems and setting goals and then to measure attainment via their own efforts. They also have an intense need for feedback on how well they are performing in accomplishing their stated goals. McClelland views entrepreneurs as having these same characteristics as high need achievers. He believes that people possessing a latent need for achievement can be taught achievement motivation, which will result in the individual undertaking either new entrepreneurial activities or a more aggressive level of his present entrepreneurial venture.

Although entrepreneurs may be characterized by their high need for achievement, it is of more interest to focus on those additional characteristics that differentiate the successful entrepreneurs from the unsuccessful ones. For example, is the successful, high growth firm differentiated from the declining or financially plagued firm by how well the entrepreneurial leader understands the marketing environment — the needs, wants and buying habits of the consumer — or how well he senses the forces resulting from changing economic, technological, political or other macro-environmental factors? How important is his sense of his product's competitive advantage? Do successful entrepreneurs accurately perceive their employees and their degree of cohesiveness and contentment with the entrepreneur's commitments? Is a high need to dominate or to hold power complementary with the high achievement motivation or with successful ventures? The following articles build on McClelland's work and each address these complex issues.

In "The R & D Entrepreneur: Profile of Success," Harry Schrage states his answer to these questions by using data obtained in his research on entrepreneurs in technologically based companies. One of his more significant conclusions is the correlation between the entrepreneur's degree of awareness of the environment and the profitability of the venture. The more successful entrepreneurs were characterized by their more accurate perception of themselves and their customers.

Forbes, "The Entrepreneur's Luck and Pluck and a Strong Succession," as well as International Management's "Idea Man Extraordinary," each offers insight into large scale business success. Forbes offers an overview on the developments within the top 100 firms while Mr. Sherman

Fairchild is analyzed in depth in the final article. One view is from the top down while the other is from the bottom up. Each has a valuable and unique perspective.

All the above authors generally agree that the entrepreneur is not motivated by money, but rather by high motivational needs, especially his need to achieve. His awareness of peoples needs and his technical knowledge enable him to perceive profitable business opportunities that others have neglected. An underlying notion from these past studies of entrepreneurs, which is primarily a phenomenon of the U.S. capitalistic system, is that the transfer of knowledge gained from studying the U.S. entrepreneurs to other less developed countries can significantly increase economic development. These characteristics of entrepreneurs are related to certain sociological factors in the entrepreneur's childhood, and then molded by personal experiences in later adult life. Further research should reveal additional parameters that will help to explain the complex individual which academicians have labeled an entrepreneur. The notion is that once he is better understood, he can be either transplanted or created for the good of an economy.

---

[1] Komives, J.L., "A preliminary study of the personal values of high technology entrepreneurs," Technical Entrepreneurship: A Symposium, Eds. A. Cooper & J. Komives, The Center for Venture Management, Milwaukee, Wis., 1972.

The Entrepreneurs

Luck and Pluck—and a Strong Succession

As many of yesteryear's Top 100 weakened or died, others rose to take their places. Here's a look at the companies that have climbed onto the Top 100 list since 1917—and at the extraordinary men who built them.

SITTING in his Beverly Hills office, the former MCA Corp. mansion, Litton Industries Chairman Charles B. (Tex) Thornton was telling how he started his company and pushed it from nothing to assets of $743 million in just 14 years. Litton, as he explained it, was born of his personal frustration. Said he, choosing his words carefully, "I saw opportunities I was unable to follow up working for other men."

Other people learn to live with the frustrations they meet in daily life. But men like Thornton are different. They balk at taking orders they do not respect. They see opportunities that others overlook. His great energy and driving ambitions blocked, first at Ford Motor and later at Hughes Aircraft, Thornton had to start his own company to try out his ideas.

In a way, Litton's story is typical of many of the new names on the 1967 list of the Top 100 industrial corporations. Almost every one of them— General Tire & Rubber, Lockheed, Georgia-Pacific—is a monument to the drive, talent and energy of a single man or of a small group of men. Existing companies couldn't hold them. Nor were they satisfied with small successes. They started companies, or took over small or faltering ones, infused them with their own zeal and enthusiasm and attracted like-minded men.

Too Many du Ponts

A close observer of the business scene puts it like this: "There are two kinds of companies in the U.S.: Those run by any tradition, by old-school

ties, by the rules; and those run by abnormal men." By "abnormal," he means abnormally ambitious, abnormally strong in motivation, in drive. These men would most likely agree with Joseph Wilson of Xerox when he says, "You have to be very naïve so as not to see how deep a risk you're taking." Such are the men who run most of the companies that outpace industry as a whole.

It's true of the recent newcomers, but it's an old story in American industry. Take Sears, Roebuck, now one of the great business organizations in the world. Sears is the lengthened shadow of two exceptional men: Julius Rosenwald, a Chicago apparel manufacturer who made Sears king of mail-order business; and General Robert E. Wood who made it the world's greatest department store chain. Wood is the kind of man Tex Thornton could appreciate. Before World War I, Wood went to work for du Pont. "He stayed there awhile," recalls Sears' ex-Chairman Charles Kellstadt, "looked around, saw a lot of du Ponts in the place and figured there wasn't much chance for him. So he got into [Montgomery] Ward where they made him a vice president. But he was a vigorous fellow and he had strong ideas on merchandising and they wouldn't listen. Someone told Rosenwald to grab Wood and he did.

"Rosenwald didn't have too much confidence in Wood's idea of getting into stores, but he did have a great deal of confidence in the General," added Kellstadt. Rosenwald gave

Wood the go-ahead to open the first Sears store (on Chicago's West Side; it's still there), and the rest is history. Wood never learned to live with his frustrations. He met them head on. In so doing he made business history.

In much the same way, the great Kaiser companies were created, not by money or monopoly, but by the will and talent of Henry J. Kaiser. Radio Corp. of America would have remained a relatively small company without David Sarnoff's visionary leadership. International Telephone & Telegraph was built by the great Sosthenes Behn; it was revived by the hard-driving Harold S. Geneen.

Geneen was cut from the same mold as the others. He never stayed long in any one place, partly because he was hard to get along with, partly because he was constantly in a hurry—in a hurry to be his own boss. He started with the New York accounting firm of Lybrand, Ross, then was chief accountant at American Can, controller at Bell & Howell and assistant to the vice president at Jones & Laughlin Steel. At Raytheon, as executive vice president, he was second in command, but he started looking around when he tired—after a scant three years—of waiting for a crack at the top job. Donald C. Power was an immensely successful attorney, but money and comfort weren't enough for him. He took the presidency of General Telephone, remade the company in his own image as GT&E. He took only eight years to make this once-sleepy telephone company into one of the great billion-dollar corporations.

No Soft Jobs Wanted

The true entrepreneur is a man who, when faced with the choice between security and a challenge, will pick the latter every time. After World War II, Continental Oil had a chance to break out of its regional, domestic boundaries by joining the industry's exploration rush. But aging, ailing President Dan Moran was not equal to the task, and succession was wanting within the company. Conoco's directors went after Leonard F. McCollum, who was making a name for himself at Jersey Standard, and negotiated two years to get him. "I was happy as a possum at Standard," said

McCollum later, as he accepted plaudits for having built Continental into a middle-sized international giant. McCollum had been poor as a youth, and the chance of the top job at Jersey must have had its appeal for him. But the greater lure to his entrepreneurial temperament proved to be the challenge of building Continental. Conoco ranked 16th among oil companies on FORBES' 1945 list, 9th on the 1967 list. The value of management? Conoco's stock price has appreciated sevenfold since McCollum took over.

The impressive thing about these entrepreneurs is that they don't necessarily need a growth industry like telephone or electronics to operate in. The late J. Spencer Love built a great enterprise, which is among today's Top 100 companies, in, of all places, the textile industry. Like the others, Love was possessed of monumental self-confidence. Everyone told him debt was dangerous, especially in a cyclical business like textiles. "Dangerous!" he sneered. "Why shouldn't I borrow when I get money at 5% and it's tax deductible and I can make 10% on it? I believe in borrowing all I can." Today, Burlington Industries' debt-to-equity ratio of 34% is among the highest in the industry.

To get borrowed capital to leverage his equity, Love used every trick in the book. He set up some 30 different operating companies, using the credit of the stronger ones to support and expand the weaker ones that had trouble borrowing on their own. Caught in a storm of technological change, he didn't try to fight it. Using his borrowed money, he kept his plants as up-to-date and modern as was humanly possible. The result is that Burlington gets more sales per employee than all but one or two of the major companies in the industry.

Change the name and the industry, throw in an even greater dose of daring and you have the same story with Owen Cheatham of Georgia-Pacific. In the mid-Fifties, some of his shrewd, conservative competitors were convinced that little Georgia-Pacific was going broke. As against $47 million in equity capital (in 1956), it had $126 million in debt. And paying fancy prices for timber reserves! What would happen to G-P when prices dropped? But Cheatham, one of the original

financial minds of this generation, was not just indulging in wild gambling. He was simply placing all the bets he could get on what he regarded as a sure thing: that growing demand and growing utilization of the entire tree were going to make timber an increasingly valuable asset. He got the Prudential and Metropolitan insurance companies, more venturesome than most, to lend him the money, using the timber itself as self-liquidating collateral. The results? Turn to page 103. There Georgia-Pacific is shown as the company among the more recent arrivals to today's Top 100 list whose stock market performance has led all the rest. From 1945 to 1967, a $1,000 investment in its common stock has grown to almost $95,000.

Find 'Em & Trust 'Em

Being human, these entrepreneurs can make mistakes. One of the most common is an egotistical failure to develop a strong successor. This is why the list of dropouts from the Top 100 includes companies built by great entrepreneurs, companies like Curtiss-Wright, American Standard and Koppers. And that is why the truly great entrepreneur is not just a risk-taker; he is also a great leader.

A case in point is Monsanto. Edgar Monsanto Queeny, now 69, took over the presidency in 1928 from his father John F. Queeny, who had built the business by breaking the German stranglehold in artificial sweeteners. To son Edgar fell the challenge to make the company greater, in fact, to build it into the giant it has become today. And he did it by acquisitions, made in a way that reveals his ability.

Queeny saw that what Maytag and others were doing to home laundering had great implications for the chemical industry. He realized that automatic washing machines would require more powerful cleaning compounds than the old elbow-grease-powered washboards. Therefore he acquired a small Alabama-based chemical company that was doing research in phosphate cleaning compounds, built a huge plant to turn out the compounds, and made Monsanto the great supplier of the basic cleaning stuff to the detergent industry.

Good leader that he was, Queeny realized he needed talent for his company; ordinary men wouldn't do. In 1936 he brought Dr. Charles Allen Thomas to Monsanto by buying Thomas' small company. Salary alone wouldn't have attracted Thomas; indeed, larger companies than Monsanto had been trying to lure Dr. Thomas and his partner, Carroll Hochwalt. So Queeny did something unusual for the time: He gave Thomas stock in Monsanto. Thomas put Monsanto into plastics and later into synthetic fibers, which, more than anything else, pushed Monsanto into the billion-dollar class.

Men Like Themselves

Herbert Dow was another who combined impatience with an understanding of the human factor. As general manager of Midland Chemical in Midland, Mich., he used that town's great brine deposits to break the German monopoly on bromides. But he wanted to go beyond that, using the brine for a whole family of chemicals. The stockholders and the board turned him down; they wanted dividends, not pie in the sky. Dow left his safe job in 1895 and started Dow Process Co. Five years later Dow took over the faltering Midland company, and Dow was well on its way to becoming the fourth-biggest chemical company in the U.S.

Like Thornton today, Wood and Dow yesterday were impatient men. If the companies they worked for wouldn't give them what they wanted, they started their own. But they were more than merely impatient. Once in control of their own destinies, they tried to create an atmosphere in which men like themselves could flourish.

Like other successful entrepreneurs, Dow succeeded in instilling his successors with his own spirit. In the late 1930s Dow pioneered in petrochemicals, being among the first to build in the now-booming Texas Louisiana Gulf Coast area.

It was at that time that Dow chemists came up with two promising discoveries, styrene and acrylonitrile; the former a basic plastic, the latter an element in plastics and synthetic fibers. Dow chose to develop styrene and therefore benefited from the demand for butadiene-styrene synthetic rubber during the war. But, having limited resources, it let acrylonitrile pass it by; and as a result, says President Ted

Doan today: "We never got off the ground, we never made money in fibers." Monsanto developed acrylonitrile, formed Chemstrand Corp., and with the growth of fibers since the war is ahead of Dow today in assets and revenues. Ironically, Dow, not saddled with the depressed fibers market, leads in net income on the 1967 list.

This much is clear: An entrepreneur, if his work is to last, must be a kind of Pied Piper of talent. Take William L. McKnight, who built Minnesota Mining & Manufacturing. Chairman Bert Cross says, "The best thing he ever did was to hire Richard P. Carlton [president from 1949 to 1953]. He was an electrical engineer by training. He was great with technical people; they gravitated to him. He got us a lot of good men." Their inventions and innovations opened up market after market. Cross gives this example: "In 1929 we bought a company that owned a hill of quartz. Dick Carlton asked our technical people, 'What do we do with it?' The ideas flowed in: Use it as chicken feed, use it in bird cages. The one that clicked was to make permanently colored roofing granules of it. Today," Cross says, "we own four quartz quarries." Because 3M challenges its people, Cross adds, "If a man can't find anything to interest him in this company, nothing interests him. He must be dead."

Again and again, in talking with the great entrepreneurs and with the men who know them, there is a recurring note: Find the right people and trust them. Julius Rosenwald trusted General Wood, even though he distrusted Wood's idea. Ernest Breech's job at North American Aviation in 1934 was to convert it from a holding company to a manufacturing company. He got the best man he knew, Dutch Kindelberger, chief engineer at Douglas Aircraft, and let him use his head. The planes Kindelberger designed and built soon had the company flourishing. In recalling the turning points in his own career, General David Sarnoff recalls a similar experience when RCA was jointly owned by General Electric and Westinghouse. "General Electric was interested in manufacturing mass items, so I began to propagandize my music box with Owen Young [GE's chairman]. They called in an efficiency

engineer and he reported to Young. His advice was: 'What's this young fellow talking about music in the home for? He's supposed to be running a communications business; make him stick to it!' Young read the report and threw it in the wastebox, and RCA as we know it today was born."

The aircraft industry has been an entrepreneurial business if ever there was one. But as the industry grew, so did the need for men who could not only build but could put their imprint on a whole organization.

This is where William Boeing of Boeing succeeded and Donald Douglas of Douglas failed. Like Douglas, Boeing was an aircraft pioneer. Quitting Yale a year before he was to have graduated, he caught the then-prevalent flying bug and started one of the two dozen or so companies then hand-building planes in the U.S. In 1927 Boeing made his big gamble: He put in a bid to fly the mail from Chicago to San Francisco. He got the contract but at a price that everyone was convinced would break him: $2.89 a pound *vs.* a bid of $5.09 from his closest rival.

But Boeing had no intention of committing economic suicide. He was convinced he could *build* a plane that could carry mail at $2.89 a pound and make money on it. He set about designing a plane around Pratt & Whitney's new Wasp engine. He bought 25 engines and built 25 Model 40-B biplanes. It was a highly efficient plane, but that wasn't Boeing's only ace. He designed his craft to carry passengers, something no other mail plane did. It carried only two of them, but the fare was $200 one way. With the aid of passenger fares, he figured he could come out ahead on each flight. He was right.

In similar fashion, Boeing was ahead of the pack in 1934. The U.S. Army Air Corps invited bids on a new multiengine production bomber. In those days "multiengine" meant *two* engines, but Boeing came up with a four-engine job, the B-17. Douglas, with a more conventional plane, got the contract, but the Army Air Corps decided to encourage Boeing's bold experiment. The company got a contract for 14 of its B-17s for flight testing.

When World War II came, the Boeing Flying Fortress, as the big plane was known, dropped the bombs that weakened Germany. Out of it, too, came the far bigger B-29 and, eventually, the B-47 and B-52 jet bombers and their refueling tanker, the KC-135. That, in turn, led to the family of jet airliners that has made Boeing the No. One commercial plane manufacturer. Its great success has been reflected in the price of its stock: $1,000 invested in 1945 is now worth nearly $56,000.

Bill Boeing dropped out of the company in 1933, but the management in depth that he built continued under his successors, including current President William M. Allen. That was where Boeing's bitter rival, Donald Douglas, went wrong.

In the Thirties Douglas captured first place from Boeing in the air-transport market with the series that culminated in the handy and efficient DC-3. Douglas was lulled into complacency when its big DC-6, successor to the DC-3, led the postwar market for piston planes. It hung back on jets, hoping that the DC-7 would constitute a new generation of piston planes. But the jets began sweeping the market and Douglas came late with its DC-8.

Worst of all, when Donald Douglas Sr. passed the presidency on to his son in 1957, he failed to provide the kind of in-depth management that Boeing had. The new team failed to cope with losses on the DC-8 and the financial problems growing out of the DC-9. The Top 100 tables tell the story: In 1945, Douglas ranked 80th among the industrial firms, Boeing 114th. On the 1967 list, however, the positions are drastically changed: Boeing is 40th, while Douglas before its recent merger with McDonnell, was only 83rd. This year Douglas was taken over by McDonnell Aircraft Co., headed by James McDonnell who ran a St. Louis aircraft company that had done a volume of only $21 million at the height of World War II when Douglas' revenues were well over $1 billion. McDonnell is able to give Douglas the management depth Douglas had not built for itself.

Big Flops, Big Successes

The great entrepreneurs are certainly not infallible. Boeing suffered several serious setbacks, one of which, involving the big Stratocruiser in the late Forties, plunged it into the red. But the important point is that Boeing had the management flexibility and ingenuity to survive the blow and come back. So did Lockheed, which was badly hurt by heavy losses on its big Electra turboprop, a serious marketing miscalculation. Douglas lacked that resiliency.

Henry Kaiser avoided Douglas' mistake. Kaiser, flushed with his shipbuilding successes in World War II, decided he could crack the auto business. His Kaiser-Frazer Corp. lost $114 million before throwing in the sponge (it survives in the fast-growing Kaiser Jeep Corp. today). But Henry Kaiser did not have all his eggs in one basket. Between 1939 and 1946, he plunged into cement, magnesium, shipbuilding, steel and aluminum as well, borrowing freely to do so. Though heavy interest payments often held down their profits, his companies grew so rapidly that today they rank second in aluminum, fourth in gypsum, ninth in cement and tenth in steel.

Why was Kaiser so successful? True to his rugged, confident self, he adopted an all-or-nothing attitude while breaking into these industries. He scoffed at those who predicted that a recession would follow the war. He expected a boom in autos, in housing, in consumer goods. He wasn't one to hedge his bets by building tiny steel or cement mills. He built big, and therefore very efficient, ones. The great demand that did in fact follow the war's end proved the soundness of his plan. And what if the pessimists had been right? What if there had been a major recession? Kaiser might have lost control but he would still have founded some great companies—as did William C. Durant, the man who founded General Motors, only to lose control to the du Ponts in the recession of 1920. Kaiser, who died three weeks ago at 85, left the empire in the hands of his son, Edgar, and a brilliant management team.

Royal Little's Textron was taking it on the chin in the late Forties, when the textile business went into the doldrums. A less flexible man would simply have ridden out the hard times. But Little was too impatient for that. Where other great entrepreneurs switch jobs when frustrated, Little did them one better; he switched industries. "I didn't see how the textile business would ever be good again in my lifetime," he says. He gradually sold off the textile properties and reinvested the money where he could get a better return. To help him, he called in banker Rupert Thompson, who pushed the company into watchbands, power saws, helicopters and more.

It was Royal Little who put Textron together; it was Rupert Thompson who made it work. Thompson realized sooner than most that the nature of the corporation was changing, and he molded Textron to the changes. "I think," he told FORBES, "that the lesson of our company is not to try to be restricted by products, but rather to be motivated by the use of capital. I don't think this type of company existed years ago." The Textron-type company, devoted not to making any particular products but to keeping capital gainfully employed, has this big advantage, according to Thompson: It protects against technological obsolescence. Steel or railroads or shoe-leather or printing may become obsolete, and product-oriented companies decline; but a Textron is in so many product lines that some are always gaining ground at least as fast as others are losing. As for the losers, they can be shucked off and the capital reinvested in growing businesses.

Thus stated, the idea seems sensible enough, but it was radical when Textron first tried to practice it. It took courage. "How could one company run so many different businesses?" the conservatives wanted to know. Textron, like Litton and others, has shown that it can—given the tools of modern management.

With assets of $501 million, Textron didn't quite make the Top 100 list this year, but at the pace it is growing it will almost certainly make the next one. Moreover, its success has influenced many another company to adopt a less rigid approach.

Tenneco Inc. didn't go quite as far as Textron in diversification, but it did shift the whole emphasis of its growth. Gardiner Symonds had the vision to foresee the dynamic growth of gas pipelining in the Forties and Fifties—and then its gradual slowing down. Over the last ten years, he successfully diversified into oil, chemicals and packaging, and this year, arranged to buy Kern County Land. Pipelines now provide only 40% of Tenneco's revenues. And Tenneco, which was just a few years old in 1945, has shot up to the 17th position in today's Top 100 companies.

How could Symonds move so fast without stumbling? "We buy companies with good management," he says. "Many people are willing to sell us their companies so they can retire to Florida. But this isn't what we look for. We want companies with young executives who will stay and run them for us. I can't run the company myself; I have to depend on others."

You've Got to Let Go

Kaiser, Little and Symonds had learned a lesson. Let Tex Thornton, speaking from his own experience, tell what it was:

"You wonder why we don't have more multibillion-dollar companies around. There are so many that start with promise, but what happens? I think it's because one, two or three men build the company to the extent of their capacity and don't let go. They feel insecure if they don't make all the decisions. Yet the company's growth has saturated their capabilities. Three times I've started small, and as the companies grew, I've had to discipline myself to decentralize. It wasn't easy the first time, but you've got to do it or you can't grow."

And it works both ways: "If you don't grow," says Xerox' Joseph Wilson, "you won't attract the kind of people you need. If the growth of copying should slow down and we were content to grow at, say, 5%, our best people would lose interest; they'd leave in droves. We *have* to diversify."

In other words you need a leader, but the leader can't do it alone. He must attract others like himself.

Another great company-builder, Dr. Henry Singleton of Teledyne, Inc.,

says the same thing in another way: "A great corporation never has to go outside for its president."

It's no different in a family-run company. General Tire & Rubber's founder, William F. O'Neil, had three ambitious sons in the company. "He didn't give us responsibility," says Michael G. (Jerry) O'Neil, General's 45-year-old president. "We took it. I grabbed a lot of it, the stuff he didn't want to do."

ITT was in bad shape in 1957 and had to create a committee of the board to look elsewhere for a new president. That was a sign of weakness, but an attempt was made to correct it—and they did find the right man. After Harold Geneen quit the second spot at Raytheon to take the top spot at ITT, things started to happen. Since Geneen took over, the company's sales have tripled, earnings per share have more than doubled.

About the same time ITT was going downhill, National Steel fell on bad times. The brilliant but cantankerous Ernest Weir, whose Weirton Steel was the key element in the 1929 merger that formed National, presided over its swift rise, based on its concentration on the lighter steels. But Weir stayed too long at the helm. Says President George Stinson discreetly, "Towards the end of Mr. Weir's tenure, he was not as aggressive in planning the company's growth as he had been." When Weir finally retired in 1957 at age 81, George Humphrey and Thomas Millsop got the company back on track, then brought in lawyer Stinson to manage its resurgence. Yet despite the work of the last decade, National's 1967 rank among the Top 100 is 12 places below its 1945 rank.

Who's in Charge?

Almost as bad as having to go outside is the case of the company that has a succession that can't measure up to the man who created the company.

That is what befell General Dynamics, the creation of hard-driving John Jay Hopkins. Starting with tiny Electric Boat Co. and merging with much bigger companies like Canadair and Consolidated-Vultee, Hopkins had by 1957 pulled together a company with sales of $1.6 billion. He died before

the nearly autonomous divisions could be brought under good managerial controls, however. While he was alive, only his dominating personality made the company hang together. The man who got the top spot when Hopkins died, leaving an uncertain line of succession, was Frank Pace. But Pace was no match for the task of whipping this sprawling company into shape. It ran aground on its biggest project, the Convair 880/990, which eventually lost $490 million. Today, under Chairman Roger Lewis, GD is well along on the road back to recovery. But it was a close call and it took Lewis, an outsider (he had been executive vice president at Pan American World Airways), to save the day.

There are interesting parallels between the near-disaster at General Dynamics and the near-disaster at Chrysler. On the surface they were different: GD's was a dramatic throw of the dice that came out wrong; in Chrysler's case, it was a slow downward drift. Both were companies that came up fast under a great entrepreneur but failed to develop depth of leadership. And both came back smartly when they got it—with the result that the work of the entrepreneur was salvaged and both stayed in the big time.

Walter Chrysler built his company from 4% of the market in 1925 to 26% in 1933; this at a time when the Hudsons, the Auburns, the Graham-Paiges were declining.

In a 1929 interview with FORBES Founder B. C. Forbes, Walter Chrysler told his own story. It was a story different in its details but not in its essentials from that of Tex Thornton or Robert E. Wood. It was the story of a mechanically minded boy who worked his way up to a responsible job with the Chicago & Great Western Railroad at 33, then quit because he realized that few men with his background ever got to the top in railroading. Besides, he had already decided that the future belonged not to the railroad, but to individual transportation as represented by the motor car.

Chrysler later cured a sick Buick operation, making a fortune in General Motors stock in the process and ending up as executive vice president. He moved on to take over and restore to health an ailing Willys-Overland at an annual compensation of over $1 million a year. That didn't hold him, either. In 1921 investment bankers brought Chrysler a moribund auto company, Maxwell Motor. Four years later, he changed its name to Chrysler and made it such a force in the industry that it was able to absorb the big Dodge Brothers company in 1928. By 1929 $1,000 worth of the old Maxwell stock purchased in 1923 had grown to $33,800.

But whereas Alfred Sloan built General Motors into an organization that could carry on, Chrysler did not. In 1935 he made K.T. Keller president, and Keller ran the company until 1950. Recalls Ernest Breech, a man who knows well what happened in the auto business at that time: "Chrysler didn't have modern financial management. K.T. Keller wouldn't let you have an organization chart. I don't want to blame Keller, but it sure went downhill." It did indeed. By 1950 its market share was just 18%. Under Lester Colbert, it fell still further, to 13% in 1954, barely half its peak share, and the company made only $18.5 million on sales of $2 billion.

Unflinching

Adds Breech: "Look what they did later when they got good management again." One of the men who gave Chrysler its good management was able George Love, now chairman of the executive committee. Says Love: "Chrysler started to fail because it didn't see that marketing was becoming more important than manufacturing. It should have seen it; General Motors and Ford did.

"A company needs the type of fellow who can find a way to meet circumstances whatever they may be. He has to have commercial ingenuity, the ability to see things that are changing for his industry, and move ahead of his competitors to meet it. He doesn't necessarily need knowledge of the industry. What he does need is a combination of mental toughness and a willingness to take a risk." In Love's view, Chrysler just didn't have that kind of man in a leadership position when it needed him. But Love found such a man in Lynn Townsend. Love says: "Spotting this type of fellow is

the tough part. That's where the judgment comes in. In fact, if you limited your *investments* to companies that had that sort of management, you'd have done quite well."

The kind of man who can do everything, the board chairman who delights in tinkering in the plant, is a familiar figure in American business. But he can be a danger to a big corporation by suffocating the initiative of other men. This may not happen, however, if the man is a real leader. Consider the case of Harold W. Sweatt who took over the presidency of Minneapolis-Honeywell in 1934 when it did a $5-million volume and ran it until 1961 and a $470-million volume. Sweatt, now honorary chairman, was a real "tinkerer" and a despiser of organization charts. All the decisions were centralized with him. But Sweatt, fortunately for his company, was a great leader.

You Figure It Out

He had about him a wry, deprecating humor. He liked to tell stories about secretaries sassing him back. Rather than killing initiative, Sweatt nourished it in his men—and he developed good men. Paul B. Wishart, who succeeded Sweatt as president in 1953, then as chairman, was head of production when Sweatt came to him, said Honeywell needed financing, that he was "tired" of doing that sort of thing and told Wishart to do it. Taken aback, Wishart protested, but asked how much money was needed. "You figure it out," said Sweatt. Wishart toiled away and came up with a $16-million figure which he took to Sweatt.

Sweatt, unimpressed, just said, "I'd figured $16 million myself. Now go and get it." Sweatt, in short, was a man who poked into everything, but he was no tyrant, no smotherer of initiative, no inspirer of uniformity. Thus, when Wishart stepped up to chairman, he was succeeded as president by James Binger, a man as different from Wishart as the latter was from Sweatt. And this continuing vitality in Honeywell management probably accounts more than anything else for the good performance of the company stock as shown in the table

The Newcomers

Fifty-seven companies have replaced the old blue chips that couldn't maintain their prominence in modern times. But they came up in different periods . . .

. . . companies which first made the FORBES Top 100 in 1929.

Allied Chemical & Dye
American Rolling Mills (Armco Steel)
Borden Co.
Chrysler Corp.
Continental Oil
Crown Zellerbach (out in 1945, back in 1967)
Firestone Tire & Rubber
Great Atlantic & Pacific Tea Co.
Montgomery Ward
National Dairy Products
National Steel
Phillips Petroleum
Pittsburgh Plate Glass
Radio Corp. of America
Shell Union Oil (Shell Oil)
Sinclair Consolidated Oil (Sinclair Oil)
Tide Water Associated Oil (Tidewater Oil)

. . . companies which first made the FORBES Top 100 in 1945.

American Cyanamid
Celanese Corp.
Continental Can
Douglas Aircraft
Dow Chemical
General Foods
International Business Machines
Lockheed Aircraft
National Distillers Products (Nat'l. Distillers & Chemical Corp.)
Penney, J.C.
Socony Vacuum (Mobil Oil Co.)
Sun Oil
United Aircraft
Weyerhaeuser Timber (Weyerhaeuser Co.)

. . . companies which first made the FORBES Top 100 in 1967.

Allied Stores
Boeing Airplane (Boeing Co.)
Burlington Industries
Caterpillar Tractor
Cities Service
Federated Department Stores
FMC
General Dynamics
General Telephone & Electronics
General Tire & Rubber
Georgia-Pacific
Honeywell Inc.
International Tel. & Tel.
Kaiser Aluminum & Chemical
Litton Industries
May Department Stores
Minnesota Mining & Mfg.
Monsanto
Olin Mathieson Chemical
Owens-Illinois
Reynolds Metals
St. Regis Paper
Sperry Rand
Sunray DX Oil
Tenneco
U.S. Plywood-Champion Papers

It's clear from these cases that truly great companies are not simply built by men who had the guts to pioneer. The builders must also be leaders. Like great politicians and great generals, great businessmen know how to make others rise above their normal limitations, know how to inspire, cajole or bribe dedication from ordinary men.

Listen again to Ernest Breech. Here's what he says it takes: "You've got to inspire men; you've got to give them goals." This General Motors graduate reorganized Ford Motor, helped build North American Aviation and Bendix and pulled TWA back from the brink of bankruptcy. Though he never founded a major company, his was the spark of inspiration that built or rebuilt a half dozen giant corporations. Concurs Arjay Miller, president of Ford Motor, "You are dealing with people, and you have to know how to motivate them and to lead them."

Perhaps, above all, the great leaders must have the self-discipline to rise above the illusion of omnipotence. They must be willing, even anxious, to pass decision-making responsibility on to others.

Tex Thornton, who has thought a good deal about the subject, puts it this way: "We stimulate people to do things and we're willing to gamble on their making a few mistakes."

What of writers, like John Kenneth Galbraith, who think that the day of the great individual entrepreneur is past? The facts simply prove him wrong. What Galbraith overlooks is this: Even a highly organized, diverse modern corporation needs leadership. It needs someone to call the tune. All the system and the organization in the world are worthless without leadership.

Will the Cheathams, the Thorntons, the McDonnells, the O'Neils be the last of the great American entrepreneurs? Not likely. There are new ones coming along every day. James Ling of Ling-Temco-Vought, Charles Bluhdorn of Gulf & Western Industries, Henry Singleton of Teledyne are creating huge new corporations right before our eyes. Not all of them will go on to greatness, but some will. And there will be new names and faces in the Seventies.

Go West . . .

Gardiner Symonds, the soft-spoken, courtly Chicagoan who founded Tenneco, tells a story that nicely illustrates the whole entrepreneurial principle. "Back when I was studying at the Harvard Business School in the Twenties, Dean Wallace B. Donham used to give a lecture to graduating seniors on the theory of Horace Greeley: 'If you stay around in one of the fine old New England companies, that would be good and it would be comfortable. But it will take you quite a while to climb up the business structure. If you go West or South, on the other hand, you only have to be right three times out of five, not three times out of three.' That is because the growth of the country and industry allows for mistakes and for the possibility of correcting them."

The entrepreneurs today don't necessarily have to move geographically —the "Souths" and "Wests" are all around them. But they still follow the spirit of Horace Greeley: By looking for new ways to do things; by trying to create industries rather than waiting for them to come in on their own; by taking tired, old, uninspired companies and turning them into lean, tough, young ones again. ■

ENTREPRENEURS ARE MADE, NOT BORN

David C. McClelland/As I See It

*Entrepreneurs are made, not born
So says a Harvard professor
who not only knows how to spot the type
but thinks he can help create them.*

Every businessman faces the same problem: how to get the maximum efficiency from his employees. And every businessman runs headlong into the same frustration: No matter what incentive plan he introduces, some employees will do just enough to get by; others will work well below their potential — which is like running a plant at 60% of capacity.

Professor David C. McClelland of Harvard's Department of Social Relations is the leader of a group of psychologists from Harvard and the Massachusetts Institute of Technology who have been studying this problem for more than 20 years. Now 52, a graduate of Wesleyan University in Connecticut who received his doctorate at Yale, Dr. McClelland's years of research have convinced him that many incentive plans fail because they are based on a false idea of why men work. The least important motive, he says, is money.

He also believes that it's possible to motivate people to put in a more productive day's work, to turn underachievers into achievers. He has demonstrated his theories, with considerable success, both abroad and in leading U.S. corporations. His ideas and methods parallel those of the noted Dr. B.F. Skinner, who formerly also taught psychology at Harvard. Together with Professor David G. Winter of Wesleyan, a former student, McClelland recently proved that even Indian businessmen, a notoriously lethargic group, can be instilled with the spirit of entrepreneurship.

Thus what Dr. McClelland has to say could be helpful in choosing investments, in raising production and cutting costs, and in turning social dropouts into productive citizens.

I have a friend. He's about 65. His wife is dead. They never had children. He's worth, I'd guess, at least $30 million. Yet, every morning, he rushes down to Wall Street to make another million. The other day I asked him, Why? He looked puzzled; finally he replied: "I don't know."

McClelland: For a psychologist that's an easy question. It's difficult only for those who think men work for money. Men really work to get various types of satisfaction from life — achievement, power. I'm not talking now about a man who doesn't have enough to eat. He works for money, certainly, but a man can eat only so much. Once you get above that bare-subsistence level, the other motives come into play.

In the case of your friend, I would guess that his two major sources of satisfaction are achievement and power; the notion that he's somebody. I am reminded of Andrew Carnegie. He said that when he made a million dollars he was going to quit. He made it at 30, then kept on going.

For people like that, money is a way of proving they're better than other people.

True, but executives love stock options. Doesn't that prove they are motivated by money?

McClelland: I think — well, that problem interests me because I'm involved right now in a lot of companies that are being started by people to whom I've given achievement-motivation training. Those people all want to start companies. They say they want "a piece of the action." An executive doesn't want to consider himself just a salaried employee. He wants to have a feeling that he owns a part of the company.

The way you describe it, beyond a certain point, money is merely a way of keeping score.

McClelland: Yes, and the reason it motivates people in a culture like ours is that we're achievement oriented. The money is a symbol that proves we're achieving.

I used to live in Latin America. A constant complaint among American businessmen there was that if you raised a man's wages, he simply worked four days instead of five.

McClelland: That's true all over the world. My favorite instance of this happened in India. A businessman from the U.S. complained to a former British colonial administrator that his people wouldn't show up for work. He said: I've raised their wages to well above what Indian companies are paying, but they still won't show up." The Englishman replied: "I have a suggestion for you: Cut their wages." The Indian worker is not achievement-oriented; he'll work just hard enough to satisfy his needs for food and drink.

What makes achievement-minded people different from these people?

McClelland: In practically every country in the world, you'll find a minority group that is very good in business; in the U.S., the Jews and Quakers; in Africa, the Ibos — the Biafrans — are very good in business, and in Ethiopia, where I was recently, the Guaragai; in Southeast Asia, the Chinese. What these minority groups have in common is a sense of being superior to other people. Once a group of people gets to believing they're better than anybody else, they'll go out and prove it.

Do these minorities you talk about have a high achievement rate because they are minorities and, therefore, feel they must try harder?

McClelland: That's what a great many people think. They'll say, "Jews are so good in business because they've been discriminated against." These same people, however, also will say, "Negroes don't do well in business because they're discriminated against." I say you can't have it both ways. My answer is that if you discriminate against somebody who's got achievement motivation, he'll counter-strive hard, but if he doesn't have achievement motivation he won't do anything. We've made studies that show that a man hears his parents keep talking about getting ahead, and picks up the idea from them.

Could you pinpoint for me why one businessman is born to succeed while another is born to lose?

McClelland: We've spent 20 years studying just this, 20 years in the laboratory doing very careful research, and we've isolated the specific thing. We know the exact type of motivation that makes a better entrepreneur. Not necessarily a better head of General Motors; I'm talking about the man who starts a business.

That man has a particular thought pattern; very simply, he's thinking all the time about doing something better, improving his performance. Now, he isn't necessarily thinking in competitive terms; sometimes he wants to beat the other guy, but that may not be essential. He's thinking in terms of constantly improving his own performance.

How can you spot such a man except by his actual performance, his track record?

McClelland: We've developed tests. For example, we'll show a man a picture of another man sitting at a desk, and he'll say: "Well, he's a man working late at night and he's very tired. He wishes he could go home and have a beer and watch TV and talk to his wife." Show that same picture to a man who is achievement motivated and he'll say: "Well, it's a guy working very hard on a new contract for a bridge. He knows it's important for his promotion, And he does it, and the next day his boss is pleased, and he's pleased and his wife is pleased."

We've been talking so far about entrepreneurs. Aren't there some people who work just because they take pride in what they do?

McClelland: The kind of man you're talking about really has what I'd call a professional orientation rather than a business orientation. Now in many cases, the man who is concerned with doing a job right is a terrible entrepreneur. Don't get me wrong. I don't want to run him down, but he often is a poor entrepreneur.

We found this in farming. In a sense, the best farmer is the worst farmer — talking in terms of profits. He gets fixed on producing the maximum amount of milk out of his cows by breeding and feeding, the whole business. This guy gets so fixated on his cows that he doesn't even think about the fact that maybe he shouldn't be in milk that much.

That's true of some companies, too. They're much more interested in making steel or planes than money.

McClelland: It takes all kinds of people to make a good world. For example, I don't want my accountant to be a good entrepreneur. I wouldn't want him taking risks with my accounts. But I wouldn't put him in charge of a new business, either.

Describe the ideal entrepreneur.

McClelland: He's interested in moderate risks. The entrepreneur type is not a gambler, because even if he wins he can't get any satisfaction from it because he didn't do it. The entrepreneur type is innovative because the old thing he did over and over again becomes too easy for him.

I tend to describe him as the ideal type, but I want to make it clear that he's different from a manager. When you have a giant like General Motors, other skills and other motives are necessary. Those guys have got to worry about managing people, power, getting decisions through, getting compromises.

All I ever think about is girls. Could you teach me achievement motivation?

McClelland: Of course. We've been teaching achievement motivation for the past seven or eight years. We've had a program in India; we've had an extensive program among black businessmen in Washington, D.C. These black businessmen turn on much faster than the Indians because, I think, the American system is a much more open system.

How do you turn them on? How would you turn me on?

McClelland: Let's go back to those pictures I talked about. The top score a man can make for his story about each picture is 11. Suppose he gets a score of 3. We tell him, "Here's how you got your 3, for this phrase and this phrase and that one. And this is why. Now here is how you can make 11 on that picture. Now rewrite it." We'll have the man keep rewriting it until he can think in those terms easily and readily. This isn't the only thing we do.

What are some of the others?

McClelland: There are some action strategies. We have found, for example, that people who think in terms of doing better generally like challenging tasks. And what's that? One that's moderately difficult, not too easy, not too hard. We have a very simple game. We put a peg on the floor in a room without furniture, give the man three rings and say, "Now throw the rings over the peg. You can stand wherever you wish." He obviously can stand right next to the peg and just drop the rings over, but he obviously isn't going to get much achievement satisfaction out of that. Or he can stand too far away to have any hope of ringing the peg. Or he can stand just far enough away to make ringing it a challenge but not far enough away to make it impossible — and that is what the person with high achievement

motivation does. He'll move back if he succeeds in ringing the peg and forward if he doesn't. He'll zero in on the place where he gets the most satisfaction, the maximum distance where he can ring the peg. Many of the black businessmen in Washington I talked about stood very close to the peg initially; they had very low levels of aspiration because they anticipated failure. A lot of our training with them had to do with getting them to set higher goals and showing them that a little risk may pay off.

We translated this into their actual business problems. Here's a guy in Washington. He's running a hole-in-the-wall dry-cleaning establishment. The wholesaler is charging him much higher prices than he charges a white, because the man buys in small quantities and the wholesaler isn't sure he'll get paid. We say, "Why don't you get together with three or four of your friends so you can buy in large quantities?" His first reaction is, "How do I know I can trust them to give me my fair share?" We get him to accept the idea of risk.

McClelland: There are a variety of ways. You can give the top executives of the company an achievement-motivation test. We did that with two companies in Mexico, both about the same size. The first was growing at a rapid rate; the second was a good, solid company, but it was growing slowly. When we gave the tests we discovered that the man who made the lowest achievement-motivation score in the first company did better than the man with the highest score in the second company.

You can make what we call "climate studies." By that I mean you can ask the workers whether they feel the company's standards are high, whether they feel they get recognition for good work, whether they feel the company is more apt to censure them if they are wrong than praise them if they are right.

There's another question you can ask: Do the workers feel the company is authoritarian or that it permits a great deal of self-direction?

You mean the company that gives its employees a great deal of freedom to decide what they should do will get better results than one that lays down strict guidelines?

McClelland: Where you find too great a demand for conformity, you'll find a low-performing company. We were called in some time ago by a soft-drink company. It was dissatisfied with the performance of its route salesmen. We talked with the salesmen; they all felt they were too severely regulated. We talked with management and management said this wasn't true. The managers said: "We keep telling these guys they should take more initiative."

It turned out that the men were right. There were regulations for everything, like, first thing in the morning, check your truck and make sure it's clean; then check your uniform, it must be laundered every three days. They had a list of rules about this long.

They also told the routemen: "This week your quota is so many cases." Now these quotas were set from the top. Management figured out what the company's growth rate should be for the year, then allocated the quotas region by region, and from the regions, the allocations went down to the guy on the route.

We said to the company: "Why don't you work it the other way, from bottom to top instead of from top to bottom? Let the men at the bottom set quotas for themselves and work up." They were a little nervous about doing this, but finally they agreed. And it worked. They did better than they'd ever done before.

It works out this way: If you ask a man, "How many cases do you think you can sell?" and he says 11,000, he's going to sell them because he's put himself on the line. He'll feel entirely differently about the goal you set for him.

I never heard of a company that operated that way.

McClelland: That's what this soft-drink company said when we made our suggestion, but they tried it, and it worked. ∎

Entrepreneurship and Technology

A basic study of innovators; how to keep and capitalize on their talents

Edward B. Roberts

One of the fascinating phenomena of the post-World War II period has been the burgeoning growth of science and technology activities. Yet within the past few years both participants in and observers of these activities have significantly shifted their concern from a focus on the process of creating new scientific and technological advances toward greater emphasis on effective utilization of discoveries and developments. Increasingly the distinction between invention and innovation has been attributed to the personal role of the innovator, the individual who championed the translation of science and technology into use.

This paper is aimed at furthering the understanding of this personally based technical innovation process. Better understanding of and management of the entrepreneur, and of this related innovation process, will lead to more rapid and more beneficial corporate and economic growth.

A Research Focus on Entrepreneurship and Technology

In September, 1964, a research program was initiated at the M.I.T. Sloan School of Management to seek better understanding of the technical innovation and of his role in transferring technology.*

EDWARD B. ROBERTS is Associate Professor of Management, M.I.T. Sloan School of Management, Cambridge, Massachusetts 02139.
* Throughout this research program I have been assisted ably by Herbert A. Wainer, now a staff member of the M.I.T. Division of Sponsored Research. Our efforts have been supported in part by research grants from the National Aeronautics and Space Administration to the M.I.T. Sloan School of Management (NSG-235) and to the M.I.T. Center for Space Research (NSG-496). Statistical analyses have been carried out at the M.I.T. Computations Center.

250   RESEARCH MANAGEMENT   July 1968

The focus of the research has been divided between studies of (*1*) the creation of new product ventures and new technology divisions in existing companies, and (*2*) the creation of new companies by entrepreneurs seeking to exploit technological advances. For simplicity these two areas are identified as "internal entrepreneurship" and "spinoff entrepreneurship," the "spinoff" label referring to the fact that the technical basis for the new company often spins out with the entrepreneur from some other existing organization.

New Concepts of Internal Entrepreneurship

From his studies of U. S. inventive resources, Donald A. Schon has identified the crucial role of the internal entrepreneur in getting major technological advances adopted.

Developments like McLean's Sidewinder missile and Rickover's atomic submarine do not fit the pattern of orderly presentation of promising technical ideas to official judges, favorable objective evaluation, and then orderly marshaling of technical resources for development. These histories look more like crusades or military campaigns, with overtones of fifth column activity and guerrilla warfare. . . .

Typically, one man emerges as champion of the idea . . . Essentially, the champion must be a man willing to put himself on the line for an idea of doubtful success. He is willing to fail. But he is capable of using any and every means of informal sales and pressure in order to succeed.

No ordinary involvement with a new idea provides the energy required to cope with the indifference and resistance that major technical change provokes. It is characteristic of champions of new developments that they identify with the idea as their own, and with its promotion as a cause, to a degree that goes far beyond the requirements of their job. In fact, many display persistence and courage of heroic quality. For a numbr of them the price of failure is professional suicide, and a few become martyrs to the championed idea.

All of these requirements apply to commercial organizations as well as to the military.[1]

More recently Jay W. Forrester has recognized the vital role of the entrepreneur as a fundamental building block for the design of a new form of corporate enterprise that is suited particularly well to the profitable exploitation of advanced technologies.

In today's "small-business" world, the risk to the budding entrepreneur is greater than it need be. In general he gets but one chance. There is no opportunity to practice and to improve ability if the first undertaking is not a success. . . . [In a more ideal process] the individual grows from initially managing his own time, to managing small projects, to becoming an entrepreneur who matches customer needs to the abilities of the organization. This evolution without discontinuity from individual worker to entrepreneur can stop or be redirected at any point.[2]

Forrester's theory of a corporate organization designed to stimulate and to depend upon internal entrepreneurship differs sharply from conventional organizational forms. Its essence bridges in concept the two research areas indicated above, the establishment of independent "outside" new enterprises with the corporate "internalization" of entrepreneurial motivations and capacities.

The Internal Entrepreneur

Both the Schon and Forrester articles propose means of achieving effective technology utilization by imaginative organizational concepts based on the internal entrepreneur. Yet little detailed empirical support has been available to assist these designs. During the past year the first of a planned series of research studies of the internal entrepreneurship process was undertaken.[3] In carrying out our pilot study in this area we developed a sample of sixteen new business ventures initiated during the past fifteen years in one large (>$500 million sales) division of an integrated electronics manufacturer. Each of the ventures selected for study was the first commercial activity of the company in the technological product area involved.

It is significant that the men who headed these new ventures for the corporation appear quite similar in key characteristics to founders of new technical companies. In median age (36), average education (master's degree), major work experience (generally R&D), and even religious background (57%, 19%, and 13% were the respective Protestant, Catholic, and Jewish representations, with 11% in other categories) the internal entrepreneurs looked very much like their "outside" entrepreneur counterparts. Thus the internal entrepreneurs and the spinoff entrepreneurs are similar; only their organizational setting is different.

The Corporate Environment toward Entrepreneurship

Of importance to understanding the entrepreneurial activity within the large corporation is recognition that both policies and attitudes of the organization often work to defeat entrepreneurial efforts.

For example it is usually felt (and supported by our research data) that entrepreneurship is characterized by youth or at least by youthful energies. Yet our research on internal entrepreneurship showed that in the corporation studied a definite bias existed against younger men taking on venture responsibility. This showed up quantitatively in a number of measures.

During the course of the project the younger men received less encouragement than the older men (.011),* they were given less latitude for independent action (.071), had less say in formulating the judgmental criteria for the venture (.136), experienced less cooperation between their venture and the company (.179), experienced a good deal of trouble in securing capital support for their project (.025), and had a lower level of sponsorship for their project (.179) —sponsorship being a term used to describe the supportive actions taken by a person or persons in higher management to advance the cause of the entrepreneur or his venture. Even after the project had attained the status of an independent venture, the younger entrepreneurs reported capital support as being a major problem (.125).[4]

It is not surprising therefore that many would-be entrepreneurs leave major corporations to create their ventures on the outside. In another of our studies we found that 39 companies had been started by 44 former employees of one large Greater Boston electronics company.[5] The 32 present corporate survivors of this group had sales in 1966 totalling over seventy million dollars—approximately double the sales of the "parent" company from which the entrepreneurs had spun-off. This suggests some of the potential gains available to the corporation that can learn to motivate its entrepreneurially oriented young men to remain with the company and to accomplish their ventures internally. Yet of the sixteen internal entrepreneurs studied a number indicated that they had already thought of going into business for themselves. Faced with corporate attitudes that discourage youthful entrepreneurs there is little wonder that such outward migration occurs.

Technology and Internal Entrepreneurship

One aspect of the internal entrepreneurship study of particular interest is the technological content of the new products developed and

---

* The figures in parentheses following a statement indicate the level of statistical significance associated with the stated relationship. Mann-Whitney U. Tests were used to determine the stated relationship. Other, usually nonparametric, tests were used as appropriate to establish other significant findings described elsewhere in this paper.

RESEARCH MANAGEMENT   July 1968   253

the factors affecting this technology. The major corporation examined has a large central research facility as well as numerous divisional developmental laboratories. Twelve of the fourteen ventures investigated were worked on in a company lab, six of them in the central research organization. The newness of the technology embodied in the product was a function of the kind of lab that worked on the venture, the central research facility accounting for the more advanced technological products (.053).

Of key significance is the fact that the ventures that employed newer technology were more successful (.084); a correlate of this finding is that the ventures worked on at the central research lab were more successful (.050). However, part of the explanation of this success seemed to lie outside of the pure technological aspect of these relationships.

In a number of the projects worked on at the central facility the people who worked on the project developed a strong sense of commitment to the project's success. This was not the case at the divisional labs where generally there was such a heavy pressure from the large work load that it was hard for lab personnel to delay ongoing work to trouble shoot the ventures's problems. . . . Thus, when technical problems arose during later stages of the venture's growth, those entrepreneurs who had previous relationships to central lab personnel were able to obtain technical help from the lab in working out their problems—in some instances the lab instituted a "crash" effort to solve the problem at no cost to the venture.[6]

These findings reaffirm not only the hypothesized importance of effective technological utilization as a basis for corporate success but also support Schon's theory of the product champion as essential to technical innovation.

Other relationships derived from our pilot study of internal entrepreneurship might be cited in regard to numerous aspects of the growth and success of new technical ventures. But the limited data base suggests that caution be exercised lest possibly overzealous, albeit empirically based statements, be made about the care and feeding of internal entrepreneurs. It is sufficient to point out that the phenomena surrounding the technical entrepreneur within the firm appear closely related to those of the spin-off entrepreneur whom we have researched more extensively over a longer period. What little we do know about internal entrepreneurship suggests that the corporation has much to gain from, and still more to learn about, effective management of technical entrepreneurship.

Entrepreneurship and the New Technical Firm

Although the on-going corporation is on occasion the active scene of technical entrepreneurship, it is in the new firm that the innovating entrepreneur flourishes. The vital interplay between entrepreneurship and technology has been explored in our studies of the formation and growth of over 200 companies founded by ex-employees of several M.I.T. labs and academic departments, a government lab, a not-for-profit corporation, and an industrial electronic systems contractor.

Detailed documentation of many of the studies undertaken on these new enterprises appears in a number of M.I.T. theses written under my supervision.[7]

The sources of new companies that have been investigated over the past three years and the number of companies uncovered from them are listed in Table I.

TABLE I

Sources of New Technical Enterprises

Sources of New Enterprises	New Companies Identified
M.I.T. Laboratories	
Electronic Systems Laboratory	11
Instrumentation Laboratory	30
Lincoln Laboratory	50
Research Laboratory for Electronics	14
M.I.T. Academic Departments	
Aeronautics and Astronautics	18
Electrical Engineering	15
Mechanical Engineering	10
Metallurgy	8
Government Laboratory	
Air Force Cambridge Research Laboratory	16
Not-for-Profit Organization	
MITRE Corporation	5
Industrial Electronic Systems Contractor	39

The companies in our sample were on the average four to five years old, ranging of course from organizations newly formed within the preceding year to companies that are over twenty years old. These companies are generally successful. As a minimum statement, they

RESEARCH MANAGEMENT   July 1968   255

seldom fail. An interesting contrast is the comparison of our findings with Dun and Bradstreet statistics that indicate that most new companies formed in the United States fail within the first few years of operation. Our new technical enterprises had a total failure rate of about twenty per cent covering their full average four to five years existence. That is, nearly all of the new-technology-based companies studied (approximately four out of every five) have survived. Our statistics also suggest that most of those still in business today will persist far into the future.

Despite the relative success of these companies, their average size is still small, though the companies are rapidly growing. At the time of study each of the companies on average had approximately one and one-half millions of dollars in sales. These sales figures range widely from the company that is new and doing perhaps one or two hundred thousands of dollars in sales to some firms that are in the many tens of millions of dollars bracket.

In Figure 1 we take as examples those companies that have come out of the M.I.T. Instrumentation Laboratory. Plotting the sales curves of each of the companies separately creates the general appearance of an exponential growth pattern.

We can identify different classes of sales growth behavior among the many firms (for example, some companies are lagging in their growth performance), but a general trend of rapidly rising sales can be attributed to the companies derived from the Instrumentation Laboratory. Of the firms studied from this lab less than fifteen per cent of the companies had failed by 1965, the time we conducted this initial study.

In Figure 2 we see how these companies as a whole compare with their source organization, the M.I.T. Instrumentation Laboratory. Here the rise in Instrumentation Lab funding is plotted over the past twenty years. With it is shown the growing curve of total current sales during the same period of all the lab's spin-off companies. This curve is of the same character as the billings of the founding organization but is significantly delayed. The delay here of about six years testifies to the technology transfer process underlying the new technical firms.

If government is to have an impact on the economy via the route of new technical enterprise spin-off, the several time lags associated with this process must be encountered before full impact is felt. The time lags involved include: the time for the individual to perform the original technical work under direct government sponsorship; the

256   Research Management   July 1968

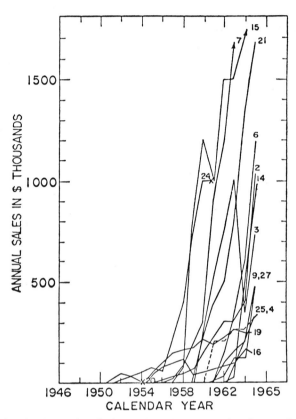

Fig. 1. Growth of the spin-off companies from the
M.I.T. Instrumentation Laboratory.

time for the entrepreneur to develop confidence that he has gained
some skills or knowledge that he wishes to transfer to the market place;
the time for establishment of the new enterprise based on transferred
technology; the time for the new company to grow to some level of
noticeable significance. These several time-consuming processes account
for approximately six years time difference between the growth of the
laboratory and the growth of its spin-off firms.   Within the past couple
of years these firms have grown to *now* exceed by a significant amount
the total sales volume of the laboratory from which the organizations
came.

   The same kind of relationship between the growth of the source
of the new enterprises and the growth of the new companies themselves has been found in other situations.   For example, Lincoln Laboratory, constrained in growth by a head count limit placed on the lab
during the late 1950s, has long since been surpassed in size by its off-

RESEARCH MANAGEMENT   July 1968   257

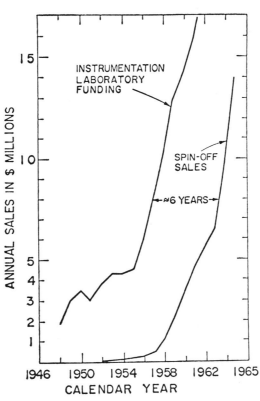

Fig. 2. Total sales of the spin-off companies from the
M.I.T. Instrumentation Laboratory.

shoots. The same rapid growth has occurred in those companies
formed out of the industrial electronics contractor studied, to the extent that the spin-off enterprises now account for double the sales
of the parent organization.

Most of the companies studied had their start as government contractors or in selling products to the defense/space markets. However, at the present stage of company development—and the companies
were only an average of four to five years of age at the time they were
studied—an average of forty per cent of the business of the M.I.T. spin-
offs comes from the commercial market. (The commercial business
percentage is much smaller for the industrial spin-off firms.) This
tendency toward non-government sales increases significantly during
each year of company history. In fact, the more successful companies
are making special efforts to become less dependent upon the government.

It is characteristic of the advanced technology markets served by

258   RESEARCH MANAGEMENT   July 1968

the spin-off companies that the Federal government's role as a customer provides the catalyst needed. Defense/space requirements for high technical performance provide support funds before the otherwise high prices would be justified by industrial or consumer markets. Yet once moving with the stimulus of the initial government market the new technologically based company seems able to penetrate into new areas of application.

The implications of these findings are important. They demonstrate that the flow of entrepreneurs out of advanced technical organizations into their own businesses can create significant technology transfer as well as impressive commercial and economic impact. When the source of these companies is a university or government laboratory, the flow is unquestionably beneficial to society. In fact, it helps the university to accomplish its objectives of education and technology movement. However, when the source of this new enterprise spin-off flow is another industrial firm, there is question as to whether indeed a net gain accrues to society. No doubt new energies and new ideas are added to the market place. However, the entrepreneurial flow may lead to disaster for the source company because its better people are among those leaving the company. In particular, those scientists and engineers who are committed to an action orientation and to the use of their knowledge are the ones who usually depart.

The combination of these results with those from the pilot study of internal entrepreneurship, demonstrates that companies ought to be concerned to discover why such people leave. Corporate and laboratory executives should seek to understand how to motivate these entrepreneurs to remain in the organization and how to manage them to produce effective new ventures for the firm. New approaches are probably needed to provide the stimuli, the incentives, and the opportunities, perhaps by drastic changes from the usual organizational forms, as were suggested by the Schon and Forrester articles cited. Otherwise the spin-off will be benefiting some other firm's balance sheet.

Let us consider implications for government policies in science and technology. It appears that policies that encourage technical entrepreneurship produce generally stable and survivable additions to the business community. During the past several years many regions of our country, several different cities, and a host of universities, as well as a number of other countries are catching on to this fact of life. They are attempting to transfer the growth potential of entrepreneurial technology transfer to the economic development of their own geographic areas. The data indicate that such attempts are worth pursuing.

The Technical Entrepreneur

Clearly, the entrepreneur is the central figure in successful technical innovation, both within the large corporation as well as in the foundling enterprise. From our research we now know many of the characteristics of these technical entrepreneurs.

First, and one of the most interesting in our opinion, is the fact of the home environment that breeds the man who becomes a technical entrepreneur. Consistently, fifty per cent of the entrepreneurs investigated have come from homes in which the father was self-employed. It is intriguing that these statistics could not have been anticipated by merely looking at any other characteristics of the entrepreneurs' fathers; their home environment, their religious background, census data on occupational patterns, or any other predictive measure that we can identify. That the home molds the characteristic careers of its offspring seems strongly supported by these figures that half of the entrepreneurs received an entrepreneurial heritage from fathers who were in business for themselves.

Secondly, we are dealing with a sample of well educated people. This is to be expected with our subjects generally being technical entrepreneurs coming from highly technical organizations. The average education of our entrepreneurs is the Master of Science degree or slightly better than that, an M.S. degree plus some additional courses. A large number of the entrepreneurs hold Bachelor degrees and some the PhD.

On the average the new company founder is in his early thirties at the time he starts his new enterprise. While this average is quite young, the age range goes down even much younger than that. Although some entrepreneurs are much older (one was in his late sixties) the age distribution curtails very quickly and few entrepreneurs are older than the late thirties.

These age and education figures for the new company founders closely match those from our study of internal entrepreneurs. With a broader data base we might have more confidence in the assertion that regardless of environment, the same kind of people, with similar education, home environment and age characteristics as our spin-off entre-

260   RESEARCH MANAGEMENT   July 1968

preneurs, are the ones who frequently transfer technology from corporate research and development laboratories into manufacturing plants and then to the market place.

One of the characteristics of the technical entrepreneurs is that in their prior laboratory work they tended to be development oriented rather than research oriented. The source laboratories do contain a wide variety of research and development work, including much basic research. Yet the entrepreneurs had tended to work near the development end of the job spectrum of the laboratories in which they participated. Furthermore, even those entrepreneurs who came from the most research oriented lab organizations generally had worked there during the periods of organizational life that had been most developmentally oriented. Development activities, or a hardware manifestation of scientific-engineering knowledge, seem to encourage the process of technical entrepreneurship.

Influences on Technology Transfer

The third group of factors observable from our new enterprise research are some of the determinants of the technology transfer itself. We studied the occurrence of technology transfer in a relatively simple, imprecise, but hopefully useful way. Technology transfer was defined by a set of four categories: one we call "direct transfer"; the second category is "partial transfer"; the third is labelled "vague"; and the fourth "none."

"Direct technology transfer" specifies those situations in which the new company could not have been founded without technology that was taken from the source organization by the entrepreneur. The transferred technology was the essential technical base on which the new company was built.

By "partial transfer" we mean that the technology from the source laboratory had been important, but that other technologies from other places also contributed to the technical strength and technical basis of the newly formed organization.

"Vague transfer" designates those situations in which some technology transfer occurred, but the transfer was of general skills rather than of specific ideas or devices. Furthermore, such a company was not felt to be significantly dependent upon the technology from the source organization, although there were ways in which the technology related.

Finally, we classified some companies as reflecting no technology transfer. In these cases we admitted to the possibility that the new enterprise might have been affected by managerial knowhow, personal growth, and improved wisdom arising from experience with people and projects gained at the source lab. But in these companies no technical knowledge stemming from the source organization could be identified as transferred into the new company.

With these categoric definitions of technology transfer, we measured the characteristics of each of the spin-off companies. We then attempted to find those factors that affect or determine the extent of technology transfer into the new enterprises.

One of the most significant influences on technology utilization is reflected in a personal measure, the age of the entrepreneur. The older the entrepreneur at the time of forming his new company, the less the source technology transferred into his organization. This appears to reflect some of the known characteristics of the technical obsolescence phenomenon. As an engineer or scientist ages he generally finds more difficulties in keeping abreast technically of what is going on in a frontier research and development organization. It is logical then that the older man generally possesses less frontier knowledge that he might transfer into a new technical enterprise.

Development-oriented source organizations and development-oriented individual entrepreneurs tend to transfer more technology into the newly established companies. This result goes beyond our earlier observation that the entrepreneurs generally tend to be development-oriented. Now we see a double filter at work. The more development-oriented individuals become entrepreneurs; the more development-oriented entrepreneurs transfer more technology.

Another discovery in this area is an interesting relationship between the time lag from leaving the organization to the founding of the company and the extent of source technology transferred. Not all of the individuals by any means directly go from the laboratory or department into the new enterprise they form. The majority of them first engage in other activities after leaving the source lab. Many go out into industry for what they regard as needed seasoning.

Figure 3, displaying data on the Lincoln Laboratory spin-offs, shows that a large number of entrepreneurs do set up their companies immediately, with a time lag of zero years after leaving the lab's employment. But most entrepreneurs spend some time elsewhere doing other things before they establish their new companies. The delay

262   RESEARCH MANAGEMENT   July 1968

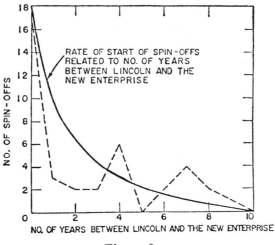

Figure 3.

extends up to nine or ten years. The average of the Lincoln-based companies is a time delay of approximately two and one-half years.

The longer the time lag between leaving the lab and setting up the new company, the less the degree of technology transfer. In the elapsed time between lab and company the technological advantage that a scientist or engineer possesses at a frontier research and development organization is in part lost. As the years pass the old lab technology is no longer as relevant, and it is reasonable that we find the degree of transfer decreasing as time from the source increases.

Factors Affecting New Enterprise Success

Our research indicates some of the determinants of new enterprise success. Success, of course, can be evaluated in a number of ways. In general, we have taken as our measure of some form of market evaluation or managerial-oriented evaluation of business success. The measures used have included: average sales; sales growth; projected sales; a weighted performance that combines company age and profitability with sales growth; Dun and Bradstreet ratings; and the entrepreneur's self-evaluation of the present success of his company. Each of these measures correlates closely with each other measure, lending confidence that our hypotheses might be tested meaningfully.

A large number of factors, ranging from aspects of home environment to education and work experience of the entrepreneur, to numerous aspects of new enterprise management, significantly affect the success of the technology-based corporation. In Table II some of the non-personality factors that affect the performance of these new enterprises are listed, as found for a subset of 84 of the firms studied.

TABLE II
Nonpersonality Factors Affecting the Performance of New Technical Enterprises

	Number of Companies	% of Sample	Factors
Higher performers	42	50	High degree of technology transfer Moderate educational level Specific business function Entrepreneur concerned about personnel matters Marketing department
Lower performers	42	50	Low degree of technology transfer High educational level No specific business function Entrepreneur not concerned about personnel problems No marketing department

The first contributing influence indicated in Table II is a high degree of technology transfer, that is high performing companies are characterized by high transfer of technology from the source. Technology transfer from a research and development organization is, therefore, not just a nicety. It is instead directly correlated with and is a causal influence on the eventual degree of new company success. A similar finding has been described for the internal enterprises discussed earlier.

The second success factor is what we call a moderate education level, by which we mean a Master of Science degree for the entrepreneur. In contrast to this Table II shows that the lower rated performers typically had a higher educational level, i.e., a PhD. Despite some notable exceptions, the PhDs as a group do not perform well as entrepreneurs. Their general temperament, attitude, and orientation are usually out of line with those needed for successful entrepreneurship.

The higher ranked performers of these new companies have included recognition of the need for specific business-oriented talents.

264   RESEARCH MANAGEMENT   July 1968

The successful technical entrepreneur is one who has recognized the importance of management skills and has brought into his organization somebody for the specific purpose of handling some of the management considerations and management activities. The lower performers do not generally indicate recognition of a need for management skills in their organizations. In this instance, however, we are not sure which is cause and which is effect: whether success is caused by recognition of the importance of management or whether recognition of management is caused by business success.

The same cause–effect quandary arises in regard to the entrepreneur's concerns about personnel matters. Those entrepreneurs that regard people as one of their key problem areas are among the most successful. Those entrepreneurs that describe other kinds of problems, but do not include people as a key problem area, are in the group with the lower performing organizations. We do not think that larger (i.e., more successful) companies necessarily have more people problems. Rather, we believe that successful entrepreneurs have become successful in part by manifesting their concern for their employees as the principal productive element of their organizations.

One differentiating element we note is the existence of a marketing department in the more successful new companies and the lack of formal marketing organizations in the less successful firms. This, in part, is related to our earlier finding pertaining to the general importance of recognizing the need for specific business functions in the corporation. More significant is the likelihood that this factor gives testimony that advanced technology needs actively to be exploited, and that even brilliant ideas do not move by their own energies into the market place.

In Table III, using data taken from a smaller sub-sample we generated, we indicate some of the personality factors that seem to correlate with high entrepreneurial success. The higher performers, when measured by the Thematic Apperception Test (a test designed to determine the need orientation of an individual), generally show high need for achievement. In contrast the lower performing entrepreneurs have low need for achievement.

Furthermore, the tests show in general a moderate need for power on the part of higher performers, with the lower-rated performers manifesting either high or low (but not moderate) need for power. Apparently high need for power manifested by the company founder drives out the possibility that others may effectively contribute to the

RESEARCH MANAGEMENT   July 1968   **265**

TABLE III

Personality Factors Affecting the
Performance of New Technical Enterprises

	Factors
Higher performers	High need for achievement Moderate need for power
Lower performers	Low need for achievement High or low need for power

organization's growth and success. The low need for power, on the other hand, symbolizes a company in which no leadership direction is being exercised—the laissez-faire situation in which every man is boss.

Entrepreneurship and Technology in Review

The technical entrepreneur has been studied within the large corporation as well as in the new firm. In both settings he has been found to be a man of youth and advanced technologically based education, coming from a work environment in which the exploitation of advanced technical ideas is being pursued. Even during childhood the eventual entrepreneur has often had home influences of career orientation toward self-employment affecting his personal development. The notion of going into business for himself has long been a serious consideration of both the internal and the spin-off entrepreneur.

Within the large corporation the young would-be entrepreneur finds attitudes and policies that discourage him and act to prevent successful technology transfer from the R&D lab to the market. Many of these young venturers cannot even get to the point of active pursuit of their interests within the firm and leave to set up new companies. The volume of this outflow is illustrated by our finding that from one major company studied 32 spinoff firms now account for sales more than double those of their parent. And those who do not quit the company may still find themselves failures as a result of a corporate anti-entrepreneurial approach. It has been suggested by Schon, Forrester, and the data analyses presented in this paper, that new forms of organizational incentives and managerial philosophies may be needed to retain and to stimulate the would-be entrepreneur.

Both internal new business ventures and external new companies were found to have their success dependent in part on the degree of

266 RESEARCH MANAGEMENT July 1968

exploitation of advanced technology. The data on the new enterprises studied permitted the identification of youth, developmental (versus research) orientation, and quickness of attempted technology utilization as influences essential to effective technology transfer from laboratory to market. Moreover, in both internal and external settings the degree of advanced technology used was found as an important stimulant of the success attained by the venture. A variety of other factors were also seen as affecting business success of the new technical enterprise, including motivational and managerial forces.

All of the results sustain the original premise that the difference between mere technical invention and successful innovation is largely attributable to the personal role of the entrepreneur. Better understanding and management of him and of the personally based technical innovation process will lead to more rapid and more beneficial technically based corporate and economic growth.

REFERENCES

1. Schon, Donald A., "Champions for Radical New Inventions," *Harvard Business Review*, March–April 1963, pp. 84–85.

2. Forrester, Jay W., "A New Corporate Design," *Industrial Management Review*, 7, No. 1, 12 (Fall 1965).

3. Buddenhagen, Frederick L., "Internal Entrepreneurship as a Corporate Strategy for New Product Development," unpublished S.M. thesis, M.I.T. Sloan School of Management, August, 1967.

4. Buddenhagen, Frederick L., "Internal Entrepreneurship as a Corporate Strategy for New Product Development," unpublished S.M. thesis, M.I.T. Sloan School of Management, August, 1967, p. 19.

5. Goldstein, Jerome, "The Spin-Off of New Enterprises from a Large Government Funded Industrial Laboratory," unpublished S.M. thesis, M.I.T. Sloan School of Management, June, 1967.

6. Buddenhagen, Frederick L., "Internal Entrepreneurship as a Corporate Strategy for New Product Development," unpublished S.M. thesis, M.I.T. Sloan School of Management, August, 1967, pp. 21–22.

7. Forseth, Dean A., "The Role of Government-Sponsored Research Laboratories in the Generation of New Enterprises—A Comparative Analysis," unpublished S.M. thesis, M.I.T. Sloan School of Management, June, 1966; Goldstein, Jerome, "The Spin-Off of New Enterprises from a Large Government Funded Industrial Laboratory," unpublished S.M. thesis, M.I.T. Sloan School of Management, June, 1967; Teplitz, Paul V., "Spin-Off Enterprises from a Large Government Sponsored Laboratory," unpublished S.M. thesis, M.I.T. Sloan School of Management, June, 1965; Wainer, Herbert A., "The Spin-Off of Technology from Government-Sponsored Research Laboratories: Lincoln Laboratory," unpublished S.M. thesis, M.I.T. Sloan School of Management, August 8, 1965.

Journal of Applied Psychology
1969, Vol. 53, No. 3, 178–184

MOTIVATION OF RESEARCH AND DEVELOPMENT ENTREPRENEURS:

DETERMINANTS OF COMPANY SUCCESS [1]

HERBERT A. WAINER AND IRWIN M. RUBIN [2]

Massachusetts Institute of Technology, Sloan School of Management

Fifty-one technical entrepreneurs were studied, focusing upon the relationships between their motivation and company performance. More specifically, the relationships between the entrepreneurs' need for achievement, need for power, and need for affiliation were related to the performance of the 51 small companies they founded and operated. The results indicate that high need for achievement and moderate need for power are associated with high company performance. The effects of need for power and need for affiliation on performance seem to be derived through their influence on leadership styles.

In an attempt to associate need for achievement (n Ach) and economic development, McClelland (1961) looks to the entrepreneur as the one who translates n Ach into economic development. The entrepreneur in McClelland's scheme is "the man who organizes the firm (the business unit) and/or increases its productive capacity [p. 205]."

The present authors' aim was to test McClelland's macro theory of economic growth at the micro level of organizational performance. The principle interest in considering McClelland's work stems from his discussions of who entrepreneurs are and of their different behavioral styles predicted from differences in need patterns. McClelland's underlying assumption is that entrepreneurs have a high n Ach and that in business situations this

high n Ach will lead them to behave in certain ways and have certain tendencies.

Based on McClelland's discussion, the present authors raised the proposition that the degree to which an entrepreneur is motivated by n Ach directly influences his skill as an entrepreneur and consequently his enterprise's performance. The major hypothesis to be tested concerns the relationship between an entrepreneur's level of n Ach and his company's performance.

Schrage (1965), in testing the relationship between the entrepreneur's n Ach and company performance, reported that companies run by entrepreneurs who have a high n Ach tend to have either high profits or losses ($\pm$ 3% of sales), while those run by low n Ach entrepreneurs tend to have low profits or losses ($\leq$ 3% of sales). Reanalysis of his data by the present authors sheds considerable doubt on the validity of his findings. The primary source of doubt was a discrepancy between the scores Schrage used for n Ach and those subsequently derived when the same protocols were rescored by the Motivation Research Group at Harvard. The fact that his results departed markedly from established theory further substantiates this concern.

In addition to the relationship between n Ach and company performance, the authors were interested in the interrelationships among three needs, n Ach, need for power (n Pow), and the need for affiliation (n Aff), with respect to company performance. n Pow is defined by Atkinson (1958) as "that dis-

[1] The research presented in this paper was supported in part by grants from the Massachusetts Institute of Technology Center for Space Research and by the National Aeronautics and Space Administration (NsG-235 and NsG-496). However the findings and views reported are those of the authors and do not necessarily reflect those of the supporting agencies. This work was done in part at the Massachusetts Institute of Technology Computation Center.

The authors wish to acknowledge the work done by Charles W. McLaughlin, a master's degree candidate in the Massachusetts Institute of Technology, Sloan School of Management, in the collection of data for this paper.

[2] Requests for reprints should be sent to Irwin M. Rubin, Room 52-538, Massachusetts Institute of Technology, Sloan School of Management, 50 Memorial Drive, Cambridge, Massachusetts 02139.

position, directing behavior toward satisfactions contingent upon the control of the means of influencing another person [p. 105]."

n Aff is concerned with the establishment, maintenance, or restoration of positive affective relationships with other people, that is, friendships. Statements of liking or desire to be liked, accepted, or forgiven are manifestations of this motive (Atkinson, 1958). McClelland's (1961) discussion of the joint product of n Pow and n Aff in relation to dictatorship stimulated this aspect of the inquiry. He found that n Pow was not related to economic growth but was related to style of leadership. More specifically, the combination of a high n Pow and a low n Aff was associated with the tendency of a country to resort to totalitarian methods as a style of leadership.

The present authors propose that n Ach has behavioral manifestations different than either n Pow or n Aff in terms of the individual's relationships with people. n Pow and n Aff are interpersonally oriented needs. Implicit in their definitions is the existence of other human beings whom the n Pow or n Aff motivated individual can influence and control, or with whom he can be friends. n Ach, on the other hand, seems to be a more internalized need. The n Ach motivated individual may need other people to help him satisfy his n Ach, but the nature of his relationship with them, or more appropriately his effectiveness with them, will be determined by other needs. The authors suggest that n Ach is a primary consideration determining noninterpersonally related behavior that leads to high company performance. n Pow and n Aff are primary considerations determining interpersonal behavior that affects company performance. n Pow and n Aff, then, can be looked upon as having strong implications as determinants of management style.

Numerous other attempts have been made to identify those personality traits which differentiate leaders from nonleaders or effective leaders from ineffective leaders. These studies have, in general, failed to find any consistent pattern of differentiating traits. In a broad sense, the present research is analogous to these prior efforts in that it seeks

to explain company performance on the basis of certain personality characteristics of the president. Steps were taken, however, in anticipation of two potential problem areas: (*a*) that personality description and measurement themselves are not yet adequate; (*b*) that the groups studied have usually been markedly different from one another and this may have concealed a relation between personality and the exercise of leadership that would have appeared within a more homogeneous set of groups or situations.

The major personality variable of interest in the present study is the need for achievement. On the basis of the existing body of research, McClelland's version of the Thematic Apperception Test (TAT) was deemed a reliable means of measuring n Ach (Atkinson, 1958; McClelland, 1961). With respect to the second problem area, a very homogeneous set of groups has been examined, thus mitigating the potential influence of the "situation."

For these reasons, the focus in this study was upon the new, small, technically based enterprise. The entrepreneur president of such a company has placed himself in a situation where his n Ach, to the extent that it exists, can readily be translated into concrete behavior. He starts the company, hires the people, and motivates them, sells, plans, takes risks, and so on. It is his personality and motivation that mold the company in its every aspect. Furthermore, in such situations, the entrepreneur's efforts and decisions are likely to be very important in determining the initial success of the venture.

METHOD

Fifty-one small technically based companies in the Boston area comprised the sample. All were at least 4 but less than 10 yr. old at the time of the study and all were "spin-offs" from one of the Massachusetts Institute of Technology research laboratories or industrial laboratories around the Boston area. They ranged in business activities from service, such as computer software development, to manufacturing, such as special purpose computers and welded modules. Company and entrepreneurial personality information were gathered from the entrepreneur president. The typical entrepreneur, based on the central tendencies for the total sample of entrepreneurs, was approximately 36 yr. of age when he started his new enterprise, was educated to the master's degree level, and had considerable

180   HERBERT A. WAINER AND IRWIN M. RUBIN

TABLE 1

MEANS, MEDIANS, AND RANGES OF
VARIABLES MEASURED

Variable	M	Mdn	Range
n Ach	5.9	5.0	−5 to 18
n Pow	9.7	9.5	0 to 19
n Aff	3.5	3.0	0 to 16
Growth rate	.40	.375	0.0 to 2.10

experience at a technically advanced research laboratory prior to starting his new enterprise. Among the information gathered were company yearly sales figures and scores on McClelland's version of the TAT for each entrepreneur. The yearly sales figures were used as the basis for determining the growth rate, defined in detail below. The index of performance was derived from the growth rate. The TATs were scored for n Ach, n Pow, and n Aff by the Motivation Research Group at Harvard University. The resulting scores were the basis for analysis of the strength of various needs in relation to performance.[3]

Growth rate is defined as follows: *annual increase in the logarithm of sales volume between the second and most recent year reported.* For example, Company A is 7 yr. old. Its second-year sales were $100,000 and its last year (seventh) sales were $950,000. These two sales values are plotted on semilog paper. The growth rate is indicated by the percent rate of change from year to year. This is, of course, constant over the 7 yr. The growth rate in this case would be approximately .56. Table 1 summarizes the general characteristics of the four variables with which this paper is concerned.

The method of analysis in all cases was a comparison of high, moderate, and low groups. Equality of sample size, within the limits of tied observations, was the criterion used in making these groupings. Standard correlational techniques were feasible in many cases, and, where appropriate, coefficients are presented in footnotes. However, since such techniques often mask nonlinear trends in relationships, the Mann-Whitney U test, one of the most powerful of the nonparametric statistical tests, was used. Furthermore, correlation techniques focused on differences between two variables based on individual differences from case to case. On the other hand, the Mann-Whitney U, a difference in medians test, analyzes differences between characteristics of groups of data. The authors feel that TAT scoring procedures are not yet precise enough to enable researchers to use individual differences as the basis for comparison.

[3] Average intercoder reliabilities of scores from the Motivation Research Group are in the high .80 range.

RESULTS

Analyses of the relationship between the three needs, n Ach, n Pow, and n Aff, and their relation to company performance are presented in this section. In addition, some exploratory results will be presented that focus on the question: Is there a pattern or combination of needs which are related to high company performance? In other words, one set of analyses will focus on the direct relationship between performance and varying degrees of strength in a single need, while a secondary focus will explore effects of several needs taken together on company performance.

Relationship between the Three Needs

The data in Table 2 suggest that, within this sample, n Ach, n Pow, and n Aff are not completely independent.[4] n Ach appears to be positively related to n Pow and negatively related to n Aff, while n Pow is negatively related to n Aff. It is important to note, however, that in all cases the relationship is non-linear. In the case of n Ach versus n Pow, for example, only the low n Ach group has a significantly different n Pow score. No differences in n Pow are observed when a comparison of the high versus moderate n Ach groups is made. A similar phenomenon is present in each relationship. In other words, the correlation coefficients reported in Footnote 4 are heavily influenced by a small subset of the total distribution of need scores.

With these qualifications in mind, it is concluded that the three needs are moderately related. Where the relationship between each need and company performance is examined, an attempt will be made to take into account this lack of independence.

Need Strength versus Company Performance

The major hypothesis in this study predicts a direct and positive relationship between an entrepreneur's n Ach and the performance of his company. No directional hy-

[4] The following are the Kendall Tau correlations between three needs (two-tailed test). n Ach versus n Pow: $T = .370$, $p < .01$, $N = 51$. n Ach versus n Aff: $T = -.259$, $p < .01$, $N = 51$. n Aff versus n Pow: $T = -.233$, $p < .05$, $N = 51$.

potheses were specified concerning the relationships between n Pow, n Aff, and company performance.[5]

Referring to Table 3, it can be seen that, within the range of moderate to high n Ach, a very marked positive relationship exists between n Ach and company performance. The growth rate of those companies led by entrepreneurs with a high n Ach was almost 250% higher (.73 versus .21) than those companies led by entrepreneurs with a moderate n Ach. Here again, however, the relationship is not purely linear since the low n Ach group has a mean performance score slightly *higher* than the moderate n Ach group but still significantly lower than high n Ach group.

n Pow, as can be seen from Table 3, is completely unrelated to company performance. n Aff, on the other hand, exhibits a mildly negative, nonlinear, relationship to company performance. The data were then examined to see if the observed relationship between n Ach and n Aff influenced the relationship found between n Ach and performance. No such contamination was found. Of those who were classified in the low n Aff group ($n = 13$), only six fell into the high

[5] The following are the Kendall Tau correlations between the three needs and company performance (growth rate). n Ach versus performance: $T = .15$, $p < .08$, $N = 51$ (one-tailed). n Pow versus performance: $T = .05$, $p < .64$, $N = 51$. n Aff versus performance: $T = -.11$, $p < .28$, $N = 51$.

TABLE 2

RELATIONSHIP BETWEEN THE THREE NEEDS

Need	Group		
	High	Moderate	Low

n Ach

	≥ 9	n	$4 \geq \times \leq 8$	n	≤ 3	n
n Pow	11.3 (A)	14	11.1 (B)	19	6.8 (C)	18
n Aff	2.0 (D)	14	3.9 (E)	19	4.4 (F)	18

n Pow

	≥ 13	n	$8 \geq \times \leq 12$	n	≤ 7	n
n Aff	2.8 (G)	15	3.0 (H)	19	4.7 (I)	17

Note.—Mann-Whitney U test results: A versus B, $p < .60$; A versus C, $p < .003$; B versus C, $p < .007$; D versus E, $p < .13$; D versus F, $p < .02$; E versus F, $p < .45$; G versus H, $p < .60$; G versus I, $p < .11$; and H versus I, $p < .09$.

TABLE 3

RELATIONSHIP BETWEEN N ACH, N POW, AND N AFF AND GROWTH RATE

Need	Code for Mann-Whitney U results[a]	Strength	Mean growth rate
n Ach	A	High (≥ 9) $N = 14$	.73
	B	Moderate ($4 \geq \times \leq 8$) $N = 19$	.21
	C	Low (≤ 3) $N = 18$	.36
n Pow	A	High (≥ 13) $N = 15$	.38
	B	Moderate ($8 \geq \times \leq 12$) $N = 19$	.47
	C	Low (≤ 7) $N = 17$	.36
n Aff	A	High (≥ 4) $N = 20$	.33
	B	Moderate ($2 \geq \times \leq 3$) $N = 18$	.30
	C	Low (≤ 1) $N = 13$	.67

[a] Results of Mann-Whitney U tests: n Ach versus growth rate: A versus B, $p < .0001$; A versus C, $p < .006$; B versus C, $p < .08$, one tailed. n Pow versus Growth rate: A versus B, $p < .80$; A versus C, $p < .90$; B verus C, $p < .80$, two-tailed. n Aff versus growth rate: A versus B, $p < .81$; A versus C, $p < 16$; B versus C, $p < .10$, two-tailed.

n Ach group. n Ach, in other words, directly affects company performance, independent of its relationship to n Aff.

The results of this section are summarized graphically in Figure 1. The percentage of companies within each subgroup (high, moderate, low), whose performance is above that of the median for the total sample of entrepreneurs, is plotted for each of the needs. Seventy-nine percent of those companies led by entrepreneurs whose n Ach was high had a growth rate which was above the median for the total sample of entrepreneurs.

Joint Products of Needs versus Performance

The previous section focused on variations in company performance resulting from each of the three needs (n Ach, n Pow, and n Aff) taken singularly. The aim in this section is to explore the question of whether or not any *pattern* of need strengths appears to be associated with high company performance. In

182   HERBERT A. WAINER AND IRWIN M. RUBIN

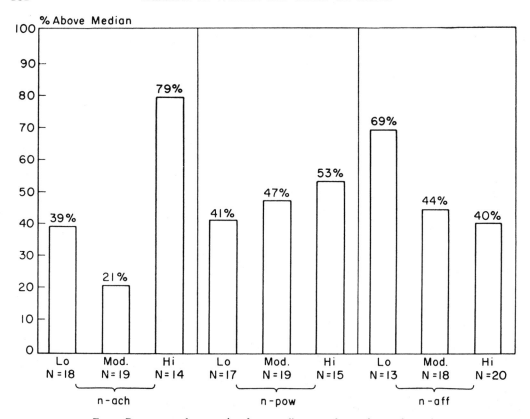

FIG. 1. Percentage of companies above median growth rate for total sample.

examining the data, it was noticed that, in addition to the very wide differences in company performance noted *between* high, moderate, and low n Ach groups, there existed substantial variations in company performance *within* each of these three groups. In other words, although the high n Ach group exhibited very high performance in comparison with the moderate and low n Ach groups, the range of performance scores *within* the high n Ach group was from .14 to 2.10. Similar within-group ranges were observed in the other two n Ach groupings.

An attempt was made, therefore, to determine whether these within-group variations could be attributed to variations in the strengths of the other two needs being investigated, n Pow and n Aff. The authors have further split the samples into high versus low performers (at the median performance score *within* each n Ach group) and compared levels of n Pow and n Aff within each of these new subgroups.

The following patterns emerge from the data summarized in Table 4. Within the low n Ach group, variations in performance are unaffected by variations in n Pow or n Aff. Within the moderate n Ach group, n Pow is identical for high versus low performers, while high performers within this group have a significantly higher n Aff. Finally, within the high n Ach group, n Aff is identical for high versus low performers, while high performers within this group have a significantly lower n Pow.

In summary, the *highest performing companies* in this sample were led by entrepreneurs who exhibited a high n Ach and a moderate n Pow. Those entrepreneurs who had a high n Ach coupled with a high n Pow performed less well than their high n Ach counterparts who exhibited only a moderate level of n Pow.[6]

_____

[6] When the authors use the phrases "moderate n Pow" or "high n Pow," they are using as their reference point the distribution of scores observed in this study sample. Their specification, for example, of

TABLE 4

RELATIONSHIP BETWEEN PERFORMANCE AND n POW AND n AFF WITHIN HIGH, MODERATE, AND LOW n ACH GROUPS

Need	High n Ach (≥ 9.0)		Moderate n Ach (4 ≥ X ≤ 8)		Low n Ach (≤ 3.0)	
	Performance					
	Low (≤.59) N = 7	High (>.59) N = 7	Low (≤.13) N = 9	High (≥.21) N = 10	Low (≤.26) N = 9	High (>.26) N = 9
n Pow	13.1(A)	9.4(B)	11.0(C)	11.0(D)	7.0(E)	6.7(F)
n Aff	2.0(G)	2.0(H)	2.2(I)	5.5(J)	4.9(K)	4.0(L)

Note.—Mann-Whitney U test (two-tailed): A versus B, $p < .08$; C versus D, $p < .40$; E versus F, $p < .50$; G versus H, $p < .50$; I versus J, $p < .02$; K versus L, $p < .25$.

Within the moderate n Ach group, higher performing companies were led by entrepreneurs who had a high n Aff.

DISCUSSION

The major hypothesis tested in this study predicted a positive relationship between an entrepreneur's level of n Ach and his company's performance. The authors' findings strongly support the conclusion that high n Ach is associated with high company performance, but the relationship between n Ach and performance is not linear across the entire range of n Ach scores. The relationship is markedly linear for the entrepreneurs whose n Ach is moderate to high. However, these entrepreneurs who scored low in n Ach were not significantly lower performers than those whose n Ach was moderate.

In an attempt to explain this nonlinearity it seems reasonable to assume that other needs or factors are influencing the entrepreneurial behavior of individuals who are not moderate to high in their level of n Ach. It is extremely likely that some threshold level of n Ach is necessary before one could assume that the strength of the need is significantly affecting the individual's behavior. In addition, it is obvious that the authors do not see n Ach as being the only (or for that matter the most important) factor that influences company

_____

high n Pow as being ≥ 13.0 was made *prior* to the analyses under discussion in this section. Consequently, classification of a mean n Pow of 13.1 as high and a mean n Pow of 9.4 as moderate is consistent with their a priori definitions.

performance. They are arguing, however, that where the need exists in sufficient strength to influence entrepreneurial behavior significantly, company performance in general will improve.

A secondary aim in this study was to explore the question of whether a certain pattern or combination of needs was most often associated with high performance. In the introduction to this paper, it was suggested than n Pow and n Aff were needs whose behavioral manifestations were interpersonal in character. Satisfaction of these two needs, by definition, involves relationships with other people. n Ach, on the other hand, is much more individualistic in character. Satisfaction of one's n Ach, although often involving contact with other people, has behavioral manifestations which are qualitatively different in nature than either n Pow or n Aff.

The results of this study suggest that the combination of a high n Ach and a moderate n Pow characterizes the highest performing companies in the sample. In other words, a high (as opposed to moderate) level of n Pow appeared to counterbalance to some extent the positive benefits of a high level of n Ach.

One possible explanation for this finding lies in the relationship between n Pow and various styles of leadership. The lower an individual's n Pow, the more permissive or laissez-faire his style of leadership, the higher his n Pow, the more autocratic or authoritarian his style of leadership. The middle of the n Pow spectrum represents a mixed influence of the two extreme styles which is

184   HERBERT A. WAINER AND IRWIN M. RUBIN

best described as democratic.[7] Prior research (Lippitt & White, 1958) has suggested that in certain situations the most effective leadership style is democratic and that performance of groups controlled in this manner is better than that of groups controlled by either of the other two styles.

Somewhat more difficult to explain is the finding concerning the positive differential effect on company performance, within the moderate n Ach group, of a high versus low n Aff level. It may be that for those individuals who have only a moderate level of n Ach, a high level of n Aff enables them to form close interpersonal relationships with their colleagues. In this way, the moderate n Ach individual· may be able to acquire the assistance he needs from his colleagues, some of whom may well have a higher level of n Ach than he himself has.

[7] The authors have assumed, of course, that high n Pow leaders are more likely to exercise an autocratic style of leadership and low n Pow leaders a laissez-faire style.

Interpretations in this area of need combinations must be viewed, at this point, as speculative and suggestive of further research. Analysis of the results of this study indicates that more complex relationships do have to be examined if a realistic view of performance determined by personality is to be gained. Future research should include replications of this study and the use of larger samples for the investigation of these hypotheses.

REFERENCES

ATKINSON, J. W. *Motives in fantasy, action, and society*. Princeton: Van Nostrand, 1958.

LIPPITT, R., & WHITE, R. K. An experimental study of leadership and group life. In *Readings in social psychology*. New York: Holt, Rinehart & Winston, 1958.

McCLELLAND, D. C. *The achieving society*. Princeton: Van Nostrand, 1961.

SCHRAGE, H. The R&D entrepreneur: Profile of success. *Harvard Business Review*, 1965.

(Received January 22, 1968)

MICHAEL PALMER

A reprint from
CALIFORNIA MANAGEMENT REVIEW
© 1971 by The Regents of the University of California

The Application of Psychological Testing to Entrepreneurial Potential

THE WORD E N T R E P R E N E U R carries a deluge of definitional and operational ambiguity. A review of the literature on entrepreneurship affords "strange and contradictory results." The entrepreneurial function has been identified with "uncertainty bearing . . . coordination of production resources . . . introduction of innovations . . . and . . . the provision of capital."[1] The literature also demonstrates the inadequacy of definitions to describe the entrepreneur in terms necessary for ex ante measurement. All definitions are ex post facto: a person is defined as an entrepreneur because of something he has done, in terms of a function. Although the functional definition may be constructed to indicate something he is *capable* of doing, the measurement problem is not solved. He still has to perform the function before he can be called an entrepreneur.

With these definitional and measurement problems sharply in mind we:

- elucidate the term entrepreneur,
- elaborate on the problems of entrepreneurial measurement,
- propose a single definition of the entrepreneurial function for possible use in psychological testing.

Before examining various definitions of the entrepreneur, it would be beneficial to speculate why an investigation such as this is important. Arthur Cole suggests that to study the businessman is to study the main figure in economic activity.[2] However, a reason such as this does not specifically answer what important consequences might ensue from such a study. As a possible answer, I might introduce the following hypothesis (for which originality is not claimed): **a priori**, there appears to be some correlation between economic growth and business formations. **Second**, important to the formation of a business is the activity of an entrepreneur. **Third**, certain areas may possess capital and resources while suffering from a scarcity of entrepreneurs; hence, in these areas we might expect to find a lag in economic development. In other areas, where numerous entrepreneurs exist along with an adequate resource base we might expect a flourish of economic activity.

A qualification to this thesis is the reasoning that in areas void of entrepreneurial talent, if the market is right, and if opportunities are available, entrepreneurs will be forthcoming. But, this assumes perfect mobility of existing entrepreneurs or that existing entrepreneurs have additional time to devote to the region.

Returning to our entrepreneurial depressed area for a moment, it now becomes obvious that if we understand the role of an entrepreneur it might be possible, as a short-run measure, to train or supervise people to act in an entrepreneurial manner. To develop autonomous entrepreneurs in the area, however, a longer-term remedy appears needed. For this, one must examine the sources of entrepreneurial talent, that is, the forces—psychological and environmental—which engendered the entrepreneurial personality. In summary, a functional definition might suffice for use as a short-run measure, but one must probe much deeper for an adequate long-run solution.

The Definitional Problem

Joseph Schumpeter noted that fifteenth century economic thinkers had established ideas about the businessman and his functions. The French economist Cantillon, the first to introduce the term entrepreneur, defined him as the agent who purchased the means of production for combination into marketable products. Furthermore, at the moment of the factor purchases, the entrepreneur was unaware of the eventual price which he would receive for his products. Thus, Cantillon introjected elements of direction and speculation into his functional definition of the entrepreneur.

Another Frenchman, J. B. Say, expanded Cantillon's ideas. Say conceptualized the entrepreneur as the organizer of the business firm, central to its distributive and production functions. Beyond stressing the entrepreneur's importance to the business, Say did little with his entrepreneurial analysis.

Adam Smith, despite the detectable influence of Cantillon upon his thinking, saw the entrepreneur as cast in a minor active role in overall economic activity—he provided real capital, but did not play a leading or directing part.[3] Generally, it appears that classical economists, for the purpose of theoretical analysis, were not concerned with the entrepreneur as a human entity, but rather treated him impersonally, as the firm itself.

In the second half of the nineteenth century examining the entrepreneur's role as distinct from the capitalist's was expedited by a growing separation of corporate ownership and management. As a result of new financing methods, the distinction between entrepreneur and capitalist became salient, and in ensuing analysis, examination of the entrepreneur was accentuated.

Early twentieth century writers conceptualized the entrepreneurial function as one of promotion. One such writer, Arthur Stone Dewing, viewed the promoter as one who transformed ideas into a profitable business. In enumerating the characteristics of a successful entrepreneur, Dewing wrote of the qualities of imagination, initiative, judgment, and restraint.[4] Dewing was quite explicit in emphasizing the promoter's importance to the creation of business organizations. "No business," he stated, "ever started itself." Other writers emphasizing the promoter during this time stressed the indispensable function of the promoter to business formations.[5]

Joseph Schumpeter contributed substantially to the literature on entrepreneurs. He excluded from the term entrepreneur all heads of firms or managers who merely operated an established business. To him, carrying out new combinations covered the introduction of a new good, the introduction of a new method of production, the opening of a new market, the finding of a new source of raw materials, and the carrying out of a new organization of any industry.[6] To accomplish this, the entreprenuer must convince money holders—bankers and private capitalists—of the desirability of his innovation. After securing the funds he merely buys the necessary means of production.

According to Clarence H. Danhof, an entrepreneur "is primarily concerned with changes in the formula of production . . . over which he has full control. . . . He devotes correspondingly little time to the carrying out of a specific formula."[7] Danhof divides the function of the entrepreneur into three major roles: *obtaining relevant information, evaluating the information with regard to profit*, and *setting the operation in motion*. Once the entrepreneur has determined what information should be gathered, the first two functions can be delegated. Basic to the entrepreneur function, in Danhof's analysis, is decision making, or judgment, under alternative choices.

Another concept is presented by Herberton G. Evans who views the entrepreneur as "the person or group of persons who has (or assumes) the task of determining the kind of business to be operated."[8] The decisions germane to this function involve the nature of the goods and services to be offered, the size of the enterprise, and the customers catered to. Once these decisions have been made by the entrepreneur, other decisions, that is decisions to achieve the previous goals set by the entrepreneur, become essentially management's. Evans notes that once these decisions have been made the role of the entrepreneur does not cease: instead, he must be continually alert and ready to make new decisions in light of changing market conditions and arising opportunities. In Evans' scheme we find a distinction between the entrepreneurial and managerial role. It's implicit in his article that the manager's role could be delegated, but not the entrepreneur's.

Another advocate of the entrepreneur as a decision maker is Robert K. Lamb. To him "entrepreneurship is that form of social decision making performed by economic innovators."[9] Lamb suggests that the major contribution of the entrepreneur is not the creation of individual firms or institutions, but a broader process of building local, national, and international communities and changing existing social and economic institutions.

All the definitions thus far examined are similar in one prominent respect—they neglect the influence of the social order on the actions of the entrepreneur. If the functions of the entrepreneur are to be thoroughly understood, all aspects contributing to his behavioral patterns must be considered social, political, economic, and psychological forces.

Joseph McGuire wrote that "Over time, and in different societies, there has evidently been a substantial change in entrepreneurial types, and presumably in the entrepreneur function."[10] In order to understand these differences, he feels one should be aware of cultural variations. Entrepreneurs in different cultures may act quite differently and these differences cannot always be attributed to economic factors, such as natural resources, money capital, and so on, for these factors may be equal. To understand the differences in business behavior, factors such as social ideology, norms and rewards for behavior, individual and national aspirations, religious doctrines, education and the like, must be examined on a comparative basis. Obviously, the need for a cultural approach is not just limited to comparative analysis, but is also indispensable for an intracultural examination of entrepreneurial behavior.

Some contemporary writers, like the earlier traditionalists, have held unwaveringly to the profit maximization motive (or some refinement of it) as the factor responsible for business behavior. They have continued to espouse this viewpoint despite the mounting evidence for other motivational factors being accumulated by the behavioral sciences.

Sigmund Freud, in his psychoanalytic theory, depicted the human being as driven by unconscious and innate drives. Essential to Freudian analysis was the influence of early childhood experiences on the behavior of the adult. For example, if a choice becomes fixated or frustrated during an early developmental stage, a resulting behavior pattern may carry over into adulthood. Nowhere in Freud's works is there mention of an economic motivation directed toward profits or material aggrandizement. An individual may seek out these material ends, but they will be incidental to the basic human motives.

According to Freud: "The sexual are amongst the most important of the instinctive forces." They may be sublimated, however, and "their energy . . . diverted towards other ends, no longer sexual."[11]

Freud's pansexualism and neglect of cultural factors promoted the development of a school of psychology known as social psychology. Among these apostates from Freudian analysis were Eric Fromm, Karen Horney, Alfred Adler, and Harry Stack Sullivan. According to the social psychologists, man is predominantly a product of the society in which he lives. His personality is not biological, but social. The notion of unconscious drives was reduced by these psychologists. Drives were provided by the social environment in which man existed. Alfred Adler, for example, declared that the driving force in man was an innate social urge—striving to attain the goal of a perfect society.

Other psychologists, known as the self-theorists, have explained man's motivation in terms of self fulfillment, or self development. Man is viewed as a driving, seeking individual, attempting to reach the ultimate goal of self completion. Within this school are such psychologists as Carl Rogers and Abraham Maslow.

Stimulus-response theorists form still another group. Advocates, such as Dollard, Miller and B. F. Skinner, visualize the behavior of the human organism as a manifestation of stimulus-response bonds. When a certain stimulus is felt by the individual, he will react according to his learned responses. Classical stimulus-response theorists explain this bond as being automatic, while instrumental theorists see its development according to the past reinforcements of the individual.[12]

In summary, behavior cannot be explained in simple terms, or as the classical economists would like us to believe, in terms of an economic motive. Perhaps the entrepreneur does seek profits, but that he has other motivational drives influencing his behavior patterns must be recognized. Therefore, to understand adequately the role of the entrepreneur, economic and psychological factors must be considered.

Now that various definitions have been examined, what can one say about the entrepreneur? To begin, all of the frameworks are disappointing in that they have been concerned with functional behavior, that is an entrepreneur is defined as an entrepreneur because he acts in a certain way. From Cantillon's incipient analysis to the economists of today, the functional stigma has remained. In addition, one cannot tell from these models (although a clue is offered by the cultural advocates) what factors initially contribute to the development of an entrepreneurial class, or how we may measure the existing supply curve of entrepreneurs in a given area, or how we may increase the long-run supply of entrepreneurs.

The Measurement Problem

Functional definitions, although limited, are essential. They are essential here because it is necessary to distinguish the entrepreneurs from the non-entrepreneurs. Thus, when a before-the-fact measurement is devised, we may compare its test predictions with actual behavior, thereby determining the validity of the measurement.

The most promising methods of before-the-fact measurement of the entrepreneur appear to be attitudinal and motivational tests. In general, the two types which might be employed are projective and pencil-and-paper tests.[13] The projective test is more nondirective and subjective in that the subject is instructed to write or speak candidly after having examined a picture or read a short story. The psychologist using such a test assumes that the subject projects himself—his feelings, beliefs, motivations, and so on—into the picture or the story, and although many of the subject's drives, motivations, and feelings are unknown even to him, they will become salient in his stories. A paper-and-pencil test is more directive in that the person is usually asked to rank himself with regard to an object or situation on a predetermined (like-dislike; yes-no) scale. Common among these testing techniques are the Likert scale, the Thurstone equal appearing intervals, and the Bogardus social distance scale.

Employing projective techniques, David McClelland has developed a promising method for measuring entrepreneurial potential. McClelland has hypothesized that the need for achievement is the psychological factor which engenders economic growth and decline. A society in which the level of achievement motivation is intense will produce energetic entrepreneurs. If McClelland's hypothesis is workable, entrepreneurship can be ascertained by measuring achievement motivation.

In the McClelland test, the subject is shown a picture (for example, a man sitting at an office desk looking at a picture of his family or a boy sitting at a piano looking out a window). After viewing the picture, the subject is asked to write a story about it. The psychologist assumes that the subject will project himself into the picture and his related story will actually be a narration about himself. In scoring the test, the experimenter checks for achievement in the subject's story; achievement being indicated by the subject mentioning one of the following incidents: (1) defining a problem, (2) wanting to solve it, (3) thinking of means to solve it, (4) thinking of difficulties that get in the way of solving it, (5) thinking of people who might help in solving it, and (6) anticipating what would happen if one succeeded or failed. The subject receives a $+1$ for each idea that shows up in his story. If none are indicated, he is given a score of -1. The test possible score would be $+36$ and the lowest possible score would be -6. McClelland claims that the "coding of the stories for achievement imagery is so objective that two expert scorers working independently rarely disagree."[14]

Certain roles have been shown to delineate entrepreneurial behavior; among these roles are risk taking, innovating, and decision making. With these roles in mind, an examination of the correlations between overt behavior and achievement motivation scores may determine whether people with high achievement motivation act in ways analogous to the theorists' definitions of entrepreneurship. In a general sense, we are trying to determine the validity of the McClelland test.

A number of significant findings are available from researchers using McClelland's approach. For example, people with high achievement motivation, relative to those with low achievement motivation, are characterized by:

- preferring tasks involving some objective risks,
- working harder at tasks which require mental manipulation,
- wanting to operate in a situation where he can get a sense of personal achievement,
- not working harder under the influence of a money reward,
- performing better under conditions where he has a positive and definite feedback,
- tending to think ahead (long-range thinking).

No correlations have been found between organizational skill and motivation achievement, but it has been shown that people with high achievement motivation prefer working with experts over personal friends.[15]

From the results of the extensive research conducted on achievement motivation, it can be concluded that people who score high on an achievement motivation test are more likely to act in an entrepreneurial way than those who score low on the test. The remaining point is, do these people end up in business? According to McClelland, "there is a tendency to bias occupational choice toward business among boys of middle (but not upper) class status with high achievement motivation."[16] He has found that in three countries (United States, Italy, and Poland) representing different stages of economic development, executives tend to score higher on the achievement test than do other professionals or specialists of comparable education and background. McClelland hypothesizes that an individual with a high achievement motivation will be attracted to the business world because the existing situations will complement his achievement motivation in terms of risks, personal achievement, unambiguous feedback in the form of profits, and specific accomplishments.

Expanding McClelland's hypothesis, it is possible to explore the sources of high achievement as a means of stimulating the long-run supply of an entrepreneurial class. Marian R. Winterbottom suggests the seeds of high achievement motivation can be traced to early childhood. Through experiments with children she has found that early mastery training promotes high achievement motivation, provided it does not reflect generalized parental restrictiveness, authoritarianism, or rejection. Generally, those children who had been urged and expected to achieve outside their home at an early age demonstrated higher achievement motivation than those who were urged at later years. Winterbottom is quick to note that too early urging on the part of the parents can be just as detrimental to the development of high achievement motivation: it may be too early for the boy's abilities, or it may be too late for him to internalize the achievement motivation.

Michael Palmer is Assistant Professor of Finance at the University of Colorado. Dr. Palmer received his doctorate from the University of Washington.

The optimum ages for parental urging and expecting, as suggested by Winterbottom, appear to be between six and eight.[17]

B. C. Rosen and R. G. D'Andrade have also conducted studies concerned with the sources of achievement motivation. They have found three variables related to achievement motivation. These factors are parental expectations, warmth, and dominance. With regard to expectations, they found that parents of boys with high achievement motivation usually set higher standards for their children than do parents of low achievement motivation boys. Further, the parents of high achievement motivation boys showed more emotional involvement with respect to their child's activities. Finally, boys with high achievement motivation had nonauthoritarian fathers. Rosen and D'Andrade suggest that an authoritarian father transfers to the boy a dependent conception of the male figure. As a result, the boy will be less likely to set his own standards of excellence and to strive for them on his own.[18]

In summary, data suggest that the sources of achievement motivation for an individual stem from the beliefs, values, and ideologies which are inculcated into his psychological system in early childhood as they are subscribed to by the parents. Unfortunately, achievement motivation tests are still in their early stages of development. McClelland notes that the test results for groups may be valid, while those for each individual are questionable. On an individual basis, the test is also subject to faking and social desirability responses. In spite of these drawbacks, the potential for entrepreneurial measurement with McClelland's or similar tests is clearly evident. What remains is the refinement of the method.

Further Research and Refinements

There exists no universally accepted definition with respect to the meaning of entrepreneurial talent. Academicians and practitioners have suggested a plethora of skills and abilities when, for example, attempting to delineate the variables which account for a successful manager or leader (or entrepreneur). All that can be noted with certainty at the present is that the nature of entrepreneurship is indeed complex.

Skills and abilities which may be necessary for

entrepreneurial success in one situation may be markedly different from those needed under changed conditions. Thus, an individual may confidently strive for entrepreneurial achievement in a particular setting, and become a passive participant in another. Furthermore, researchers have suggested the need for more than one type of leader when relating to the attainment of group goals. Robert F. Bales has found two types of leaders with a group: "task specialist" who controls the activities of the group, and the "social specialist" who manages the stresses and strains of the participants in the group.[19] Furthermore, Bales' research suggests that it would be rare for one person to perform both leadership functions.

Differences in motivations would appear to account for this. Bales suggests that task specialists are motivated by strong desires to control the activities of others while maintaining their own freedom. Social specialists appear to be motivated by desires for affiliation and affection. In addition, the task specialist, because of the nature of his position, will probably be low on likeability; while the social specialist will generally be the most popular person in the group.

One area of research would appear to involve the delineation of entrepreneurial functions. That is, *how* do we differentiate an entrepreneur from a nonentrepreneur, and *what* skills and abilities are necessary to the performance of the entrepreneurial function?

A second area in need of further research relates to the testing techniques. This appears especially relevant in the case of intercultural measuring for achievement motivation. Undoubtedly, what needs to be developed is a series of different pictures (or a series of different tests) applicable to varying cultures. Another measurement problem involves differences in interest among individuals. Psychologists should probably use a fairly large number of pictures (or tests) in an attempt to negate any personal differences in interest.

A third area open to further research involves cause and effect analysis. Investigations should attempt to answer why certain people possess higher entrepreneurial motivation than other individuals. Cross-discipline research—involving all the behavioral sciences—appears to be needed.

In summary, while present psychological testing allows us some measure of entrepreneurial potential, contemporary research would appear to be needed in the areas of defining the skills and abilities of an entrepreneur, refining the testing techniques as they relate to these defined skills, and pro-

viding answers relating to the sources of entrepreneurial motivation.

Suggestions

Decision making under varying degrees of uncertainty appears to be an underlying feature of entrepreneurship. For the most part, however, the element of uncertainty has only been implied by most writers. Cantillon, for example, introjected the element of price variability with regard to the entrepreneur's product. Schumpeter noted the innovating nature—developing new methods and enterprises—of the entrepreneur. Frank H. Knight, of course, was more explicit. In his *Risk, Uncertainty, and Profit*, in which he defines the entrepreneur as the "central figure of the system," he notes uncertainty as an integral factor in business decision making.[20]

Decision making under uncertainty appears to offer a suitable framework for the measurement of entrepreneurial potential. As suggested, previous entrepreneurial definitions appear to encompass functional activities under conditions of uncertainty, for example, uncertainty with regard to: pricing (Cantillon), innovating (Schumpeter), promoting ideas into business operations (Dewing), determining the type of business (Evans), and making decisions under alternative choices (Danhof), or changing market conditions (Evans).

In spite of McGuire's position that "over time, and in different societies, there has evidently been a substantial change in entrepreneurial types, and presumably in the entrepreneur function,"[21] the need to make decisions under conditions of uncertainty appears to be a relatively consistent part of the entrepreneurial function. For example, whether we are operating within an agricultural or an industrial society, within a small or large business organization under private or public leadership (or even within a micro versus a macro framework), the element of uncertainty cannot be eliminated.

The willingness of an individual to deal with uncertainty, therefore, would appear to be an appropriate measure of entrepreneurial potential. **Successful entrepreneurship, within this proposed framework, would involve a (1) determination of the types and degrees of uncertainty confronting the performance of a particular operation and (2) the ability to make the appropriate decision necessary for goal attainment.**

Conclusions

I would argue that the entrepreneurial function involves primarily *risk measurement* and *risk taking* within a business organization. Furthermore, the successful entrepreneur is that individual who can correctly interpret the risk situation and then determine policies which will minimize the risks involved (for example, converting uncertainty into fixed costs), given a particular goal aspiration. Both functions, I would argue, are essential for successful entrepreneurship. Thus, the individual who can correctly measure the risk situation, but is unable to minimize that risk, would not be defined as an entrepreneur. As suggested earlier, risk cannot be eliminated; the successful .entrepreneur, however, can minimize the risk situation.

In addition, I would suggest that psychological testing (such as the McClelland achievement motivation) be directed most toward the measurement of an individual's perception and handling of risk. Cause and effect research should be concerned with an investigation of the motivational determinates of risk bearing versus risk aversion. Specific research in this area should be directed at a determination of the psychological and environmental sources which produce a risk functioning individual. Last, research should concern the extent to which programs can be developed for the successful training of risk measuring and risk taking.

REFERENCES

1. B. F. Hoselitz, "Entrepreneurship and Economic Growth," *American Journal of Economic Sociology* (1952), p. 97.

2. Arthur H. Cole, *Business Enterprise in Its Social Setting*, (Cambridge: Harvard University Press, 1951), p. 28.

3. Joseph A. Schumpeter, "Economic Theory and Entrepreneurial History," in *Change and the Entrepreneur* (Cambridge: Harvard University, 1948), prepared by the Research Center in Entrepreneurial History, pp. 63–66.

4. Arthur Stone Dewing, *The Financial Policy of Corporations* (New York: Ronald Press, 1919), pp. 245–254.

5. E. S. Meade, *Corporation Finance*, 1915, p. 23; R. E. Heilman, *Journal of Political Economy* (November 1915), 895.

6. Joseph A. Schumpeter, *The Theory of Economic Development* (Cambridge: Harvard University Press, 1934) in E. Okun, *Studies in Economic Development*, pp. 91–94.

7. Clarence H. Danhof, "Observations of Entrepreneurship in Agriculture," *Change and the Entrepreneur* (Cambridge: Harvard Univerity Press, 1949), p. 21.

8. Herberton G. Evans, "A Century of Entrepreneurship in the United States With Emphasis Upon Large Manufacturing Concerns, 1850–1957," in *The Entrepreneur*. Papers presented at the annual conference of the Economic History Society at Cambridge, England, April 1957. Published by the Research Center in Entrepreneurial History, Harvard University, p. 50.

9. Robert K. Lamb, "The Entrepreneur and the Community," in *Men in Business*, William Miller (ed.) (Harvard University Press, 1952), p. 91.

10. Joseph McGuire, *Theories of Business Behavior*. (Englewood Cliffs, N.J.: Prentice-Hall, 1964), p. 238.

11. Sigmund Freud, *A General Introduction to Psychoanalysis* (New York: Washington Square Press, 1920), p. 27.

12. See Calvin S. Hall and Gardner Lindzey, *Theories of Personality* (New York: Wiley 1957), esp. pp. 114–155, 324–327, 420–499.

13. For empirical observations on the two types of tests see: Irwin G. Sarason, *Contemporary Research in Personality*, pp. 1–81.

14. David McClelland, "Business Drive and National Achievement," *Harvard Business Review* (July-August, 1962), 101–102.

15. Elizabeth G. French, "Motivation as a Variable in Work Partner Selection," *Journal of Abnormal Social Psychology* (1956), 96–99.

16. McClelland, "Business Drive and National Achievement," 102–103.

17. Marian R. Winterbottom, "The Relation of Need for Achievement to Learning Experiences in Independence and Mastery," in J. W. Atkinson (ed.) *Motives in Fantasy, Action and Society* (New Jersey: Van Nostrand, 1958), pp. 468–71.

18. B. C. Rosen and R. G. D'Andrade, "The Psychological Origins of Achievement Motivation," *Sociometry* (1959), 185–218.

19. Robert F. Bales, "Task Roles and Social Roles in Problem Solving Groups," *Readings in Social Psychology*, E. Maccoby, T. Newcomb, and E. Hartley (eds.), (New York: Holt, Rinehart, and Winston, 1958), pp. 437–447.

20. Frank H. Knight, *Risk, Uncertainty, and Profit*. (New York: Houghton Mifflin, 1921), chaps. I and VII.

21. McGuire, p. 238.

CHARACTERISTICS OF SUCCESSFUL ENTREPRENEURS[1]

50

JOHN A. HORNADAY AND JOHN ABOUD

Babson College[2]

Introduction

IN an earlier article in *Personnel Psychology*, Hornaday and Bunker (1970) discuss the importance of achieving a better understanding of the psychological nature of the successful entrepreneur through a research program designed to identify and measure the personal characteristics of those persons who have successfully started a new business. Such knowledge would be of much interest to lending organizations such as banks, to enfranchising organizations such as oil companies and restaurant chains, and to federal government programs, both domestic (in loans to small businesses and in such efforts as the poverty programs) and international (as in using foreign aid more effectively to help strengthen the economy of underdeveloped countries). Further, colleges of business administration can make significant contributions in entrepreneurial education if it is possible to understand the nature of entrepreneurship and if workable programs can be developed from the results of the research.

The earlier research led to the development of a structured interview guide sheet as well as the selection of three standardized, objective tests that appeared promising in differentiating successful entrepreneurs from men in general. Although McClelland (McClelland, Atkinson, Clark and Lowell, 1953) has reported success in using both the Thematic Apperception Test (Murray, 1943) and in using his own test for this purpose, these tests are *projective* in nature and can be administered and interpreted only by a highly-

[1] This study was supported by a grant from the Babson College Board of Research.

[2] The authors wish to express their appreciation to Margaret Courtnay Stone who aided in the data collection.

trained psychologist. The goal of this study was to develop *objective* tests which will be valid and will have the advantage of a simple format and ease of administration and interpretation.

Further, McClelland approaches the problem of predicting entrepreneurial success by measuring, specifically, individuals' need for achievement (*n Ach*) and he emphasizes that this characteristic is to be considered even to the exclusion of other factors. In a recent interview for *Forbes* (McClelland, 1969), he stated, "We've spent twenty years studying just this [why one businessman succeeds and another fails], twenty years in the laboratory doing very careful research, and *we've isolated the specific thing. We know the exact type of motivation that makes a better entrepreneur.* [Italics ours.] Not necessarily a better head of General Motors; I'm talking about the man who starts a business." He went on to say that the specific characteristic is the individual's need for achievement.

Need for Objective Approach

The earlier research by Hornaday and Bunker and the present study of entrepreneurs are predicated on two assumptions: (1) that there would be great value in a system of selection that is *objective* and *structured* so that non-psychologists could administer it, and (2) that in addition to the admittedly important *n Ach* there may be other factors which should be measured. The latter point is that our prediction of success would have higher validity if measurement were made of several factors, each of which makes some independent contribution to the ultimate success of the entrepreneur.

The need for objectivity in measuring need for achievement is emphasized by Hermans (1970). He says, "During the past twenty years, there have been a great many studies in the area of achievement motivation. These vary from psychometric investigations to theoretical discussions. One of the most difficult problems in this area is that of measurement. Projective techniques have been the principal devices used to quantify the strength of the achievement motive. . . . With regard to the projective needs for achievement measures, several critical problems arise. Klinger (1966) pointed to their lack of internal consistency, lack of test-retest reliability, their deficient validity against performance criteria, and the low intercorrelation among several projective *n Ach* measures. . . . The need for a new measure for *n Ach* still exists."

The pilot study indicated that three objective tests held promise of differentiating entrepreneurs from men-in-general. For the present study, therefore, these tests, along with the structured interview, were administered to successful entrepreneurs. As in the pilot study, the "successful entrepreneur" was defined as a man or woman who *started* a business where there was none before, who had at least eight employees and who had been established for at least five years. These criteria were selected because it was desired to eliminate the "Mom and Pop" stores and because the first five years are the most difficult. The criteria are similar to those established by Collins et al. (1964) in their entrepreneurial studies. The three tests applied to the entrepreneurs were: Kuder Occupational Interest Survey, Form DD (Kuder, 1970), Gordon's Survey of Interpersonal Values (Gordon, 1960), and a questionnaire composed of three scales drawn from the Edwards Personal Preference Scale (Edwards, 1959). Throughout this paper the abbreviations for these tests will be, respectively, OIS, SIV, and EPPS.

Forty "successful entrepreneurs," as defined above, were interviewed and tested in the summer of 1970. The sample was selected without regard for geographic location (all were located in either North Carolina, Rhode Island, or Massachusetts), but care was taken to obtain twenty black and twenty white entrepreneurs. That racial selection made possible a tentative investigation of the null hypothesis relative to racial differences.

In addition to these forty entrepreneurs, use was made of the twenty entrepreneurs who were interviewed and tested in the pilot study (Hornaday and Bunker, 1970) since they were given essentially the same interview and the same tests. The number of cases used for the several analyses varied because some entrepreneurs completed only a part of the forms. For all sixty, however, interview responses are available; most of the questions in the interview were the same in the two studies.

Hypotheses

Specifically, the hypotheses investigated in this study were:

1. A number of personal characteristics differentiate successful entrepreneurs from men in general and these characteristics can be measured by objective, standardized tests. Entrepreneurs are significantly higher on scales on the EPPS that measure need for achievement, need for autonomy, and need for aggression. On the SIV, the examinees are expected to score higher on scales measuring the importance attached to recognition, independence, and leadership.

2. Because of the nature of scoring the OIS, the scores of entrepreneurs could not be compared to men-in-general. The Form DD scores of OIS are lambdas (Clemans, 1968; Kuder, 1963), and the na-

ture of those scores does not permit comparison of an individual to a group. The hypothesis for the OIS, therefore, must relate to the scales on which entrepreneurs are higher relative to their other scales. Entrepreneurs should score high on scales relating to business occupations and business college majors. The greatest value from the Kuder Occupational Interest Survey, however, would be gained from an entrepreneurial key for the OIS, and development of that key must await the gathering of considerably more data.

3. In answering the questions covered by the interviewers, entrepreneurs are expected to indicate that they work long hours, that the work interferes with their family relationships, that they rebel against regimentation, and it was felt that their family background might reflect, generally, a rebellion against an attitude in the father that they perceived with distaste. A number of additional areas were investigated in the interviews as a further exploration into characteristics which might be significant. On these, no specific hypothesis could be formed nor is there any control group of the general population to serve as a basis of comparison. Thus, the interview was largely exploratory.

4. On a self-rating form in which entrepreneurs subjectively compared themselves to the general population, it was hypothesized that the subjects would be above the general population in all of the significant items (a few items were "fillers"). Those are such items as: need for power over people, self-reliance, innovative tendencies, and other characteristics as listed in Table 3.

5. Relative to race, the null hypothesis is to be tested for all scales of the tests and items of the interview. Our hypotheses are that no racial differences will be found between black and white entrepreneurs. Data, therefore, are presented for the races separately and, where no difference is found, combined.

Procedure

The subjects of this study consisted of a total of sixty entrepreneurs. The distribution of the sixty by race and sex is as follows:

34 white males
22 black males
2 white females
2 black females

During the early work of this study, which began in the summer of 1969, a total of twenty entrepreneurs were interviewed. It was in the process of these interviews that the Interview Schedule was developed. Development consisted primarily of devising items, reordering most of them, and, subsequently, deleting or adding a very few items. Also during this early phase of the work, the three tests used to assess the personality traits of the entrepreneurs were selected. Because some experimentation with the formats and content of these measurement devices was necessary, not all of the entrepreneurs were subjected to identical items. As will be seen later, this, plus the failure of some entrepreneurs to complete all of the forms, resulted in the sample's containing somewhat less than sixty for the various forms employed. Early experimenting with procedures of testing and interview also yielded unequal numbers of completed forms for the various questionnaires employed.

The forms which held the most promise in the pilot study and were used in this study are:

The Standardized Interview Schedule
The Kuder Occupational Interest Survey (Form DD)
The Gordon Survey of Interpersonal Values
A modified form of the Edwards Personal Preference Schedule
A five-point scale of personal self-estimates called The Self-Evaluation Scale

Results

Analyses were made separately and in combination for the white males (34) and black males (22). Because of the small number of cases for women (two white and two black), no meaningful comparative analyses could be made by sex. Inspection of the data indicated differences between the female and the male entrepreneurs, and it could not be established that the sexes could be reasonably combined; therefore, only the male entrepreneurs were used in subsequent analyses.

The structured interview was used with the full group of sixty entrepreneurs. Many of the items were administered to the total of sixty, but a few items were introduced or revised at some time during the first twenty contacts. For the last forty the interview schedule was kept constant. The sample size for interview items, thus, may vary between 40 and 56 (since the four female entrepreneurs were not included).

Table 1 presents data for black males and white males on all of the interview items that lend themselves to quantification. The items on which significant differences occurred were:

TABLE 1

Analyses of Quantifiable Items of the Structural Interviews

	Statistic	White Male (N ≤ 34)	Black Male (N ≤ 22)
Time required for interview	Mdn.	90	75
Number of employees	Mdn.	24	15
Years in this business	Mdn.	13	8
Hrs. work/week at start	Mdn.	68	70
Hrs. work/week now	Mdn.	60	60
Age of entrepreneur	Mdn.	46	42
Age started business	Mdn.	33	34
Previous ent. effort?	% yes	20	27
Special person import. in getting started	% yes	25	9
Special idea import. getting started	% yes	58	18
Never married	% yes	0	0
Divorced or separated?	% yes	6	32
Graduated high school?	% yes	94	82
Graduate college?	% yes	82	32
Level of school achievement	Mdn. eval.	Above Av.	Average
Serious in school	% serious	79	25
Consider dropping out	% yes	36	38
Active in extra-curricular activities in school	% yes	75	62
Financed coll. primarily through own effort	% yes (of coll. group)	45	84
Accepts regimentation?	% yes	77	68

(1) Length of time in business. White males averaged 13 years and black males averaged eight years. This perhaps is a reflection of the more recent encouragement given blacks to go into business for themselves.

(2) Frequency of separation and divorce from wives. In this study 6% whites and 32% blacks were divorced or separated. This may reflect a general cultural difference rather than a characteristic of entrepreneurship. (Divorce and separation is considerably higher among the blacks in the U. S. according to the *Statistical Abstract of the United States, 1970*.) In fact, the per cent of divorce and separation among all entrepreneurs is below that of the general population (16% among all entrepreneurs combined; approximately 33% in the general population).

(3) The frequency of a special idea as the basis of the development of the enterprise was much greater for white entrepreneurs than for blacks. This may have been a reflection of the types of entrepreneurs in the two groups. A much higher

percentage of the whites were in manufacturing, where a specific original idea might have been particularly important. Almost all of the blacks were in sales and services; of the three blacks who were in manufacturing, all had moved into the field because of their having an innovative idea.

(4) Differences in per cent graduating from college and "seriousness" in school, as well as differences in self-support in college. Again these may reflect cultural differences and differences in socio-economic background.

On all other characteristics investigated in the interview, insignificant differences between races were found. It appears that each of the obtained differences resulted from socio-economic differences or from special considerations in sample selection, as in (3) above, and it does not appear that any racial differences for entrepreneurs as such were evident. The null hypothesis, therefore, cannot be rejected on the basis of interview results.

Table 2 presents the objective scales of the EPPS and the SIV for the two racial groups, separately and combined. Inspection of the raw data indicated no justification for combining the sexes in this study. In comparing black and white males, however, we find that on all scales except Benevolence there are no significant differences. The only exception was a t of 2.48 produced by the very low score of whites on the Benevolence scale. Because of the ipsative nature of the SIV, and because of the very high scores by whites on Independence and Leadership, the low Benevolence scores are interpreted as *relatively* low for the entrepreneurs, not necessarily low compared to the general population. Since the SIV is not normative, only interpretation of relative values is appropriate. The t-tests were applied for this survey only to point to direction and relative magnitude of differences. Because of the small differences between blacks and whites found in Table 2, the results of the two races are combined in the last column.

Compared to men in general, entrepreneurs are significantly higher on scales reflecting need for achievement, independence, and effectiveness of their leadership, and are low on scales reflecting emphasis on need for support. Again the low need for support score may result from the high scores on other scales of this ipsative survey.

Note that only three of the EPPS scales were investigated in this study. Only those three scales were investigated since it was assumed that they were the most likely to relate to entrepreneurship. It is recommended that, in later research, the full fifteen scales of the

TABLE 2

Comparisons between Black Entrepreneurs, White Entrepreneurs, and the General Population on Nine Personality Scales

Scale[a]	Black		White		Combined		General Population[b]		White-Black		Black-Gen. Population		White-Gen. Population		All Entrepreneurs-Gen. Pop	
	M	SD	M	SD	M	SD	M	SD	Diff.	t	Diff.	t	Diff.	t	Diff.	t
Achievement	15.4	2.97	18.4	5.78	17.3	3.89	14.4	4.80	3.0	1.81	1.0	.76	4.0	3.60**	2.9	3.40**
Autonomy	13.5	3.26	15.2	4.61	14.7	4.28	13.5	4.79	1.5	1.07	.2	.15	1.7	1.60	1.2	1.34
Aggression	12.6	2.65	12.4	5.12	12.5	4.48	12.5	4.74	(.2)	.14	.1	.08	(.1)	.09	.0	.00
Support	12.1	3.69	11.2	5.64	11.6	5.05	15.0	5.70	(.9)	.53	(2.9)	1.87	(3.8)	2.91**	(3.4)	2.66**
Conformity	13.4	7.12	11.1	6.04	12.0	6.53	14.8	6.50	(2.3)	1.03	(1.4)	.77	(3.7)	2.50*	(2.5)	1.86
Recognition	8.9	4.34	11.5	5.03	10.7	4.86	11.2	5.20	2.6	1.58	(2.3)	1.62	.3	.25	(.5)	.39
Independence	20.1	7.17	21.9	6.13	21.5	6.76	16.9	7.40	1.8	.80	3.2	1.57	5.0	2.99**	4.6	2.76**
Benevolence	17.5	6.18	12.9	4.46	14.7	5.76	15.8	6.80	(4.6)	2.48*	1.7	1.06	(2.9)	2.22*	(1.1)	.80
Leadership	17.9	6.63	21.1	7.09	19.9	7.08	16.1	7.70	3.2	1.34	1.8	.85	5.0	2.86**	3.7	2.15*

[a] Scores on Achievement, Autonomy, and Aggression were derived from the Edwards Personal Preference Schedule. The other scales are from the Survey of Interpersonal Values.
[b] Population is being used here to denote the norms provided in the test manuals of the Edwards Personal Preference Schedule and the Survey of Interpersonal Values.
* Significant at the five per cent level ($p \leq .05$).
** Significant at the one per cent level ($p \leq .01$).

EPPS be included in the investigation if cooperating entrepreneurs would be agreeable to answering the full 225 items of that test.

Discussion

It is surprising that the EPPS Autonomy scale yielded no significant t value ($t = 1.34$) since interest in independence *is* a characteristic of successful entrepreneurs and since the SIV Independence scale is highly significant ($t = 2.76$) and is correlated with the Autonomy scale .49 (Gordon, 1963).

On the OIS, the numbers cannot be treated as raw scores since the figures are not quantitatively comparable from one person to another. It is the relative standing that is significant. The highest 10 occupational scales and highest 10 college major scales were examined for blacks and whites separately, and striking differences were evident. Both college and occupational scales related generally to the occupations and avocations of the entrepreneurs. Since there were more manufacturers (particularly in electronics and related areas) among the whites, engineering scales were frequently high; for blacks they were infrequently in the top five scales. The interviews (Table 1) indicated that education level was significantly higher for the whites, and the kinds of occupations ranking toward the top for them reflected higher educational requirements. For example, whites frequently ranked high on computer programmer, engineer, psychologist, and travel agent. Blacks frequently ranked high on television repairmen, plumbing contractor, automobile salesman, and florist. Both rank high on manager, architect, and buyer.

It is of interest to note that lambdas greater than .60 were attained on one or more scales by 40 per cent of the white entrepreneurs but by none of the black entrepreneurs. Lambdas above .50 were attained by 80 per cent of the whites and only 30 per cent of the blacks. That difference is interpreted to mean that the interests of the black entrepreneurs are not as highly developed and are more diverse; interests of white entrepreneurs tend to be more sharply developed. This again is probably the result in a large measure of the difference in educational background.

Over-all, the OIS was not significant in selecting entrepreneurs or in differentiating blacks and whites of comparable educational level, but it still may prove to be fruitful if a scale for entrepreneurs can be developed. This aspiration is reinforced by the fact that for many blacks Business was a first or second preference as a college major. The OIS was also useful in the present study in that the V scale, a measure of accuracy of the test-taking by examinees, was checked

TABLE 3

Analysis of Self-Ratings on The Self-Evaluation Scale for White and Black Entrepreneurs, and Their Combined Scores, in Per Cent Selecting Each Position.

		5	4	3	2	1
1. Energy level	White	57	27	17	0	0
	Black	47	26	26	0	0
	Combined	53	27	20	0	0
2. Physical health	White	79	15	5	0	0
	Black	58	25	19	0	0
	Combined	64	21	15	0	0
3. Need Achievement	White	70	18	12	0	0
	Black	56	28	14	0	0
	Combined	65	22	13	0	0
4. Willing to take risks	White	60	27	9	3	0
	Black	56	28	14	0	0
	Combined	58	27	11	4	0
5. Watch T.V.[a]	White	0	9	30	47	13
	Black	0	11	17	22	50
	Combined	0	10	24	36	29
6. Creative	White	47	37	10	7	0
	Black	43	43	14	0	0
	Combined	45	39	12	4	0
7. Need for affiliation	White	6	9	10	16	20
	Black	19	14	29	24	14
	Combined	11	13	20	24	32
8. Desire for money	White	21	35	35	9	0
	Black	55	10	25	10	0
	Combined	33	26	32	9	0
9. Tolerate Uncertainty	White	30	27	20	13	10
	Black	43	29	10	14	5
	Combined	35	28	16	14	8
10. Desire for candy[a]	White	9	0	0	9	81
	Black	0	0	0	6	94
	Combined	4	0	0	7	89
11. Authoritarian in Business	White	38	38	19	6	0
	Black	35	30	12	12	12
	Combined	24	35	27	6	9
12. Liking for sports[a]	White	0	27	27	18	27
	Black	6	19	6	25	44
	Combined	4	22	15	22	37
13. Get along with employees	White	54	35	8	0	4
	Black	47	35	12	0	6
	Combined	51	35	9	0	5

TABLE 3 (continued)

		5	4	3	2	1
14. Organized	White	12	41	41	0	6
	Black	24	52	10	14	0
	Combined	31	30	19	13	7
15. Self-Reliant	White	72	21	3	0	3
	Black	55	40	5	0	0
	Combined	66	28	4	0	2
16. Likes to Collect Things[a]	White	9	9	9	0	72
	Black	0	13	6	13	69
	Combined	4	11	7	7	70
17. Singleness of Purpose	White	12	31	18	31	6
	Black	18	18	24	12	30
	Combined	15	24	21	21	18
18. Need for Power	White	15	9	27	21	27
	Black	10	14	14	33	29
	Combined	13	11	22	26	28
19. Patience	White	35	18	6	24	18
	Black	30	30	18	12	12
	Combined	32	24	12	18	15
20. Competitiveness	White	33	28	22	11	6
	Black	53	24	12	12	0
	Combined	66	20	6	6	3
21. Take Initiative	White	69	27	0	0	4
	Black	70	30	0	0	0
	Combined	70	28	0	0	2
22. Confidence	White	53	47	0	0	0
	Black	77	24	0	0	0
	Combined	65	35	0	0	0
23. Versatility	White	39	50	11	0	0
	Black	53	30	6	6	6
	Combined	46	40	9	3	3
24. Perseverance	White	63	31	6	0	0
	Black	77	24	0	0	0
	Combined	70	27	3	0	0
25. Resilience	White	59	29	12	0	0
	Black	65	30	6	0	0
	Combined	62	29	9	0	0
26. Innovation in Business	White	45	39	12	3	0
	Black	78	16	0	0	6
	Combined	41	41	15	4	0
27. Leadership Effectiveness	White	32	39	26	3	0
	Black	38	33	19	10	0
	Combined	35	37	23	6	0

[a] Indicate "filler" items which were inserted so that entrepreneurs would have the opportunity to use the entire range of the scale.

to determine if the answers were valid. In only one case was the V scale out of the acceptable range and for that individual all of the forms were returned to the entrepreneur with the request that he take them a second time more carefully. Since they were not returned, he was not used in the test analyses.

The Self-Evaluation Scale is so highly subjective that it is of little value. To be interpreted meaningfully, it would have to be given to a standardization group for comparison. As a matter of information only, the distribution of answers for the 34 whites and 22 black entrepreneurs is presented separately and combined. Inspection of Table 3 reveals a very high similarity of self-ratings by the two races so that combination is most meaningful. Both races rate themselves significantly above average on need for achievement, self-reliance, competitiveness, initiative, confidence, versatility, perseverance, resilience, innovation, and physical health.

In addition, as part of the structured interview each entrepreneur was asked what qualities were necessary for success in business. The characteristics listed by both blacks and whites are similar, but there was some difference in emphasis.

The blacks mentioned most often the need to have "Knowledge of the Business." Also frequently mentioned was either skill in management of finances or a source of financial advice. Frequently mentioned, but not as often as Knowledge of Business, was: honesty, having a good character, possession of inner drive, willingness to work hard, and pleasing personality. This latter list corresponds very well with the characteristics most frequently mentioned by white entrepreneurs: willingness to work hard, perseverance, single-mindedness of purpose, and the ability to work with people.

Conclusions

Both the EPPS and the SIV yielded scales that significantly differentiated entrepreneurs from men in the standardization groups for those tests. These scales were achievement, support, independence and leadership (Table 2). It is recommended, therefore, that these two forms be used in further study of the entrepreneur. It is also recommended that continued use of the OIS may be fruitful in order to gather sufficient data for developing an entrepreneurial scale.

The interview items have not been analyzed for their effectiveness in differentiating entrepreneurs from men in general, but the items have been sharpened for clarity, and the authors' experience with these sixty entrepreneurs indicates that the items as given elicit meaningful responses from entrepreneurs. Compared to the laborious procedures and technical training necessary for interpreting projective tests, the administration and scoring of the objective tests is easy and accurate. Furthermore, not only does this procedure yield *n Ach* scores but also other information, obtained by structured devices and objectively evaluated, which further sharpens the differentiation of the successful entrepreneur. It is yet to be determined whether these scales will differentiate between the successful entrepreneur and the individual who has made an *unsuccessful* attemp to be an entrepreneur but this study establishes (insofar as judgment can be made on a small number of cases) that the structured interview and tests used here are objective indicators of entrepreneurship.

REFERENCES

Clemans, William V. An analysis and empirical examination of some properties of ipsative measures. *Psychometric Monographs*, 1968, 14.

Collins, Orvis F., Moore, David G., and Unwalla, Darab B. *The Enterprising Man*. East Lansing: Michigan State University Press, 1964.

Edwards, Allen L. *Manual for the Edwards Personal Preference Schedule*. New York: The Psychological Corporation, 1959.

Gordon, Leonard V. *Manual for Survey of Interpersonal Values*. Chicago: Science Research Associates, 1960.

Gordon, Leonard V. *Research Briefs on Survey of Interpersonal Values (Manual Supplement)*. Chicago: Science Research Associates, 1963.

Hermans, Huber, J. M. A questionnaire measure of achievement motivation. *Journal of Applied Psychology*, 1970, 54, 353–363.

Hornaday, John A. and Bunker, Charles S. The nature of the entrepreneur. PERSONNEL PSYCHOLOGY, 1970, 23, 47–54.

Klinger, E. Fantasy need achievement as a motivational construct. *Psychological Bulletin*, 1966, 66, 291–308.

Kuder, Frederic. A rationale for evaluating interests. *Educational and Psychological Measurement*, 1963, 23, 3–10.

Kuder, Frederic. *Manual for the Kuder Preference Record: Form DD*. Chicago: Science Research Associates, Inc., 1970.

McClelland, David C. In *Forbes*, June 1, 1969, 53–57.

McClelland, David C., Atkinson, J. W., Clark, R. A., and Lowell, E. L. *The Achievement Motive*. New York: Appleton-Century-Crofts, 1953.

Murray, Henry A. *Manual for the Thematic Apperception Test*. Cambridge: Harvard University Press, 1943.

Statistical Abstract of the United States. U. S. Department of Commerce, Bureau of the Census, Washington, D. C., 1970.

CHAPTER 2

THE IDEA STAGE

Where do ideas come from? What makes a good idea for a new business? Polaroid, Xerox, Digital Equipment Corporation, and IBM are companies built around a good idea. The entrepreneurs in these cases were significantly innovative to build a strong and profitable market position. These companies were founded on truly new ideas, from significant technological developments. These were truly new ideas and the level of success of each company is legend. Usually, however, the more common method of founding a new business is more one of combining existing fields of technology or repackaging the old into a new product or service. Most companies are not built on truly new ideas.

The route might be depicted as follows: An individual gains specialized technical knowledge, senses a gap in the market that is not being filled. Gaining support for his idea from one or two associates or from the financial community, the entrepreneur's new business venture is born. The business is established amidst an aurora of excitement and convictions based on the entrepreneur's perception that what is being offered is a unique innovation satisfying an untapped expanding need. A market opportunity existed, a product idea was born, the technology selected; a company is started.

The entrepreneur and his associates then develop the manufacturing technology and processes to produce prototype products or services. The prototype is tested and refined. The ideal product candidate has been crudely developed and now, the creative development and marketing cycle of a new business enterprise is initiated.

The new venture will then find the market response to its product favorable, or unfavorable. This will only be determined in a real test in a free market-place. The unique ideas, which are not just repackaging other existing product concepts, stand a better chance of being successful. The first time a customer exchanges money for the product the new enterprise attains a significant milestone known as "the product notion." Up until this crucial stage, the enterprise remains as an incubating idea waiting to be born. Below is the sequence:

Idea - - >bread board - - >prototype - - > product notion - - >first sale - - >repeat sale - - >product profitability - - >profitable enterprise.

How are unique ideas created? The history of this process offers few conclusive facts but one can reasonably conclude that placing creative people in an unconstrained environment, with organizational deterrents, policies, and procedures removed, optimizes the flow of ideas. Bell Telephone Laboratories has been the mother of many of the new technologies and this is the model which they employ. It is often these organizational restrictions and the overbearing emphasis on short term goals that cause entrepreneurs to leave their employers and start their own businesses. Many good ideas are never born because of the short term demands of other tasks. Creative contact with other entrepreneurs and professionals, will soon result in the entrepreneur shaping his initial idea and then formulating more significant product innovations. This is as true for the internal as well as the external entrepreneur.

The crucial step in the profitable exploitation of a new idea is to select the proper technological combination — a selection that will result in a short product development time, high value to cost ratio, and economies of scale in manufacturing. However, all these crucial variables are unknown at the idea stage. In fact, the idea is usually only partially developed and one must ask "How can I judge the economics of scale" at so early a stage of product development?

The entrepreneur is faced with considerable risk. He must make guesstimates on limited data. Judgement is the word of the moment. In the first article, Michael Palmer discusses psychological testing to determine entrepreneurial potential. He specifically discusses an individual's risk taking abilities. Based upon these data he draws conclusions on an individual's entrepreneurial capabilities.

Michael Palmer also attempts to answer other investigative questions about entrepreneurs. Historically, the entrepreneur is perceived in many ways: 1) as an organizer of the business firm; 2) as the person innovating the new products or process, developing the new market, or finding new resources; and 3) as a risk taker, innovator and decision maker. Among the several characteristics that seem to indicate entrepreneurial potential are the person's need for achievement and his ability to make decisions under uncertainty. Thus, according to Palmer we find the entrepreneur engaging in business activities which provide concrete feedback on performance (profits), some degree of risk taking, and opportunity for personal achievement.

The budding entrepreneur will perceive both risks and rewards from founding a new business venture. Will he be able to raise sufficient start-up and operating capital? What are the most important start-up problems to resolve first? Who does he seek out for advice and consultation when he has difficulties? Has he really considered all the risks? What is the very first thing one must do to found a business?

"Why should a prospective founder of a new technologically-based firm be concerned with specific regions in the nation where concentration of technologically based firms exist?" are the issues covered in an article by Arnold Cooper. Based on his research into the formation of a wide range of technologically-based firms on the West Coast, Professor Cooper discusses regional factors that support a differentiation between the environment in general and the more specific entrepreneurial environment. He claims past entrepreneurial activities within a region will enable the prospective founder to develop a keener awareness of venture capital sources and individuals and institutions which provide help and advice. Thus, the region in which the business is to be located should be examined as carefully for availability of the required resources as the product idea. Just as farmers need fertile soil to start new farms for new crops, entrepreneurs are also significantly effected by the new business climate in a specific geographical region, according to one of the more meaningful authorities, Professor Arnold Cooper of Purdue University.

Donald Schon addresses the issue of Product Champions within larger organizations. He suggests solutions to the dilemma of supporting new technologies and products within an old organization. New products are the life blood of old companies. One earlier study[1] indicated that the products which will be on the market in ten years are not presently available. Secondly, of the new products which are introduced in the next ten years, more than one-half of them will fail. Taken together, these two statements are staggering. In simple

words, there is a great need to focus on this new products problem.

Before discussing the remainder of this reader, I shall digress for a moment to face the new product issue squarely. The articles in the reader offer specific advice to entrepreneurs and as such are included. However, I should mention that my own interest in this topic has been substantial and, for a broader perspective may I suggest the following three articles. I have chosen not to include them in the reader but for a greater insight into managing products I believe all three can be helpful.

1. Murray Harding, "Customers Give N.E.I. Answers to Marketing Problems," Industrial Marketing (August 1966), pp. 66-68.
2. Mancuso, Joseph R, "Why Not Create Opinion Leaders for New Products Introductions?" Journal of Marketing (July, 1969), Vol. 33, No. 3, p. 20-26.
3. Mancuso, Joseph R., "How to Manage Products," Management Today, January, 1973, pp. 74.

Whether an internal or external venture activity, the entrepreneurial spirit must exist to provide the driving force behind the risky market development cycle. There are differences, however, in how the corporation perceives and tolerates individual mistakes, and this is related to the organization structure. In another article, Robert Adams reviews his company's established process for internal product innovation as it seeks to tap new and profitable markets.

In another of the articles, Dr. Edward Roberts, on the faculty at M.I.T., states his views on entrepreneurial characteristics which relate to their successful technologically based ventures. Professor Roberts judges the entrepreneur to be the most central ingredient in successfully exploiting advanced technology. Roberts' studies were based in Massachusetts and were concentrated on the Route 128 industrial complex. How the entrepreneur views the need for management versus technical skills, his concern for personnel, the process of technology transfer, and his level of education are all presented as non-personality factors that directly correlate with venture success. The invention of a new or improved technical product or process does not necessarily produce a profitable business. To successfully build a business based upon the invention requires an individual or product champion who is willing to break down barriers and to take risks in his campaign to meet development and marketing objectives. The cliche of building a better mousetrap and the customer will beat a path to your door is expanded to now say "Build a technologically based firm and profits will beat a path to your pocket" by Professor Roberts as he explains why neither cliche has proven accurate in the real life world of business.

Mr. Hyman Olken suggests sources of product ideas from the Government's R & D programs. Large companies as well as small firms can benefit by comprehending the vast resources of government sponsored research and development. These "spin-offs" are a potential source of new product ideas for both internal and external entrepreneurs.

Recapping, I conclude that ideas usually result from creative people finding solutions to problems. Whether the idea is unique enough to capture a specialized and profitable market share must be determined in a free marketplace. Sufficient analysis is required to test the new idea against market needs, producibility, profitability, competition, market growth, and other factors related to changing consumer needs. Generally, the risks involved in exploiting the idea will be directly related to the potential rewards.

---

[1] Elizabeth Marting, New Products, New Profits (New York: American Management Association, 1965), p. 9, Conrad Jones, "An Action Philosophy for the Corporate Entrepreneur," Printers' Ink , Vol. 287 (May 29, 1964, p. 20. This estimate was based upon a sample of 65 well-managed firms engaged in research and development activities; Peter Hilton, New Product Introduction for Small Business Owners, Small Business Management Series No. 17, (Small Business Administration, 1961), pp. 63 - 66.

An Approach to New Business Ventures

Robert M. Adams

From time to time new terms or expressions for old situations rise to common usage in our everyday vocabulary. Such terms become so popular and so prevalent, so discussed and so disputed that we are led to presume that they describe some amazing new social, scientific, or economic phenomenon. Who has not heard about the "establishment" or the "generation gap;" the "brain drain" or the "conglomerate;" "escalation" or the "new politics." Our parents and grandparents and more ancient generations knew the phenomena described by such words, even if they didn't use these words. And so it is today with "new business ventures," an increasingly popular expression among businessmen, investors, and managers of research and development.

Our nomadic ancestors launched new ventures virtually every day of their lives. Certainly the first merchant to send goods across Europe and Asia by camel caravan was involved in a new enterprise on which he hoped to make a substantial profit. The advent of the Industrial Revolution quickened and dramatized the new business thrust of capitalism; but the Industrial Revolution is more than 200 years old so we can hardly claim that new businesses based on new technologies are recent phenomena.

If, then, new business ventures are not new, why are they the subject of so much attention and discussion these days? Why are they high on the list of suggested theme subjects for meetings of the I.R.I., an organization of people and industries committed not to what's old, but to what's new?

The answer is not simple. It's not sufficient to say that desire for growth is the answer because this merely leads to the question of why we want growth. The complete analysis of that question would yield a complex mixture of social, economic, scientific, philosophical,

DR. ROBERT M. ADAMS, General Manager, New Business Ventures Division, 3M Company, Saint Paul, Minnesota 55101. This and the two following articles were presented at the IRI New Venture Management Seminar in Los Angeles, October, 1968.

RESEARCH MANAGEMENT, Volume XII, Number 4 (1969)   255

and psychological reasons. For some of us, the driving force is simply corporate policy, usually dictated by such factors as competition or an investment image. For others, it is the opportunity to convert the raw ore of scientific discovery into refined products for human wants.

We can accept the fact that new business ventures are regarded as necessary and presently desirable things in our business life. How, then, do we achieve such necessities and satisfy such desires?

It is my intention to discuss only one aspect of this subject: new business ventures developed within a sizable and growing industrial corporation. It will necessarily be a somewhat narrow view of the subject since my first-hand experience is largely with a single company, albeit one that has been unusually successful in this area. It is not my objective to discuss acquisitions or the formation of new businesses to exploit already established markets with known technology, although these are both well used and often suitable routes. Please note, however, that the term, "developed within", does not exclude finding new ideas, inventions, or technologies outside the company. The important point is that the development from the idea or invention stage to commercial reality comes from within the company.

Converting new technologies or new products or new business concepts to successful enterprises is not the province or property of any single organization or individual. If any company had a tried and proved answer to new business ventures that assured success for every start, that company would guard such knowledge zealously. Such a key to success would be carefully protected proprietary information. It is possible only to describe some general principles which have been found useful and to recommend them to you for our own evaluation.

A new business venture in the context of this presentation will be considered truly new only if it produces new sources of sales and profits for its sponsor from presently untapped markets. Success in such ventures hinges on many factors, not the least of which is sheer good luck. However, consistent performance cannot be achieved without three absolutely essential elements: the proper corporate climate; a good organizational approach; and people. It sounds easy, but is it?

Favorable Climate Necessary

Climate is an average condition established over long periods of time. Like the climate which prevails in our natural environment, a corporate climate is composed of several parts: attitudes, actions, and approaches. Also, like our natural environment, climatic conditions frequently start at the top. Generally, a favorable climate for new business ventures results when a company's top management demonstrates its personal interest and enthusiasm in new business activities on a daily basis; when it points with pride to a success in a new venture and is eager to try again; when it accepts a failure with constructive concern but is eager to try again. Such management must be absolutely convinced that new ventures based on new products and new technology are essential to the future of the corporation. It can be quickly recognized that a favorable climate is not easily created nor is it easily maintained. It should also be recognized that even a favorable climate is marked by the day-to-day variations which we call weather.

One other aspect of "climate" should be mentioned here: the corporate attitude toward the company's inventors, entrepreneurs, and new venture managers. More will be said about the subject of people a little later. It is sufficient here to note that those ventures promising the greatest reward are normally the ones that require the greatest risk for the company and for individuals. Mistakes are more likely to be made in probing new products, new processes, new markets, and new business concepts. Management must, therefore, learn to differentiate between mistakes made in attempts to do something new, and mistakes made as a result of inherent inability. No one expects praise for failure; neither should a man be unfairly criticized for venturing a new approach. None of this is meant to imply that inventors, entrepreneurs, and new business ventures managers should be coddled or pampered. Experience indicates just the opposite attitude works best. The key is management's willingness to move forward with a minimum of hindsight criticism and a maximum emphasis on what's next.

Development Activities Best in Separate Unit

The second essential ingredient in my recipe for successful new business ventures is a development concept or plan. It starts with the basic question of where the new venture work is to be done in the company. As a simple illustration, let's look at a corporation having three operating divisions, each with its own sales, production, and technical departments. These established operations are concentrating daily on producing goods, distributing them, selling them, and improving them, all within the framework of sales forecasts and profit objectives. This leads to a multitude of short-term programs and pressures which greatly limit the division's freedom to explore wholly new developments, especially in business fields not related to the existing business. New business development is a long-term proposition; if it is too closely associated with operating functions, it tends to be neglected, restricted, or even cannibalized when operating problems occur.

For such reasons as these, new venture development activities have the greatest chance for success when organized as an independent corporate function. Top management then has the opportunity to determine directly the corporation's commitment to enter brand new business fields. It can establish recognized and permissible amounts of deficit financing or investment dedicated to future long-term gains. Being closer to the new enterprises, it can be more sensitive to their progress, programs, and people.

Having found a place for our new business development activities, we must now find some ideas which promise future new businesses. Briefly, here are the usual sources of such ideas: company laboratories, observant salesmen, outside inventors, patent literature, market studies, licensing organizations, and consultants. Those charged with the responsibility for reviewing these ideas must be imbued with the power of positive thinking. If they come to a negative conclusion, it must be because they could not find a suitable answer to the positive question: "How can this idea be made into a profitable business?"

Further evaluation of promising ideas and inventions needs people competent to determine product potentialities and market possibilities. This requires technical experience and marketing experience properly blended for the selection of the best new business opportunities. My company has found that such a blend is most effective when the marketers are physically located in the same laboratory facilities used by the technical people. In fact, one scientifically trained marketing manager reduced the significance of this approach to a formula. Simply stated, the formula says that the probability of commercial success of an unrelated new venture is inversely proportional to the square of the distance between the technical point of view and the marketing point of view. Or, in other words, the chance of achieving commercial success with a new business is very low and approaches zero if the marketing view of it is a great distance from the technical view.

Following this approach, we house our technical men and marketing men side by side. We send the scientists and engineers into the market occasionally, and we involve the marketers in testing and using the products. We do all we can to get each man to appreciate the other's point of view and thereby increase our chances of commercial success.

Entrepreneur Spearheads Venture

Assuming it has been demonstrated that there is a worthwhile basis for initiating a new business venture, what's next? Continuing with my own company's concept, an entrepreneur is named to spearhead the effort to prove the business concept. He hires the people he needs from the technical and marketing staffs. He finds the facilities he needs wherever suitable space is available. He is a "venture manager," the counterpart of the president and chief executive officer of a new small company. He proves that his products have customer appeal and utility, that they can be made by feasible processes, and that they can be sold at prices which will build future profits as volume expands. He begins to establish the roots for a long-term business by creating a proprietary position with patent protection, technical know-how, and pioneering marketing methods.

Those small, new product companies which thrive and grow (many never make it) eventually assume the status of an official corporate project, though still a part of the New Business Ventures Division. Project status is a prize achieved by the small company as recognition for its achievement in proving the concept and content of the new business. This is the point at which management satisfies itself that there is a desirable new business and that the venture manager is sufficiently committed and capable to carry the business to its full potential. With management's vote of confidence, the new project manager now assumes full responsibility and authority for all aspects of the venture, including technical, manufacturing, and marketing. In every instance, his goal is to develop and establish the new business with a maximum amount of sales and profit potential, consistent with the real values that are created for the customer. He is accountable for the success or failure of the project.

This concept of new venture development has as its advantages at least the following: (1) defined individual authority and responsibility; (2) measurable results and recognition; (3) emotional involvement and commitment of people who have this project as their only job; (4) freedom from the inhibitions and pressures of an established operating group; and (5) direct top management interest and support.

Throughout this talk there have been references to people: management people, venture people, entrepreneurs, and inventors. It is impossible to talk about successful new business enterprises without talking about people.

The importance of people to business success was given a significant twist in a speech last year by 3M Company's Vice President for Research and Development, Dr. C. W. Walton, who said, "A vital ingredient in business success is excitement, primarily *people* excitement . . ." If we added dedication to that statement, we might have a nearly complete description of the new venture manager or entrepreneur. Excitement will help him to sell his ideas and concepts and products, but dedication will keep him at the task during the inevitable setbacks and downturns of new business development.

These are the kinds of qualities we look for in the people whom we select to manage our new ventures and to carry them through the process which has been described earlier. Sometimes it's the inventor who exhibits these characteristics. Often it's someone who has had to evaluate an invention in the laboratory or marketplace and has seen the outline of a promising new business. Occasionally, and we wish it were more often, it's an entrepreneur from one of our operating divisions seeking the freedom to develop his own ideas.

Of course, talent and capability are required and it takes courage and energy and a host of other virtues to be a good new business venture manager. But if there is a lack of excitement and no depth of dedication, the project is in danger. In fact, these are important signals for which to watch in judging whether to launch or to continue a new venture.

More can be said about people and their role in new business ventures, but the objective of this discussion is limited to calling attention to the need for an entrepreneur whose excitement and dedication will favorably affect all those with whom he may come in contact.

To summarize, then, internally generated new business ventures have the best chance to succeed when the corporate climate is favorable; when a development concept is adopted that gives freedom of action, individual responsibility, a chance to become wholly involved, and adequate rewards; and when the project is placed in the hands of an entrepreneur who is excited by the potential business and dedicated to making it go, go, go. . . .

By MAURY DELMAN

THE FATE OF small business in the United States is not altogether rosy. According to the U.S. Statistical Abstract, private businesses of all sizes have shrunk from 39.5 per 1,000 population in 1948 to 29.8 per 1,000 in 1967. Small businesses have increased in number, but not in proportion to the population growth.

U.S. Department of Commerce studies show that about half of new small businesses never make the third year. Retailing suffers the most, with only 29% surviving three-and-a-half years. Wholesaling shows best with a 48% survival after the same period.

Nevertheless, Dun & Bradstreet figures suggest that more than 400,000 firms are started annually with about an equal number being discontinued.

Survival depends upon a variety of factors. Dun & Bradstreet people have been able to pinpoint nine major reasons for failures of new businesses.

Topping the list is simply lack of managerial experience. Even those who have managed other businesses successfully have come quickly to bankruptcy when operating businesses they knew little about. For example, take the case of a young Pennsylvanian who went into the building business after nine years as an insurance agent. With his cash tied up in real estate and "receivables," suppliers were willing to sell him on a cash basis only. He couldn't buy enough to keep going. After four years, he filed a voluntary petition in bankruptcy with liabilities twice the size of his assets.

A middle-aged Texan gave up a successful career as an insurance salesman to become an air-conditioning and heating contractor. He, too, ended up in a bankruptcy court when most of his capital got tied up in slow receivables. A West Virginia doctor teamed up with a restaurant owner to build a shopping

Pitfalls to Avoid in Starting Your Own Business

A look at why small businesses fail, with some useful hints and sources of help and information.

center and became a bankrupt after construction costs got out of hand.

A "receivable" is simply money somebody owes you that you can't get your hands on yet. If a builder, for instance, has given so many people long-term credit that he hasn't enough ready cash or credit of his own to pay his workmen and buy supplies to put up a new building, he has to pass up the bids on the new jobs. People who are new to business easily get themselves trapped with a shortage of enough funds on which to keep operating. In their eagerness to get their very first customers they may extend attractive credit which turns out to be suicidal for them. Experience selling insurance is hardly good training for another business that requires buy-sell judgment and heavy day-to-day expenses before the profits roll in.

But even with specific experience in some line there is no assurance of suc-

New businesses now fail increasingly.

cess. The importance of experience is not the time spent but what is learned. Successful businessmen underscore the need for balanced experience. This includes knowledge of your product, financial handling, buying and selling.

Insufficient starting capital ranks just under lack of experience as a cause of all business failures. The notion that a few thousand dollars and very hard work will bring success has held very little validity since the 1930's. An experienced women's-wear retailer says, "Anyone going into business now without plenty of capital in back of him should have his head examined." Even if a new business venture should survive its first year with limited capital, this disadvantage takes many years to overcome.

Borrowing the needed capital often seems an easier solution than it is. Those who don't calculate exactly how much the interest on the borrowed money will

Small Business Administration staff volunteer (rt.) counsels small business owner.

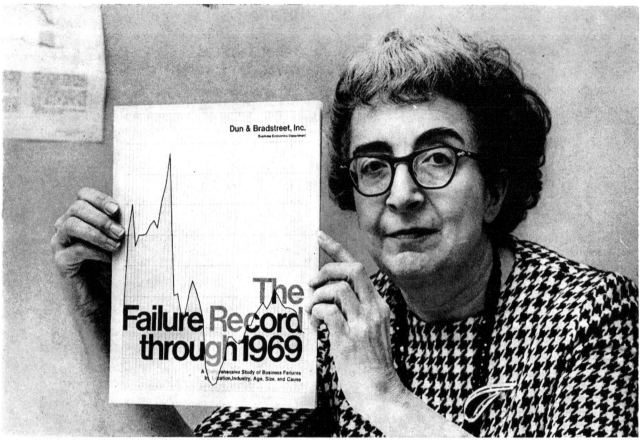

Dun & Bradstreet's Rowena Wyant displays company's report on business failures that pinpoints reasons behind them.

cat into their expected profits often come to grief—discovering too late that they've only been working for the bank. A man who earns 9% "clear profit" on capital that he borrowed for 9% can have a great time running his own business until he starves to death.

Yet, the attractions of being "independent" have been known to induce new "businessmen" to close their eyes to the hard fact that they won't earn a cent for themselves until they have met all operating costs *and* the interest.

Today, anyone starting a new business must first figure his normal operating expenses plus his salary. For safety, the expense figure should be adjusted upward from 25% to 50%. There are always unforeseen costs. Then, he'll have to determine the volume of business he must do to cover these expenses. The cost of supplies, merchandise, etc., to produce this volume must be figured. Finally, what fixtures are needed and what receivables will have to be carried if credit is granted to customers? In essence, what capital is needed to produce income enough for a reasonable net profit after expenses. A surprising number of people go into business without doing this hard arithmetic.

The third business pitfall is the wrong location. Inexperienced people are prone to look for inexpensive locations. Good locations are bound to cost money but the volume realized from a good location can more than offset the higher rent.

Once a business is under way it can readily fall victim to the fourth pitfall —inventory mismanagement. The common warning, "don't get too much inventory," should be modified to, "don't buy too much of the wrong merchandise."

The management of inventory is an art, if what you are doing is selling something that you keep in stock. Its ABC's are simply put, even if its XYZ's are not. The dollars you have invested in inventory must earn you money at a desirable rate. Fast turnover will earn money on goods that are priced at a small profit margin. Goods that turn over slowly only pay well if the markup is large. The great inventory tragedy is found in goods that sit on your shelves without any buyers. They represent dollars invested by you that are not earning anything—in short, precious capital that's tied up. This is all just as obvious as it can be, but, oh, the businesses that go on the rocks because of ill-judged inventory.

In the big, successful retail stores there is not love, humanity, sentiment or personal whim in the matter of inven-

tory. The hard questions are: "What sells, at how fast a turnover, for what markup?" and buyers of stock succeed or fail on their ability to solve that equation most profitably. By contrast, I know of a successful man who quit his profession to invest his all in a store selling a "cultural" product that he thought the people "ought to" have. It bankrupted him because people buy what they want, not what you think they "ought to."

Pitfall five is too much capital going into fixed assets. Any money invested in fixtures or real estate will most likely come from your working capital or will be borrowed. Money tied up in frozen assets that aren't necessary to your business is working capital that may not be available when you need it for either a crisis or an opportunity.

The sixth pitfall is poor credit granting practices. The temptation to let customers "put it on the books" can be very strong, particularly if your competition is coming from low-margin, big-volume cash competitors. If you offer easy credit in order to get the business, some customers may be so slow to pay that they'll give *you* "the business." When you force credit on people you are in danger of attracting the poorer payers. One of the shocks lying in wait for new businessmen is that well-heeled customers are very often the slowest to pay their debts.

In granting credit two fundamental questions must be answered: Do I have enough capital? Do I know how to collect?

A general rule is that you must have additional capital on hand equal to one-and-a-half month's credit sales in order to give customers 30 days to pay. Credit granting and collecting takes skill. Many people just don't have it. One retailer with 25 years experience commented, "When I first started I also tried to sell on credit but found that I wasn't a good collector, so after several months I made all sales for cash and have since conducted a cash and carry business."

Pitfall number seven is taking too much out for yourself. It's an easy habit to fall into. Many new business starters pledge to themselves, "We're not going to take anything out of the business." And of course they can't stick to it. What's the purpose of going into busi-

Inventory management can make or break a firm. Here, a volunteer retired executive looks over the stock of a New York clothing firm that the S.B.A. is assisting.

ness if you aren't going to take something out? The approach to what you take out for yourself should be flexible and realistic. When profits decline owners must curtail their drawing.

The eighth pitfall can come from too much success. Business is so good you decide to expand—but unplanned expansion can be ruinous. Generally businesses grow in two ways: Slow and steady from within—marked by increased sales and profits, or by rapid expansion through addition or acquisition.

Rapid expansion must be carefully planned since it requires skills to manage new people you must hire as well as additional capital. One storekeeper found out the hard way that two stores weren't twice as profitable for him as one. With one store doing well he opened another across town. But the managerial help in his second store failed to grasp his successful methods. The owner had to supervise both stores with his wife helping out. When she got sick the load was too much. Eventually, physical and capital strain required that he sell the second store. Today, he operates one store profitably and without undue headaches.

Pitfall number nine—the wrong attitude—ruins many. Some businesses fail to prosper or come to grief because of wrong attitudes of their owners. Being in business is plain hard work, demanding full diligence. Some owners figure that since the business is theirs they'll work hours only to suit themselves. Others get involved in outside interests to an excessive extent. They may even tell themselves that social and civic interests help promote the business when all they do is take the owner away from affairs that need tending. Greed kills off still others. When products are misrepresented or shoddy, it is always found out. A well-known chain of fine restaurants had to be sold off because their owner evaded income taxes. The penalties levied by the Internal Revenue Service in addition to a jail sentence

forced the sale of that restaurant chain.

But, even with all the hazards, the dream of having your own business can be realized. There are ways to overcome the obstacles and succeed. A prime source of help lies with the Federal Government through its agency, the Small Business Administration, set up in 1953 to aid small business. The S.B.A. with its network of 88 field offices in principal cities, as well as in Guam and Puerto Rico, is available to assist new business hopefuls as well as established small businesses. The available offices are listed at the end of this article and can be found in the phone book under the classification "U.S. Government."

Most people associate the S.B.A. solely with loan assistance but this is only a part of the important services the agency performs. Actually, the S.B.A. is structured to provide a wide range of advisory services to help businesses operate better. Anyone who's in trouble with his small business should at least ask the S.B.A. for advice. Maybe it can't save him—but maybe it can. And it often sets up clinics, workshops and management courses for small business owners. In addition, it guides established business owners in procuring government contracts set aside for small business.

The S.B.A.'s doors are open to anyone who seeks counseling and guidance on going into business for himself. At the S.B.A. office he is assigned to a management counselor who interviews him to determine his business objective and his qualifications for reaching it. The interview is controlled by a four-page questionnaire which probes for such information as education, work experience, knowledge of a particular business' needs, capital requirements and other pertinent data needed to evaluate fitness to start a venture.

Some people are only technically equipped, which isn't enough. For example, the young vet who served a year's apprenticeship repairing radio and TV sets before entering the military. He learned more from electronics training in the Army. Upon discharge he wanted to set up shop for himself. But while he could make a radio or TV work wonderfully, he actually knew nothing about running a business.

"Even worse, some people come through the door armed with no more than a burning desire to be free and work for themselves. They haven't got the foggiest notion of what business they'd like to get into or what knowledge is needed," confides Charles Spano, management counselor for New York's Small Business Administration regional office. "In such cases I encourage them to participate in one of our work-

Jean Taylor's Long Island, N.Y., store, House of Nine, is a successful franchising venture.

shops for prospective business owners."

S.B.A. workshops are usually conducted on a one-day-a-month basis, teaching basic principles of financing, taxes, federal regulations and sales promotion. Workshop leaders stress additional sources of advice and assistance and encourage their students to use them. The workshops are valuable in a number of ways, Mr. Spano points out. "They teach business principles and they show up the weaknesses of many aspiring business entrants, dissuading them from going into business when they aren't truly ready."

In cases where a would-be entrant shows strong potential, the S.B.A. is prepared to act further. A counselor may help him get a loan to start the business. Once started, counselor guidance may continue until the fledgling business is on its feet.

While the S.B.A. now rarely makes direct loans, it does get involved with "participation" loans. One type, the guaranty plan, requires that a bank make the loan which the S.B.A. guarantees up to 90%.

Before the S.B.A. will involve itself in a loan it insists that an applicant first seek a direct bank loan. Only after a turn-down will the S.B.A. consider participation. Borrowers are expected to furnish such information as their experience, a financial statement reflecting all personal assets and liabilities, a detailed projection for the first year of operation and a list of all collateral at present market value.

A more modest loan is available through the S.B.A. under the Economic

Opportunity program. These loans are offered to the economically "disadvantaged," particularly the minorities, who have the capability to operate a business but can't get loans through usual channels. The maximum amount of an Economic Opportunity loan is $25,000 for up to 15 years.

The S.B.A. can also put you in touch with ACE, a group of active business executives who have volunteered to help guide those in small businesses. S.B.A. has another such corps of volunteer counselors made up of retired executives. They are called SCORE. (S.B.A. also seeks more executives and retired executives who would care to volunteer for ACE or SCORE.)

Beyond personal counseling and loans, the S.B.A. produces and publishes a variety of publications of interest to the

ALL PHOTOS FROM BLACK STAR

small businessman. These include lists of available books, pamphlets, technical aids, management research summaries and annuals. Many are free and are obtainable by writing your S.B.A. field office. Others sold at a nominal charge can be purchased from the Superintendent of Documents, Government Printing Office, Washington, D.C. 10402. Recommended reading includes:

Checklist for Going Into Business (Management Research Summaries No. 120). Free;
Factors in Small Business Success or Failure (Management Research Summaries No. 145). Free;
The First Two Years: Problems of Small Firm Growth and Survival (Small Business Research Summaries No. 2). $1.00;
Problems of Small Business (Management Research Summaries No. 42). Free;
Starting and Managing a Small Business of Your Own (Starting and Managing Series No. 1). $0.25.

An excellent source of information for anyone interested in starting a busi-

ness is a trade association. Trade associations exist in every major industry and many minor ones. They are sources of surveys and studies that do economic analyses of such factors as salaries, wages, sales and labor conditions. A letter addressed to a trade association asking about the feasibility of entering an industry will often be answered with a packet of materials outlining such matters as growth trends, capital equipment, new technology, operating ratios and other pertinent data. A full listing of trade associations can be found in the *National Trade and Professional Associations of the United States.* $7.95. Columbia Book Publishers, Room 300, 917 15th St., N.W., Washington, D.C. 20005.

Chambers of Commerce, both state and local, can help to get a new business started. Generally, they can assist in such

Leonard Morris made a go of his franchised Management Recruiter Service.

matters as site location, labor information, referral work, setting up introductions and making appointments with vital sources, and they may even make loans. Thomas N. Stainback, executive vice president of New York's Chamber of Commerce and former president of the Jersey City Chamber of Commerce points out that ". . . while the services of Chambers vary widely, to overlook their facilities is a mistake since they can save people time, money and headaches along the way."

Public libraries can be gold mines of information to potential owner-managers of small businesses. Libraries offer indices to business periodicals, newspapers and select subjects. They keep such government documents as censuses of population, business and agriculture, the *Census of Manufacturers*, the *Census of Business* and *County Business Patterns*.

Libraries hold copies of existing local, state and federal laws, as well as pending legislation. The statistics needed to make important decisions, and the precise information found in directories are all free for the asking through public library sources. Although a local library may be small and unable to furnish a particular publication, it can still be of help by borrowing the volume you want through interlibrary loan channels.

THE FOLLOWING references are helpful in using the public library to get information on running a business:

Sources of Business Information, by Edwin T. Coman, Jr., Revised 1964. $8.50. University of California Press. 2223 Fulton Street. Berkeley, Calif. 94120.

Selected Business Reference Sources. 1965. $2.00. Harvard University. Baker Library, Boston, Mass. 02138.

How to Use the Business Library, by H.W. Johnson. 3rd edition. 1964. Paperback, $2.00. South-Western Publishing Company. 5101 Madison Rd., Cincinnati, Ohio 45227.

Basic Library Reference Sources for Business Use. Small Business Bibliography No. 18. Small Business Administration. Sept. 1966. Free. S.B.A., Washington. D.C. 20416. (Or nearest S.B.A. office.)

Starting your own business is one thing. How about obtaining a ready-made business? A franchise is a possibility. There are perhaps 1,200 franchise companies and between 400,000 and 600,000 franchise outlets that annually generate from $80 to $110 billion in sales in the United States. Franchises account for nearly 10% of the gross national product and 26% of all retail sales. Ninety percent of all existing franchises sprang up in the last ten years and franchising as a way of American business life is continuing to grow.

A prospective franchisee's choices are virtually unlimited. The variety of products and services available would cover the yellow page directory. Most prominent are the fast foods, employment agencies, financial services, tool and equipment rental, convenience grocery stores, cleaning stores and women's ready-to-wear shops.

Essentially, a franchise is a license to do business under a company's trademark. Usually the trademark covers a known or proven product or service. Along with the license goes a formal contract of continual relationship with the franchisor. The prime attraction of a franchise is the opportunity to start an independent business with limited capital and experience. Other benefits are initial training and follow-up guidance, promotional assistance and possible savings through bulk buying. Generally, franchises require an investment fee plus a continuing royalty, usually a percentage of the gross. Sometimes an advertising fee is tacked on which goes into the company's promotion fund. This is customarily a percentage of the gross, too. If products are involved, the franchising company reserves the right to sell them to the franchisee at company-fixed prices. Franchisors perform a variety of services for their franchisees, including financing, site selection, fixturing, purchasing of initial durable equipment and record keeping.

Franchise investments can be as low as $1,000 or as high as $100,000. Annual incomes from single, successful franchise operations range from $10,000 to $250,000. Because the franchise idea appeals to the "be-your-own-boss" instinct it attracts people from every walk of life and occupation.

Leonard Morris, 46, a New Yorker, had a radio tube distribution business, now operates a plush Management Recruiters employment agency on Wall Street. John Hannon, 42, a Mississippian, left a $135-a-week packing job in 1963 to buy a fried-chicken franchise from the original Colonel Sanders. Today, he has nine stores employing 75 people with a gross yearly volume of over $2,500,000. Jean Taylor, a secretary for the Santa Fe Railroad at Fort Worth, Tex., now runs a House of Nine dress shop on Long Island. It grosses $400,000 a year.

With the astounding number of franchisors now in the market, the question arises—are they safe? Figures compiled by the International Franchise Association based on an analysis of its members over a period of years would indicate they are. The I.F.A. claims that the average franchise operation has approximately an eight to one better chance of being in business after ten years than the average small business started by an individual operating on his own.

Despite the statistics presented by the I.F.A., franchises have proved a disaster for hundreds of innocent investors. At least five states have introduced franchise disclosure laws. The Federal Trade Commission is conducting investigations of its own. Why all the furore about a business structure which seems to be the modern day fulfillment of the American dream? Bernard Goodwin, a prominent New York attorney and franchise expert, testifying before the Texas legislature in June 1970, said: "Well, the con-boys moved in on this thing (franchising), the bunco boys, the soft-shoe operators. They said, 'Wow, we're not in the stock market anymore because we've got the SEC there watching us or the Blue Sky laws all over the country watching us, and we can't operate like we used to operate. Franchising—this is a heaven. Where did this come from? We can go around selling franchises. And who cares what happens afterwards. We collect our franchise fee, and we disappear.' "

Harold Brown, a Boston attorney and author of the book *Franchising Trap for the Trusting*, is an outspoken critic of much in franchising. He castigates such practices as kickbacks; overcharging franchisees for products, services and equipment; proliferation of outlets so as to force owners to sell back to the parent company at a fraction of their value, and arbitrary termination of contracts on flimsy grounds.

Louis J. Lefkowitz, Attorney General of the State of New York, after investigating thousands of franchises, strongly supports a full disclosure law. In particular, he finds much in franchise promotional literature which is inadequate, misleading, wholly lacking or blatantly false as to facts necessary to make a sound business decision. Take, for example, a pet-grooming service franchise seeking a $10,000 investment from a franchisee for fully equipped grooming trucks, including kits for gourmet dog food, as well as grooming supplies. It represented that potential profit of "up to $40,000 per year" was within easy reach—even without experience. The fact was that the company had only one small grooming truck, no record of performance(!) and no financial backing.

A home protective service, luring investors with the promise of earning $30,000 annually, stated to Lefkowitz's staff that it could not answer the attorney general's questionnaire. With only a few months in business they hadn't "enough of a background." Other franchise companies involved in bankruptcy reorganization continued to solicit franchisees without even a hint of their financial condition.

A random sampling of 84 different franchisors and 10,620 franchisees showed that 65.5% of the persons investing in franchises earned less than $15,000 a year in their prior occupation. It was also found that 36% of the franchisors managed to stay in business two years or less. It was further found that at least half of the franchisors went into it to make their money from the franchisees, rather than from the success of their product.

If you're considering a franchise, heed the warning of the National Better Business Bureau, Inc., which advises "investigate before buying."

The Bank of America issues a checklist of 50 questions it thinks you ought to have answers to before contracting with a franchisor. That's more than we can print here, but if you that interested and aren't near a Bank of America office, send a stamped, self-addressed return envelope to "Franchise Questions, The American Legion Magazine, 1345 Ave. of the Americas, New York, N.Y. 10019." Do *not* send a letter. The coded address tells what you want. Your envelope will be returned with a list of the Bank of America questions in it. This offer ends March 1, 1971.

Harry Kursh's big book, *The Franchise Boom—How You Can Profit in It*, is a veritable encyclopaedia of franchise information. The revised 1968 edition sells for $9.95. Publishers are Prentice-Hall, Englewood Cliffs, N.J. 07632.

FRANCHISES are listed in the "Business Opportunities" section of some newspapers and in the Wall Street Journal. Other sources of franchise information include:

1970 Directory of Franchising Organizations. $2.00. Pilot Books, 347 Fifth Ave., New York, N.Y. 10016.

The Monthly Report. $13 per year. National Franchise Reports, 333 North Michigan Ave., Chicago, Ill. 60601.

Modern Franchising Magazine. $3.00 per year. Modern Franchising Magazine, Inc., 1033 First Ave., Des Plaines, Ill. 60016.

Franchising Today, by Charles L. Vaughn. 1969 edition. $19.50. Farnsworth Publications Co., Inc., 381 Sunrise Highway, Lynbrook, N.Y. 11563.

Franchise Company Data, Task Force for Equal Opportunity in Business. July 1969. Free. U.S. Department of Commerce, Washington, D.C. 20230.

The Franchise Annual, 1968, $2.50, National Franchise Reports, 333 North Michigan Ave., Chicago, Ill. 60601, is published by the International Franchise Association, Inc., an organization which can supply important information on member franchises.

There is also the alternative of buying an existing non-franchise business. This approach is both advantageous and disadvantageous. On the plus side, it avoids the time and headaches involved in locating a site, negotiating a lease, fixturing, buying merchandise, installing record systems and hiring personnel. Important, too, going businesses have momentum—something a starting business lacks and must overcome. Moreover, going businesses are, for the most part, predictable as to their volume and earnings.

Hunting for a good, going business for sale can be costly and time-consuming. Acquiring a business warrants serious investigation before you lay your cash down and take title. For this, you will have to call upon the expertise of lawyers, accountants and bankers. Because a business is going it can be costly to buy—but this may still be better than starting one yourself and failing.

As a rule, service businesses can be bought for less than manufacturing or wholesaling operations. They also need less working capital to operate since large sums aren't tied up in inventory and receivables. On the other hand, service businesses have the poorest survival rate.

One road to finding a business for sale is through a business broker. They are easily found in the yellow pages of the phone book under the classification "Business Brokers." Some specialize in particular lines of business, while others handle anything that comes through the door. Telephone listings, however, are no guide to a broker's reliability. To get a reference on a good broker ask your bank.

Good brokers won't accept listings of outright lemons. They demand financial statements proving the income and net worth of a concern as well as other important details of its history. Beyond merely getting the buyer and seller together, a good broker can be instrumental in setting up the terms of the sale and sometimes steering an over-anxious buyer away from involvement in a business he couldn't handle.

Fritz Loeb, 30 years a broker with the 50-year-old David Jaret Corp. in New York, states: "A good broker makes every effort to weed out bad listings. If this is not done it is easy to ruin a reputation earned over a lifetime of service." He adds: "Many buyers are naive in that they seek to find out why the seller is selling. What really counts is the merits of the business as it stands and its future."

Another source of quick leads is the classified listings found in the "Business Opportunities" sections of newspapers. Most of them are typical small businesses such as small motels, stationery stores, cleaners, bars, restaurants and retail specialty shops. In most cases, newspaper ads give minimum information. They seldom disclose more than gross sales or weekly income, length of lease and seller's price. From that point on it will be up to you to do much investigating.

The idea that you'll come upon a real "sleeper" involves about the same odds as your breaking the bank at Monte Carlo. Generally, a business up for sale is first offered to relatives or a trusted executive, then to suppliers or even competitors. Advertising a business for sale has perils which sellers prefer to avoid. It can cause a pulling in of supplier's credit, send customers to buy elsewhere and induce key employees to begin to look for other jobs. By the time a business appears in the classified columns there can be something seriously wrong. This does not mean it should be ruled out completely. If you can recognize and cure the ills you may have a terrific bargain bought at a rock-bottom price.

Inserting your own ad to seek a business should be done with care. Your wording should be precise as to the kind of business you seek, its location and the price you're willing to pay. An imprecise ad, for example, offering to invest cash and managerial participation for a partnership will yield hundreds of replies from sour businesses, shaky start-ups and wacky inventors. Even the better replies will entail days of researching

before any decision can be made. In a nutshell, it's a long and aggravating way to search.

Better sources for leads are lawyers, bankers and accountants. In the course of handling clients these professionals come into contact with businesses of all sizes and descriptions. Equally as important, they are often privy to intimate knowledge of the businesses they recommend.

Let's assume that after sifting various proposals you narrow your choice to one. This is the time to make a close scrutiny before signing. It is advisable to ask yourself such questions as: What is the growth potential? Am I buying mainly physical assets, goodwill or momentum? Could the business be duplicated more cheaply by starting my own concern? Is this a profitable investment at the price? Do I know the market? Who are the customers? Why do they buy this product or service? Is the product or service growing in popularity? Is strong foreign competition or obsolescence likely? What is the competition from larger and better capitalized firms? What is the business' reputation in trade channels? Is the business linked to the skill or reputation of the present owner? These and many more questions should be considered. In buying any business "let the buyer beware" is still the rule.

Once you've decided to buy a business, it pays to give heed to a tax plan that permits maximum cash available in the first year's operation. (Usually this is done by charging off assets as rapidly as possible, converting everything allowable into expense.) Other tax strategies are possible which will allow you a lower purchasing price yet a higher net return to the seller. A certified public accountant should be consulted to guide you with these strategies.

Upon closing title there are other details which require your attention. For example, how will accounts that are receivable when you take over be handled? Will they be assigned to the buyer or seller or to factors? Are you taking on the debts of the seller? What obligation do you assume from the seller's union contract? Here, a good attorney is well worth his fee.

If all the pitfalls and technicalities involved in modern-day business seem a bit discouraging, many people still overcome them. Beyond personal satisfaction found in operating a successful business, being in business for yourself has many tax advantages. It's about the only way an individual can accrue capital. When you consider that quality common stock may not yield 4%, a good small business returning 20%, 30% and even 40% is well worth the effort and headaches—if you know how to do it.

Small Business Administration field offices, found in phone books under "U.S. Government," are located in:

Alabama: Birmingham.
Alaska: Anchorage, Fairbanks, Juneau.
Arizona: Phoenix, Tucson.
Arkansas: Little Rock.
California: Fresno, Los Angeles, San Bernardino, San Diego, San Francisco.
Colorado: Denver.
Connecticut: Hartford.
Delaware: Wilmington.
District of Columbia: Washington.
Florida: Jacksonville, Miami, Tampa.
Georgia: Atlanta.
Guam: Agana.
Hawaii: Honolulu.
Idaho: Boise.
Illinois: Chicago, Springfield.
Indiana: Indianapolis.
Iowa: Des Moines.
Kansas: Wichita.
Kentucky: Louisville.
Louisiana: New Orleans.
Maine: Augusta.
Maryland: Baltimore.
Massachusetts: Boston, Holyoke.
Michigan: Detroit, Marquette.
Minnesota: Minneapolis.
Mississippi: Gulfport, Jackson.
Missouri: Kansas City, St. Louis.
Montana: Helena.
Nebraska: Omaha.
Nevada: Las Vegas.
New Hampshire: Concord.
New Jersey: Newark.
New Mexico: Albuquerque, Las Cruces
New York: Albany, Buffalo, New York, Rochester, Syracuse.
North Carolina: Charlotte.
North Dakota: Fargo.
Ohio: Cincinnati, Cleveland, Columbus.
Oklahoma: Oklahoma City.
Oregon: Portland.

Pennsylvania: Philadelphia, Pittsburgh.
Puerto Rico: Hato Rey.
Rhode Island: Providence.
South Carolina: Columbia.
South Dakota: Sioux Falls.
Tennessee: Knoxville, Memphis, Nashville.
Texas: Corpus Christi, Dallas, El Paso, Harlingen, Houston, Lubbock, Marshall, San Antonio.
Utah: Salt Lake City.
Vermont: Montpelier.
Virginia: Richmond.
Washington: Seattle, Spokane.
West Virginia: Charleston, Clarksburg.
Wisconsin: Eau Claire, Madison, Milwaukee.
Wyoming: Casper.

Idea man extraordinary

Sherman Fairchild's exploits as a technological entrepreneur make him one of the most creative businessmen in the US

HIS NAME adorns so many different enterprises, one might almost think there are several Fairchilds. But no. There's just one Sherman M. Fairchild. However, his interests range from optical equipment to electronics to aircraft.

At 72, he is the largest stockholder in IBM, with 509,000 shares worth $158 million (£65.8m.), a fortune built from a $2 million (£833,333) inheritance. He is also founder and chairman of Fairchild Camera & Instrument Corp., with sales last year of $220 million (£91.7m.) and of Fairchild Hiller Corp., an aerospace company which sold about $260 million (£108.3m.) last year.

In addition, he holds 84,860 shares in Conrac Corp., an industrial and aircraft equipment maker he helped to launch. From just these four interests alone—and he has many others—he earns an income of nearly $1.5 million (£625,000) a year in stock dividends.

Yet, at an age when most executives have retired and are thinking only of grandchildren and golf, this tall, plump innovator—and confirmed bachelor—continues practising his unusual brand of entrepreneurial magic. He is applying his growth touch now to four small companies he owns completely.

At a time when society admires the well-disciplined professional, he has been an amateur because he wants to be. He likes to be the outsider who can move inside when he chooses. He reminds one of a medieval patron of the arts, but the art he subsidizes is technology. And he doesn't worry too much if the companies and products that come out of it fail to turn a profit—so long as he's captivated by what they're doing.

New technology forever fascinates him. Transforming it into the shape of a company—and perhaps into profits—fascinates him just as much. His motivation, he says, is "to build the best and the most advanced."

Fairchild's interests range from photography to electronics to aircraft

At his private laboratory, his passion for technology is gratified as he personally tests the prototype of a new high-quality intercom system, the Fairchild Forum. (His name pops up on products that vary from printers' equipment to semiconductors to aircraft.) Beaming at the flexibility and performance of the system that his Fairchild Recording Equipment Corp. is about to introduce, he brags: "It's our best effort yet."

But Fairchild the technologist never eclipses Fairchild the entrepreneur. And any work week provides a kaleidoscopic display of his talents. A recent week's schedule included:

● A trip to Los Angeles to explain to film executives how his Front Projection system—the kind used so successfully by Stanley Kubrick to film

large segments of "2001, a Space Odyssey"—could be applied to commercial film-making.

● A talk with Edward G. Uhl, president of Fairchild Hiller, about disposing of an unprofitable product line.

● A telegram from IBM Chairman Thomas J. Watson Jr. advising him (as a board member) of a government antitrust suit against the company.

● A taping session in his New York City town house. He brought Hubie Blake, the 85-year-old jazz pianist, there to record, as he does with many musicians.

● A filming test of some new colour film, done in his living room, which has photographic lights and electronic strobes in the wall fixtures.

Ideas fly from Fairchild like sparks from a welder's arc. His enthusiasms

Fairchild

include photography, aviation, audio systems and electronics. For a short time in 1921 he became so interested in the music business that he started publishing music. Today he is planning a book publishing venture.

And, through the years, he has been a connoisseur of good food, pretty girls and lively parties. In 1917, he attended the Cordon Bleu cooking school in Paris largely to be close to a young lady who had caught his fancy. The byproduct: a lifelong taste for gourmet food and fine wines.

Indeed, even by today's standards, Fairchild was a swinger when he was young. He was fond of night-clubbing, often with his close friend Howard Hughes (but he has not seen him for 11 years). He still throws three or four parties a year.

Nevertheless, he has hardly been a playboy. The energy centre of his life has been technical pioneering, and all of Fairchild's companies have been started to manufacture something nobody else would make.

Over the years, Fairchild Recording, one of the four companies he owns completely, has spawned 42 technical "firsts." This is a phenomenal performance for a company virtually unknown outside the broadcasting equipment industry. It developed such esoteric products as the first commercial feedback amplifier, the first professional tape deck, the first stereo

pickup and the first recording of sound on aluminium discs. Now, as it brings out the new Forum intercom, the company is expected to double or triple its $1 million (£416,667) sales of last year. Since it is moving into a market wider than the broadcasting industry, its name will be changed soon to Fairchild Sound Equipment Corp.

In fact, Fairchild thinks the time of expansion has now come for all four of his companies that operate in the photographic and audio markets. Last year, in a burst of typical corporate enthusiasm, he packaged Fairchild Recording and the three other photo-audio companies into what he jokingly calls a "mini-mini conglomerate."

Conglomerates usually are constructed from different parts. This is a group of related firms. Into it, with Fairchild Recording, went:

• Front Projection Corp., which manufactures a system for simulating location shots inside a studio.

• Cine Magnetic Inc., a company that Fairchild bought in 1967 when an old friend, Everett Hall, ran out of money. It has a system that makes four 8mm. films at one time from a 16mm. or 35mm. master.

• Projection Systems Inc., a companion corporation that rents and maintains audio-visual equipment for corporate clients.

All told, Fairchild has invested $4 million (£1.7m.) in the group. And now some rich returns are on the way. The Forum has the biggest potential. Cine Magnetic is about to reap the benefits of a switch to 8mm. film by industrial

users and television stations—the result of wide acceptance of the new Super 8 film size, which puts a bigger picture on the screen. And Front Projection will be hard-pressed to keep up with orders from film-makers and television stations.

Fairchild himself helped perfect the Front Projection System. The way it happened is typical of his method of operating.

His interest was first aroused when he read about a new material 3M Co. had developed to reflect heat from fire fighters. It consisted of a sheet of plastics bubbles, each with a metallic mirror on one side to improve its reflecting power. Intrigued, Fairchild bought some to try it as a reflector of lights for indoor photography. He found it reflected so much light he could project slides or films on it and rephotograph them as a background.

What's more, if persons or objects were placed against this background and photographed through a half-silvered mirror, they looked as though they were actually moving about in the background scene.

Getting control—But others had done similar experiments and Fairchild learned about them. Some had taken out patents. Fairchild snapped up most of the patent rights and perfected the process.

To prepare his four companies for such growth, he assigned Warren Farrell, a business consultant, to take charge of the lot. Farrell, who normally works for Fairchild personally, managing some of his investments, was made chairman of each of the four. Each has the same vice president for marketing, too.

The sudden action developing in these four companies is also typical of Fairchild. He has always allowed his companies to ramble along at their natural pace until some technical development fires them into growth. Sales of Fairchild Aeroplane were only $3 million (£1.25m.) a year in 1940, but then the company started building a trainer and a cargo plane for World War II. By 1943, sales were $102 million (£42.5m.).

Similarly, it took 37 years for sales at Fairchild Camera to reach $37 million (£15.4m.). In next 10 years, however, its entrance into the semiconductor business increased sales sixfold.

In each case, technology set the entrepreneurial pattern. From the very beginning, Fairchild has operated this way. He would tinker with an idea

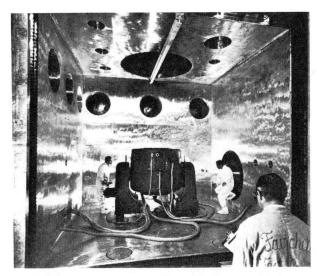

Equipment undergoes space chamber test at Fairchild plant

Pilot trains in simulated aircraft cockpit

until he produced a working prototype; when no one would manufacture it, he would.

Fairchild started tinkering early with various mechanical devices. Sent to Arizona in his teens to cure a sinus infection, he took up photography and has worked with it ever since.

He was unable to finish Harvard because of a threat of tuberculosis, so he transferred to the University of Arizona where he was introduced to flying. Because aeroplanes and cameras were more exciting than college, he left school.

Flying game—In 1919 he designed an aerial camera for the US Signal Corps, and when nobody else would manufacture it he set up shop in a loft in New York City to build cameras. That company led to Fairchild Aerial Surveys. This was a familiar caption on almost every aerial photograph published during the 1920s, until the company's name was changed to Fairchild Camera & Instrument Corp.

In 1924, when he needed an aeroplane to take aerial photographs, an adequate one was not available. So he started another company, the forerunner of Fairchild Hiller, to build the planes. His first model, designed by Igor Sikorsky, was a monoplane with a number of technical innovations such as flaps to slow speed on landing and an enclosed cabin for the pilot.

As the Depression worsened in 1930, he went looking for subcontracts to

keep the precision metalworking capacity of Fairchild Camera busy. He met a man named Crook who was looking for someone with a strong technical background to develop equipment that would put sound on aluminium discs. Previously, records were made from wax and shellac.

Fairchild was interested by the technological progress made possible by aluminium. He was also impressed by the briefcase full of contracts for aluminium records Crook had from radio networks. So he decided to take on the project. Terms were cash on delivery for equipment that worked.

"We had just about completed the design of the equipment," Fairchild reminisces, "when we discovered that Crook was more than the man's name. All those contracts he had were forged. He disappeared and left us with the almost-completed equipment for cutting aluminium records."

Into broadcasting—Fairchild persevered anyway. The company finished the work on its own and became the first to put sound on aluminium. It was the start of doing business with the broadcasting industry. Over the next 15 years, Fairchild Camera developed a large number of high-quality devices, built for a limited market of broadcasting stations.

In 1948, with Fairchild Camera flooded by postwar subcontracts, its management decided to sell off the audio portion of the business. This was proving unprofitable, mainly because the products were so good they were too expensive. Nobody else would buy it, so Fairchild did—and called it Fairchild Recording. Today it's on the verge of booming.

Of course, Fairchild has been helped not a little by the money he inherited. His father was a wealthy manufacturer of business machines, a founder of IBM and the company's first chairman. Fairchild's smartest move, possibly, was to hold on to the $2 million (£833,333) worth of IBM stock that he received from his father.

A side benefit from this was his long association with IBM—as a major stockholder, a member of the board since 1925 and a member of the executive committee since 1956—which exposed him to what he believes is the best management in industry. But his efforts to translate the IBM way to his companies has not met with so much success. He has often had management trouble.

His basic philosophy on manage-

ment is "get the right man and let him run it." And he has gone to great lengths to apply that doctrine. One of his favourite methods has been to search out the best second man in somebody else's company and pay him to join one of his.

Just last August he offered to lend C. Lester Hogan $5.4 million (£2.25m.) to make a stock purchase if the semiconductor executive would leave his post as executive vice president of Motorola Inc. and become president of Fairchild Camera.

But in at least one memorable instance, this method ended in grief. In 1938, he engaged J. Carleton Ward Jr. from United Aircraft Corp. to be president of Fairchild Engine and Aeroplane Corp. In 1946, after repeatedly clashing with him over what kinds of planes the company should make for the postwar market, Fairchild resigned and let Ward run the company his way.

Three years later, when he no longer had control of the company, Fairchild was angered by what he felt was a too liberal retirement plan for Ward. He launched a proxy battle, won it and replaced Ward with Richard Boutelle.

Criticism—Ward, for his part, complained that Fairchild was always butting in, telling engineers what to do. Fairchild is sensitive to criticism of the management of his companies and he appears to have learned from his worst experiences. Today, he lets a company's management give all the orders to technical people, though he is not above bombarding them with clippings —and potential new ideas—from the 150 technical journals he reads omnivorously.

Grief over management problems has afflicted Fairchild Camera, too. In 1957, after the board had selected a different candidate, Fairchild went out and picked his own man for chairman, John Carter, then one of the brightest young vice presidents at Corning Glass Works.

With Carter apparently doing a superb job, sales exploded from $37 million to $220 million (£15.4m. to £91.7m.) in 10 years, and Fairchild withdrew to the sidelines. But much of the growth was due to one fortuitous move: the start of semiconductor manufacturing. Elsewhere, things were not going well.

In 1967, Carter resigned under pressure from the board and Fairchild came back on the scene. Recalling the mess that resulted, he says sadly, "I waited too long with John Carter. But at what point do you make such a decision?"

After Carter left, Fairchild resorted to another favourite stratagem he has employed to tide a Fairchild company over a difficult period. He formed a management committee to run Fairchild Camera while he looked for a new chief executive.

The result was not unmixed joy. In fact, Fairchild was accused of being "committee crazy." "Calling it a committee was the worst mistake I ever made," he says defensively. "It was a management team. I'll never form another committee."

New ideas—But if committees have gone to limbo, Fairchild must still keep himself constantly surrounded by people. For him, the life blood of his activity is exposure to people who might stimulate an idea.

Each morning the postman brings him a stack of mail eight inches high and there are many proposals in it. Many are absurd, like one suggesting the installation of huge magnets on cars to prevent collisions by repelling vehicles that are about to bump.

No matter how ridiculous the idea, Fairchild answers each one. To the proposer of the magnet scheme, he sent two magnets and the suggestion that the writer measure the repelling force to calculate how big and heavy the car magnets would have to be, in order to work.

From almost any kind of conversation, Fairchild's interest may suddenly catch fire. When an admiral, who was making small talk, told him how difficult it had been to write an accurate history of a naval battle, it occurred to Fairchild that it would also be very difficult to write an accurate history of aviation. So he quickly engaged a writer and a researcher to put together a series of books on aviation pioneers.

In almost predictable style, he plans to publish the series himself. "That's the only way I can be sure it will be done the way I think it should be," he says, enunciating the first law of the Fairchild entrepreneurial method—better than anyone else could. **End**

It is in the nature of a large organization to oppose upsetting change and innovation, yet change and innovation there must be. The answer to the problem is . . . .

Champions for
Radical New Inventions

By Donald A. Schon

• Why do small companies, large corporations, military laboratory employees, and independent inventors find it so difficult to sell really new inventions to the military services?

• What is the nature of resistance to innovation in military and business organizations?

• What does experience show to be the requirements of successful technical innovation?

• What steps can management take to ensure that the necessary development work will go into promising proposals for radical new products and processes?

The military services hold up to the business community an enormous and only slightly distorted mirror in which patterns surrounding technical innovation stand out clearly. Goaded by the threat of competition and a perceived need for corporate growth, industry seeks new products. In order to "win the arms race" and "meet the Soviet threat," the military seeks new weapons systems. Both depend on technical innovation and lean on technical resources for producing change. Both are caught in the gap between the wish for deliberate and systematic methods of innovation and the uncertainty and risk inherent in this activity. In both, there is a discrepancy between formal organization for innovation and the informal organization and process by which it is sometimes accomplished (though in the military, perhaps because it is a superorganization, the informal routes are more clearly visible).

In this article I shall examine the significance of the resources for invention that are being wasted and the reasons (many of them all too human and understandable) that this waste continues to go on. Then I shall turn to the measures we can take in business and government to cope with the problem. The first and most essential step is recognizing resistance to change and accepting it rather than "driving it underground." There are a series of measures, one of the most important of which has to do with the "product champion" concept, that we can take to promote the development of promising new inventions.

Much of the information and thinking in this discussion is based on a study conducted by Arthur D. Little, Inc., under a contract administered by the National Inventors Council and supported by the military services.

Significant Resource

In the traditional sense, "inventor" means an amateur, untrained, and independent genius of the kind supposedly typified by men like Thomas A. Edison and Samuel F. Morse. Whether or not technical heroes ever did fit this mold, it is clear that they do not fit it now. The growing technical complexity of military and industrial life has made it impossible for individuals to invent effectively without extensive technical experience. Moreover, in our culture today, the official idealization of inventors masks an unofficial contempt. "Inventor" is very nearly a dirty word. With few exceptions, industry and the military alike tend more and more to protect themselves from the apparent dangers of deal-

77

ing with individuals as individuals; and as a result the individuals who might once have called themselves "inventors" are now forming small businesses or filtering into the ranks of large corporations.

For these reasons, "inventors" in the old sense are not the resource we ought to be interested in here. We should be concerned, rather, with innovative, technically trained individuals who have proved their ability to develop new products and processes and who have done so as individuals, without organizational support. We find these people operating as professional independents and in a variety of organizational settings: universities, research institutes, small and large corporations, and the military itself. What is more, our concern should be with radical innovation, such as Robert H. Goddard's early work on rockets and Sir Frank Whittle's work on the jet engine. When it comes to this kind of innovation (which is always easier to identify in retrospect than in advance), a man's residence in an organization does not guarantee him organizational support.

From this point on, when I refer to "inventors" and "inventions," I shall use the terms in the ways just described.

Number of Inventors

How many such men are there; how much have they contributed? This question can be answered only indirectly and by approximation. On the basis of our own estimates and interviews with technical people in military laboratories and large corporations, heads of small businesses, and professional independent inventors themselves, a good guess is that today there are several thousand independent inventors in the United States. To mention some of the pieces of evidence gathered in our study:

• The United States Patent Office was able to give the National Inventors Council a list of 500 inventors who had accumulated many useful patents, working independently. Jacob Schmookler estimates that 40% of the patents currently granted are assigned to such individuals.[1]

• There are about 310,000 small businesses in the United States ("small" by the Small Business Association's standards — less than 500 employees and less than $10,000,000 in annual sales).

• We interviewed 42 small companies which, through technically trained individuals in their employ, had developed an impressive array of new products and processes.

We have no way of estimating the number of independent innovators working without organizational support *in* military laboratories and large corporations.

Value of Contribution

How important a role have such people played in innovation? Evidence for their actual and potential contributions is, as might be expected, elusive. Nevertheless, several different kinds of evidence have been gathered:

❧ Although patents are a doubtful sign of technical innovation, patent studies have been made which are at least indicative. Jacob Schmookler's study covering patents granted during the last decade reveals that a surprisingly high percentage were assigned to individuals working as individuals, rather than to organizations. Indeed, 40% to 60% of the patentees worked outside the organized research teams of industrial laboratories. And John Jewkes, David Sawers, and Richard Stillerman made a study which showed that between 1936 and 1955, in both the United States and Great Britain, the percentage of patents issued to individuals, as opposed to corporations, remained between 40% and 50%.[2]

❧ In a paper presented to the Joint Economic Committee on September 24, 1959, Professor Daniel Hamberg of the University of Maryland stated that 12 of the 18 inventions he had examined resulted from the work of independent individuals and relatively small companies. The authors, in their *The Sources of Invention,* show that 40 of 61 important inventions made since 1900 were the product of independent innovators, working alone, unaffiliated with any industrial laboratory. Another 6 were the product of investigation conducted in small- to medium-size organizations. Their list cuts across technical disciplines and industrial areas, ranging from Bakelite and cellophane to safety razors and ball-point pens.[3]

❧ In the course of our study, we assembled a list of inventions important for military uses, made within roughly the past 50 years. Individuals working without organizational support were either entirely responsible for these inventions or played a major role in their evolution:

Jet engine — Sir Frank Whittle
Gyrocompass — H. Anschütz-Kaempfe
Helicopter — Igor I. Sikorsky
Rockets — Robert H. Goddard

[1] "Inventors Past and Present," *Review of Economics and Statistics,* August 1957, p. 321.
[2] *The Sources of Invention* (New York, St. Martin's Press, 1959), p. 105.
[3] Ibid., pp. 72, 73.

Many varieties of automatic guns — e.g., the
  Lewis gun
Suspension tanks — George Christie
Doron body armor — General Georges F.
  Doriot
Noiseless and flashless machine guns —
  Stanley Lovell
Cryotron — Dudley Buck
Atomic submarine — Admiral Hyman G.
  Rickover
Sidewinder missile — William B. McLean
Project Astron — Nicholas C. Christofilos
Stainless steel — Elwood Haynes
Titanium — W. J. Kroll

Bear in mind that many of these developments,
as well as a number of others which could have
been included, occurred *after* the beginning of the
organized research and development which has
characterized the last 50 years.

It is clear, then, that in recent times individuals working without organizational support
have been responsible for an extraordinarily high
percentage of important, radical commercial developments. In spite of the problems in contributing to the military, they have also been responsible for a number of significant military
changes. Also, these individuals have shown
themselves to be particularly well equipped
to do innovative exploratory work and to do
it quickly in comparison to the research teams
of large corporations. However, as we shall see
presently, much of their potential value to business and the military has been wasted.

What are the reasons for this waste? Let us
begin with a look at the military screening offices, then turn to companies and individuals
who are doing (or might be doing) defense
work. Later we can examine the interesting
parallels with commercial innovation.

Failure to Get Through

Within the military, there is official recognition of the need for technical innovation. Military research and development chiefs and civilian advisers emphasize the need for radically
new developments, for "ideas," and for more exploration. They are apt to express this need in
terms of "meeting the Soviet threat," "winning
the Cold War," "defending the Free World,"
and the like — phrases which play for the military very much the same role that "growth" plays
for the industrial corporation.

The formal channel by which the ideas of

individuals may enter the military is the military screening offices. The major research and
development agencies of each of the three services have such offices, as do major operating
groups like the Army Ordnance Corps and individual military laboratories like the Army Signal Corps Laboratories. The function of these
agencies is to receive and screen the ideas of
individuals, inside and outside the military, and
to pass on to appropriate technical personnel
those ideas which seem to have most merit.

How much innovation goes through this channel? We interviewed 14 men from 7 screening
offices which receive from 40 to 2,000 ideas a
month. The chief question asked of each man
was whether he could identify an invention
submitted through his office and later used by
the military. *In not one case could he do so.*

For this reason we were led to conclude that
as a means of helping the military to use resources of invention which are not now adequately used, these screening offices are virtually a hindrance. They can be best understood
as a wall, rather than as a screen. They protect
the main body of military R & D from the dis-
turbance of outside inventors and inventions;
they are a device for maintaining good public
relations.

Many of the men we interviewed were perfectly open about this. They had long ago concluded that inventors may as well not submit
inventions to the military services. They pointed to their own problems: cuts in budget, too
few personnel, overlap and repetition of function within and among the services, and difficulties in getting feedback on ideas from the working laboratories. And although these men are
charged officially with a constructive function,
they work under conditions that permit them to
perform only a secondary, defensive one.

In brief, there are significant resources of innovation for which there is expressed need, and
there is a screening organization whose main
function is to serve as a buffer against them.
This is not the simple case of a large organization's discrimination against certain individuals.
The case is much more that of a complicated
social tangle in which people on all sides of the
issue are caught, in spite of their best efforts.

Why Inventors Fail

The problems of contributing to the military
are experienced in different ways by individuals

in varying settings. Let us take a look at four groups — people in the military, large and small business, and independent inventors.

Federal Employees

Individuals in military laboratories, who are inventive and technically competent, have a unique value as a resource. They know what the technical problems are. They have access to prior art in their fields. They are subject to minimum security restrictions. And, unlike individuals in other settings, they are already organized as a resource. It is particularly significant, therefore, that where figures are available, military screening offices report that the rate of rejection of ideas submitted internally through formal channels is as great as the rate of rejection of ideas submitted from the outside.

Some of the reasons for this came out in our interviews with technical personnel in military laboratories. In spite of the fact that many of these people had records of outstanding technical contribution, there was a general sense of discouragement about the possibility of contribution apart from assigned work. The men gave several reasons for this attitude:

(1) In their view self-initiated innovation was not expected of them. And where their function was not limited to testing or administration of contracts, their superiors seemed to fear that self-initiated work would distract them from assigned tasks.

(2) While there was a civilian award program for self-initiated contributions, substantial awards were rarely given. (An exception was the $25,000 award given for the development of the Sidewinder missile at the Navy's China Lake Laboratory.)

(3) Most important of all, discouraging delays were encountered when the men attempted to go through formal channels. This they attributed to a "reverse natural selection" among technical civil service personnel. Relatively low salaries tended to drive many good innovative technical men out of government work, and the dedicated inventors who stayed on had to cope with the remainder — many of whom come into positions of responsibility only through seniority. One laboratory experimented with an "Operation Blue Sky" in order to solicit new technical ideas. But the ideas submitted were reviewed by the same men who were believed to have blocked innovation in the past, and the experiment produced nothing but frustration.

Small Business

In the case of small business, many innovators come from universities and large corpo-

rations precisely in order to be freer and more effective in technical innovation. They tend to be men who show unusual enthusiasm for new technical developments and who, by and large, have demonstrated an unusual ability to move quickly from new technical ideas to prototype development. But they do not contribute significantly to the military for these reasons:

(1) Many technically based small companies have not even attempted to gain military R & D contracts. They attribute this to the unprofitability of such contracts, inability to capitalize on later production contracts, the difficulty and cost of selling R & D to the government, and competition with large corporations.

(2) Relatively few small businesess are successful when they attempt to gain technical development contracts with the military, and the successful ones tend to conform to a pattern. Thus —

(a) They gain contracts in a specialized technical area in which one or two of their staff members have considerable technical prestige.

(b) They have a man (or two) in top management experienced in dealing with the military.

(c) They either bid on contracts where the technical requirement is already clearly recognized by the military, or they sponsor their own development work and apply to the military for optimization contracts.

(d) In general, they do not make money on such contracts; they are lucky to break even.

All of this suggests that, in spite of efforts by the military and the Small Business Administration to increase the small business share of R & D contracts, there is still a resource of technically trained innovative individuals in small firms throughout the country whose contributions the military is not getting. This is particularly true of technical needs that the military has not yet clearly recognized and of small companies lacking the qualifications mentioned above.

Big Business

Large corporations are entirely distinct from individuals without organizational support. But the large corporation's advantages in approaching the military — its proven name, its large sales force, its capital, its ability to carry out production contracts — apply only to projects officially sanctioned by top management. Innovative, technically trained individuals within a corporation frequently have technical ideas that never get official sanction. Ideas of this kind may not look to the top management like a source of long-range profit, they may not seem to have commercial application, or they may even lie outside the corporation's pattern of technical growth. And yet they may be of great value to the military. To illustrate:

During World War II, technical staff members of a large corporation proposed water-filled protective capsules for pilots of high-speed aircraft and a new kind of aircraft thermometer. Both ideas were rejected at the time and later produced successfully elsewhere. Most technical directors of large corporations are familiar with similar cases.

Inevitably, corporate managers make some mistakes in judging the value of a proposed development for the corporation, and in many more cases they correctly judge as inappropriate for them a development which might be of great value to the military. The originator of such a development must either sell the idea "uphill" in his own organization; or he must sell it essentially as an individual to the military. The double obstacle is usually insuperable. And, what is more, the technical man usually has no incentive to overcome it. He will have signed away his patent rights, so that he cannot profit from them. He is not eligible for the civilian award program. If his project succeeds, he is likely to gain some status and prestige. But if it fails, he may very well suffer for having wasted time and money.

Independent Operators

Independent inventors constitute a special case in that their problems in relating to large organizations, both in the military and in private business, are classic.

First, there are difficulties inherent in the relation itself. Witness, for instance, the mutually frustrating, but finally successful, efforts of Alexander Zarchin to interest the Israeli government in his salt-water conversion process, and the mutual harassment that characterized the interaction of many inventors in one U.S. industry — an interaction which in the case of at least three major inventors (Rudolph Diesel, Wallace H. Carothers, and William G. Armstrong) ended tragically.

In the case of the U.S. military, this relationship has certain special features. For example, each of the services views itself as being harassed at present by one or two voluble inventors, skillful in appeal to Congressmen, who have made that service their particular target. Unfortunate-

ly for R & D administrators in each of the services, the word "inventor" is apt to conjure up an image of their particular tormentor.

What makes the situation even more delicate is that these men cannot easily be dismissed. There are the stories of Professor Robert H. Goddard who tried in the 1930's, for the most part unsuccessfully, to interest the U.S. military in rocketry; of George Christie, inventor of the suspension system for tanks — rejected by the U.S. Army, later adopted successfully by the Russians; and of Nicholas C. Christofilos, "the crazy Greek" who turned up with Project Astron.

The difficulty with these rare geniuses is that they can be recognized easily only in retrospect, never in prospect. You never know for certain that your present-day tormentor, whom you *think* is a crank, may not turn out to be another Goddard, another Christie, or another Christofilos.

Furthermore, the inventor himself may often show considerable aggressiveness, not to say eccentricity, in his dealings with the military. In many cases, his motives appear to be primarily to show up the professional military man, the professional scientist, or the professional engineer. He may present his invention so aggressively as to suggest that he is aiming not at having it accepted but at being able to complain of its unfair rejection.

At best, the preliminary judgment of new technical developments is precarious, particularly for men who do not have great technical sophistication in the field in question. Often the technical administrator must base his judgments on the soundness of the man at least as much as on the promise of the development itself. And when the man appears in sneakers and an open shirt, when he behaves queerly, or when he refuses (moved by his own perhaps legitimate and perhaps excessive fears about protection of his idea) to reveal the principle of his invention until he has been paid, he makes it extremely difficult for the military decision-maker to act favorably toward him.

While these difficulties are sharpest for the men who call themselves inventors, they extend generally to all kinds of individuals mentioned earlier. For the military, feeling that it has been burned so frequently in its dealings with individual inventors, tends to apply its defensive attitude to *all* "organizationless" individuals. Thus, we are confronted here by a vicious circle of protection and aggression, practiced by both parties.

Need to Resist Change

So far, the complicated social tangle responsible for the record of the military screening offices has been presented mainly from the side of the would-be contributors. But there is another side as well. And here we find striking parallels between military and commercial organizations.

"Normal" Opposition

Individuals approaching the military tend to be inattentive to the military administrator's problems. These problems make it difficult for him to invest in radically new technical developments for which there is no obvious and immediate requirement — especially when these are at the "idea" stage and are to be undertaken by individuals working without organizational support. These problems have to do, in part, with the so-called "weapons systems" approach which characterizes much of the military's technical development work:

"To ensure that no time, money, or effort will be wasted on blind alleys, almost all of the planning is done in terms of the end products that are supposed to emerge from the program — the weapon systems. Before any major project is begun, the planners painstakingly figure out what performance characteristics the weapon system is supposed to have and the technological innovations it will contain. The development program is spelled out stage by stage and then reviewed by numerous agencies within the armed services, by special committees, and by the staff of the Assistant Secretary of Defense for Research and Engineering. After the program is under way, progress is monitored at every step." [4]

Within this sort of approach, certain general technical routes to the goal are chosen. "Technical problems" are problems in implementing these routes. A military technical administrator operating within such a system cannot easily shift his attention to radical technical ideas not obviously related to his requirements, and so he finds it even more difficult to invest in risky individuals who will not be able to carry their innovations into production later on.

There is an even more general sort of resist-

ance to radical technical change. Elting Morison describes it elegantly in his study of the introduction to the Navy of continuous-aim firing (a new combat-tested method, presenting major advantages over old ones, had been rejected by Navy officials until President Theodore Roosevelt intervened):

"The Navy is not only an armed force — it is a society. In the forty years following the Civil War, this society had been forced to accommodate itself to a series of technological changes. . . . These changes wrought extraordinary changes in ship design, and therefore in the concepts of how ships were to be used; that is, in fleet tactics and even in naval strategy. . . . To these numerous innovations, producing as they did a spreading disorder throughout a service with heavy commitments to formal organization, the Navy responded with grudging pain. It is wrong to assume, as civilians frequently do, that this blind reaction to technological change springs exclusively from some causeless Bourbon distemper that invades the military mind. There is a sounder and more attractive base. The opposition, where it occurs, of the soldier and the sailor to such change springs from the normal human instinct to protect oneself and more especially one's way of life. Military organizations are societies built around and upon the prevailing weapon systems. Intuitively and quite correctly the military man feels that a change in weapons portends a change in the arrangements of his society." [5]

What Morison characterizes as the "normal human instinct" to oppose technological change is as true of the military today as it was in Theodore Roosevelt's time.

Justified Ambivalence

We come now to a most important point. Resistance to change is not only normal but in some ways even desirable. An organization totally devoid of resistance to change would fly apart at the seams. It *must* be ambivalent about radical technical innovation. It *must* both seek it out and resist it. Because of commitments to existing technology and to forms of social organization associated with it, management *must* act against the eager acceptance of new technical ideas, even good ones. Otherwise, the technical organization would be perpetually and fruitlessly shifting gears.

This is true in the military and also in almost all walks of private industry. As a matter of

[4] Burton Klein, "A Radical Proposal for R & D," *Fortune*, May 1958, p. 112.

[5] "A Case Study of Innovation," *Engineering and Science*, April 1950.

fact, most corporations are, if anything, *more* intensively defensive than the military. Taking the case of proposals from outside the organization first, only a few companies have maintained a tradition of receptiveness to such ideas. For in addition to sharing with the military reasons like those mentioned, many companies are afraid of being sued. Because some companies have had to pay damages to inventors, most companies have built up elaborate legal defenses. And because some companies have stolen ideas from inventors, many would-be inventors have become gun-shy.

But the most interesting analogies refer to inside, rather than to outside, innovation. Here, too, most large corporations share the military's ambivalence over radical proposals. On the one hand, there is official enthusiasm for growth, expansion, diversification, progressiveness, getting ahead of the competition, and maintaining share of market — all backed up by the axiom that those who do not forge ahead fall behind, as well as by the *Alice in Wonderland* notion that you must run very hard even to stand still.

There is plenty of reality behind this axiom, as witnessed by the fate of many sleepy industries tied to outmoded products and processes. (I seriously wonder, however, if growth is always required for corporate health and whether new products are *always* the means to salvation.) The fact stands, nevertheless, that radical product innovation means radical changes in all phases of the business — new technologies, new product techniques, new channels of distribution, and perhaps even a new conception of the market.

Novelty in these areas challenges accepted ways of doing things and long-established skills. It may throw a company, including top management, into areas where it feels inept and uninformed. Also, as in Morison's example of continous-aim firing, changes in technology tend to carry with them major changes in social organization, threatening established hierarchies, undermining the security of positions based on old products.

Moreover, the more radical the product innovation, the higher, in general, the cost of developing it. And this cost curve tends to rise sharply after the preliminary work in which the first models are built and the first market concepts are achieved. In fact, the whole process is marked by increasing risk and takes place in a context where most new product efforts fail. It is not surprising, in view of these tendencies, that a ground swell of covert resistance to change comes into conflict with official enthusiasm for it.

The pernicious part of this problem for both the military and industry is not the resistance to change, but the failure to recognize it. Here again, the rule applies to almost all types of organizations.

In the case of the military, resistance is masked by official assumptions to the effect that the services are wholeheartedly in favor of technical innovation in weapons systems and accept or reject all new ideas objectively, strictly on their merits. These assumptions conflict with reality and mislead potential innovators. For they go hand in hand with other assumptions. It is held, for example, that "civilian resources of invention are ready to be tapped" — that is, solutions to urgent technical problems are there for the taking, in the form of already worked out developments. If this is so, it is only prudent to reject solutions which have not yet been fully developed — and this, of course, includes most ideas submitted to the military.

In short, official assumptions, masking what is often legitimate resistance to change, drive that resistance underground, as in the case of the idea-screening operation itself. Once underground, this resistance to change goes out of control. Thus, the question of its legitimacy never comes up, and potential contributors to the services are bewildered by the discrepancy between words and action.

In industry, too, once resistance to change goes underground, it becomes capable of destroying most product innovation. Underground resistance paves the way for disguised defenses against change. In screening new ideas, many large corporations employ formal committees which are, in effect, buffers against new ideas. Assumptions are found to the effect that new ideas are wholeheartedly desired and are evaluated objectively, strictly on their merits — together with the further assumption that new ideas should be fully developed and ready for plucking. For instance:

In some large companies, the "new idea forms" which must be filled out by innovators require a fullness and precision of detail impossible early in the life of a new product idea. Such screening mechanisms require that each idea be developed before support is given for its development; they have the effect either of discouraging submission of new ideas or of forcing development work underground.

Pattern of Success

Despite the complicated buffers and screens I have described, innovation does take place in government and industry. Radical inventions do find acceptance, and the fact that they do, and the reasons that they do, are tremendously important. Since the military is such a superb case in point, let us take its experience first.

Developments like McLean's Sidewinder missile and Rickover's atomic submarine do not fit the pattern of orderly presentation of promising technical ideas to official judges, favorable objective evaluation, and then orderly marshaling of technical resources for development. These histories look more like crusades or military campaigns, with overtones of fifth-column activity and guerrilla warfare. They present clear illustrations of four major themes.

1. *At the outset, the idea encounters sharp resistance.*

Like Goddard's work on rockets, Whittle's work on the jet engine, and virtually every other significant military technical development, the Sidewinder and the atomic submarine at first were met with indifference and in some cases active resistance from military officials. These innovations appeared to run counter to the most sensible and established technical commitments. They looked expensive and unfeasible.

2. *Next, the idea receives active and vigorous promotion.*

In spite of the myth that valid technical ideas do not need internal sales, it is characteristic of successful technical innovation within the military that the new idea requires and receives active promotion. Often, as in Morison's description of the introduction of continuous-aim firing, there is a division of labor as to invention and promotion. In that instance, the inventor was not equally talented as a promoter, and so a second figure emerged who was able to carry the fight for its introduction and development into the highest Navy circles. In our own time, Admiral Rickover's skill in defending and promoting his ideas is legendary. Techniques for promoting new technical ideas are a matter of serious concern, even at the highest military levels, as shown by the use for this purpose of outside publication and appeal to Congress.

3. *For the introduction, promotion, and development of these ideas, their proponents make use of the informal, rather than the official, military system.*

In the early stages of development, when the idea was still in its infancy, the Sidewinder was not funded through official contracts from any of the Navy bureaus, but from the small sums detoured from official programs. Only when enough work had been done to show the strength of the idea did it fall into official contract channels. The use of such "bootlegged" research funds is only one example of the use of the informal military network. In many instances ideas now under development or test were submitted originally through personal contracts; in the matter of technical development, particularly across departmental lines, a network of good personal contacts is a cherished resource. The buffering function of the official screening offices virtually forces such a network into existence.

4. *Typically, one man emerges as champion of the idea.*

Many people do know of Goddard, Whittle, Rickover, and McLean. But in the case of less famous developments, for example, the Navy's "Ribbon in the Sky" and the introduction of frangible bullet firing as a training method in World War II, individuals also emerged as champions. There is nothing incidental or exceptional about this happening. Where radical innovation is concerned, the emergence of a champion is required. Given the underground resistance to change described earlier, the new idea either finds a champion *or dies.*

Essentially, the champion must be a man willing to put himself on the line for an idea of doubtful success. He is willing to fail. But he is capable of using any and every means of informal sales and pressure in order to succeed.

No ordinary involvement with a new idea provides the energy required to cope with the indifference and resistance that major technical change provokes. It is characteristic of champions of new developments that they identify with the idea as their own, and with its promotion as a cause, to a degree that goes far beyond the requirements of their job. In fact, many display persistence and courage of heroic quality. For a number of them the price of failure is professional suicide, and a few become martyrs to the championed idea.

All of these requirements apply to commercial organizations as well as to the military. As just one example, Arthur K. Watson has testified to the importance of the third condition at IBM:

"The disk memory unit, the heart of today's random access computer, is not the logical outcome of a decision made by IBM management. It was developed in one of our laboratories as a bootleg project — over the stern warning from management that the project had to be dropped because of budget difficulties. A handful of men ignored the warning. They broke the rules. They risked their jobs to work on a project they believed in." [6]

Product Champions

But perhaps the most challenging part of the pattern described, at least for corporate executives, is the product-champion concept. How can it be made to work (yet not work so well that the organization is in chaos)?

To begin, it is clear that the product champion must have considerable power and prestige in the organization; otherwise he will not have the freedom to play his role. He must know and know how to use the company's informal system of relationships. Also, his interests must cut across the special interests (technology, marketing, production, and finance) which are essential to the product's or the process's development.

But attention to these requirements has a curiously futile ring to it. For one thing, it is extremely difficult *in practice* for top management to admit the need for such a man, since the implication in doing so is that something is wrong with what is euphemistically called the organization's "climate for creativity." Moreover, once the need is admitted, what can be done about it? Is management to bring in individuals whose overt function is to disrupt the company order which has been so carefully built up over the years? And, if it is to do so, what evidence is there that product champions can be selected and fostered?

In fact, there is some evidence that these men can*not* be hired and "developed" the way some others can. In more than one case, com-

panies have brought in men who were specially chosen to initiate radical product change; but since these men were chosen, in part, for their thick-skinned aggressiveness, they succeeded in alienating others on whom they depended, even to the point of ensuring failure. In still other cases, companies brought into this new product role men who were well received within the organization but who lacked the aggressive, risk-taking properties of the product champion, and failed for the opposite reasons.

Nevertheless, there have been instances in which product champions have been successfully introduced from outside, or recognized and supported within, a company. This kind of activity has occurred in at least two different ways:

(1) Management resorts not to sweeping across-the-board change, but to a model for change. It sets up a pilot operation staffed by only a few men but capable of carrying ideas through preliminary development and promoting them vigorously in the informal channels of the organization. This pilot operation can be headed by a man selected because he has the characteristics of the product champion described previously, with the exception of overt aggressiveness, which often is not necessary. The function of the operation is to provide a model of product innovation, small at first, but capable of taking root and spreading.

(2) The company's management makes the decision to adapt to its new technology and to the product champions who accompany that technology, rather than to force innovation into the mold of the established organization. Such a decision crucially affects the company's policy of corporate growth and diversification, since it does not require that new products mesh with existing means of production and distribution. Essentially, it gives support to certain product champions as entrepreneurs, allowing them to push their product through from beginning to end, and establishing a new division for the resulting business (that division need be only loosely related to the existing corporate structure).

More often than not, the champions are drawn from within the organization. They are given freedom to take a technical, production, marketing, and management view of their new product — in effect, to approach its development as though they were setting up a small business with corporate funding and support. They are held responsible for the success of that business, in turn, as though they were an independent corporate entity. The corporation resulting from consistent pursuit of such a policy has the aspect of a loose confedera-

[6] Address to the Eighth International Congress of Accountants, New York City, September 24, 1962.

tion of businesses which may or may not fall into the same product family.

Both of the foregoing patterns share recognition of the need for the product champion, a need created by the organization's own powerful underground resistance to change. The patterns are devices by which top management, shrewdly assessing obstacles to innovation, attempts to manipulate the organization. The success of the manipulation, at least on a temporary basis, is shown by the number of organizations for which one or another of the patterns described has become a standard procedure.

Needless to say, these patterns do not represent the only alternatives. Once the need for the product champion has been recognized, there are many possible social inventions for selecting and supporting him. The important point is that *some* such invention is required.

Conclusion

In perspective, the problem of significant innovation in business and the military raises some basic questions. For instance, it seems fair to ask if the most important aspect for top management is not formal organizational procedures but the social tangle which necessitates bringing the product champion into being in the first place. Why must legitimate resistance to change go underground? Why is it not possible to deal openly in a company with the dangers of innovation, even while proceeding with development work? Why should penalties for failure fall so heavily on one or two men, when the organization as a whole demands innovation?

The product-champion approach grows out of the sharp division between those in top management who dispose and those, lower in the organization, who propose. Product champions would be needed less if the risks of product change were more evenly distributed, that is, if top management were to give up some of its prerogatives to dispose of what others propose. This may be seen as too steep a price to pay for innovation. But a willingness to face the price of innovation is a major part of the problem of technological progress.

Reprints of Harvard Business Review articles are available at the following prices:

Single reprint	$ 1.00	Additional 100's up	
Two reprints	1.30	to 1,000, each	$ 20.00
Three reprints	1.50	First 1,000	215.00
Four to 99, each	0.40	Additional 100's	
First 100	39.70	over 1,000, each	15.00

These prices apply to total quantity of reprints (whether for the same or assorted articles) ordered at one time. When ordering individual articles, please list by author, month, and year rather than title. Postage is prepaid on orders shipped via parcel post or third class mail. Allow 21 days for normal delivery. For faster service add 50¢ for special handling charges on orders of over 100 reprints.

Reprint Service
Harvard Business Review
Soldiers Field, Boston, Massachusetts 02163

JOHN T. DOUTT

Product Innovation in Small Business

Does the formula for survival involve the use of technical factors, or the acceptance of challenges to managerial philosophy and ingenuity?

The charge that small businessmen are using too much system and procedure, too much organization, too technical an approach to problem solving is a strange sound indeed. More commonly they are accused of being casual in adoption of "more business-like methods." Recent observations by the author suggest that businessmen do look on problems of product innovation and development as being technical in origin and solution. And their attempt to solve them has led them on occasion to activities that are both costly and fruitless. Findings indicate that small manufacturers tend to view the problem in terms of these concepts:

- Research efforts should prove rewarding in proportion to the money and personnel that are given to them.

- A useful tool for making decisions about new products is the check list. This will save time on products that "just don't fit".

- Technically trained people can be hired who will generate new product ideas and will aid in developing them.

- Management problems attendant to new products that are developed can be delegated to someone who is brought in to administrate the commercial aspects of the new product.

The Mechanical Approach

Perhaps the most amusing ideas embraced are those that hold that research is something like selling life insurance in that the more money spent and the more effort made, the more certain and the more rewarding the results will be. And, much as the life insurance man is taught to believe, all one has to do is to redouble his efforts, and his redoubled reward will be forthcoming. In a rather simple simile, doubling the amount of fertilizer applied and doubling the number of gardeners does not necessarily produce a double size bloom on the flower. The climate in which new product ideas flourish cannot be purchased by simply doubling the offering price nor can new products be expected to blossom twice as large or twice as fast by doubling the number of technically trained personnel engaged in the effort.

One of the most generally used tools in product research is the check list. Here one can ascertain at a glance whether or not a given idea fits with some preconceived notion as to what would be a "good" product for the company to develop. While the range of items on the check lists runs from freight rates to adaptability to currently owned equipment, the common theme throughout is the belief that here is a time saver and an automatic device to screen the "good" ideas from the "bad" ones. The fact that some "good" ideas (in terms of germination potential and possible adaptability) are discarded at the very outset is accepted rather casually as inevitable. At least, management had evolved a policy, an approach, a framework for dealing with the different problem of product development.

The Formula

The desirable qualities or characteristics that a new product should possess to be attractive to a small manufacturer can be summarized easily: it should serve some unique purpose in fairly wide-spread applications and should lend itself to patents or the de-

velopment of a specialized market niche that will not invite or attract too much competition. The realization of this formula is almost certain to result in a product of some pulling power and with sufficiently high profit margin to make the producer happy. And the specialized market niche permits the manufacturer to schedule his manufacturing operations in a fairly serene atmosphere, the customer taking his turn at the gate and never mentioning pricing practices.

The fact that some manufacturers do find products with just these characteristics does not seem to help them in finding additional products to add to their line. Rather than regarding the experience as being unique, the finding of the proverbial needle in the haystack, the general reaction is simply to add one more criterion to the checklist — and this one well-nigh excludes any real product innovation for some time in the future. It might be better for the manufacturer to regard his finding of such a product as the grandest kind of luck and rather than spend his time looking for another needle he might do better to turn his attention to the more pedestrian products that make up the product line for most manufacturers.

CURIOSITY AND CONCERN

The fact of the matter is that finding another product with the rare combination of characteristics described above is something that cannot be assured by any mechanical approach to the problem — neither amount of effort at product innovation nor the time-honored check list. The premium quality here is an intense curiosity and concern that is centered on the product by individuals within the organization — individual men who are thoroughly immersed in the notion of "doing something with our product" or some new product which they have thought about largely on their own. And, as with religion, it would sometimes appear that the best way to kill it is to organize for it, delegating, assigning, parceling out until the responsibility for the product (and the zeal for it) are pretty well dismembered.

If this quality of concerned curiosity is to be developed and implemented, top management must see their own responsibility in creating the climate so essential for its advancement. As with most characteristics of the business, this one starts at the top. If the company has been living in an atmosphere of comfortable circumstances with little or no innovation in the day-to-day tasks undertaken by the management echelon, it is unlikely that one will find any wellspring of curiosity and new ideas anywhere in the company. The zest for innovation and progress is indeed a permeating and contagious sort of thing. It cannot be purchased, pigeon-holed, channeled and controlled as one would a pound of pig iron for the store room.

The Management of Improvement

Nor can one wait until such time as he needs a more imaginative approach to his product line and then proceed to instruct his people to think imaginatively, creatively. It is not a sort of current that lends itself to switch control. And bringing in an innovator or idea man to be superimposed on an uninspired organization is only to dramatize and accentuate the problem of the

company's plodding pace. It will hardly solve it. The management of improvement is a continuing part of the management responsibility and the attitude or climate so essential for it to flourish in cannot be hired, delegated, or controlled by gimmick or device.

The company that is blessed with top management possessing this quality will be characterized by a questioning attitude throughout the organization — a ferment that soon involves all phases of the operation of the enterprise. Personnel earmarked by their intensity of curiosity will be hired for both sales and production, and they will get their greatest encouragement here not from the pay check but from top executives who are themselves responsive to this trait.

A second characteristic of the innovating company will be its concern with the finding of problems that need solutions. Involvement with solutions as such (an inevitable by-product of the research laboratory) or the purely commercial activity of new applications of the present line are not just a lesser order of the imaginative mind. They are more likely to be an actual distraction to it. If some unique purpose is to be served and some specialized market niche is to be found, it is more likely to result from the quest for problems to be solved than it is from the making of minor adjustments in the usefulness of our present product to its present customers. Herein lies the failure of much of that which is called "market research".

Survival of the Small

But the competition is keen, and it is here that the large company may find an edge over the small producer. With its reputation and larger sales force, it gains more exposure to problem situations, and when they arise, it is in a position to spend great amounts of time and money on the solving of a particular problem knowing full well that the solution could lead to a whole series of product developments. Obviously, if the small producer is to survive in such an economic arrangement, it will be by the excellent quality of what he does and not by any quantitative attempt to meet the large producer on his own playing field. His sensitivity to problem situations must be keen, his ideas unusual.

The Academic Fountainhead

It is becoming increasingly common for executives in the industrial world to turn to academic people for aid on this topic of product innovation. One case observed will be described by way of illustration. Believing that teachers in universities would be in the vanguard of new ideas and latest developments in scientific and technical areas, the chief executive of a small manufacturing concern contacted a number of university professors in a broad number of areas and arranged a loose organization whereby they would be called in as the need would arise. It was his hope that these people would become a fountainhead of new ideas, some of which might become the product with the unique characteristics described earlier.

Despite some lapse of time, the academic program has not turned up any ideas worth developing commercially. Apparently there is little correlation between intelligence and the sort of creative imagination required here. In fact, the more informed mind often

turns out to be the more critical, not only of the efforts of others but of its own as well. The result is a barrenness in which creative ideas cannot take root.

AN ORGANIZATIONAL PROBLEM

The problem receiving the least attention from top management is the question of what they would do with a new product idea if they did get one and how they would integrate it into their present organization. In at least one case studied, the chief executive was actively seeking one or more new products to be added to the line, but confessed quite openly that he did not have the management team to handle the new product or the increased burdens that expanding production and sales would place on his present organization. In still another instance, the owner-manager of a fairly large operation (125 employees) admitted that he had surrounded himself with narrowly trained executives hired to do specific tasks, and that he had made no effort to weld them into a working team. Any new product developed, he observed, would mean that he would have to bring in some one to handle it. Just how it would relate to his present product line or how his new product manager would fit in with his going organization were problems that had been given but casual consideration.

In still another instance, the chief officer of the company claimed to be looking for new products, maintaining that his present plant and capital structure could easily support a sales volume three times its present size. While his manufacturing operations were quite systematically controlled, made possible by the fact that his chief product was free from the usual harassments of a competitive market, he relied on a constant round of visits among the executives themselves to maintain control and coordination in the higher echelons of the business. And he himself was actively engaged in reviewing inventory records of finished stock and initiating a work order for replenishment when he judged it desirable to increase quantities on hand. It is doubtful if even the slightest increase in sales volume or diversity of product line could be experienced without placing serious strains on his present administrative devices.

The New Perspective

It is apparent from these few observations that product innovation is far from the mechanical problem that it often appears to be. The priceless ingredients here are a management philosophy, an attitude, a sensitivity, a curiosity that the top executives generate and encourage and which flows from the top down through every department of the organization; it permeates every office and every function of the enterprise. In one instance this attitude was evidenced by a number of home-made machines in the shop which incorporated bicycle wheels and peculiar mechanical linkages because, as the owner explained, "nobody makes the kind of machines we need".

Until the chief executives of a company see this problem in terms of the perspectives outlined here, they will probably continue to rely on the old precepts of product development: research budget, technical personnel, and check list, complete with 5 gradations of opinion. But the race is not to the swift nor the struggle to the strong. It is to those who grasp the true nature of a problem and react with some intelligence to what it suggests.

CHAPTER 3

THE START UP PROBLEM

What is involved in starting a business? The prospective entrepreneur is confronted with an overwhelming assortment of problems and tasks during the planning and start-up stages. Inevitably, the founder must decide on a board of directors, a banker, a lawyer and an accountant. How to hire employees is also a central issue. Results are accomplished from resources. On the other hand, resource allocation is never as difficult as during the start-up phase when resources are scarcest. When results are needed quickly in a wide area of tasks, and resources are minimal, what is done first and second and third is crucial to the long run success of a firm.

The entrepreneur must digest and balance all the interrelated factors that are determinants of business success. Does the company really have a unique product or service to offer the marketplace? Which type of financial source is the best choice to provide risk capital to the business? Has a contingency plan been conceived in case product development, marketing or financing difficulties are encountered? If the firm can be launched on the right foot, instead of the left, the firm can avoid the problems inherent in a series of false starts. Unfortunately, this is the exception, not the rule for the new venture.

Murphy's law declares that "If anything can go wrong it will." It's universally true and especially applicable at the start-up phase of a new business. In addition, Mancuso's corallary to Murphy's law states, "it'll happen when you least expect it." Keep these two laws which govern business in mind and the start-up of a new business can be controlled but not made much easier. For your enjoyment and puzzlement, I've taken a page out of my newest book and added it to the reader. The book is entitled, "No Guts — No Glory" — how to fight dirty against management. The page I offer to you is a compilation of Murphy's laws. I think you'll enjoy them. And they are best read and believed during the start-up phase of your new business.

The entrepreneur's strategies for accomplishing his established goals and objectives must be documented in a business plan. Various forms of the plan will be used to sell his idea and himself to the financial community, to potential customers, and to suppliers who may consider his business

a credit risk. The business plan is the foundation of the business itself, and it provides a road map for start-up decisions. A good one is invaluable. May I suggest you refer to the appendix of "The Entrepreneur's Handbook" for "sources of help" on this vital issue. I'd suggest two excellent sources for you. They are Number Four and Five on the Table. The first is "The Business Plan" by LeRoy Sinclair at Technimetrics in New York and the second is a chapter in Donald Dible's book "Up Your Own Organization."

Writing a good plan ensures that a complete and integrated examination has been made of the product, market, manufacturing process, physical facilities, product cost structure and the abilities of the management. This plan pulls it all together. It should be done and done well. An article listed last in this "start-up" section addresses this issue. May I suggest you read the article by Hauser and Bricher entitled "Business Plan for the Scientific Entrepreneur" in detail. The reason it's listed last is because it is an excellent summary not because it is last on any scale.

The first article in this section is a check list from the Small Business Administration for prospective entrepreneurs to use in evaluating their qualifications and readiness for business start-ups. What are the entrepreneur's personal qualifications? Does he possess leadership abilities, strong perserverance, an endless supply of energy, and applicable experience? What is the market plan and how will it be affected by changing economic conditions? Will the product be distributed through direct or indirect channels? How will the consumers needs be affected by changing technological, political, cultural or economic environments? These and other important questions are offered in this checklist format for an individual intending to found a new business. Another checklist is offered by Don C. Hoefler from an Electronic News article in December of 1969. This is also valuable because it highlights issues for technical firms. Another excellent checklist is offered in a book mentioned in the bibliography. It is broad and very good. The book is "How to Organize and Operate a Small Business" by Baumback, Lawyer & Kelly — Prentice Hall, 5th Edition, Appendix B, p. 583.

The SBA checklist and Hoefler's checklist

compliment the information in Delman's article presented in another Section and the Hauser and Brickner planning checklist presented as an article in this section. These checklists should not be ignored. They can turn up areas of concern you've overlooked. So may I suggest you look them over now, it's the best ounce of prevention presently available.

Up to now the readings have discussed factors related to entrepreneurial activities in already established businesses. But given a good idea, or a strong desire to be your own boss, how does one proceed to establish himself as head of a business enterprise? What are the major factors to consider if the business venture is not to become a business failure statistic — as nine out of ten do?[1] What sources of information and help are available? Is there a better chance of success in acquiring an on-going business or buying into a franchise chain, rather than starting a new business from the ground up? In another article, Maury Delman discusses these questions, lists the major reasons for business failures, and provides sources of help for making these initial trade-off decisions. Delman emphasizes the need for the prospective entrepreneur to thoroughly understand the operational and financial considerations involved in starting his own business.

The last readings by Stuart Hauser and William Brockner discuss the need and development of a business plan for the successful start-up of a scientific business venture. This article was referenced earlier under the discussion of the business plan. The article indicates how a plan becomes a documented means for uniformly communicating the entrepreneur's strategies for producing and marketing his product according to these authors. It establishes a reference framework for the future use in measuring the company's progress. Venture capitalists, bankers, potential employees and the company's accountant and lawyer are all intertwined in the business and this document becomes the game plan for succeeding. It should indicate whether or not the founder has the experience, leadership qualities and resources required for profitably exploiting his product concept. And in the final analysis, preparing the plan provides the entrepreneur with a greater awareness of himself and his chances of success in the new business venture.

The entrepreneur will experience severe difficulties during his first few years of business. The company will be unprofitable and as such it is still not a viable business. Delivery dates must be met, products must be reliable, and suppliers must be paid. But mainly, the entrepreneur must convince potential customers that his product is either better or less costly, and that this business has a long life expectancy. The entrepreneur must be aware of and confident in his entrepreneurial abilities, and committed to the successful exploitation of his product concept. Stick-to-it-tiveness is often used to supplement other weaknesses in the business plan.

Both his abilities and his strategies will be documented in a business plan, and this is then used as a reference framework to measure both levels of performance. Consequently, the plan should not be optimistic or unreal because it often comes back to haunt a business after the start-up.

---

[1] May I suggest you consult Dun and Bradstreet which offers statistics into small business failures. Contact your local D & B office for the latest data.

A COLLECTION OF
MURPHY'S LAWS

Some authorities have held that Murphy's Law was first expounded when he stated that "If anything can go wrong, it will — during the demonstration."

Nothing is as simple as it seems.

Everything takes longer than it should.

The more innocuous a change appears, the further its influence will extend.

All warranty and guarantee clauses become void upon payment of invoice.

The necessity of making a major design change increases as the fabrication of the system approaches completion.

Firmness of delivery dates is inversely proportional to the tightness of the schedule.

Dimensions will always be expressed in the least usable term. Velocity, for example, will be expressed in furlongs per fortnight.

An important Instruction Manual or Operating Manual will have been discarded by the Receiving Department.

Suggestions made by the Value Analysis group will increase costs and reduce capabilities.

Original drawings will be mangled by the copying machine.

In any given miscalculation, the fault will never be placed if more than one person is involved.

In any given situation, the factor that is most obviously above suspicion will be the source of error.

Any wire cut to length will be too short.

Tolerances will accumulate unidirectionally toward maximum difficulty of assembly.

Identical units tested under identical conditions will not be identical in the field.

The availability of a component is inversely proportional to the need for that component.

If a project requires n components, there will be n-1 units in stock.

A dropped tool will land where it can do the most damage. (Also, known as the law of selective gravitation.)

Probability of failure of a component, assembly, subsystem or system is inversely proportional to ease of repair or replacement.

A transistor protected by a fast-acting fuse will protect the fuse by blowing first.

Left to themselves things always go from bad to worse.

Nature always sides with the hidden flaw.

If everything seems to be going well, you have obviously overlooked something.

Technical entrepreneurship: what do we know?

Arnold C. Cooper, *Purdue University**

Abstract. The factors influencing the birth of new, high-technology firms have been investigated in a number of separate studies. This paper summarizes and reports upon this research.

New, technologically-based firms have had, in the aggregate, substantial economic impact. The birth of these companies has been concentrated in particular places and at particular times.

The decision to found a new company appears to be influenced by three major factors. The characteristics of the entrepreneur, including the many aspects of his background which make him more or less inclined toward entrepreneurship, are important. The organization for which he has been working, which might be termed 'the incubator organization' also influences the entrepreneurial decision in various ways. A third factor consists of a complex of external influences, including the availability of venture capital and the collective attitudes toward entrepreneurship. Feedback processes appear to be at work such that past entrepreneurship makes future entrepreneurship more likely.

What do we know about how new, technologically-based firms are founded? What factors influence the birth of such companies? The phenomenon of technical entrepreneurship has been investigated in a number of places by a number of individuals; this paper summarizes and reports upon that research.

New, technologically-based firms contribute in a variety of ways to the growth and vitality of the economy:

1. They are important sources of innovation, sometimes achieving great success in matching developing technologies and market needs.
2. They add to the vitality of industry, serving as new sources of competition and complementing and spurring the efforts of established firms.
3. They offer alternative career possibilities for those engineers and managers who do not function most effectively in large organizations.
4. From the standpoint of regional economic development, they make pleasant neighbors, producing relatively little noise and pollution, employing highly paid technically-trained people, and broadening the regional economic base, thus lessening the reliance upon a few organizations.

Although many of these firms have enjoyed only modest success and others have failed, some have been extremely successful businesses. Companies such as Metals Research Ltd. and Nuclear Instruments Ltd. in England and Digital Equipment, Raychem, and Memorex in America have enjoyed great success. Compared to other kinds of new businesses, technically-oriented firms in America have experienced relatively low failure rates

[Draheim, *et al.* (1966), Roberts (1972), Cooper (1971)] The employment provided by new firms, considered in the aggregate, can be substantial. For example, spin-off firms from the major laboratories affiliated with M.I.T. provided, within a few years of founding, substantially more employment than the parent laboratories [Roberts (1969)].

The birth of these new firms seems to be concentrated in particular places and at particular times. In America, cities such as Boston, Los Angeles, San Francisco, and Minneapolis have had in recent years large numbers of new firms. There are other regions which, although they employ large numbers of technical personnel, have had relatively few new companies founded. Some of the regions in which technical entrepreneurship has been studied are indicated in Exhibit 1.

Exhibit 1
HIGH-TECHNOLOGY FIRMS STUDIED

Areas	Number of Firms Studied*
Ann Arbor, Michigan	76
Austin, Texas	31
Boston, Massachusetts	250
Buffalo, New York	42
Canada (nationwide)	47
Erie–Niagara, New York	43
Minneapolis–St Paul, Minnesota	142
Oak Ridge, Tennessee	21
Palo Alto, California	250

* These do not represent all new firms founded in the areas indicated, only those studied.

Understanding what has been learned to date about technical entrepreneurship should be of interest to a number of groups, including engineers or technical managers who envisage becoming entrepreneurs, those concerned with regional economic development, and managers of organizations interested in alternative ways of exploiting technology.

INFLUENCES UPON ENTREPRENEURSHIP

The founding of a new firm is, in a basic sense, a decision made by one or several entrepreneurs. The influences upon this decision might be organized under three general headings:

1. *The entrepreneur* himself, including the many aspects of his background that affect his motivations, his perceptions, and his skills and knowledge.
2. *The established organization* for which the founder had previously been working, which might be termed an 'incubator organization'. Its characteristics influence the location and the nature of new firms, as well as the likelihood of spin-offs.
3. *Various external factors*, many of them regional in nature. These include the availability of capital, collective attitudes and perceptions relating to entrepreneurship, and the accessibility to suppliers, personnel, and markets.

* This paper was prepared during a period spent with the R & D Research Unit, Manchester Business School, in 1972.

ARNOLD C. COOPER

Exhibit Two

INFLUENCES UPON THE ENTREPRENEURIAL DECISION

Antecedent Influences Upon Entrepreneur

1. Family and religious background.
2. Educational background.
3. Psychological makeup.
4. Age at time(s) of maximum external opportunity and organizational 'push'.
5. Earlier career experience.
6. Opportunity to form entrepreneurial groups.

Incubator Organization

1. Geographic location.
2. Nature of skills and knowledge acquired.
3. Motivation to stay with or leave organization.
4. Experience in 'small business' setting.

External Factors

1. Examples of entrepreneurial action and availability of knowledge about entrepreneurship.
2. Societal attitudes toward entrepreneurship.
3. Ability to save 'seed capital'.
4. Accessibility and availability of venture capital.
5. Availability of personnel and supporting services; accessibility to customers; accessibility to university.
6. Opportunities for interim consulting.
7. Economic conditions.

[Diagram: the three groups above connect to a box labeled "Entrepreneur's decision"]

The various influences on the entrepreneurial decision are shown in Exhibit 2.

THE INDIVIDUAL ENTREPRENEUR

What are the characteristics of these people who choose to take the unusual step of starting new companies? What prepares and propels them toward this unique activity? The longest history of research in entrepreneurship centers on the individual founder. Although the technical entrepreneur has been studied much less extensively than his non-technical counterpart, the following characteristics emerge:

1. Founders of high-technology companies often form groups to start new companies. The percentage of new firms started by groups of two or more was 48% in Austin, 61% in Palo Alto, and 59% in a study of 955 geographically diversified firms [Susbauer (1967), Cooper (1971), Shapero (1971)]. Groups permit a more balanced mangement team, one less likely to have major areas of weakness. They also provide psychological support at a time when the individual may be wondering whether he is taking the right step.
2. Founders tend to be in their thirties when starting high-technology companies. The average age of founders studied was 34 in Austin, 35 in Philadelphia, and 32 in Boston [Susbauer (1969), Industrial Research (1967), Roberts (1968)]. Apparently, at this time in their careers, they have sufficient experience and financial resources, yet are still willing to incur the necessary sacrifices and risks.
3. The typical American technical entrepreneur had at least a B.S. or first degree, usually in engineering. In Boston and in Austin the median educational level was an M.S. degree [Roberts (1969), Susbauer (1969)]. Since these new companies' competitive advantages are based upon the founders' knowledge, this is not surprising.

Earlier studies of *non*-technical entrepreneurs emphasized that they tended to have modest educational qualifications. Often, they got along poorly with their fathers, their teachers, and their employers; they often left school at an early age [Collins & Moore (1964)]. Available evidence on technical entrepreneurs suggests they do *not* fit this mould, at least with respect to their tolerance for formal education.

4. Founders appear to be more single-minded in their devotion to careers than hired executives. Within the semiconductor industry, they had fewer outside civic and sports activities [Howell (1972)].
5. Studies involving psychological tests and very limited numbers of respondents showed that entrepreneurs rated higher than average in aesthetic and theoretical orientations, leadership orientation, and achievement orientation. They rated low in religious orientation, need for support, need for conformity, and practical mindedness. Interestingly, they did *not* have high scores in regard to economic values [Komives (1972)]. The high scores in need for achievement are consistent with a considerable body of research focussing upon the importance of this factor in entrepreneurial activity [McClelland (1961)].
6. A disproportionately high percentage of founders are from homes where the father was in business for himself [Roberts & Wainer (1971), Shapero (1971)].
7. In some instances, an unusually high percentage of founders are from particular segments of the population. In Canada, 50% were immigrants; in Boston 16% were Jewish [Litvak & Maule (1972), Roberts & Wainer (1971)].

THE INCUBATOR ORGANIZATION

When a founder starts a new company, he typically leaves some organization. The characteristics of that organization, which might be termed the 'incubator', influence entrepreneurship in a number of ways.

1. The incubator organization affects the location of the new firm. Even though technical founders may have been geographically mobile at earlier stages of their careers, they rarely move at the time when they are founding new firms. The percentage of new companies started which involved at least one founder who was already working in the area was 97·5% in Palo Alto and 90% in Austin [Cooper (1971), Susbauer (1972)].

2. Established organizations also influence the nature of the new businesses established. In Palo Alto, 85·5% of the new companies served the same general market or utilized the same general technology as the parent company [Cooper (1971)]. In Ann Arbor, 83·7% of the new firms had initial products or services which drew 'directly' on the founders' previous technical employment experience and knowledge [Lamont (1971)]. The founder typically starts his new firm to exploit that which he knows best. Thus, families of related companies grow up, such as hearing-aid companies in Mineapolis or chemical firms in Buffalo [Draheim (1972)].

   One study showed that spin-off firms from universities initially concentrated on providing services—R & D, testing or consulting. Spin-offs from small firms tended to provide standard products, while those from large firms tended to provide custom products [Lamont (1971)].

3. The established organization also appears to influence, to a marked degree, the motivations of the entrepreneur. In brief surveys such as questionnaires, founders tend to report the socially acceptable reasons as to why they became founders; these include the desire for independence, financial gain, etc. [Howell (1971), Roberts & Wainer (1971)]. However, depth interviews often disclose that the founder is 'pushed' from the parent organization by frustration. In one study, 30% of the founders quit their previous jobs with no specific plans for the future; 13% had to leave because of factors such as plant closings, and an additional 40% said they would have left their previous positions even if they had not become entrepreneurs [Cooper (1971)].

   Studies of spin-offs from individual organizations also show that internal factors influence spin-off rates. Thus, internal problems of Univac in Minneapolis and Tracor in Austin were both associated with subsequent spin-offs [Draheim (1972), Susbauer (1972)].

SPIN-OFF RATES

Spin-off rates appear to vary widely, even among firms in the same geographical region. Some organizations function as incubators to a much greater extent than others. In Palo Alto, the range in spin-off rates for firms with more than 3 spin-offs during the decade of the 60's was about 200 to 1. Many organizations had no spin-offs; others had as a major product—entrepreneurs [Cooper (1972)].

What kinds of firms have high spin-off rates and what kinds have low spin-off rates? In Palo Alto, small firms considered as a class (less than 500 employees) had spin-off *rates* 10 times as high as large firms considered as a group [Cooper (1971)]. Studies of four major M.I.T. laboratories also showed that spin-off rates were inversely associated with laboratory size [Forseth (1966)]. Consistent with these findings, another study showed that where a city is dependent upon one large, dominant firm, the development of new firms rarely occurs [Draheim, *et al.* (1966)].

Very limited data suggest that, within large industrial firms, spin-offs occur chiefly from the 'small businesses' within the firm and rarely from the large, dominant divisions [Cooper (1971)].

Clearly, incubator organizations influence entrepreneurship in a number of ways and some organizations make better incubators than others.

ROLE OF UNIVERSITIES

Some of the major complexes of new firms have grown up around universities—such as Boston, Palo Alto, and Ann Arbor in America. Some observers have concluded that universities play a central role in the development of local entrepreneurship [Deutermann (1964), Allison (1965)].

The extent to which universities have functioned as incubators, with students or staff spinning off to start new firms, has varied widely. In Boston, Austin, and Ann Arbor, substantial percentages of the new firms studied were direct spin-offs from a university or one of its laboratories [Roberts (1969), Susbauer (1972), Lamont (1971)]. Where direct spin-offs from the universities have occurred, they have rarely involved faculty giving up full-time positions to become founders. Although faculty have been involved in a variety of roles, including sometimes being the 'driving force' and sometimes giving only advice, their commitment has usually been only part-time [Roberts (1972)]. Many spin-offs have occurred from university contract research laboratories engaged heavily in government contract research; notable examples are the Instrumentation Laboratory and Lincoln Laboratory at M.I.T.

However, a variety of other patterns also exist. In Palo Alto, only 6 of 243 firms founded in the 1960's had one or more full-time founders who came directly from a university [Cooper (1971)]. In that complex, the role of the university as an incubator appears to have been relatively more important in the earlier years. In both England and America, there are universities strong in science and engineering which have been associated with very little entrepreneurship. There are also instances of substantial entrepreneurship without the presence of a strong university. Shapero found that of 22 technical complexes studied, only 7 had major universities. Several had no colleges when the technical company formation process was getting started [Shapero (1971)].

Universities have undoubtedly played a role in attracting able young men and women to particular regions, and sometimes in giving the firms located there competitive advantages in recruiting and retaining these people. They also provide sources of consulting assistance and opportunities for continuing education for professional employees. However, the degree to which universities play a central or essential role in technical entrepreneurship appears to vary widely.

EXTERNAL FACTORS

A complex of factors external to the individual and external to the parent organization appears to influence entrepreneurship. Research to date provides us with only a limited understanding of many of these factors. Yet it is clear that they interact to create climates more or less favorable to entrepreneurship. It is also clear that climates can change over time and that, to some extent, past entrepreneurship makes future entrepreneurship more likely.

The decision to found a business is affected by the entrepreneur's perceptions of risks and rewards and his knowledge of sources of venture capital and of individuals and institutions which might provide help and advice. Past entrepreneurship creates what might be termed an 'entrepreneurial environment', in which the prospective founder is surrounded by examples and enveloped in knowledge about the process. A number of researchers report that the credibility of the act of starting a company appears to depend, in part, upon whether the founder knows of others who have taken this step [Shapero (1971), Cooper (1971)].

Societal attitudes toward business and entrepreneurship are also undoubtedly important in influencing an individual's decision. Although decisions to found technically-oriented companies have not been studied in this context, studies in a variety of countries show that some cultures are more entrepreneurially inclined than others [Hagen (1971), McClelland (1961)].

VENTURE CAPITAL

Venture capital is supplied both by the founders themselves and by external individuals and institutions. In one American study, 40% of the technically-oriented firms were started primarily with founders' capital; in a Canadian study, 35% of the firms were initially financed by the founders [Cooper (1971), Litvak & Maule (1972)]. The extent to which founders can save sufficient capital depends upon salary and taxation levels. Observers believe that entrepreneurship in the United Kingdom and Canada is seriously hampered by the difficulty in saving 'seed capital' [Bolton (1972), Hodgins (1972)]. In the American electronics industry, stock options, which are often intended to bind executives to firms, sometimes make it financially feasible for them to become entrepreneurs [Cooper (1971)].

Institutions and individual investors vary substantially in the extent to which they are willing to invest in new, technologically-based firms. The prospective founder seeking capital must thus try to make contact with the 'right' sources of capital, those whose experience and attitudes make it more likely that they will assist this kind of venture. In areas of active entrepreneurship, well-developed communication channels may have developed, such that it is relatively easy for the prospective founder to make contact with experienced venture capital sources [Baty (1964)].

In Palo Alto, externally supplied capital for the new firms of the 1960's often came from the successful entrepreneurs of the 1950's. Some of them had become venture capitalists after selling their businesses; others still active in their businesses, advised both entrepreneurs and venture capitalists and served as vital communication links [Cooper (1971)].

Attitudes toward investing in new, technically-based firms can change substantially over time. The success of Control Data in Minneapolis and Tracor in Austin apparently helped to change the local investment climate and made the raising of capital by subsequent waves of entrepreneurs much easier [Draheim (1972), Susbauer (1972)]. Of course, the reverse can happen also; the collapse of the American 'new issue' market in 1961 was followed by a period in which institutions and individuals were extremely sceptical of this kind of venture.

LIVING CONDITIONS

To what extent are attractive living conditions essential if a complex of new firms is to develop? Clearly, established organizations consider whether they will be able to attract and keep highly trained, mobile, scientific personnel in deciding where to locate branch plants and laboratories. These organizations, in turn, can become the incubators which bring potential entrepreneurs to a region. However, available evidence suggests that, although attractive living conditions may attract technical people to an area as employees, they rarely attract men who are in the act of founding companies [Cooper (1971)]. Furthermore, one study of 22 areas of active entrepreneurship showed that only 8 had unusually attractive living conditions [Shapero (1971)]. Some men leave parent organizations and become founders, because, in part, they do not want to be transferred from a region they like [Susbauer (1972)]. However, in most instances living conditions do not appear to bear directly upon the decision to found a company.

ECONOMICS OF LOCATION

How important are the economics of location, including transportation costs and the development of complexes of related firms which buy from and sell to each other? Although more research is needed to determine the relative importance of these factors, it does appear that the growth of a complex conveys many benefits to new firms. These include pools of trained labor and the development of specialized suppliers. Although transportation costs may not be very important with many high-technology products, the ability to work closely with customers is sometimes essential. Location in a complex may be particularly important for those new firms which provide custom manufacturing services and which serve as satellite suppliers. An additional benefit is the development of specialized expertise among local accountants, bankers, and lawyers relating to the special needs of small, high-technology firms [Shapero (1971)].

Location in a complex of related firms also provides opportunities for consulting; these opportunities are particularly important for those founders who quit previous jobs with no specific plans for the future and who need to support themselves while plans are crystallizing and capital is being raised [Cooper (1971)].

EXPERIENCED ENTREPRENEURS AND SMALL FIRMS

Past entrepreneurship creates within a particular region many new, small, technologically-based firms. As indicated earlier, these firms, as a class, tend to have high spin-off rates and to be almost ideal incubators. In addition, past foundings create experienced entrepreneurs. Later, when the founder sells out or when disputes cause the founding team to break up, what does the experienced founder do? Sometimes, he starts another firm, drawing upon his prior experience [Cooper (1971)]. In an area of active entrepreneurship, there may be hundreds of experienced founders. Their presence makes future entrepreneurship more likely.

THE DEVELOPMENT OF AN ENTREPRENEURIALLY-ACTIVE AREA

How does an entrepreneurially active area develop? There have been few studies involving systematic comparisons between regions or of environmental influences as they change over time. However, studies to date suggest that the following processes influence the regional climate for entrepreneurship.

If an area is to develop and maintain technical entrepreneurship, organizations which can serve as incubators must be present, be attracted, or be created. Since founders tend to start firms where they are already living and working, there must be organizations which will hire, bring into the area, and train the engineers, scientists and technical managers who may someday become technical entrepreneurs.

However, the nature of these organizations is critical in determining whether spin-offs actually occur. It is certainly not difficult to point to cities where thousands of engineers are employed, but where there is little entrepreneurship. Exhibit 3 indicates the characteristics of firms and the industries in which they operate which

may be associated with high or low birth-rates of new firms.

If the established firms serve markets that are stable or declining, there is little incentive for the prospective entrepreneur to enter the field. If the established firms are in industries which require large capital investments or substantial organizations to compete, it will be difficult to assemble the critical mass needed to get a new firm started. If the potential incubator firms hire relatively undynamic people, train them narrowly, and organize them so that engineers talk only to engineers, and so forth, it will be difficult to assemble a well-rounded founding team with the requisite knowledge and skills in marketing, engineering, and manufacturing. If the established firms are well-managed and avoid periodic crises, there may be little incentive for potential founders to leave comfortable positions.

Under such conditions, a would-be founder will find the going difficult. If he seeks to bolster his confidence or to gain advice, he will find few successful founders who have preceded him. If he seeks to support himself as a consultant while formulating his plans and raising capital, he may find this difficult if there are few small companies in the region.

Sources of venture capital experienced in investing in new, technologically-based firms are probably not available locally and making contact with possible investors may be laborious and time consuming. In such an environment, the prospective founder's personal experience is likely to have been in large, established firms. He is likely to know little about what is involved in starting and managing a new firm.

How does the first new firm become established in such a region? Sometimes it involves those rare instances in which the founder comes from another geographical location or starts a new company not related to the business of the parent firm he has left. Sometimes, it involves a technically-trained person who was working in a non-technical organization [Shapero (1971)].

The rate of entrepreneurial activity appears to be accelerated or diminished by a number of factors, al-

Exhibit 3
INDUSTRY AND ORGANIZATIONAL ATTRIBUTES
RELATED TO THE BIRTH-RATE OF NEW FIRMS

Characteristics of Industry

Low Birth-Rate	High Birth-Rate
slow industry growth	rapid industry growth
slow technological change	rapid technological change
heavy capital investment required	low capital investment required
substantial economies of scale	minor economies of scale

Characteristics of Established Incubator Organizations

Low Birth-Rate	High Birth-Rate
large number of employees	small number of employees
organized by function	product-decentralized organization
recruit average technical people	recruit very capable, ambitious people
relatively well-managed	afflicted with periodic crises
located in isolated area of little entrepreneurship	located in area of high entrepreneurship

All of the attributes in a given column are not necessarily found together nor are they required to bring about a given spin-off rate. Various combinations may exist.

though this is another subject deserving additional research. One of the most important factors is the development of the markets and technologies on which the area's industry is based. If the rates of market growth and technological change decline, then technical entrepreneurship will decline, for potential founders will find fewer areas of opportunity. In America, public attitudes relating to new issues of stock from recently-formed companies are also important, for they affect substantially the availability of venture capital.

However, if these factors are favorable, a self-reinforcing process takes place. Past entrepreneurship makes future entrepreneurship more likely and, in time, a high rate of entrepreneurial activity may develop.

REFERENCES

Allison, D. (1965) 'The university and regional prosperity', International Science and Technology, April.

Baty, G. (1964) 'Initial Financing of the New Research-Based Enterprise in New England', Boston, Mass.: The Federal Reserve Bank of Boston.

Bolton, J. (1972) 'Small firms', Speech to Management Forum, University of Manchester, 26 April 1972.

Collins, D. F. & Moore, D. G. (1964) 'The Enterprising Man', East Lansing, Mich.: MSU Business Studies, Michigan State University.

Cooper, A. C. (1971) 'The Founding of Technologically-Based Firms', Milwaukee, Wis.: The Center For Venture Management.

Cooper, A. C. (1972) 'Spin-offs and technical entrepreneurship', I.E.E.E. Transactions on Engineering Management, Vol. EM-18, No. 1.

Deutermann, E. (1966) 'Seeding science-based industry', New England Business Review, December.

Draheim, K., Howell, R. P. & Shapero, A. (1966) 'The Development of a Potential Defense R & D Complex', Menlo Park, Cal.: Stanford Research Institute.

Draheim, K. (1972) 'Factors influencing the rate of formation of technical companies', Technical Entrepreneurship: A Symposium (eds. A. Cooper & J. Komives), Milwaukee, Wis.: The Center For Venture Management.

Forseth, D. A. (1965) 'The Role of government-sponsored research laboratories in the generation of new enterprises—a comparative analysis', S.M. Thesis, Cambridge, Mass.: M.I.T. Sloan School of Management.

Hagen, E. E. (1971) 'How Economic Growth Begins: A Theory of Social Change', Entrepreneurship and Economic Development (ed. P. Kilby), New York, N.Y.: The Free Press.

Hodgins, J. W. (1972) 'Management challenges to the entrepreneur', The Business Quarterly, Vol. 37, No. 1.

Howell, R. P. (1972) 'Comparative profiles—entrepreneurs versus the hired executive: San Francisco Peninsula Semiconductor Industry', Technical Entrepreneurship: A Symposium, op. cit.

Komives, J. L. (1972) 'A preliminary study of the personal values of high technology entrepreneurs', Technical Entrepreneurship: A Symposium, op. cit.

Lamont, L. M. (1972) 'The role of marketing in technical entrepreneurship', Technical Entrepreneurship: A Symposium, op. cit.

Lamont, L. M. (1971) 'Technology Transfer, Innovation, and Marketing in Science-Oriented Spin-Off Firms', Ann Arbor, Mich.: Industrial Development Division, Institute of Science and Technology, University of Michigan.

Litvak, I. A. & Maule, C. J. (1972) 'Managing the entrepreneurial enterprise', The Business Quarterly, Vol. 37, No. 2.

McClelland, D. C. (1961) 'The Achieving Society', Princeton, N.J.: D. Van Nostrand, Inc.

Roberts, E. B. (1969) 'Entrepreneurship and technology', Factors in the Transfer of Technology (eds. W. Gruber & D. Marquis), Cambridge, Mass.: The M.I.T. Press.

Roberts, E. B. & Wainer, H. A. (1971) 'Some characteristics of technical entrepreneurs', I.E.E.E. Transactions on Engineering Management, Vol. EM-18, No. 3.

Roberts, E. B. (1972) 'Influences upon performance of new technical enterprises', Technical Entrepreneurship: A Symposium, op. cit.

Shapero, A. (1971) 'An action Program For Entrepreneurship', Austin, Texas: Multi-Disciplinary Research, Inc.

Susbauer, J. C. (1969) 'The technical company formation process: a particular aspect of entrepreneurship', Ph.D. Dissertation, Austin, Texas: University of Texas.

Susbauer, J. C. (1972) 'The technical entrepreneurship process in Austin, Texas', Technical Entrepreneurship: A Symposium, op. cit.

Susbauer, J. C. (1967) 'The science entrepreneur', Industrial Research, February.

ADDITIONAL READING

Bruce, F. R. (1972) 'Spinoff industry', Oak Ridge National Laboratory Review, Spring.

Cooper, A. C. (1970) 'The Palo Alto experience', Industrial Research, May.

Cooper, A. C. (1970) 'Entrepreneurial environment', Industrial Research, September.

Goldstein, J. (1967) 'The spin-off of new enterprises from a large government funded industrial lab.', S. M. Thesis, Cambridge, Mass.: M.I.T. Sloan School of Management.

Mahar, J. & Coddington, D. (1965) 'The scientific complex—proceed with caution', Harvard Business Review, Vol. 43, No. 1.

Mahar, J. & Coddington, D. (1965) 'Academic spinoffs', Industrial Research, April.

Roberts, E. B. & Wainer, H. A. (1968) 'New enterprises on Route 128', Science Journal, December.

Roberts, E. B. (1969) 'What it takes to be an entrepreneur . . . and to hang on to one', Innovation, Number Seven.

Rogers, C. E. (1966) 'The availability of venture capital for new, technically-based enterprises', S.M. Thesis, Cambridge, Mass.: M.I.T. Sloan School of Management.

Shapero, A., Howell, R. P. & Tombough, J. R. (1965) 'The Structure and Dynamics of the Defence R & D Industry', Menlo Park, Cal.: Stanford Research Institute.

Teplitz, P. V. (1965) 'Spin-off Enterprises from a Large Government Sponsored Laboratory', S.M. Thesis, Cambridge, Mass.: M.I.T. Sloan School of Management.

Thurston, P. (1965) 'The founding and growth process of new technical enterprises', S.M. Thesis, Cambridge, Mass.: M.I.T. Sloan School of Management.

—— (1967) 'Technical Innovation: Its Environment and Management', U.S. Department of Commerce, Washington, D.C.: U.S. Government Printing Office.

CHECKLIST FOR START-UPS

By Don C. Hoefler/Manager's Casebook

IN THE BEGINNING was the word.

The would-be entrepreneur must convince his would-be financial backers that he has an idea for forming and running a company, which will make a market-acceptable product, and operate at a profit.

Although he may do a fair amount of verbal pleading, he probably will not even get a hearing unless he carries in his hand a piece of promotional literature known as a "business plan." Although he has probably not written a line of selling copy in his life, now the promoter is faced with the need to open doors to the financial community by telling investors what they want to hear.

Since not many new-company promoters are equipped by education or experience for the task of business plan preparation, not many business plans are as effective as they might be in turning on the financial community.

"Despite the fine educational job being done by leading business schools and management organizations, the subject of developing, financing and managing a new venture remains largely an untreated topic," says Robert R. Kley, who heads his own consulting firm in the venture planning field, at Ann Arbor, Mich.

Mr. Kley has assembled a 24-point checklist for preparing a business plan, and he says: "If you are starting a new company, organizing a new division or subsidiary, facing plant expansion or considering an acquisition, these are the critical questions for you to consider."

1. **PROVIDE A 1-PAGE SUMMARY** of the venture idea.

2. Describe the key goals and objectives. Specify what you are setting out to achieve, particularly your sales and profitability goals.

3. Provide an in-depth market analysis. If you can support your own probe with some solid numbers from a prestigous researcher such as Stanford Institute or Arthur D. Little, so much the better.

4. List the names of six close competitor firms, and briefly analyze their strengths and weaknesses.

5. List the anticipated selling price to your ultimate consumer for each product in the projected line. Include also a brief summary of comparison prices.

6. Provide a list of potential customers who have expressed an interest in your projected products.

7. Provide a one-page summary of the functional specifications of each product in your over-all spectrum. Make them good and definitive, and cover the total line, but don't get down to individual models.

8. **SHOW THE PHYSICAL FORMS** of the products, with photographs of prototypes if possible, or in art renderings.

9. Provide a profile of key patents.

10. List and categorize the key technologies and skills required to develop and manufacture the products. Indicate which frontiers of the art are being pushed hardest.

11. Describe the alternative channels of sales distribution, and indicate whether you intend to sell direct, through reps, or to OEMs.

12. Describe the basis for determining if your products will be typically lease or buy items. This will depend upon the propensities of your potential customers, who must be sorted out.

13. Describe the type and geographical distribution of your anticipated field service organization.

14. Tell how you can modularize your product line with interchangeable sub-assemblies. This is critical from an inventory point of view, and can mean tremendous cost savings.

15. Show cost-volume curves for each module, with breakdown for material, labor and factory burden.

16. Describe the manufacturing process involved, and illustrate it with block diagram.

17. Describe the types and quantities of capital equipment needed, and when.

18. Present a flow-event-logic feedback chart, illustrating achievement milestones and showing stepped levels of when and how additional funds should go into the venture.

19. Project staff and plant space requirements over a five-year period.

20. Describe the rationale for choosing any single manufacturing plant location.

21. Present cash flow projections, monthly for the first 24 months, and then quarterly for the next three years.

22. Provide pro-forma balance sheets for five years.

23. Provide pro-forma P&L statements for five years.

24. Present your position on the degree of ownership control you seek, and the limits to which these can be varied with time and profitability.

There it is, an even double-dozen. Use it and prosper.

A reprint from
CALIFORNIA MANAGEMENT REVIEW
© 1966 by The Regents of the University of California

HYMAN OLKEN

Spin-Offs:
A Business Pay-Off

*Is the enormous stockpile of data from the
government's research and development programs providing
the seed for the growth of advanced technology in industry?
How can an industrial concern find and put to use
the research reports most valuable to its progress?*

❦ THE UNITED STATES government's vast expenditures for research and development (R&D) in space, in defense, and in atomic energy have profoundly altered the basic industrial structure of this country. Most of the industrial growth resulting from these programs has been concentrated in only a few areas —California, Texas, Florida, and a limited area of New England (Route 128 around Boston).

The profitable types of industry have become those which possess the tremendous technological sophistication and complexity necessary to meet the goals of these programs; this has fostered the belief that the industrial future of an area depends upon advanced technology. Hence, there has been a nationwide upsurge in "Industrial Parks," "Research and Development Institutes," and other attempts to create the climate required for the growth of new technical industry in a particular area. It is now widely believed that the future of industry lies in the highly technical fields and that each state or region must develop the tools and resources to bring about the flowering of such industries.[1]

Corollary to this is the belief that the future

growth of civilian (consumer) industry along these lines will be achieved mainly by the use of "spin-offs," that is, by the profitable implementation of the technological advances being made in the course of achieving the federal government's vast space, defense, and atomic energy programs.[2] A number of measures have been taken recently to improve the machinery for obtaining and using such spin-offs. These include:

• The National Clearinghouse for Federal Scientific and Technical Information which is the central agency for the dissemination of all unclassified United States government research reports.

• A $4-million-a-year "Technology Utilization Program" by the National Aeronautics and Space Agency (NASA) to disseminate its technical advances to industry.

• The newly enacted "State Technical Services Act" (HR 3420) which sets up state agencies to promote technological industries, chiefly by utilizing the stockpile of federal research reports to achieve spin-offs.

All of these measures are predicated on the assumption that the technological information resulting from the federal government's annual expenditure of over $10 billion on research and development constitutes an enormous treasury or gold mine that can be converted into profitable new products, new processes, and other technological advances. Such spin-offs would make technical industry flour-

Mr. Olken was educated at Harvard in Economic History and Electronic Engineering. He has spent many years promoting spin-offs to private industry from R&D technological advances.

ish all over the country as it has in the San Francisco Bay area, the Los Angeles area, and the Route 128 area around Boston.

Vital Questions

This raises important questions; some have already been raised by congressional critics.[3] Does the stockpile of government research reports really provide the seed for the flourishing of technological industry? If it does, are the right measures being taken to bring about this hoped-for flourishing of technological industry? Finally: How does an industrial concern gain a position on the band wagon toward the new era in a technologically sophisticated industry? I will attempt some answers to these questions.

Spin-Offs Not New

Historical perspective. Although spin-offs became a serious issue when government R&D activities reached the multibillion-dollar-a-year scale, they are not new, and efforts by the government to make them available to private industry date back several decades.

Probably the earliest and greatest accomplishment in this field was achieved by the Agriculture Department when it brought its research results directly to the farmer and helped him apply them through the valuable Agricultural Extension Service. The Agriculture Department has also made research contributions of great value to industry, and its funnelling of those results to industry has been equally effective. Some eminent examples are the process for the production of penicillin, the dialdehyde starch process, and a number of processes for producing better cotton textiles (wrinkle-resistant cloth, wash-and-wear, etc.).[4]

Other valuable technological advances have been made and their application diffused throughout industry by the Bureau of Standards (instrumentation and fire-resistant materials), the Tennessee Valley Authority (fertilizers), the Bureau of Mines (metallurgical processes and oil extraction from shale), and NACA, the predecessor of NASA (aircraft fuels and lubricants).

At the end of World War II, a tremendous mass of technology was acquired from Germany, and, at the same time, much of our classified defense R&D

work was declassified for public use. Both these accumulations of valuable technology were turned over to the Office of Technical Services (OTS) of the United States Department of Commerce to funnel to industry. Spin-offs had by then become a formal activity of the federal government.

Growth of Importance

Recent activities. When the federal government's R&D expenditures rose to over ten billion dollars a year, government agencies began to stress the valuable by-products or spin-offs that "fall out" to civilian and commercial industry, in part to justify their enormous expenditures. Hence, in recent years, those agencies which generate a great deal of R&D technical information have undertaken extensive "technology utilization" programs which pick out the commercially applicable technical advances and serve them up with the invitation to industry to help itself.

Furthermore, there is at present a movement to recognize the spin-off as a vital aspect of government research activity and to put it on a uniform, government-wide basis. The effort to achieve this is spearheaded by Assistant Secretary Holloman of the Commerce Department through an "industry extension" program (the "State Technical Services Act") that would help the industrial enterpreneur in the same way that the Agricultural Extension has been helping the farmer for generations.[5]

Spectrum of Services

Extent of government spin-offs activity. Spin-offs are now an extensive area of government activity, and many government agencies provide a whole spectrum of facilities and services in support of spin-offs.

The most widely known is the **Clearinghouse for Federal Scientific and Technical Information.** This is the vastly expanded version of what was for many years the Office of Technical Services of the Department of Commerce. When I was employed there in 1951–1953, its staff for promoting the diffusion of technical advances consisted of myself and one secretary; I produced the material actually publicizing the government reports, with the aid of a few technical specialists and librarians who published the monthly list of new report abstracts and handled the reference work. Our facilities consisted of several roomfuls of library card files and a storage area for the printed copies of reports. The sale of reports was about $14,000 a month; the total staff (half of which served other functions) was 48; and the total annual budget was $200,000. The same agency now has a staff of 292, an annual budget of $4 million, and an annual volume of sales of over $1 million.[6]

The **NASA Technology Utilization Program** prepares printed matter (technical briefs, reports, etc.) on technical advances made in the space program; it also subsidizes universities which prepare reviews in various areas of technology developed by the program and which help industry to make use of the accumulated technological advances produced by the program. This includes the support of a $5-million data processing center (ARAC at the University of Illinois) for matching a firm's technical interests to the data flowing out of the space program.

Other agencies heavily equipped with multimillion-dollar facilities and large staffs, which engage entirely or partially in the spin-off functions, are:

◆ **Department of Defense.** DOD publishes and distributes research reports through the Institute for Applied Technology in the National Bureau of Standards. It operates a $60-million Defense Documentation Center at Alexandria, Virginia, as a clearinghouse of DOD reports.

In addition, DOD is spending over $7 million yearly to set up "Information Centers" for different subject-matter areas, each of which is responsible for "keeping abreast of the world's literature in their own very limited areas of science and technology, and able to answer questions and prepare state-of-the-art summaries covering the entire range of their disciplines." Included are the Defense Metals Information Center (Battelle), the Infra-Red Information Activity (University of Michigan), the Plastics Technical Evaluation Center (Picatinney Arsenal), and the Electronic Properties Information Center (Hughes Aircraft Company).[7]

◆ **Atomic Energy Commission.** The AEC Division of Technical Information Extension (Oak Ridge) disseminates complete "packages" of technical material (reports, drawings, etc.). It publishes Nuclear Science Abstracts of its research and development reports, keeps these reports on hand at AEC regional depository libraries, and sells them through the National Clearinghouse.

The AEC also issues reviews of various areas of technology, translations of foreign articles, and complete packages of drawings, specifications, etc., on equipment developments. These packages are sold through the National Clearinghouse.

Details on all the various technical information-disseminating activities are given in the AEC booklet TID 4550.[8]

◆ **Library of Congress.** It conducts the National Referral Center for Science and Technology, which is not a cumulation of reports, but a register of significant information sources in all areas of science and technology. "Its principal function is to put any scientist in need of information in contact with the systems or places that can best provide it."[9]

◆ **Smithsonian Institution.** It conducts the Science Information Exchange which collects and stores information on current research activities. This does not provide reports or abstracts, but can advise "who is currently working on what projects."

The Smithsonian issues a one-page record (Notice of Research Project) that includes: the name of the agency supporting the work, title of the project, location of the work, names of investigators, level of effort, and a 200-word summary. It prepares 75,000 of these notices a year, which cover about 90 to 95 per cent of projects in life sciences, but fewer industrial research projects.[10]

Altogether, over $400 million[11] worth of data processing equipment and correspondingly sized staffs are engaged, at an annual cost of $200 million, in the government's activities in promoting spin-offs.[12]

Industry's Demands

Extent of industry involvement in spin-offs. Comments from private industry that the stockpile of government research reports offers little that an industrial firm can use to create new products (or that this can not be done without prohibitive expenditures) are still common, though less frequent than in years past. However, the truth is that private industry already does exploit this new technology on a huge scale. This can be indicated by some comparative figures. While I was employed at OTS (from 1951 to 1953), sales of government research reports increased from $9,000 to $14,000 a month. The present sales of government reports by the National Clearinghouse for Federal Scientific and Technical Information run in the hundreds of thousands of dollars each month. Although part of this is to fill the requests of DOD contractors, the flow of information to industry is huge and represents a very considerable effort by industry to "cash in" on the new technology.

Another indication of the extent of industry's efforts to achieve spin-offs is the fact that over thirty firms each pay some $5,000 a year to obtain rapid information of new reports that match their interests through the NASA-supported ARAC program.[13] The other government agencies engaged in spin-off activities can cite equally great demands for technical information from industry.

Of course, these demands for reports give only an indirect indication of industry's pursuit of spin-offs. Direct information, such as case histories of spin-offs achieved by industrial firms, would be far more desirable, but the following two factors make firms reluctant to disclose such information:

• A firm which finds a technological bonanza in the government research report collection is not going to help its competitors to share in the bounty by announcing that its valuable new advance was acquired from a source open to all.

• Firms in private industry which devote huge advertising budgets to the creation in the consumer's mind of a belief similar to "progress is our most important product" certainly do not want to destroy this belief by stating that a considerable part of this "progress" is the result of government-sponsored technological developments available as a windfall to anyone willing to pick them up.

However, despite the lack of direct information provided by industry, it can be seen that spin-offs are heavily used by industry to achieve its technological advances. This shows through, like the exposed fault lines that reveal a geological formation, in those cases where an entire industry has been forced to a new level of technological sophistication by advances disclosed in government research reports. Examples of this are the universal shift to integrated circuits by the electronics industry and the shift to numerical control by the machine tool industry[14]; both of these advances were first developed by government contracts and made accessible to industry through government R&D reports. I have selected eighteen other examples from the AEC program (see Appendix).

Spin-offs are no longer an insignificant grab bag from which a few industrial concerns may pluck an occasional windfall as a valuable addition to their area of business. Instead, spin-offs are a significant, costly government activity which is a primary factor in the technological progress of private industry. Hence, almost any industrial concern must become engaged in achieving spin-offs as a basic part of its business activity or perish.

However, this does not mean that the industrial concern which has not previously been active in spin-offs is condemned to a period of costly floundering until it can develop the capability of achieving successful spin-offs. Only a minimum level of appropriate know-how is required to develop this capability.

R&D Contracts

Types of Spin-Offs. There are three major categories of spin-offs:

◊ The first is that in which the product of the development project done by the company for the government fits in with the company's product line. A good case of this is the development of a process for manufacturing a widely used electronic component—the electrolytic capacitor—by using tantalum as the basic metal foil instead of the conventional aluminum.

The superior capacitor thus produced gave the General Electric Company, which developed it under a government R&D contract, a great commercial lead in its manufacture of this component, and GE, for some time thereafter, dominated the market for this important component in the electronics industry.

To achieve the utmost in spin-offs of this kind is a matter of getting the right government research and development contracts, a subject which has been treated extensively elsewhere.

New Product Areas

◊ The second type of spin-off is that in which a valuable technological development is produced by the company for the government, but the development does not fit into that company's product line. A good example is the case of the digital computer created (on a government contract) by the small firm of Eckert and Mauchley which later became part of Remington-Rand. This was the first electronic computer (the Eniac, later the Binac) which contained all the essentials of a general purpose computer suitable for business use (stored program and ability to handle alpha-numeric quantities). However, it was the IBM Company which capitalized on this computer, built a vast and profitable new market for it, and has dominated this market.

In spin-offs of this type, there are three major approaches that can be followed:

• The company can develop marketing capability in the field called for by the spin-off. For example, the North American Aviation Company, in the course of a government research project, developed the process of forming metal objects with the help of powerful forces exerted by magnetic fields which were generated by brief pulses of very heavy electric currents. They went further, devised equipment for industrial application of the process, and set up a subsidiary firm to design, build, and market the equipment. This subsidiary has become a profitable addition to the parent company.[15]

• Another approach for cashing in on spin-offs not related to a company's product line is to buy or merge with a concern that has the needed marketing capability. This approach is analyzed in some detail in an article in the *Harvard Business Review*.[16]

• A third approach, one which appears to have come into use recently, is that in which the company sets up those of its personnel who pioneered the spin-off development that is unrelated to its product line in a separate business based on the spin-off. This business is supported by the parent company and becomes an affiliate or subsidiary. In essence, the parent company acts as banker to a new business which will give it a footing in the new product area. Apparently, a number of these have been successful, and the use of the "turn your own employees into entrepreneurs" approach is increasing.[17]

Success in this type of spin-off requires a management capability adequate to meet the marketing problems posed by the new technical development. Some firms have it; others do not. A good discussion of this subject is provided in the section on the textile industry in an Arthur D. Little, Inc., report on innovation in industry.[18]

Adapting Spin-Offs

♦ The third type of spin-offs is that in which a firm pulls a technological advance out of the government's R&D report stockpile, adapts it to its own product line, and thereby creates a large and profitable new market for itself. The following is an example.

One firm, which built food-processing equipment for restaurants, was accustomed to designing equipment to insure complete sanitation. This firm learned of a government-supported development (the arterial bypass) that would enable people with kidney ailments to be hooked into a large "blood washing" machine in the hospital that would perform the kidney function and periodically alleviate kidney malfunctioning. The firm immediately thought of the possibility of a kidney machine which the patient could use at home and thus avoid the expense and trouble of going to the hospital. They surveyed the potential market for such a kidney machine and found the price level at which it would be commercially feasible, then developed one accordingly. This has become a whole new area of profitable commercial activity for that firm.[19]

This third type of spin-off constitutes the great mass of the spin-off iceberg that lies below the surface. It is the area of spin-offs which are most readily available to those small firms not particularly associated with defense or space R&D, and it is the effective exploitation of these spin-offs that will assure the successful conversion of civilian industry, on a national scale, to the advanced technologies produced by the government R&D.

Finding the useful spin-offs. Regardless of the facilities and services provided by the government to publicize this spin-off iceberg, finding a technological advance which will produce a valuable new product for a firm is still very much a "do-it-yourself" activity. The firm that takes the trouble to acquire the know-how needed to prospect and work this mine of industrial ore will benefit enormously by doing so. The rudiments of this know-how follow.

Quantity Pays Off

Make the digging a continuous, extensive activity. Looking up one or two reports will yield little, but scanning a few thousand will reveal several possibilities close to your firm's product and, probably, one technological advance that could be developed commercially without too much difficulty or cost. For instance, a chemist, who took the trouble to study confiscated reports on the technological advances in Germany, learned of the German chemical industry's work with new greases which contain a lithium-based soap (rather than the sodium-based soap then common) and of the valuable advantages of these new greases. Using the information in these documents, he developed lithium-based greases and processes for making them that could be patented. These he exploited by licensing and became independently wealthy.

Careful Study

Do the job intensively as well as extensively. It is not merely a matter of studying a great number of reports. That is, not only abstracts but a good condensation or the full text of the report should be read, because, in the majority of cases, the authors of research and development reports do not do a good job of revealing the really significant technical information, and rarely does it occur to them to emphasize that point in the report from which a commercially profitable product or process could be extracted. A practical example will bring home the truth of this.

At OTS following World War II, where it was my job to publicize those reports that contained potentially valuable developments for industry, I read between five and six thousand government research reports. One of these had the rather uninteresting title of "Application of Foot Measurements in the Development of Last Systems." It appeared to be a considerable (54-page) accumulation of tables of the anatomical dimensions of men's feet. Nothing could seem less interesting, especially from the technological point of view. But a closer study of the report showed that the anatomical tables were worked up in order to evolve a better system of men's shoe sizes which would greatly reduce shoe inventories and improve the fitting of shoes. What a boon this would be to the shoe industry! So I studied this report quite thoroughly and sent out a press release summarizing its contents and their value to industry to the trade magazines in the shoe and related industries. The result? Over six hundred copies of this report were sold. And, though the shoe industry is reluctant to admit that this bit of government research helped them, the fact is that a number of shoe manufacturers have applied these ideas for a good shoe-sizing system to their products and are benefiting millions of customers as well as increasing their profits.

The Right Agency

Pick out the government agency which produces developments closely related to your company's product line. For example, for food and clothing, follow the reports of the Army Quartermaster Corps; for heat-resistant and abrasion-resistant paints and coatings, follow the reports by NASA, which is sponsoring research on coatings for the protection of re-entry vehicles.

To find the agency which produces developments related to your product line, one approach is to scan abstract services which list the reports from many different agencies (such as AEC, NASA, Air Force, Army Quartermaster Corps). A more direct approach is to study the lists of research and development projects that different government agencies are engaged in. A good example is the Air Force Research Résumés.[20]

Qualified Searchers

Employ people with the right skills and knowledge to do the searching of reports. That is, use only people well qualified for research application engineering—people with the ability to translate a technical advance into a potentially valuable commercial product or process—and able to do it at a glance. This naturally requires an innate capability to begin with, but the following spectrum of experience is important.

In the first place, the person should be a competent engineer with several years of professional experience—in the laboratory, in product design, or in process development. This should be followed by a couple of years of sales engineering; one never knows what a customer expects from a product until one experiences, at first hand, the potential user's reaction to it. With this experience, the engineer learns to recognize the commercial possibilities in an industrial product or process. Finally, his experience should include a couple of years as a technical editor on one of the commercial technical magazines (trade papers). This develops an aptitude for recognizing valuable technical ideas, even when inadequately expressed.

A person with this combination of experience will have the capacity to review a stream of technical reports rapidly and to quickly extract from each one any commercially valuable information it may contain.

Ingenuity Important

Develop an ability to discern future commercial product needs and some ingenuity in converting a technical advance into a new product. The ability to discern future product needs comes from understanding the nature of the process of technological growth. Ingenuity is, of course, a native talent with which one must be endowed in some measure, but the talent one has can be developed by training, like a singer's voice. In the case of technological ingenuity, such training has long been advocated and has achieved some measure of development. In particular, an on-the-job training course that would be effective in developing the ingenuity needed to uncover new product or process possibilities from research reports has already been suggested.[21]

REFERENCES

1. V. J. Danilov, "The Seduction of Science," *Industrial Research,* May 1965, pp. 38–50.

2. Robert A. Solo, "Gearing Military R&D to Economic Growth," *Harvard Business Review,* Nov.-Dec. 1962, pp. 49–60.

3. See "Sniping at NASA on Space," *Business Week,* May 11, 1963; "Will Space Research Pay Off on Earth?" New York *Times Magazine,* May 26, 1963; and other references on p. 6 of Richard S. Rosenbloom, "Technology Transfer-Process and Policy," *National Planning Association, Special Report No. 62,* July 1965.

4. For a more definitive list, see "Expenditures by the Government for Research & Development," Remarks by Senator Long of Louisiana, *Congressional Record,* May 4, 1965, pp. 43–52.

5. J. Herbert Holloman, "The Brain Mines of Tomorrow," *Saturday Review,* May 4, 1963, pp. 46–47.

6. Private Communication from Eric A. Tietz, Institute of Applied Technology, National Bureau of Standards, U.S. Dept. of Commerce, Washington, D.C.

7. "When a Computer Needs a Friend," *Business Week,* March 6, 1965, pp. 146–152.

8. "What's Available in the Atomic Energy Literature," TID-4550, 10th rev., Feb. 1965. Available from AEC Div. of Technical Information Extension, Oak Ridge, Tenn.

9. John F. Stearns, "Tomorrow's Acquisition and Use of Technical Information," *Research and Development,* Jan. 1965, pp. 24–26.

10. Harvey Marron "Science Information Exchange," *AEC Technical Information Bulletin No. 11,* Dec. 1964, pp. 27–29.

11. Private communication from D. Schone, Head, Institute of Applied Technology, National Bureau of Standards.

12. "When a Computer Needs a Friend," *Business Week, loc. cit.*

13. B. M. Kerr, "Spin-off from Space," *Science Journal* (London: July 1965), pp. 85–90.

14. Robert L. Hatschek, "NC (Numerical Control) Today," *American Machinist,* Nov. 22, 1965, pp. 109–116.

15. "Magnetic Forming," in "Metal Forming Techniques," *NASA Technology Utilization Report, SP-5017,* May 1965, pp. 42–47. See also "Modular Magneform Equipment" in *Magnefor/Pulses,* II : 2 (April 1965), General Atomics Div. of General Dynamics Corp.

16. John G. Welles and Robert H. Waterman, Jr., "Space Technology: Pay-off from Spin-off," *Harvard Business Review,* July-Aug. 1964, pp. 106–118.

17. Remarks by Donald Schone, Head, Institute of Applied Technology, National Bureau of Standards, at U.C. Extension Seminar on Creation of New Industry, in San Francisco, Calif., May 6–8, 1965.

18. "Patterns and Problems of Technical Innovation in American Industry," *Report to National Science Foundation by Arthur D. Little Inc.* Available from Clearinghouse for Government Research Reports.

19. "Freezer Manufacturer Builds a Life Saver," *Business Week,* March 6, 1965, pp. 88–92.

20. *A Survey of the Research Activities of the Office of Aerospace Research,* U.S. Air Forces, OAR-016 1963, 578 pp. Available from National Clearinghouse for Federal Scientific and Technical Information, Springfield, Va. 22151. Better still, consult the Science Information Exchange of the Smithsonian Institution, Washington, D.C., which maintains an index of all government research activities in progress.

21. H. Olken, "Creativity Training for Engineers; Its Past, Present and Future," *IEEE Transactions on Education,* E-7, 4 (Dec. 1964), pp. 149–161.

APPENDIX

The following spin-offs are from AEC research and development programs:

For the Chemical Industry:

1 / **New chemical processes:** achieved by irradiation; particularly for producing new types of plastics. SOURCE: S. A. Parker, "Radiation Processing," *Discovery,* March 1965, pp. 18–21.

2 / **New chemical processes:** achieved by high temperature plasmas. SOURCE: Gibson and Weidman, "Chemical Synthesis via the High Intensity Arc Process," *Chemical Engineering Progress,* LIV:9, 53.

3 / **Radioactive materials** (nuclear fuels); extraction and production processes. SOURCE: *The Nuclear Industry 1964,* Div. of Industrial Participation, U.S. Atomic Energy Commission, Nov. 1964, pp. 1–15.

4 / **Activation analysis:** inducing radioactivity in materials and using the resulting emitting radiation to detect ultraminute quantities of component materials. SOURCE: *The Magnet,* IX:5 (Berkeley: Lawrence Radiation Laboratory, University of California, May 1965), 1–3.

For the Metal-Working Industries:

1 / **Magneforming:** shaping metals by powerful, fast-pulse, magnetic fields. SOURCE: H. A. J. Dennison, "Magnetic Forming," *Science Journal,* Dec. 1965, pp. 66–71.

2 / **High-precision tracer lathes.** SOURCE: J. B. Bryan, J. E. Bowerbank, Jr., E. D. Holland, O. Mohl,

"Upgrading Tracer Lathe Machining Operations," American Society of Tool and Manufacturing Engineers, Technical Paper 362, LXI, Book 1, 1961.

3 / **Improved measurement of surface finish.** SOURCE: J. B. Bryan and O. Mohl, "Microinterferometric Scanning for Full Surface Metrology," American Society of Mechanical Engineers, Paper 64-W.A./Prod-15, presented at ASME Winter Meeting, New York, Dec. 4, 1964.

4 / **Gauging techniques for micro-inch tolerances.** SOURCE: J. B. Bryan, W. Brewer, E. R. McClure, and J. W. Pearson, "Thermal Effects in Dimensional Metrology," American Society of Mechanical Engineers, Paper 65, Prod-13, presented at ASME Metal Engineering and Production Engineering Conference, Berkeley, Calif., June 9–11, 1965.

For the Electrical and Electronic Industries:

1 / **Improved high power ignitrons.** SOURCE: D. B. Cummings, "Development of Switching Tubes for Controlled Fusion Research," *Electrical Engineering*, Nov. 1960.

2 / **Better energy storage capacitors.** SOURCE: *Proceedings, Symposium on Engineering Problems of Controlled Thermonuclear Research*, held at Lawrence Radiation Laboratory (LRL), Livermore, Calif., May 4–7, 1965. UCRL Report CONF-650512, Technical Information Division, LRL, Livermore.

3 / **Improved high power thyratrons.** SOURCE: *ibid.*

4 / **Better vacuum system components.** SOURCE: *ibid.*

5 / **Cryogenic magnets.** SOURCE: *ibid.*

6 / **Super-sensitive semiconductor radiation detectors.** SOURCE: *The Magnet*, June 1965 (Berkeley: Lawrence Radiation Laboratory, University of California), pp. 6–9.

7 / **New (radiation) semiconductor production process.** SOURCE: "Semiconductor Devices Produced by Neutron Irradiation in Dies with Slit Pattern," Brookhaven National Laboratory, Report BNL-790.

For the Construction Industries:

1 / **Rock melting as a drilling technique:** incandescent metals drill lava rock at 50 feet per day at power consumption of 1 calorie per cm^3. SOURCE: Los Alamos Scientific Laboratory, Report LA-3243.

2 / **Drilling of very large holes to great depths:** new drilling rig and technique permit drilling holes up to 13 ft. 4 in. in diameter to depth of 5,000 feet. SOURCE: Contact AEC Nevada Operations Office.

3 / **Prestressed concrete pressure vessels.** SOURCE: Contact General Atomics, San Diego.

The findings of the new study reported here are important to investors, lenders, and suppliers, as well as business associates.

The R & D Entrepreneur: Profile of Success

By Harry Schrage

Three physicists leave their positions with a large corporation or leading university to establish their own company. They pool their funds, secure a research contract from the government, obtain a loan from a friendly bank; and a so-called "R & D company" is born — that is, a company based on a new technology. Hundreds of such organizations have been started in the United States in the last decade. Their importance to the sustained growth of our economy has become a widely recognized fact. Leading economists call research and development the key to rapid growth of the gross national product; the President of the United States has stressed the importance of research and development; and the industrial community has shown its agreement by allocating ever-increasing sums of money to this effort.

In all this exuberance, one of the many questions remaining unanswered is: Who should run an R & D organization? Should our three physicists seek a "business manager" to head their organization while they devote their time to scientific pursuits, or should one of them run the company? Underlying both inquiries is the key question: What qualities should the man chosen possess to maximize the chance of being successful? This article deals with the answer to that question. It is an answer which is of

great importance, I believe, to managers of technologically based companies, as well as to all those who have an interest in such firms — investors, banks, competitors, larger companies looking for acquisitions, SBICs, and others.

Veridical Perception

To determine the qualities that make a successful R & D entrepreneur, I have used a method which is currently gaining widespread use by psychologists in establishing personality requirements for many occupations. It works like this:

Step 1: Choose at random a group of men engaged in the occupation which interests you. (In this case, the occupation is heading up an R & D company.)

Step 2: Measure the degree of success attained by each man, and rank your group, starting with the most successful and going on down to the least successful one.

Step 3: Apply psychological tests which measure behavioral aspects relevant to the men's job performance (in this case, their success in developing profitable operations).

Step 4: Score each man on each test, assigning to him a numerical "grade."

Step 5: Compare the grades of each behavioral test with the degree of success attained by each re-

56

spondent. Use statistical tests to determine the validity of each set of relationships.

Step 6: Define the "ideal" performer, using *only* those aspects of personality which show significant change up and down the "success" scale.

I began with one premise: *the R & D company president can only be successful to the extent that he veridically perceives his environment.* Lest my key phrase, "veridical perception," sound overly technical, let me emphasize that it is simply the best term I know for a certain kind of executive behavior. Veridical perception may be defined as the act of recognizing people, things, or situations as they truthfully are, rather than attributing to them qualities which are the products of one's emotions or imagination. Why should this quality be of great importance? Mainly because the establishment and conduct of a young R & D company is a unique experience. While the manufacturer of some long-established consumer product can — with at least relative ease — assess national demand, compare his product to others, hire experts in his field, and observe long trends in pricing, distribution, and profitability in his industry, the R & D man must continually improvise in his search for success. Some very urgent questions which he faces are:

- What new product or service should be developed?
- How long and costly will development be?
- What price can be charged, and what volume will sell?
- What types of engineers, scientists, and salespeople are needed to do the job?

Observing Reality

The answers are rarely obvious. Even under ideal circumstances, the R & D entrepreneur proceeds by trial and error. He makes certain assumptions about the nature of the world around him, then moves ahead for a while. Next he *observes* the results. Were his original assumptions right? Are things moving in the predicted direction? Is the market responding favorably? Are the employees satisfied that the

company is here to stay and has a good future, or are they looking around for other jobs? The correct answers to these questions are vital. If he now perceives his environment — or at least its most relevant parts — veridically, he will make the proper corrections, change his course if necessary, and proceed again. If he does not perceive his environment veridically, only luck can save him.

Suppose a businessman-engineer commits his company's resources to the design of "the best vacuum-tube amplifier on the market," and, when asked why he does not turn to transistors, replies, "Because that's somewhat out of my line." This man simply has not learned to perceive his managerial role veridically; he sees him-

---

In this article Harry Schrage draws a new picture of the entrepreneur of the technologically based company. The author, himself a manager of two small enterprises in the past, bases his conclusions on a study he completed earlier this year as a Sloan Fellow at Massachusetts Institute of Technology. His findings will surprise many readers. Contrary to many common beliefs, entrepreneurs of profitable R & D firms do *not* rank consistently high in achievement motivation or needs to dominate, he reveals, and they *do* have much anxiety and self-awareness. Most important, the profitable R & D entrepreneur has a passion for knowing customer and employee situations firsthand. — *The Editors*

---

self as an engineer. And how about his perception of the market? Implicit in his decision is the notion that vacuum-tube amplifiers enjoy an equally attractive market — indicating that his perception of that area is not veridical either.

Suppose our man states, "My products are superior to those of my competitors," and, pressed for the details, is unable to substantiate his claim with anything more than, "I have to feel this way; otherwise, I would have no right to be in business." Now he displays magnificent faith but no knowledge of the *facts*. Does his creation last longer, use less power, or require less maintenance than the others? If he knew the answers, he might be able to justify a higher price, reduce the cost, or announce the advantage to his customers. Any of these could increase his profits.

Employee relations — the personnel function in general — is another area where veridical perception makes a tremendous difference. If our R & D manager insists, when asked about personnel problems, "All my female employees are only interested in meeting the right man," and indicates that he is really serious, how can he begin to deal constructively with the problem of high turnover?

Is veridical perception important only in the field of R & D companies? Social scientists have recently pointed to the fact that a necessary prerequisite to the successful direction of *any* organization is the leader's accurate perception of the field in which he operates:

◖ Jay W. Forrester, in discussing the growth of young companies, stresses the need for accurate assessment of the market's response to the company's prices, service, and quality.[1]

◖ Peter F. Drucker attributes corporate success to management's ability to determine the needs of the market and to direct the company toward the fulfillment of those needs.[2]

◖ Edgar H. Schein maintains that accurate perception of the nature of each person within one's organization is of prime importance.[3]

◖ Fred E. Fiedler goes a step further by showing, on repeated trials, a strong correlation between a man's ability to accurately perceive differences among his subordinates and the effectiveness of his organization.[4]

Nature of Study

Armed with all this evidence (which verified my own observations as a company manager), I chose, at random, 22 R & D companies. These firms ranged from pure service or consulting organizations to those whose prime emphasis was on manufacture of proprietary products designed and developed by their own staff of scientists and engineers. None was more than 10 years old.

Each president-founder was asked for:

1. Sales volume for each year since the company's establishment.

2. Annual profit or loss after making the following two adjustments:

(a) Comparison of personal salary drawn by the president to the salary that would have been paid to a stranger holding the same job. (I subtracted the resulting deficit or added the resulting surplus to profits.)

(b) Subtraction from profits of all capitalized amounts spent on proprietary R & D.

The respondents were interviewed at length concerning their attitudes, methods of decision making, and management problems. (See Appendix A for the approaches used in the interviews.) The profits (or losses) of each firm were computed as the average percent return on sales during the reported history of the company.

What do the results indicate? They prove that the entrepreneur's accurate perception of *the market's response to his firm's products or services* as well as a keen understanding of *the determinants of his employees' morale* are directly related to high profitability.

Personality Theories . . .

What other aspects of the chief executive's personality are related to this spirit of inquiry which helps him run his firm profitably? I decided to test three personality factors derived directly from David C. McClelland's description of the entrepreneur in his book, *The Achieving Society*,[5] and from *The Enterprising Man* by Orvis F. Collins, David G. Moore, and Darab B. Unwalla [6] (for detailed descriptions, see Appendix B). These factors were:

1. Achievement motivation.

2. Power motivation.

3. Awareness of impaired performance under tension.

Why were these three factors chosen? In his study McClelland maintains that achievement motivation is the single factor that draws a man to the entrepreneurial role. He further claims that this stimulus causes the individual to become inquisitive about the progress of his firm and — in brief — to adopt all such behavioral characteristics as are required for success. In *The Enterprising Man* resentment of authority, much akin to power motivation, is seen as the only relevant motive for entrepreneurship. This model illustrates how the very drive that places

[1] "Dynamics of Corporate Growth," an address delivered at the conference on "Management Strategy for Corporate Growth in New England," Massachusetts Institute of Technology, November 12, 1963.

[2] *Managing for Results* (New York, Harper & Row, Publishers, 1964).

[3] "Organizational Psychology" (Massachusetts Institute of Technology, unpublished manuscript, 1964), Chapt. 5.

[4] "Psychological Distance and Team Effectiveness," *Personnel Administration*, November–December 1958, p. 21.

[5] Princeton, D. Van Nostrand Co., Inc., 1961; see also McClelland's "Business Drive and National Achievement," HBR July–August 1962, p. 99, and "Achievement Motivation Can Be Developed," p. 6, this issue.

[6] Lansing, Bureau of Business and Economic Research, Michigan State University, 1964.

the entrepreneur in the role causes him to distort information about his firm and to engage in self-defeating behavior. Both theories insist that for various reasons the businessman frequently experiences anxiety and therefore finds his performance impaired.

How valid are these claims and findings for the R & D entrepreneur? To answer this question was an aim of the study.

. . . vs. Flesh & Blood

Before turning to look at the findings concerning personality, let us attempt to sketch the R & D entrepreneur as he appeared during the interviews. The findings should have more meaning if we know something about the man, the ambitions he expressed, and the problems he claimed to have encountered.

All but one of the respondents were scientists or engineers. All appeared to be well above average in intelligence. All were college graduates; six held Ph.D. degrees. Some had continued teaching while running their companies part-time. Practically every respondent stated that he had entered the R & D field because in it he found something important and challenging — a means of putting his talents to use.

Some were without doubt similar to McClelland's model of the entrepreneur. Their high achievement scores, their apparent talent for surrounding themselves with competent men, and their ceaseless efforts to produce profits attested to that fact. *Others* showed signs of fitting the Collins, Moore, and Unwalla model. These would talk about their "stupid" former bosses or the "lousy" organizations they had worked for. They would refer to fights they had engaged in with bankers, former partners, directors. Some resented authority to the point where, faced with seemingly insurmountable financial problems, they rejected as "unthinkable" any schemes whereby their companies would have become adequately financed at the price of their losing absolute control.

However, the achievement-motive and power-motive models seemed to fall at random on the success scale. Several men were quite low in achievement motivation and surrounded themselves with friends rather than experts, but ran moderately profitable companies. Some defied the power-motive model on almost every count. They had enjoyed their schooling; relinquished control of their companies at the start; and showed every evidence of a healthy dependence on their bankers, directors (who theoretically could fire them), and authority figures in general.

If we accept this composite picture of the entrepreneur as well as the previously described idea of veridical perception, we can ask some highly relevant questions and learn much about profitability through their answers:

• *Does* achievement motivation really improve the entrepreneur's performance by making him a more active information seeker?

• *Is* power motivation really wasteful of the businessman's energy by causing him to concentrate on issues of authority rather than to seek accurate information?

• *Is* anxiety, or perhaps the individual's *awareness* of being nervous, really a plague which prevents him from running his firm profitably?

Motives & Effects

First, let me summarize my research findings in capsule form. The pattern that emerges is one never before described:

(1) Achievement motivation does increase the man's awareness of his customers and employees. Its effect on operations, however, is to increase profit *or* loss! (See Part A of EXHIBIT I)

(2) Power motivation, as predicted, fogs the individual's perception of customers and employees. But instead of simply hurting profits, it causes either profits *or* losses to decrease! (Part B)

(3) Awareness of impaired performance in tight or difficult situations — what I shall call self-awareness — goes hand in hand with awareness of customers and employees. Presidents high in one are generally high in both; those low in one are also low in the other. (Part C-1)

(4) Self-awareness, including a measure of what is often called "anxiety," is strongly related to profitability. Greater self-awareness leads to higher profits. (Part C-2)

(5) Power motivation has a negative effect on self-awareness. The highly power-oriented men report little, if any, impairment of performance in tight situations. (Part C-3)

(6) When self-awareness scores are added to market- and employee-awareness ratings, their sum — representing "total awareness" — exhibits a strong influence on profits. *Total awareness increases profits significantly.* (Part D)

These are the cold findings. Let us now examine the meaning of each of the relevant aspects of personality and consider why the results

EXHIBIT I. ROLE OF PERSONALITY FACTORS

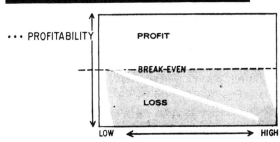

A. ACHIEVEMENT MOTIVATION AND ···

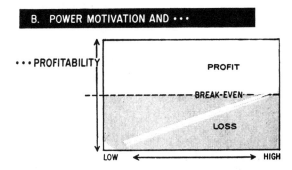

QUESTION. Are the customers generally satisfied with your product?

▼ *Winner*: "The response is mixed but improving. Our sales representatives or I always visit our customers periodically — not to land orders but to find out what complaints they have, if any. Our deliveries are still a little slow to some accounts, but we haven't had a major complaint on quality for over six months."

▲ *Loser*: "You bet they are. They wouldn't be buying from me if they weren't." Despite several

B. POWER MOTIVATION AND ···

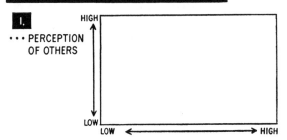

turned out as they did. In the discussion I shall depend heavily on the wealth of uncoded and perhaps uncodable data collected during the course of numerous hours of depth interviews.

Awareness of Customers

What precisely does awareness of customers and employees imply? How does the entrepreneur go about gaining such awareness? The following are examples of those parts of the interviews dealing with customers, with answers of successful men or "winners" contrasted with answers of "losers":

QUESTION. Do you feel that the use of your device will increase or decrease in the future?

▼ *Winner*: "I have asked most of my customers what their anticipated volume will be in the foreseeable future. Their replies indicate that I can expect the current level of demand to continue for at least the next year."

▲ *Loser*: "I am convinced it will increase with time. I have always developed absolutely the finest in this line of equipment. The trouble is that each time I get going with a particular design, they [government] change their minds and decide that they want something else. This time I'm sure, though, because I have a good amount of back orders on hand."

C. SELF-AWARENESS AND ···

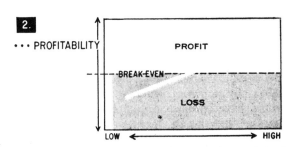

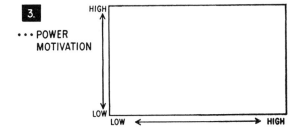

more questions along the same line, the man quoted was unable to add any further information to this statement.

QUESTION. How can you tell what it is about your products that your customers like and dislike?

▼ *Winner*: "Every two or three months I visit each of our recent customers all over the country. I never tell them that I am president of this company. I just tell them I'm the man who is supposed to find out what troubles they are having with our product. People seldom complain to a president; but since they think I just work here, they really squawk about every little problem they have had. This has helped me tremendously in making our product really good."

▲ *Loser*: "Our products are better, and the price is right." This was a phrase used several times during the interview by the man quoted. When asked, "Well, do they tell you this?" he answered, "They don't have to tell me a thing. I know it every time they reorder!"

QUESTION. Is there a way to anticipate future sales in your business?

▼ *Winner*: Talked of his constant efforts to find out what this nation's military needs will be in the near future. He explained that for a number of years he had maintained contact with military people in Washington, D. C. Several years ago, when the need for a particular scientific device became apparent, he founded his company expressly for the purpose of developing that item. He had no trouble in getting capital, landing a contract, or attracting good people to his organization. He had maintained his vigilance since. Each time a new government need arose, he shifted the emphasis of the company to it.

▲ *Loser*: Explained that there was no way. He added that he had always taken much pride in developing newer and better devices. "The darned trouble is that many customers don't appreciate the fact that my products are better than anyone else's. So I sell one or two units and never get to write off the cost of developing the product."

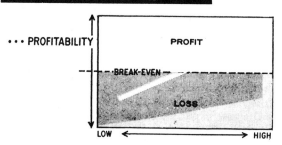

D. "TOTAL AWARENESS" AND ···

··· PROFITABILITY

PROFIT

BREAK-EVEN

LOSS

LOW ←———→ HIGH

What do these examples tell us about the difference in approach between the winners and the losers? The losers either "know" the answers without looking or decide that it is useless to try to find out. Their thoughts seem to revolve about their inventions. They have little concern for what goes on "out there" (the market), filling this void with their own preconceived notions.

The winners, on the other hand, appear to admit that they do not know enough and spend much time looking for the answers in the marketplace. They sound as if they have managed to transfer some of their scientific curiosity to business matters.

Awareness of Employees

Here are some questions and answers, recorded at interviews, dealing with employees:

QUESTION. How is morale in the shop?

▼ *Winner* (company of about 50 employees): "I have some men who are usually optimistic and others who frequently see doom ahead." When asked, "How do you know this?" he answered: "My office is located so that every man who comes in or goes out of the building passes by my door, and the door is always open. They know that they are welcome to come in and tell me their troubles. I know this takes much of my personal time, but it pays off. My scientists are absolutely the finest anywhere."

▲ *Loser* (company of about 50 employees): "Morale in my company is excellent. We recently landed a number of contracts, and people always feel good when there is plenty of work ahead. I have decided that engineers and scientists usually become unhappy when they're not doing a good job. Then they just get depressed and leave." When asked, "How do you know this?" his response, after a pause, was, "Experience."

▼ *Winner* (company with several hundred employees): "Morale is mainly a function of the departmental boss and of the individual employee. In some departments it's better than in others. When my company was small, I used to spend much time with the people in the shop. Now I instruct my supervisors to stay close to their people and to find out whenever something bothers them. Then there are some of the older employees who have been with us from the start. They frequently come to see me at my office and tell me what is going on."

▲ *Loser* (company with more than 100 employees): "I keep away from my company as much as I can. There are always some gripers among employees. They come and tell you that this is wrong and that is wrong. But you can't believe them. People often invent reasons when it's actually they who are to blame for problems that arise."

Once again we find the same contrast. The losers sound quite involved with themselves and appear to be projecting their own problems onto their employees. For instance, the first loser sees his own elation over incoming orders as the prime determinant of morale in the shop; and the second loser sounds reluctant to become involved in other people's problems.

On the other hand, both winners appear genuinely interested in finding out what really goes on in their companies. Their spirit of inquiry has extended to the area of employee morale. They, like the winners in the section on customer perception, admit to themselves that they do not know unless they are told. Therefore they listen and perceive veridically.

A word of caution: though other areas of veridical perception (e.g., suppliers, investors) showed no significant correlation to profits, I am convinced that it would be very dangerous to dismiss them as irrelevant. The unprofitable entrepreneur is likely to find himself thrown into frequent contact with his banker, his stockholders, and his suppliers. He is also occasionally forced to resort to accounting controls in order to satisfy his creditors. Although veridical perception in such situations did not seem to have the consistent impact that it did with customers and employees, I can only conclude that the *tests* failed to show significant relationships.

Achievement Drive

Why did achievement motivation cause profits *or* losses to increase rather than exert a positive influence toward success? I propose an explanation based on the other results of this study.

If we accept McClelland's findings, i.e., that achievement motivation causes the individual to try harder to succeed, then the increasing absolute value of profits or losses with rising achievement motivation may well indicate that he does try harder, but that the existence of another factor — his ability to perceive — causes his increased effort to swing results toward success or failure, depending on whether the perception is good or poor. Since we already know that veridical perception is vital, we can attempt to reconstruct the events as follows when the R & D entrepreneur builds his company:

◖ The *accurate* perceiver proceeds for a while with a tentative plan, checks his results, modifies his plan to remedy the observed problems, and resumes along modified lines. Since he perceives veridically, his corrections will tend to improve the performance of his company. The higher his achievement motivation, the more vigorous his pursuit of profits.

◖ The *inaccurate* perceiver, by contrast, after his first run, either fails to verify the results or attributes to them his own meaning. Since his diagnosis tends to be incorrect in either case, he now resumes, taking the wrong course. The higher his achievement motivation, the more vigorous his actions and the greater his losses.

In light of this explanation, the observed relationship between achievement motivation and profitability becomes meaningful.

Patterns of Power

How does the power motive affect the R & D entrepreneur's performance? Let us look first at the men who are low in power motivation.

We find that men unconcerned with power tend to delegate downward in the organization and to accept suggestions from cofounders, directors, and stockholders. What are the implications of this?

It indicates that awareness of the facts becomes a highly critical factor with these individuals. If they take the trouble to choose their subordinates carefully, the freedom given to the subordinates can produce highly successful results. Similarly, competent partners and superiors tend to produce fine results.

The converse, however, also holds true. If the choice of subordinates, partners, and sources of capital is undertaken in the absence of factual assessment of their strengths and weaknesses, the results can be disastrous.

Why are the profits *or* losses of the highly power-motivated men so much less (see Part B of EXHIBIT 1)? Here we observe two patterns:

(1) The behavior of the "manipulators" leads to all sorts of spectacular one-man maneuvers which sometimes produce high profits — *and occasionally large losses.* Hence the *average* net return over the life of their companies tends to be small.

(2) The cautious high-power individuals, on the other hand, tend to hold a tight rein over their subordinates and to accept no advice or control from authority figures. Since highly dominant management produces cautious subordinates, and tight financial control generally leads to early cor-

rections of losses, it appears reasonable that this group should also show small profits or losses — in this case, not because high profits tend to cancel out high losses, but because profits and losses both are consistently small.

Anxiety About Performance

Why does awareness of (or, some would say, "anxiety" about) impaired performance in short-lived stress situations appear to facilitate the success of R & D entrepreneurs, whereas in the case of trainees, salesmen, engineers, and production employees, research findings indicate that such self-awareness is maladaptive? (See Appendix A.)

If the trainee's anxiety causes him to forget, to misread, or generally to panic during an examination, he obviously will suffer. The salesman who loses his composure, forgets, or cannot reason clearly while trying to close a deal will lose his sale. The engineer or production employee who cannot think and becomes unnerved while facing his boss will probably be classified as poor in "success potential" by the latter. All of the foregoing, if subject to impaired performance in their moments of appraisal, will logically suffer. But the entrepreneur does not derive his profits through effective performance in short-lived stress situations. Successful performance of the entrepreneur depends mainly on his ability to perceive things clearly and to take proper corrective action when necessary.

Thus the simple answer to our question is that anxiety is not debilitative to the entrepreneur. But why should it help him?

Value as a Prod. The responses of several of our subjects suggest one answer. One entrepreneur, when asked about employee performance, replied:

"I have found out one thing about these people [his employees]; if you leave them in peace, they tend to go to sleep at their jobs. So I periodically manufacture emergencies for them. Whenever I get them good and anxious, they work long hours and really perform."

Was not this man projecting his own traits onto his subordinates? Was he not really saying that anxiety makes him work hard and that whenever his level of anxiety drops, he tends to go to sleep at his job? The responses of several other subjects revealed the same tendency toward projection. This leads us to conclude that the capacity to recognize and acknowledge personal anxiety, rather than hurting the entrepreneur's chance of success may actually increase it.

Honesty With Self. Observation of our subjects during and after their completion of the Achievement Anxiety Test (see Appendix A) leads me to suspect that the less successful ones tend to be *less honest with themselves* than the more successful ones are; i.e., they are just as anxious, but they will not admit it. One head of an unprofitable company, after completing the test, was asked if he had any final comments to make. He related an incident which he had observed some months earlier:

He knew of a man who had left an industrial position to join the Civil Service. When the man was asked why he made the change, he replied, "I couldn't stand being on the firing line all the time. I wanted security." Our respondent thought this strange. He said, "Most people don't admit to themselves that they are afraid." Thus he made an important confession. He had scored himself low on debilitative-anxiety response and, barely aware of his deception, had communicated it to the interviewer.

The entrepreneur in our society tends to see himself as brave, aggressive, always full of ideas, always able to produce in tight situations. Debilitative-anxiety responses characterize almost the exact antithesis of these traits. Is it not then natural that the individual whose self-esteem is already threatened by losses should tend to protect himself from further loss of face by denying any traits that might further disqualify him from his role? The successful individual, on the other hand, should perceive far less threat to himself in admitting to occasional debilitative responses.

The trainee, salesman, or engineer sees his role as demanding intelligence and skill. If unsuccessful, he should readily "confess" to debilitative response under stress. What a magnificent way of preserving his self-esteem by admitting that nervousness has hindered recognition of his "perfectly adequate" talents! Thus we have another reason for the reversal of anxiety results with entrepreneurs.

Total Awareness

As Part C-1 of Exhibit 1 shows, awareness of impaired performance in tight situations correlates positively with awareness of customers and employees. Part C-3 shows another unexpected result: anxiety scores show a strong negative correlation with power motivation. Since power impulses are viewed as suspect in our culture, few people admit to themselves or to others that what concerns them most is a desire to control people or an aversion to being led or influenced by others. In fact, psychologists have observed that power impulses are extremely anxiety-arousing, causing the individual to deny them even to himself as a defense.

With this additional information, our picture of the entrepreneur becomes quite clear. If high in power motivation, he *denies* anxiety, frequently projects, and therefore fails to perceive veridically. We can now view the individual who *admits* to anxiety — the high-anxiety scorer — as the man who tends not to project and who perceives veridically.

Our ideal entrepreneur can now be thought of as being totally aware of his own feelings and aware of others'. And high self-awareness plus high awareness of customers and employees, as reported in our results, is our best index to profitability!

Before leaving this concept of "total awareness" let us examine one other observed advantage that this set of personality attributes appears to impart to the entrepreneur. One universal problem that has been described dozens of times in the literature, and also by practically every respondent in my study, is the transition that an R & D entrepreneur has to make from the role of scientist or engineer to that of businessman. In the present study, several men projected their conflict between these roles onto their subordinates, disclaiming any personal involvement in it. Yet this disguise seemed quite transparent in the light of candid statements by others of being very much involved in the problem themselves. The following are quotations recorded at interviews with different men:

Executive A: "The biggest problem in the path of success of an R & D firm is the desperate need to form a bridge between the scientific part of the organization and the administrative functions."

Executive B: "The thing that is wrong with all my scientists is that they get completely hung up on their ideas and completely forget about time, costs, and the need to show a profit."

Executive C: "What's wrong with R & D companies is that the scientists keep thinking that all their customers are boobs and that eventually a really intelligent one will come along and shower them with profits."

Executive D: "I used to think that there was some magic to running a business. So I would hire a businessman and tell him to run the company and leave him alone. Only I kept picking the wrong men. So now I am learning to run the business myself."

Executive E: "The biggest mistake I ever made was to think that if my product were technically excellent, everything else would take care of itself."

Executive F: "I always knew that I had no talent for accounting and things like that; but when I realized the trouble I was getting into, I took in a top financial man as a partner, and things have been a lot better since."

These are only a few in a multitude of comments dealing with the same problem. This problem, which appears central to the R & D entrepreneur, remains unsolved by the "unaware" man. Executives A, B, and C project their dilemma onto their subordinates; they do not perceive it as their own problem. Mr. D gave his problem away to someone else, expecting him to solve it. Executives E and F are "aware" enough to perceive the problem as theirs. Mr. F has actually pinpointed a specific weakness in himself and has found a satisfactory solution.

Conclusion

What qualities should the R & D entrepreneur possess to maximize his chances of being highly successful in terms of company profits? We now have our answer. Parts A, B, and C-1 of Exhibit I tell us that *the most successful individual is high in achievement motivation, low in power motivation, and high in awareness of self, the market, and his employees.* A word of caution: another glance, at Part C-2, shows us that the most unprofitable man, who shows loss after loss each year, differs from the successful manager only in that he lacks awareness!

What are the implications of these findings for the active or prospective R & D entrepreneur? Psychologists tell us that our behavior is partly a function of our perception of the role we occupy, not only of our basic personality. We need only look at the tough-fisted cop who comes home to his family and suddenly becomes a lovable teddy bear to see what they mean.

The business world is changing rapidly, and yesterday's models of leadership frequently do not apply today. While the perfect entrepreneur, only a few decades ago, was seen as highly aggressive, independent to the point of taking advice from nobody, and insensitive to his own or other people's feelings; today's R & D success exhibits different behavior. The heads of the most profitable companies in our sample have a very human quality about them. They display much interest in people and in themselves. They readily admit to their weaknesses, to uncertainty about their work, to many things they have failed to do. They are good readers — some to the point of being familiar with much of the recent work in the behavioral sciences. Above all, they are curious — about science and its progress, about business affairs, about people.

Can those of us — business associates, bankers, suppliers, and others — who deal with R & D entrepreneurs in our daily work gain by these results? If our interest lies in the assessment of a man's future potential, the questions which should yield the most reliable results are:

(1) Does he appear to really know the nature of his customers? Is he aware of why they buy his products or services? Does he know what they like and dislike about his company? Above all, *does he appear to have made an active effort to find out?*

(2) Does he really know his employees? Can he distinguish between the more- and less-effective ones? Or does he stereotype all his employees with one brief description? Can he distinguish several factors that make for good morale and others that tend to destroy it? And again, *has he taken the trouble to really find out for himself,* or does he just appear to be theorizing?

(3) How curious is he about people? Indications of curiosity are frequently a good sign of awareness. One of the entrepreneurs in this study was so curious that after the first 15 minutes of interview he knew more about the interviewer than the latter knew about him! I later looked at his scores and discovered that he had rated extremely high in "total awareness," very high in achievement motivation, and very low in power motivation! His company's profits had averaged better than 10% of sales during its seven-year life span!

(4) Does he tend to look up and compare his company to highly successful ones, or does he look down to failures for comparison? An as yet unreported characteristic of the highly successful entrepreneurs is their tendency to be critical of their own performance. When asked how well they have done so far, they typically refer to General Electric, Du Pont, or General Motors and conclude that they have made a very modest start by comparison. This is in sharp contrast with the losers, who generally report having been fairly successful with emphasis on the fact that others have not done nearly as well!

Educators and men interested in training and improving the caliber of tomorrow's executives might well give some thought to the "optimal managerial style" indicated by the findings of this study. The findings indicate that tomorrow's manager should exhibit little power-motivated behavior, much achievement motivation, and — above all — a high degree of awareness of himself as well as of others on whose reactions he depends. The first two criteria suggest democratic, participative, problem-solving activity. The awareness criterion overshadows these two in adding the highly important requirement for frequent and careful assessment of results.

I believe that the corporate executive, much like the R & D entrepreneur, is frequently far better equipped to make sound decisions, given the facts he needs, than he is to seek the information telling him how well he is doing. But who will give him such information? Who *can,* other than himself? It is the rare manager who relentlessly pursues the facts — sometimes good and sometimes bad — which he must have in order to navigate his way surely to success.

Appendix A. Methodology

Here are some additional details about the research approach.

Veridical Perception

What areas of information available to the entrepreneur must be perceived veridically in order to assure profitability of the firm? I decided to test all those areas which might be relevant, allowing the statistical results to answer the question. The following are the sources of information and the nature of feedback which I assumed might be of importance.

Source 1: Stockholders or directors

Is the president aware of their approval (or lack of it) related to his conduct of the company? Does he accept advice, help, or criticism from them? If he is unaware of how they feel and unmindful of their suggestions, he may find himself unable to raise additional investment capital — if needed — and may be depriving himself of a valuable source of advice.

Source 2: Banks

Is the president in close enough contact with his banker to perceive veridically the bank's willingness (or lack of it) to extend short-term credit to him? Lack of veridical information in this area might lead to unnecessary cash shortages.

Source 3: Credit agencies, such as Dun & Bradstreet

If the R & D entrepreneur neglects this source of information, he may find difficulties with suppliers and financial institutions simply because his D & B rating is poorer than he thinks.

Source 4: Internal accounting controls; such as periodic P & L statements, balance sheets, and so on.

If the entrepreneur fails to install sufficient controls and financial reports, he has no basis — other than intuition — for determining how well he is doing, how much to invest, whether a given policy is helping or hurting the company, whether or not sales are living up to expectations, and so forth.

Source 5: Competitors

Accurate and up-to-date information on competitors should allow the chief executive to judge his relative status in the industry. It should help him to answer such questions as:

- "Is my overhead just about in line?"
- "Is my company more or less profitable than the others?"
- "Am I growing as fast as the rest?"
- "Are the others about to introduce a product which will obsolete mine?"

Source 6: Suppliers

Are the executive's suppliers satisfied that he is a valuable and sound customer? The prices he pays, the quality he receives, the credit terms available to him — all depend in part on his suppliers' opinion of his firm.

Source 7: Customers

What are the customers' current and future needs? Are they satisfied with the quality of the firm's goods or services? Are prices and delivery delays satisfactory?

Source 8: Immediate subordinates

Do subordinates have suggestions or talents which are being ignored? Are they putting all their effort into their work, or are they hunting for other job opportunities?

Source 9: Other employees in the organization

Are other employees offering useful ideas and abilities? Are the ideas and abilities being used?

Are they going all out for the company, or are they job-hoppers?

Source 10: Turnover

Accurate perception of reasons for which employees leave the service of the company can frequently tip the entrepreneur off to poor morale, low salaries, and numerous other difficulties within his organization.

Source 11: Salary and wage levels

Is he overpaying or underpaying his executives and other employees? Lack of accurate information in this area could lead to a high turnover rate, poor morale, or excessive costs.

The method selected for testing was to interrogate the respondent concerning each area, making it appear as if the content of his report — instead of its veridicality — were the issue. By extracting from him his method of obtaining the data in question, I could readily ascertain whether the information was factual — obtained from verbal or written reports through active search — or inferred from preconceived notions, fragmentary evidence, or just wishful thinking.

Each of the 11 areas of feedback was rated at every interview. The respondent received one of the following four ratings on each item:

Score	Behavior
+2	Subject *approaches* source.
+1	Subject *accepts* feedback originating from this source.
−1	Subject *distorts* feedback.
−2	Subject *avoids* feedback from this source.

The resulting numerical scores, ranging from −2 to +2, were recorded separately for the 11 sources of information. Scores of 0 resulted occasionally. Such a score would be the consequence of a double rating which was made, for example, when a respondent was found to "accept" (+1) some information from a source and to "distort" (−1) other information from the same source.

The veridical perception scores were individually compared to profitability, and those showing statistically significant relationships were classified as representing relevant sources of decision-making information.

Achievement & Power Motivation

McClelland's version of the Thematic Apperception Test was used. This test is the one which has been used in recent years in numerous research projects dealing with achievement and power motivation. Pictures are shown to respondents, who are asked to tell stories about them. The pictures represent scenes which usually suggest stories dealing with problem solving (achievement), the boss-subordinate relationship (power), or family and friendship (affiliation). Coding of the stories was performed by an experienced scorer whose reliability has been established by frequent cross-checks over a period of several years.

Anxiety Appraisals

Psychologists have defined two types of anxiety:

(1) That which the individual experiences generally, regardless of the task he may be performing or the situation he may be in, is termed "general anxiety." Each individual is presumed to possess a relatively constant degree of general anxiety.

(2) The other type, defined as that which is aroused only in response to a specific situation, is called "specific anxiety."

Our concern in this area rests with anxiety directly related to the performance of the entrepreneurial role, viz., the second type described. While several tests have been developed for the measurement of general anxiety, none have been devised for the measurement of anxiety specific to the entrepreneurial occupation. We therefore adapted the Alpert-Haber Achievement Anxiety Test (AAT) for this purpose. Psychologists Richard Alpert and Ralph N. Haber designed the AAT to measure anxiety specific to taking of examinations by students.[7]

What theory underlies the AAT test? Let me describe it briefly:

In 1950, George Mandler and Seymour B. Sarason devised a similar test, the TAQ, which lists a number of symptoms of anxiety such as accelerated heartbeat, increased perspiration, and loss of self-confidence. Their questionnaire asked the student to indicate the strength of each symptom he experienced while taking examinations. Mandler and Sarason reasoned that every individual experiences three drives related to the exam situation:

(1) A learned, task-relevant urge to do well, finish the exam, follow instructions.

(2) A task-related anxiety response to rapidly and efficiently complete the task in order to regain composure.

(3) A task-irrelevant drive consisting of feelings of inadequacy, helplessness, heightened somatic reaction, anticipation of punishment, anticipation of loss of status and esteem, and implicit attempts at leaving the test situation.

They named the conflict between the task-relevant and the task-irrelevant responses the direct cause of "test anxiety."[8]

[7] Richard Alpert and Ralph N. Haber, "Anxiety in Academic Achievement Situations," *Journal of Abnormal and Social Psychology*, September 1960, p. 207.

[8] George Mandler and Seymour B. Sarason, "A Study of Anxiety and Learning," *Journal of Abnormal and Social Psychology*, April 1952, p. 166.

[9] *An Introduction to Motivation* (Princeton, D. Van Nostrand Co., Inc., 1964), Chapter 9.

[10] See Richard Alpert and Ralph N. Haber, op. cit.

John W. Atkinson, investigating the relationship between TAQ scores and the performance of students of equal intelligence, discovered a definite negative correlation between these two.[9] Alpert and Haber based their AAT on these findings. Their questionnaire explores both task-relevant (facilitative) and task-irrelevant (debilitative) responses to the test situation. The AAT has been found to have somewhat stronger correlation with student performance than the TAQ.[10]

The AAT has been modified by changing all references from exam-taking to trying situations faced by salesmen. The modified questionnaire was tested on a group of salesmen. It again showed a negative correlation to sales performance. The same test, modified to apply to anxiety-inducing events faced by engineers and production employees, also showed negative correlation between reported achievement anxiety and a superior's rating of the man's "success potential." Would the AAT, modified to contain trying situations faced by the entrepreneur with customers, bankers, and stockholders, also show a negative correlation to profitability? This was one of the questions we sought to answer.

The following are examples of our modified questions. (The respondent is instructed: "Place an X in the space that most accurately describes you.") The first two deal with debilitative responses to short-term stress situations; the latter search for facilitative responses:

• When tackling a problem in an area with which I am not familiar, my fear of coming up with a poor solution cuts down my efficiency.

Always ___ ___ ___ ___ ___ *Never*
     (5) (4) (3) (2) (1)

• When I am asked a pointed question by my banker (or stockholder), my mind often goes blank for a while before I am able to think clearly.

Almost always ___ ___ ___ ___ ___ *Never*
     (5) (4) (3) (2) (1)

• When I am under great time pressure to complete a job, nothing distracts me.

Always true ___ ___ ___ ___ ___ *Never true*
     (5) (4) (3) (2) (1)

• I like to be placed under pressure in situations where coming up with the right answer is very important.

Always ___ ___ ___ ___ ___ *Never*
     (5) (4) (3) (2) (1)

All questions were scored between 1 and 5, corresponding to the "never" to "always" extremes. The scores were classified, added, standardized, and combined to give one "anxiety" index.

The Interview

Each respondent was assured that his company would not be identified in the final analysis and that no facts or figures identifying any specific company would appear.

68   *HBR Nov.–Dec. 1965*

The first 15 minutes were devoted to the following six "warm-up" questions:

1. Please define, in your own terms, success of a company such as yours.

2. How successful has your company been by these criteria?

3. Please name some very successful young R & D companies.

4. Please name some unsuccessful ones.

5. If starting from the beginning now, what three things would you do to assure your company's success?

6. What three things would you avoid in order to avert failure?

The interviewer made supportive comments to all the replies indicating that they were "good" answers. The next hour was devoted to the "perceptual veridicality" questions. Next the subject was asked for his financial figures. And, finally, the Thematic Apperception Test was administered (about 30 minutes), followed by the Anxiety Test. The total interview time came to approximately two hours.

APPENDIX B. PSYCHOLOGICAL MODELS

In *The Achieving Society*, referred to earlier, David C. McClelland links entrepreneurship with achievement motivation. He defines this drive as the desire to do well in competitive situations where results of one's efforts can be measured objectively. Whether the competition is against another contestant or against an objective measure of success is immaterial; the high achiever seeks success in both of these situations.

On the basis of a series of experiments, McClelland has developed an objective method for obtaining a quantitative estimate of the strength of an individual's achievement motivation. The person is asked to tell brief imaginary stories in response to a series of pictures (a special form of the Thematic Apperception Test). Scoring of these stories is based on the theory that motivation manifests itself in a person's daydreams or fantasies. The high achiever, when asked to "fantasy," tends to

---

For an interesting extension of McClelland's ideas, see his article, "Achievement Motivation Can Be Developed" (Thinking Ahead), on page 6 in this issue. — *The Editors*

---

compose stories which deal with problems that must be solved, means of solving them, and their solutions; while the low achiever's thoughts do not run along these lines. The achievement-related references contained in the stories are counted, and a numerical score representing motive strength is computed.

People high in achievement motivation generally show the following preferences:

1. They like situations in which they take personal responsibility for finding solutions to problems.

2. They tend to set moderate achievement goals and take "calculated risks."

3. They want concrete feedback as to how well they are doing.

4. They dislike repetitive, routine work.

5. They prefer experts over friends as their working partners.

McClelland adds that accurate knowledge of results is also a source of anxiety because "it cuts both ways: it provides not only proof of success but also inescapable evidence of failure."[11] Each attempt at ascertaining customer acceptance of his products or services, each probe into employee morale, and every inquiry aimed at determining the extent of satisfaction of the board of directors, bankers, or other financial institutions exposes the entrepreneur to the risk of discovering failure in some aspect of his work.

McClelland's "achieving" entrepreneur thus supplies us with the first two variables which seem to have relevance to the profitability of the firm. *Achievement motivation leads to problem-solving and information-seeking behavior, while anxiety is seen as a possible deterrent to either of these.*

A somewhat different picture of the entrepreneur is presented in the recent study by Collins, Moore, and Unwalla, which was also mentioned earlier. The value of this model to our study lies in the fact that it approaches our subject in the context of Freudian theory leading to somewhat different interpretations of the entrepreneur's need to achieve and of the source of anxiety. This study employs depth interviews and the Thematic Apperception Test. When active entrepreneurs in the manufacturing industry are tested, the findings show that the entrepreneur, unlike the executive employed by a company not his own, chooses his occupation because of intolerable emotional tension when dealing with a boss (authority figure). The following is a paraphrase of the explanation given by the authors as to the origin of this tension:

The combination of an emotionally close and rewarding mother and a more distant, passive, and nonauthoritarian father causes the child to feel that through his own achievement he has succeeded in winning his mother's affection and has therefore displaced his father. This situation brings on strong guilt feelings in the boy, causing him to fear revenge by the father. As the child grows up,

[11] David C. McClelland, *The Achieving Society*, p. 231.

this fear gradually spreads to all authority figures. The individual then rationalizes the tendency, recalling his father as having been too demanding yet unrewarding and unreliable, or simply as having been a failure. He is quick to discover real or imaginary weaknesses in all authority figures with whom he comes in contact.

Collins, Moore, and Unwalla list eight resulting tendencies often observed in their subjects:

(1) If the individual is employed by someone else, he tends to feel uncomfortable and is often incapable of good performance. Success on the job may bring on anxiety produced by a subconscious fear of invoking the jealous wrath of his father.

(2) He feels that the company (a symbolic mother figure) must not be dominated by a strong father figure.

(3) His own company (symbolic mistress) allows him to act out his needs without incurring the wrath of jealous male authorities.

(4) His business becomes a symbolic "bad (seductive) mother" and must not be shared with a partner.

(5) The business (bad mother) helps him to demonstrate his maleness.

(6) Since this solution is "immoral," it may lead to feelings of *"groundless anxiety"* when the company is successful. The subconscious need for punishment may now bring on the failure of the business.

(7) Financial losses may lead to relief from anxiety, producing magnificent behavior in the face of reversals. His inability to tolerate success brings on deficient behavior when the company is running well.

(8) His career pattern is therefore frequently marked by a series of ups and downs.

Two observations by the authors illustrate a relevant point. The entrepreneur functions satisfactorily in dealing with his subordinates only when their relationship is patriarchal or patronly. *He tends to project onto them his own undesirable impulses* — seeing them as lazy, disloyal, and so forth. He perceives male authority figures as shadowy, remote beings, not sought out for help or looked up to as models to be emulated.

We now have a second formulation of entrepreneurial anxiety. It is subconsciously generated through fear of retribution by an imaginary father figure. It can lead to *distortion of perceptions* related to or information coming from authority figures. It can also lead to *inaccurate perception* of subordinates. Finally, it can, if intense enough, lead to self-defeating behavior generated subconsciously by the need to be punished for one's own success.

People who seek positions of authority, who show much concern over influencing others, and who resent being influenced by authority figures, are defined by psychologists as being high in *power motivation.* We can therefore borrow, from Collins, Moore, and Unwalla, power motivation as a relevant dimension of the entrepreneur — one which *leads to much concern over authority issues rather than successful problem solving.* The highly power-motivated individual should perceive his environment non-veridically and, based on our original assumption, should therefore run his firm unprofitably. *Anxiety again appears as a deterrent to success.*

What are the differences and similarities in these two psychological models of the entrepreneur? McClelland sees the entrepreneur as an individual who seeks veridical feedback on how well he is doing and experiences anxiety only because the feedback might be negative. Collins, Moore, and Unwalla, on the other hand, observe the entrepreneur as projecting his own fantasies onto the sources of feedback — therefore not perceiving veridically — and experiencing anxiety whether the information is good or bad, but especially when his company is running well.

If the latter model were accurate, then we should expect most entrepreneurs to be unsuccessful in business and very difficult to deal with. This picture somehow defies our observations of the business world. If, however, McClelland's model applied to all entrepreneurs, then we should expect them all to be high in achievement motivation, to incessantly seek accurate feedback about their companies, and to be anxious *only* in the face of bad news. We also find this view difficult to accept.

Since current research in the field of personality recognizes man as being highly complex rather than simple, why not adopt the view that *both models may well have merit.* There certainly exist entrepreneurs who display much resentment of authority. Some ignore information about their firms. Others display all the characteristics of the high achiever. Many seek accurate feedback. All experience anxiety related to their work some of the time. Some appear to be anxious most of the time. And so on. Is not such a view more realistic? And does it not help us to ask better questions of the entrepreneur and to get more useful answers from him?

Men may construe things after their fashion, clear
from the purpose of the things themselves.
                    William Shakespeare, *Julius Caesar*

Business plans for the scientific entrepreneur

In the 1960's the popular thing to do with a new discovery was to form a company. Now some are in trouble. This article tells what is really needed to start a successful enterprise

by Stuart Hauser
Industrial Economist, Stanford Research Institute
and William H. Brickner
Brickner Associates

The 1960's saw the emergence of a relatively new phenomenon in the U.S. business and academic communities—the successful research scientist turned successful entrepreneur. The real life successes are well known and include some of the nation's leading businesses. Their success has spawned a large number of venture capital seeded enterprises based upon technology. However, the more numerous—but less publicized—stories of failure, poor stock market performance, and the now wary business venture capitalists will make this dream considerably more difficult for scientists in the 1970's to realize.

For the scientist considering turning entrepreneur, this article outlines key problems that he must consider in establishing a business and discusses a methodology by which these problems can be handled. It deals primarily with the need for, and the development of, a business plan.

The scientist-entrepreneur needs to consider the following eight important topics during the startup phase of his business: Identifying the basic purpose of the enterprise, describing the products or services it will market, evaluating the market potential for the proposed product, developing strategy to do the job, defining the required resources, securing funds and financing the enterprise, identifying alternative courses of action for key goals, and the organizational structure and allocation of duties.

Crucial: The start-up process

Before the entrepreneur opens his door for business, there are several steps he should consider in detail. Effort spent on start-up activities will tend to facilitate the later success of the business. In fact, we believe that the viability of a new enterprise is often determined by the attention given to these crucial but largely overlooked factors.

Assess and specify the personal objectives of the key group of founders. The goal-setting process is difficult because each individual may subscribe to the accepted group goals even though these may be at odds with his personal (and sometimes unrecognized) goals. The founding group should expect to spend adequate time on mutual goal exploration and then articulate these objectives in terms of the immediate future and the next five years. It is vital that the founders recognize the distinction between their privately held goals and their publicly stated goals, and the possible consequences if there are significant divergences between them. A new business simply cannot afford the cost of conflict of interests.

A few examples will illustrate the importance of goal definition. Assume that for one founder the most important goal is complete independence of action. Perhaps a one-man consulting business will best meet his needs, leaving his potential colleagues free to continue on their separate path. For another group, accustomed to working as a team in a unique technology, the goal may be technological leadership in the fabrication of their special kind of product. The aggressive individuals who form a group for the primary goal of rapid accumulation of wealth are an entirely different breed. Obviously conflict will arise if half of a founding group is oriented toward the technological goal and the other half toward the monetary goal.

Form a founding group with the smallest number of people who can plan the growth of the business successfully. This may necessitate the acquisition of talents not already available within the founding group. Major functions common to all business should be covered: marketing, manufacturing, finance, product development, and production engineering. Many scientist-enterpreneurs fail to understand the value of the nontechnical functions, especially the marketing activity. Consequently, one or two key people may need to be added to the original group, for part of the "action," of course. It is unrealistic to presume that a technical specialist can learn new disciplines quickly enough to save the business.

Locate and hire key advisors as necessary. Key advisors could include an accountant, corporate and patent attorneys, a business planner, and perhaps a public relations specialist. Such specialists will require either cash or equity, but they will repay their cost many times over by their counsel. The corporate attorney should probably be contacted before agreements among the principals are completed. He can draw up an agreement that will provide fair treatment for the founders and the enterprise in the event of later unresolvable disagreements.

Carefully selected advisors will assist in preparing papers of incorporation, meeting state laws and local requirements for the new business, and solving more personal matters that often arise among the principals. Two specific examples where advisors are useful are in negotiating the firm's financing and developing the most advantageous organization for tax purposes.

An additional benefit derived from properly selected advisors is their assistance in establishing good contacts in the financial community and among the appropriate trade journals. Such contacts may pay off both immediately and in future years.

Prepare the business plan and review it with key advisors before implementing any of its significant provisions. For example, patent counsel might advise on the suitability of describing details of a technical process before patent applications have been filed, or, conversely, on a potential liability resulting from incorporating ideas which could be the property of others.

Implement the plan and institute a program of periodic reviews. A fledgling business doesn't need the control and review procedures of a large corporation, but there should be a rational plan for reviewing decisions and events against the business plan, particularly if the decisions call for financial investment.

Recognize the possibility of conflict. Founders are liable to face conflict at some point. Conflict may even provide a healthy vehicle for developing creative solutions to problems. In any case, the severity of problems will be diminished simply by the fact that the group accepts conflict as an ever present possibility.

Developing the business plan

The first major task facing the founders as a cohesive business group is the development of the business plan. The plan is not a prospectus, nor a vehicle to enhance the technical reputations of the founders, nor a forecast of U.S. or world economics. The business plan is a document that identifies the product and goals of the enterprise, required resources, methods and alternatives for achieving set goals, and initial decisions that must be made during the first few months. If properly constructed, the completed plan will be a useful day-to-day guide for important activities. If it is tucked away on a shelf and not used as an

---

A business plan—what should be in it?

Here is a suggested outline listing major items that should be included.

1. Executive summary — A **one** page summary giving the key elements of the plan.

2. The organization (1-2 pages). Structure: Partnership, corporation, or other. Basic purpose: Description of product or service and markets.

3. Background and history (1-2 pages). Description of development or identification of business opportunity. New markets or technologies to be opened.

4. Management and ownership (1-2 pages). The founders: A paragraph on each of the key people describing background and talents. Key management personnel. Present or proposed distribution of ownership.

5. Product strategy (3-5 pages). Description of family of products or services to be provided. Summary of strengths and weaknesses of the proposed approach.

6. Marketing strategy (3-5 pages). Classes of customers to be served and their buying profiles. Total potential market of available customers. Market growth rate. Competition: Companies, products and prices. Distribution and field service channels. Special marketing strategies. Estimated market share: Preliminary sales forecasts. Timing schedule for introduction of the proposed products.

7. Product r and d programs (3-5 pages). Description of required projects. Schedules of expenses in terms of production milestones and goals. Estimates of probability of success. Identification of key technical problems.

8. Production and manufacturing strategy (3-5 pages). Production costs as a function of production volume: Economies of scale and impact of the production learning curve. Major make versus buy decisions. Quality control requirements. Financing the inventory.

9. Personnel and staffing (3-5 pages). Essential skills. Availability of required personnel. Proposed benefits and compensation incentives.

10. Financial strategy (3-5 pages). Financial forecasts of P and L, Balance sheet, cash receipts and disbursements, working capital needs for financing, inventories and receivables, rate of return on investors equity for at least three years. Financing alternatives. Product pricing.

11. Summary (1 page). Key strengths to be emphasized. Benefits to investors, key employees, and customers.

12. Appendix A. Biographies of key personnel and consultants.

13. Appendix B. List of key assumptions.

---

operating tool, something is wrong with either the plan or the attitude of the founders toward it. In either case, corrective measures need to be taken immediately.

In general, the contents of the business plan should include the topics outlined on page 15. A good plan can be prepared in 15 to 30 pages of text excluding tables and charts. The document's style should accommodate the backgrounds of the intended users and readers. For example, if the plan will be used to interest technical specialists who may join the organization with long term working capital, it will have a different emphasis from a plan designed to be used to locate venture capital support. While the emphasis for different readers may change, the basic content of the plan should not.

After the executive summary, the next three items of the plan answers the questions: What is the company? Who is in it? What do they have that is unique? These items will describe the founders and their talents as resources for the business.

Product strategy is where serious original work begins because only the founders can develop the product plan. This plan will include a simple description of the product or service and the means by which the basic product concept will be exploited. For instance, assume that our entrepreneurs have developed a data acquisition system in which analog data can be encoded redundantly in digital form on audio quality magnetic tape, using portable audio quality electronics but with the quality and reliability of computer tape. Their first products are to be a series of low cost, on-site recorders for field-based analog air and water pollution data collection systems. If our entrepreneurs are primarily pollution oriented chemists, their total product strategy might involve the subsequent development of a series of elemental detection systems specifically for the pollution market. If they are digital engineers, their product strategy might include the development of a series of recorders for other industrial process oriented markets.

The emphasis of product strategy is on the unique technology of the group and its embodiment in a specific product. Obviously a realistic assessment must be made of the capabilities of the product compared to competing techniques.

Marketing strategy is an area where research scientists may need a great deal of help. At this point, customer classes or markets must be identified, annual sales of all similar products to each market over a period of several years must be calculated, alternatives for marketing and field servicing the product must be worked out, and estimates of possible market shares and the impact of competing products must be made. The founders should consider using outside sources for their market data unless they know these customer groups intimately. The price of misjudging markets can be fatal if it is the first market for the first product.

Gathering market data involves literature field research. Sometimes market information can be purchased from one of several excellent organizations engaged in techno-economic research. An alternative is a proprietary research project, but this may be too expensive for the newly founded organization. Whichever route is used, the credentials of the people conducting the research are important.

Rather than purchase the required data, the principals can themselves do the painstaking library and field work. The information they gather must be highly specific and quantitative or it will have little value. The phrase "a large and growing market" is often used to describe a market opportunity. Consider a total market of 1000 units in 1970, growing at the rate of 15 per cent per year through 1975, for example. This might be excellent for a highly proprietary system selling for $10,000, especially if the product has no immediate competition. But the same market size and growth for a $50 product in an existing competitive market is hardly an exciting prospect.

Identification of markets may seem deceptively easy until one realizes that locating ultimate users of the product or service is not enough. Our entrepreneurs must also determine the current purchasers of the product. In fact, there may be several purchasing groups, each with its own unique characteristics. Miniperipherals, for example, developed for use with minicomputers have several customer groups: minicomputer manufacturers, OEM users of minicomputers, systems houses, and end users. However, a new peripheral which requires extensive interface hardware or software might not be suitable for the last group of minicomputer customers.

Having identified the market, many sources of data can be used for estimating the total market size in units and dollars, and the market growth rate. The necessary information is available from trade associations, trade publications, U.S. Department of Commerce publications and related literature. The market can be segmented, if desired, in terms of product price range, major operating features, or other differentiating characteristics.

Total market estimates should include two or more years of history as well as the current year's sales, and projections for at least three years. The validity of all forecasts will depend upon how well assumptions about the environment are quantified and stated somewhere in the business plan.

Several proposals for field sales and service activities suitable for the products or services being offered should be included too. Conversely, field sales and service limitations may dictate which markets a small enterprise should seek to penetrate. In our miniperipheral example, a small company with limited sales force consisting of a few key engineers might select customers among the few OEM users or larger purchasers of minicomputers, even if such sales must be allowed large discounts.

Questions to be answered are: Does the company use sales reps or hire its own sales engineers? Is there a ready made manufacturers sales organization already selling related products? What kind of incentive program does the company's unique situation allow? Does the organization's newness present a difficult recruiting problem? What kind of service and warranty policies are required to keep customers happy? Is field service to be provided by the company's engineers or by contract with a national organization?

The market share analysis is essentially the company's booking forecast for the period under study. This forecast should be in the form of annual order receipts in units and dollars. The figures need to bear a reasonable relation to the marketing program. Except for entirely new products, there exist figures for average annual sales per salesman in each industry. However, innovative marketing programs can dramatically increase salesmen productivity. Assumptions supporting the quantitative information should be included in the plan.

Finally, a realistic assessment of competitive products and companies must be made. a good way to compare products is to prepare a table showing critical features, such as price, performance, and specifications, including the advantages of the competitive products. A brief paragraph on the strengths and weaknesses of each company rounds out the analysis.

Product r and d programs are familiar to senior engineers and scientists. We won't dwell on them except to note the more deadly r and d sins common to small companies. First, miscalculations are often made about the time and money required to complete a product design and build prototypes to specifications. Second, misjudgments are made concerning the difficulty of solving technical problems to bring scientific feasibility to the level of engineering art. Third, overdesign of the product often creates problems in pricing and uses by customers.

If the r and d program involves expenditures of a hundred thousand dollars or more, the business plan should include a budget of these expenditures and target dates for important milestones. Difficult technical questions should also be identified.

Production and manufacturing strategy is considered after the new product is designed. Here again, specialists may be required, including a cost accountant and a manufacturing engineer. The basic problem is to produce, test, and ship the product at target cost and specifications. The answer might be to build or buy a manufacturing plant, or farm out production of subsystems, leaving only final assembly and testing to the company's own production staff. The exact strategy adopted should be determined by inventory financing and related nontechnical questions as well as purely production questions. Innovative but practical alternatives might be worked out that would provide a significant cost advantage over competitors. Would it be feasible, for example, to use the excess production capacity of a manufacturer of a related product to mutual advantage?

Financial strategy is one of three critical topics of the business plan. This should include annual proforma financial statements for a three to five year period. It is very desirable to show the first year by quarters, as this is when most new ventures may experience financial control troubles. These forecasts should be prepared, or at least reviewed, by a CPA or other professional who has experience working with managers. If he also has had direct experience in your product area, he may bring insights of success and failure to bear. The financial strategy should portray the financial resources and assets required, and the generated cash and earnings flow, including return on investment. Here is where the consequences of selecting various alternatives will be most visible, and it may be useful to show the financial consequences of major alternatives.

Assume a hypothetical situation where all questions about the product, market, and production have been worked out, and the significant alternatives have been identified. However, the marketing plan is not resolved between establishing a factory-based sales force and using an existing nationwide sales rep organization. The sales rep company is ideally suited for the product, but wants a per cent discount from listed retail price to industrial customers. Preliminary estimates would indicate that most profits on sales are somewhat lower if reps are used. Financial analysis might reveal that with a rapid market penetration during the first three years, the representative sales force allows a greater accumulation of profits with higher return on investor equity, reducing working capital requirements significantly.

Summary should be brief. It should summarize the key strengths and unique features of the basic product concept, its implementation in the business plan as described, and benefits to key employees, investors and customers.   □

A success profile

An entrepreneur may successfully work his way through the start-up process as discussed in this article. However, while he now has a fledgling enterprise, he and his cofounders are not yet guaranteed business success. Eventually they will need to bring in additional managers, employees and working capital. By then the founders will have encountered experts in evaluating start-up enterprises for the purpose of deciding to commit further resources. Some of the questions that these experts will ask the founders should be considered. The questions suggest a profile typical of enterprises run successfully by scientist-entrepreneurs.

Industry skill and experience. Do the key people know their way around the technologies and markets served by the products or services offered, or are they reinventing the wheel?

Motivation. Do the managers indicate a real willingness to make personal and business sacrifices that are essential to a new business? Experience shows that most start-up situations require loss of evenings, weekends, and holidays with the family in order to breathe life into the struggling company. Circumstances may further require acceptance of a lower standard of living (hopefully temporary) by founders families.

Integrity. Are the top people capable of facing the truth, admitting mistakes, and adopting corrective action? For instance, the company's president must be able to kill a pet project when its prospects for success are obviously poor. He must also be able to deal effectively with poor performance of an employee, even those in important positions. Is the top man capable of making decisions which may result in personal sacrifices?

Leadership. Does the group have a well defined leader who commands the respect and attention of his associates and can speak for them at crucial times? Can the leader bring in new talents on the management team without any of the founders feeling threatened? Does the leader have sufficient staying power to stick through the uncomfortable and trying moments of the organization's formative years?

CHAPTER 4

VENTURE FINANCING

The entrepreneur will typically require financing during three phases of the enterprise development sequence. During the first phase, the entrepreneur requires seed money to purchase the materials, rent the space, hire the accountant and lawyer, pay the necessary state and government fees, and pay his employees throughout the time it takes to establish a productive organization. To obtain sufficient financing for this stage, the entrepreneur must invest a substantial part of his personal net worth into the venture to indicate his commitment in making the business a success. The entrepreneur's enthusiasm alone is not enough. He must commit a large share (if not all) of his personal net worth. Even then, conventional sources of financing still may not be willing to provide start-up funds during this highly speculative start-up period when the reward potential is difficult to ascertain. Private placements and venture capitalists are the preferred sources of high risk start-up funds. Funds from relatives and friends are the more common source but the entrepreneur must trade-off the dangers of still living with friends in the event of bankruptcy with the need for start-up funds.

During the second or growth phase, the business will usually require second phase financing to cover the costs of additional new product development, building the new plant, hiring more full time employees and the necessary manufacturing equipment to meet the initial demand for the company's product. By this time the product has been successfully developed and marketed, giving the business and entrepreneur a track record with a measure of achieved success. Commercial banks, insurance companies, and the SBA generally become interested at this stage, along with less venturesome venture capitalists. Supposedly this is a less risky stage of financing because more factual information is available about the entrepreneur and his business plan.

In the final stage of venture financing the enterprise has matured to the point where neither traditional small business financial sources nor friends and relatives can provide the magnitude of funds required for further plant and staff expansion. Investors with large sums of money must now be located — usually through the public sale of stock, a larger financial institution, or through a merger. Capital is the blood for new business growth, and all but a few firms need several infusions of fresh new blood to provide the stamina for rapid growth. While it varies from industry to industry, and company to company, there are several common elements to venture financings.

To recap, here are the elements:

A) <u>Sources of equity capital</u>

Friends and Relatives	High risk High reward

Angels (successful private individuals

Venture Capitalists

Institutional Investors	Low risk Low reward

B) 1. Seed Money
2. Venture Financing
3. Private Placement
4. Public Offering

When the entrepreneur has successfully maneuvered through these financing phases proving he has managed to communicate effectively with the financial community, he has then established himself and his enterprise in the business community. He is no longer an entrepreneur running a new venture, but a manager running a large company.

The first reading by Victor Danilov presents an overview of the principal financial sources for small business ventures. He claims the start-up or seed money stage of the venture when the risks are highest is the least attractive to traditional financial sources. The aspiring entrepreneur must be cognizant of the many financial sources and how their investment guidelines and decision criteria differ in matching his firm's financial needs to the characteristics of the financial community. Danilov concentrates on the venture capital groups and how they rank management factors against the product concept, the type of financial returns they expect, and the preferred combinations of equity and debt investments. The entrepreneur usually appoints a representative from the financial group to his board of directors, and thereby trades ownership and control in return for cash and possibly management assistance. The entrepreneur also reaches other compromising agreements in overcoming obstacles to finance the development of his enterprise according to Danilov. May I suggest again that the appendix to "The Entrepreneur's Handbook" offers further assistance. On the one hand, a listing of (SBIC's) Small Business Investment Companies is offered as well as a listing of venture capital opportunities. Items in the sources of help appendix numbered 2, 3, 4, and 5 address this issue directly.

Even after the financial sources are known, located, and their objectives understood, to compete for these funds the entrepreneur must present a comprehensive and factual business plan. Many times, especially in times of tight equity money, the only source of funds is bank debt. Arnold Ruskin examines this essential interaction from a banker's point of view. In accomplishing the basic objective of realistically assessing the venture risk level, Professor Ruskin discusses the various qualitative and quantitative informational needs that exist. He looks at entrepreneurs and his business plans through the eyes of the banker.

The additional articles by Sanchagrin, Adams and Kelly, also focus on these issues. Each approaches the same issue from a different point of view. Taken together, this grouping of views offers a broad insight into a complex field. This is such a crucial and difficult area that I choose to offer a variety of views, rather than endorsing a single approach.

Product, employees, markets and environmental factors will be considered, along with a measure of the entrepreneurial and leadership characteristics of the founder, by the financial sources. Does the entrepreneur understand what is encompassed in his product development and marketing efforts? Will his entry into the market result in a meaningful market share and a strong position against traditional or potential competition? Has the entrepreneur assembled a talented and cohesive team, all striving for the same goal? Is the environment in terms of suppliers, technological assessments, legal and economical factors viewed realistically? These are all questions that a banker or any other

financial source must answer to evaluate the entrepreneur and his venture plans. Funds for financing a new or growing business are usually available for good plans. However, a good plan depends on the entrepreneur's ability to convincingly provide the information required by the venture capital sources. These authors answer these issues in an easy to read format.

While the entrepreneur is organizing his venture plans, he should be cognizant of the many sources of financing and how his attractiveness to these sources may be affected by his corporate structure. Hence, the corporate structure is intertwined with the venture financing. The second to last article discusses special tax inducements available to equity investors in companies that qualify under Section 1244 of the 1958 Small Business Investments Act. The main tax advantage of this structure is the tax shield of capital losses from ordinary income for stockholders, while gains are treated at the capital gains rate. To raise funds for risky ventures, this popular tax incentive provides a downside advantage to the venture capital investors. Section 1244 restrictions are not too cumbersome and they allow up to $50,000 in capital losses to be applied as a tax shield in a single year whereas without 1244 stock only $1,000 can be applied as a tax loss in the event the business fails. This is significant for any potential equity investor. The Business Week article is quite old but not dated; the issues are still the same. May I suggest you consult your lawyer and accountant on the latest interpretations on this section.

Sources of capital fall into two basic categories: debt (loans) or equity (stock). Equity is provided by the stockholder. Long term debt is usually obtained from commercial banks, with the possibility that the Small Business Administration (SBA) will guarantee the more risky loans. The SBA seldoms lends its own funds to a small business but will countersign a bank debt. A Small Business Investment Company (SBIC) can also provide either debt or equity. These SBIC's are also arms of the SBA. The final article by Anthony Chase and Jim Proctor offers insight into the SBA financing program. May I also suggest you read note No. 1 in the appendix on Sources of Help. It can refer you to your local SBA office for the latest advice on financing. Also, as an appendix to the "Entrepreneurs Handbook", a complete listing of SBIC's is offered.

RAISING FUNDS FOR SMALL BUSINESS

FINANCE/BUSINESS WEEK

Section 1244 companies provide large tax inducements
for investors in less-than-$500,000 issues.
Little-known method is attractive for well-heeled risk-takers.

A little-known part of the Small Business Investment Act of 1958 — the same law that gave rise to small business investment companies — is gaining fresh notice as a device by which small companies can raise equity capital. Labeled Section 1244, it offers a large tax inducement to investors: Losses from investing in "1244" stock can be deducted from ordinary income, while gains are treated at the capital gains rate.

As defined by the law, a "1244" company in effect is a corporation with less than $500,000 in capital and paid-in surplus and whose total equity, even after a new stock offering, won't exceed $1-million. There are a number of other limitations — only one class of stock can be outstanding, and more than half of income has to come from things other than rents and royalties — but the capital restrictions are the practical qualifications. In fact, a number of corporations have changed their corporate structure to be in a position to qualify under "1244."

Estimates. Yet "1244" has been ignored by all but a few small business concerns — and by the investment bankers that might lead them to this route. No exact figures are available — neither the Securities & Exchange Commission nor the Small Business Administration has kept tabs — but Wall Street men guess that only $10-million or so has been raised this way. This figure does not include the small but growing number of "1244" companies being privately formed by attorneys to take advantage of the favorable tax treatment.

The Wall Street offerings have been made mainly on a non-registered private placement basis or through Regulation A filings (issues of $300,000 or less in which neither full disclosure nor an independent certified accounting are nec-essary) arranged by a few Wall Street underwriters, such as Carl M. Loeb, Rhoades & Co., Kidder, Peabody & Co., McDonnell & Co., Inc., and Smith, Barney & Co.

All told, perhaps 25 such offerings have been handled by Wall Street houses. But it's hard to tell since underwriters are secretive about their "1244" business. It's a small-scale operation for all of them, and they do not want to encourage a flood of money-seekers.

Advantages for all. Carter believes that any offering under $500,000 (the limit on "1244" issues) should be handled in such a way that investors will get the "1244" tax advantages, provided the company qualifies in other respects. Since "1244" tax treatment is available only to the first purchasers of the stock, this means that shares must be sold directly to investors instead of being sold first to an underwriter and then resold by him, which is the more usual method of financing.

If the issue is handled so that it qualifies for "1244" tax treatment, Carter says, everyone concerned can profit. The underwriter who sets up the deal can be rewarded, not by the usual underwriting fee, but by appreciation on stock obtained in advance below the offering price. The company gets its funds — which might not have been possible otherwise — and gets them cheaper than it could through a regular stock offering, since there are no underwriting commissions. Original investors get capital gains treatment when they sell out.

If things go sour, all bets are off, but the investor at least has some downside protection in being able to deduct losses from ordinary income.

In Carter's format, the company places its own stock. Carter, Berlind acts as a financial advisor, and may refer subscribers to the company.

But it is considered an "underwriter only to the extent that the spread between any shares it purchases and their eventual sale will be treated as an underwriter's fee. So far, SEC has taken no exceptions to this way of doing business.

Good results. Some houses have had surprisingly good luck with these investments, given their speculative nature, and their activities are attracting fresh interest. In addition, a small underwriting concern, Carter, Berlind & Weill, has advised several companies recently to offer their securities publicly through the "1244" device to facilitate obtaining equity capital.

Actually, the slow start of "1244" companies is not very surprising. Congress itself didn't foresee a big demand for them when it passed the 1958 law. Its chief aim was to put muscle into the SBICs so that they in turn could provide financing for small businesses, which don't enjoy the same access to equity financing as large corporations.

To tap additional private funds for small business, Congress offered tax benefits directly to original investors in "1244" stock. Under the tax code, up to $50,000 on a joint return can be written off current income if a "1244" stock investment is disposed of at a loss. This privilege extends only to original purchases. This part of the effort to help small businesses has fared less well.

Speculative. Companies that fall into the "1244" category are obviously in a gray area for financing. They are small, speculative, sometimes just a few persons starting out with a new idea. The risks of investing in them are apparent. Gene M. Woodfin of Loeb, Rhoades says "it's like drilling a wild-catter."

High-bracket investors are willing to take this sort of risk if it is offset by favorable tax treatment. That's why "1244" stock has caught on with some Wall Street houses that have a clientele that can buy such shares.

Most underwriters, though, frown on selling "1244" stock publicly, preferring to control its placement as much as possible. They argue that the companies are too small, their management and sales problems too large for broad distribution. Woodfin says: "This is only seed-corn we're handling out. Shares of "1244" companies should be purchased only by those able to gamble." He adds that distribution of such shares is limited within his own firm.

Other firms say that they, too, keep "1244" stock in "strong" hands, even when they make Reg A filings. Arthur Carter of Carter, Berlind goes along, insisting that a discriminating list of investors is needed whenever "1244" stock is involved. But he advocates a more direct approach in bringing "1244" to the attention of both corporations and investors.

Carter's view may be self-serving, but he gets support from some underwriters who aren't involved in any way. "After all," says one, "if the tax benefits are there, why not take advantage of them to ease a small company's way to equity capital

Expenses cut. According to Carter, the public sales of "1244" stock offers a big advantage over private placement in that investors get a market value for their shares. At the same time, Carter thinks a "1244" offering is more advantageous to a company seeking — and able — to raise public money than a normal stock issue that is underwritten. The big factor here is reduced expenses.

Carter points out that Arista Truck Renting Corp, a New York City outfit, netted about 13% more in a recent $500,000 issue than it would have if it had a regular underwriting. It netted roughly $483,000, compared with the $425,000 it would have obtained otherwise. As an official at Arista says, "In our business where capital is a key, $50,000 is a lot."

Other underwriters back up Carter. On Reg A filings, for example, underwriting charges now cost a company about 12%-15% of the total, while legal expenses account for another chunk.

For this part, Carter takes cheap stock below the offering price, ordinarily using book value as a yardstick. In the Arista deal, Carter, Berlind & Weill bought for its investment account 25,000 shares of common at 1 cent a share; the offering was at $5 a share. The firm also has a three-year agreement to provide financial advice at a $1,000 annual fee.

Pitfalls. As inside counselor, Carter, Berlind hopes it can keep its investment off the shoals. But this doesn't mean it can't go aground; some "1244" firms are already hurting.

A number of companies that have raised funds via "1244" have good words for it. But one company official says: "The trick is to pick the investment banker who isn't looking for a financial gimmick, but one who has laid out a sound financial approach for when — and if — your company starts to grow." **End**

Financial Aid and Venture Capital

Chase and Proctor

Programs at SBA

*Financing independent business may be a banker's bag—
but he just might find some new ideas by taking a closer
look at the. . .*

PERHAPS NO OTHER AGENCY of the Federal Government is as beleaguered and at the same time as actually and potentially productive as the Small Business Administration. The Small Business Act,[1] the Small Business Investment Act (SBI Act),[2] and a number of other statutory provisions have armed SBA with an impressive array of weapons with which to stimulate and defend the small business sector of our free enterprise system.

We will discuss one SBA activity—its role in providing venture capital and other kinds of financial assistance to small businesses. SBA's full range of programs also includes its extensive activities in the areas of federal procurement, management assistance, minority enterprise and on behalf of small business before other governmental bodies.

By law, SBA is prohibited from granting financial assistance unless the assistance is unavailable from private sources on reasonable terms.[3] On the other hand, SBA is admonished by the same statute that its loans must be "of such sound value or so secured as reasonably to assure repayment."[4] Its role is not to subsidize dying businesses nor to conduct a give-away program, nor does it compete with the private banking industry. Rather, SBA's role is to make financing available to potentially profitable small concerns that cannot fit into the priority framework of the private capital markets.

SBA's guaranteed loan program is well-known; less familiar are its recent efforts to make that program more attractive to banks. Its disaster loan program is also well-known, yet it is scarcely realized that SBA aids not only victims of natural disasters but also those affected by the federal bulldozer, by product disaster, by international trade concessions, and by health and safety legislation. SBA also has a special loan program for low-income individuals, and makes unsecured long-term loans to state and local development companies and to small business investment companies. Finally, SBA can guarantee the rentals of small concerns to their landlords, thus making them more attractive tenants.

THE SBA EXPERIENCE

Despite the risks inherent in its lending policy, SBA's loss rate has not been excessive. Many would argue it should be higher. On regular business loans the rate of loss has been approximately two percent—high enough to be unacceptable to commercial bankers but low enough to demonstrate that it is a true loan program and not a system of subsidies.

In its 17 years of existence, SBA has approved over 200,000 direct and guaranteed loans for a total of more than $6 billion. In the most recent fiscal year, some 32,000 loans were made in the amount of almost $1 billion. Small business investment companies, licensed and partially financed by SBA, have provided 37,000 financings to small business concerns in the amount of $1.8 billion in the ten years since that program was activated.

While SBA assistance has reached significant dollar amounts, it has not gone far enough toward meeting the real needs of vast numbers of eligible concerns across the country.

Of all the independent businesses in the United States, 95 percent are considered small by SBA standards and might qualify for SBA assistance. This sector of the economy contributes roughly 37 percent of the gross national product and is responsible for over 40 percent of U.S. employment, giving SBA a potential clientele of impressive proportions. In times of high interest rates and low liquidity, the credit needs of these businesses become especially acute. Yet the aggregate level of SBA assistance has largely not been responsive to increased levels of need by small business. Clearly, there is room for SBA to expand its financial assistance role, especially at the present time. It is equally clear that no amount of government dollars alone can provide an adequate level of assistance.

No problem of SBA is more important, nor is any receiving more attention, than that of making SBA's programs and procedures more attractive to private lenders. The most extensive changes have been made in the business loan program.

THE BUSINESS LOAN PROGRAM

SBA's business loan program, under Section 7(a) of the Small Business Act, is its primary means of providing financial assistance. Under this program, SBA will guaranty up to 90 percent of a loan by a private financial institution, usually a commercial bank, to a small business concern that cannot otherwise obtain credit on reasonable terms. The private lender puts up 100 percent of the money on each such loan and stands at least 10 percent of the risk of loss. The lender also is responsible for servicing the loan. Where even guaranteed credit is otherwise unavailable, SBA may advance part or all of the loan funds itself; but the large majority of loans are now on a guaranty basis.

In Fiscal Year 1970, 84 percent of the new funds disbursed in the business loan program were private dollars, the highest proportion in SBA's history. The maximum amount of a guaranty or direct loan to a single borrower is $350,000,[5] although lower limits have been set administratively on direct loans; the maximum term of a loan is ten years, but 15-year loans are possible for certain construction projects.

Banks are permitted to charge "legal and reasonable"[6] rates of interest on guaranteed loans. The bank pays SBA an annual guaranty fee of ¼ percent on the balance of the guaranteed portion of the loan.

Several recent innovations will make participation in the program infinitely more convenient to the banker:

• *Blanket Guaranty.* SBA has eliminated the necessity of a separate guaranty agreement between the bank and SBA for each loan. SBA now executes one blanket agreement with the lender, under which many loans can be made, approved by SBA and thereby guaranteed. This so-called Simplified Blanket Loan Guaranty (SBLG) program has eliminated an untold amount of paper work and clerical burden. A one-page application form is used for the guaranty, separate long-form loan authorizations are eliminated, and reporting requirements are reduced. Under SBLG, SBA approves or denies each individual loan application within ten work days.

• *3-Day Loan Approval.* In some eight areas SBA now processes every loan application within three days; if SBA has not rejected an application within three days, the guaranty automatically becomes effective. The burden is squarely on SBA to act quickly on the application. The three-day plan is now in full operation and expected to become nationwide within a few months.

• *Immediate Payout.* In July 1970, SBA instructed its field offices that upon default of a guaranteed loan and demand by the lender for payment of the guaranty, SBA will now make prompt payment without a prior audit of the loan. The former practice was to investigate the activities of the lender in closing, disbursing and servicing the loan before paying on the guaranty— a process that often consumed months and aroused the displeasure of lenders. In eliminating the waiting period, SBA reserves the right subsequently to audit and take legal action to recover for losses arising out of misfeasance by the lender.

• *Elimination of Forms.* The number of forms a lender must use in making guaranty loans is constantly being reduced. Banks may now use their own mortgage forms and other collateral instruments, although SBA will provide them on request for the use of small lenders. In July 1970, certain optional clauses were eliminated from SBA note forms, making it possible to arrive at a single form of note that can be used in all cases. Reporting requirements have been lightened—reports to SBA on the status of guaranteed loans are now semi-annual instead of quarterly.

• *Revolving Credit.* SBA is currently adding a new tool to its business loan program, making available revolving lines of credit to small construction contractors. A pilot program with a major bank is now in the final stages of preparation. Within overall limitations set by a single guaranty agreement, the bank will advance funds to finance performance of multiple contracts, against pledges of contract rights by the borrower. The bank lender will be permitted to use all of its own loan closing and servicing forms, including note forms. The duration of each line of credit will normally be one year, and longer terms may be authorized. Competitive interest rates would be charged, and the maximum amount of guaranty is $350,000 or 90 percent of the loan, whichever is less.

• *Bank Sale of SBA Paper.* In recent years, low bank liquidity has inhibited the level of SBA-guaranteed financing. While SBA has primarily guaranteed loans by commercial banks, it has occasionally issued guarantees to other lenders that can exercise adequate credit judgments and perform the servicing function. Under present legislation, however, SBA has not issued guarantees directly to the bulk of the institutions, such as the insurance companies, pension funds, and foundations.

SBA has cooperated in arranging sales, to several state (public) pension funds, of the guaranteed portions of SBA-guaranteed loans. Under the normal arrangement the bank originating the loan sells the 90 percent "guaranteed portion" to the state pension fund, with SBA consent, retaining a 10 percent risk exposure and continuing to service the loan. The pension fund, since it invests in only the guaranteed portion, has a 100 percent guaranteed investment. Since the bank continues to service the loan, the fund can continue to be a passive investor.

SBA hopes to make these procedures, now used by the state pension funds, attractive to the private institutions. It is thoroughly reviewing the "packaging" of the guaranteed portions of loans into convenient investment units, that will be necessary to market them to a broad range of institutional investors and provide adequate secondary market facilities that will insure investors of a degree of liquidity. This is most difficult and may require legislation.

SPECIAL PROGRAMS

The business loan program is only one of SBA's tools. SBA's full flexibility is not generally recognized, and this lack of awareness has led to under-utilization of many of its programs.

SBA is generally known to provide disaster assistance—the ordinary disaster loan is made to a property owner of businessman to compensate for physical loss of other economic injury suffered in natural disasters.[7] The $150 million of assistance guaranteed after Hurricane Camille is evidence of the scope of this activity. It is less well known that SBA is authorized to make disaster-type loans (that is, long-term, low interest rate loans) in situations other than natural disasters. For example:

▲ *Displaced Business Loans*[8] can assist small businesses that have suffered economic injury by reason of being displaced by, or located in or near, a federally-assisted construction project, including urban renewal and highway projects. These loans, with no dollar limit, have up to 30-year maturity at an interest rate which is currently 5¾ percent. Most of the funds for the program have come directly from SBA, but there has been a degree of bank participation (at 8 percent interest).

▲ *Product Disaster Loans*[9] are available to assist small businesses that suffer economic injury as a result of inability to process or market a product for human consumption because of disease of toxicity due to natural or undetermined causes.

This authority was enacted by Congress in 1964, as a result of the botulism scare that injured scores of small firms in the Great Lakes fishing industry. The limits of SBA's authority in making these loans have not been tested, as there have been no loan applications.

▲ *Trade Adjustment Assistance Loans*[10] are available to assist any business, large or small, to adjust to increased competition from imports. This authority was enacted in 1966 and supplements the Trade Expansion Act of 1962.[11] Under the original provisions of that Act, domestic firms could apply for assistance if they could show that U.S. trade concessions were the major cause of increased imports and that increased imports were the major factor causing injury to the firm. Early applications for assistance were unsuccessful. Recently however, firms in the upright piano, sheet glass and barber chair industries have received presidential authorization to apply to the Secretary of Commerce for assistance.[12] As of this writing, only one application has been received by SBA. Pending legislation[13] would make trade adjustment assistance more readily available to industries and firms injured by import competition.

SBA has other disaster-type authority as well, such as its ability to assist small coal mine operators to meet the requirements of recently enacted *Coal Mine Health and Safety* legislation.[14] Similar bills have been introduced in Congress to enable SBA to extend disaster-type assistance to small businesses that must meet the requirements of local, state or federal *anti-pollution* laws.[15]

Economic Opportunity Loans

Title IV of the Economic Opportunity Act of 1964[16] authorizes SBA to make or guarantee loans to small business concerns that are (1) located in urban or rural areas with high proportions of unemployed or low income individuals, or (2) owned by low income individuals. EO loans cannot be granted unless other financial assistance (including a regular SBA business loan) is unavailable. The maximum loan size is $25,000; SBA may lend the money directly, or may guarantee up to 100 percent of a bank loan. Despite the guarantee, only about 1/3 of the new funds going into the program are from private sources; the small size of the loans and a higher delinquency rate have discouraged bank participation. Nevertheless, the program has been quite active and over 17,000 loans have been granted, totalling approximately $200 million.

It should be noted that the Urban Affairs Committee of the American Bankers Association has been extremely active in creating a framework for increased lending to the urban poor. Among other projects, minority lending seminars have been scheduled to be held eventually in 54 cities.

Development Company Loans

Under Section 501 of the SBI Act,[17] unsecured loans are made to State Development Companies (SDCs) incorporated under specific state enabling laws. These corporations have as members (or stockholders), banking institutions, federal savings and loan associations, building associations, pension funds and insurance companies who agree to lend to the SDC certain funds for investing in small business concerns within the state. The economic growth of the affected area is of primary importance. Once the members or stockholders have made their capital contributions to the SDC, SBA will lend funds to the SDC in an amount not exceeding such contributions. The SBA loans are for a maximum of 20 years at the same interest rate as the SDC borrows from its members, but not more than 8 percent per annum. Forty-one states now permit the incorporation of SDCs. SDCs initially confined their activities to long-term collateralized loans but more recently have invested in equity securities of small business concerns.

The Local Development Company (LDC)[18] has proven to be a flexible means of promoting economic development, particularly in rural areas where money is often extremely difficult to obtain for small businesses. Local development companies are private profit-making or non-profit corporations composed of citizens and businessmen of the local area. A minimum of 25 members or stockholders, all of whom reside or do business in the area of operations, must control at least 75 percent of the voting stock of an LDC. SBA loans money or guarantees up to 90 percent of loans by other lending institutions to LDC's to assist "identifiable" small businesses in plant construction, conversion or expansion, including land acquisition. The maximum loan or guaranty is $350,000 for *each* small business to be assisted. The loans may not be used for working capital; however, an ordinary business loan or SBIC companion loan could be made to the same business concern for working capital.

For each project assisted by an LDC, local sources must normally inject at least 20 percent of the project cost; but in some locations, including "target areas" of high unemployment or predominately low-income individuals, a 10 percent (or lower) local injection is required.[19] Loans to LDC's bear interest at 5½ percent, for as long as 25 years. Banks may charge any legal and reasonable interest rate and the loan may be 90 percent guaranteed by SBA. While LDC's have been successful in rural areas, those in urban areas have had difficulty raising the "local injection," and there is some indication that SBA may have to waive part or all of the local injection requirement in many cases.

Lease Guarantee

Another little-known vehicle of SBA assistance is the Lease Guarantee Program.[20] SBA, usually in cooperation with a participating insurance carrier, will guarantee the payment of rental by a small business tenant to its landlords, in effect making the small concern a triple-A tenant for credit purposes. This program enables him to compete with larger firms for space. The resulting strength of the lease may also help the landlord obtain financing for the construction of the leased premises. Leases may be guaranteed for terms of from five to twenty years.[21]

SBICS

Small Business Investment Companies (SBICs) are licensed and regulated by the SBA pursuant to the SBI Act. SBICs are privately owned and operated corporations created in order to fill the "gap" in equity capital and long-term loan funds available to small concerns, and to provide management assistance to such firms.

In order to become licensed, an SBIC must have a minimum private capitalization consisting of $150,000 of cash or eligible Government securities (though $150,000 is now rarely considered sufficient private capital by SBA). Generally speaking, SBA is authorized to furnish an SBIC with so-called "matching funds" by purchasing SBIC debentures in an amount up to twice the SBIC capitalization, but not to exceed $7.5 million.

The SBIC industry has a number of tax advantages. An SBIC shareholder may treat gains on sales of his stock as long-term capital gains or, if he is not so fortunate, he may take an unlimited ordinary-loss deduction on losses arising from disposition of the stock. SBICs are granted relief from the tax on excess accumulations of surplus from the tax on excess accumulations of surplus and may qualify for relief from the tax on personal holding companies. The Internal Revenue Code allows SBICs to take full deductions against ordinary income for losses they sustain on convertible debentures, or on stock received through conversion of debentures.[22]

A total of 841 SBIC licenses have been issued since the beginning of the program. The number of SBICs actively operating in the program has now declined to 338. Many of the early minimum size companies have defaulted on their obligations to SBA or incurred regulatory difficulties occasioning their departure from the program. In addition, a relatively small number of larger SBICs have surrendered their licenses, reportedly because of low profitability and their dissatisfaction with federal regulatory requirements. Most recently, several former SBICs have formed "two-tier" structures with an unregulated venture capital company as the parent of a subsidiary licensed SBIC.

It was not until 1966 that the SBIC industry as a whole showed a net return on invested capital (2.5 percent).[23] Today, the industry may be approaching health and stability.

Bank Ownership

Congress attempted to remedy the early plight of the industry by enacting the SBI Act Amendments of 1967.[24] According to a study prepared by SBA in 1967, an SBIC required a minimum capitalization of $1 million in order to constitute a sound financing organization, i.e., "to assure adequate income, to employ competent management, to make the company attractive to private investors, to allow diversification of investments and to enable an SBIC to have reasonable expectations of a successful long-time operation."[25]

In support of resulting 1967 legislation to increase an SBIC's minimum mandatory capitalization to $1 million, SBA took the position that bank-owned and bank-affiliated SBICs were among the best operated companies; in view of the requested increase in minimum SBIC capitalization, banks should be permitted to invest up to 5 percent of their capital and surplus (as opposed to the previous 2 percent) in SBIC stock. Congress finally approved an amendment permitting a bank to purchase SBIC stock not exceeding 5 percent of the bank's capital and surplus but did not increase the required minimum capitalization of an SBIC, which remains at $150,000.

A new provision was added at the insistence of the House conferees prohibiting banks from thereafter acquiring 50 percent or more of any class of voting securities of an SBIC.[26] In support of this new restriction the House Banking and Currency Committee stated that—

Commercial banks presently own or have an affiliation with 84 small business investment companies, 24 of which are wholly owned by banks. Your committee feels that this is an undesirable situation and one loaded with dangerous monopolistic potential.[27]

Statistics as of September 1969 indicate that there are 62 bank affiliated SBICs including 26 that are wholly owned by banks. Their combined paid-in capital and surplus amounts to $157.4 million and their investments in small concerns outstanding as of the end of September 1969 consisted of $46.9 million long-term loans, $68.4 million debt obligations with accompanying stock warrant or conversion privileges and $54.1 million of capital stock. In addition to their combined capital stock and surplus, the bank affiliated SBICs were financed with $33.2 million of funds borrowed from SBA under the SBI Act. The rate of private capital to Government funds among bank affiliated SBICs is 4.7 to 1, comparing favorably to the ratio of 6 to 5 for all SBICs.

Matching Funds

A major concern of the SBIC industry in recent years has been the irregularity of government funding. Legislation enacted last December authorized an increase of $70 million in the level of SBA "financing functions."[28] During the six months following this enactment, SBA received 104 applications for SBIC funding totaling $115.7 million and approved 99 debenture purchases for a total of $59.5 million. For Fiscal Year 1971, an SBIC program level of $65 million has been set, but SBA's ability to use a portion of this is contingent upon its ability to guarantee loans to SBICs by private investors. A backlog of applications already exists, and pending applications for the refinancing of maturing debt add to the burden.

The SBICs will not solve their funding problems without reducing their dependence on direct government lending. Under the original Act, SBA was clearly authorized to guarantee loans by private lenders to SBICs. A quirk of the 1967 Amendments has cast a cloud over this aspect of SBA's guarantee authority and private investors have since been unwilling to place full reliance upon it, despite favorable rulings by the Comptroller General.[29]

From time to time, SBA has been able to sell blocks of SBIC debentures to the private market as an indirect source of funds for new lending.

MESBICs

The President has recommended that (1) the SBI Act be amended to allow a bank to become a 100 percent equity owner of a Minority Enterprise SBIC, or MESBIC (subject to the "5 percent of assets" limit), (2) MESBICs be permitted to organize and operate under state nonprofit corporation statutes and (3) ordinary income tax deductions be allowed for contributions to nonprofit MESBICs.[30] "MESBIC" is defined as a special purpose SBIC "the investment policy of which is that its investments will be made solely in small business concerns which will contribute to a well-balanced economy be facilitating ownership in such concerns by persons whose participation in the free enterprise system is hampered because of social or economic disadvantages."[31]

SBA has already amended its regulations to permit regular SBICs to own MESBIC subsidiaries and to permit MESBICs to be under common ownership with existing SBICs. An SBIC owning a MESBIC must own at least 20 percent of the MESBIC's voting securities unless it demonstrates that it will be an active participant notwithstanding a lesser percentage of stock ownership. Non-SBIC investors may also acquire a portion of the equity securities of such a MESBIC.[32]

To encourage the formation of MESBICs, SBA has issued licenses to MESBIC applicants sponsored by strong parent companies (or individuals) despite the fact that the MESBIC will have private capital of only $150,000. A MESBIC can succeed with this minimum amount of initial private capital only if its strong parent will absorb all or part of its operating expenses and stand ready to inject additional private capital as the need develops. In order to attract large firms into the MESBIC program, recognizing that returns on investment can be delayed for many years, it was considered appropriate to permit MESBIC sponsors to commit capital only to the extent necessary to cover specific investment opportunities and operating expenses.

The first MESBIC, licensed by SBA in August 1968, was Arcata Investment Company of Palo Alto, California.[33] As of September 2, 1970, 16 licensed MESBICs were in operation, with 12 license applications in process and approximately 80 "commitments" (indications of serious intent on the part of potential MESBIC sponsors). The 16 operating MESBICs had aggregate original private capital of $3.1 million supplemented by $1.4 million borrowed form SBA. MESBICs have made or committed an estimated 98 financings to disadvantaged concerns for over $1.5 million.

CURRENT PROPOSALS

A variety of legislative proposals affecting small business are now before Congress.[34] These proposals place additional emphasis on increasing private participation in financing small business.

Whereas SBA can now extend its guaranty only to lenders that qualify as "banks or other lending institutions," the new proposals would enable SBA to guarantee loans made by persons or organizations "not normally engaged in lending activity." For the first time, SBA could directly guarantee loans to small business made by trusts, foundations, pension funds, churches and community groups, as well as service the loans made by these occasional lenders.

In order to cut red tape and minimize the time required to process a guaranteed loan, the legislation would authorize SBA to delegate authority to selected lenders to approve loans for guaranty without advance SBA approval in each case. A dollar ceiling would be imposed on the total amount of a lender's non-approved loans. SBA's advance approval of each loan is now required, even under the Simplified Blanket Loan Guaranty and the three-day approval plan.

The basic economics of an SBA-guaranteed loan would be affected by the new legislation in two ways. First, small businesses would be eligible to receive an interest subsidy during the first three years of an SBA guaranteed loan, which could reduce the effective loan interest rate by as much as 3 percent. The grant would go directly to the small business concern and not to the bank lender; special care would be exercised to assure that the bank did not increase its ordinary interest rate as a result of the subsidy. Within the 3 percent limit the subsidy could not exceed one-third of the total annual interest rate and could not reduce the effective interest rate below SBA's direct loan rate of 5½ percent. From the lender's standpoint the legislation would provide for an income tax deduction (with certain limitations) of 20 percent of the gross income derived by corporate lenders from SBA guaranteed loans.

In addition, the proposal would (1) exempt MESBICs from the provision preventing more than 50 percent ownership of an SBIC by a bank, (2) permit the incorporation of non-profit MESBICs, contributions to which would be deductible for income tax pusposes, and (3) permit SBA to guarantee the timely payment of 100 percent of principal and interest for the full term of debentures issued by SBICs.

Tax Aspects

The tax provisions of the proposed legislation are designed to attract trained personnel and management talent to small business. Subchapter S of the Internal Revenue Code provides that certain small businesses may elect to be taxes as partnerships. A principal advantage is that operating losses, common in the early years of a business, may be deducted directly against ordinary income of its shareholders. The new proposal would increase from 10 to 30 the permissible number of shareholders in a Subchapter-S corporation (enabling a company to issue employee stock options) and would permit a MESBIC to be a shareholder without the MESBIC's shareholders being counted against the new total of 30.

The tax treatment of early losses in a business would be liberalized by extending the present tax loss carry forward period from five years to ten years. This will be of particular use to new businesses that find it necessary during the early years to spend large amounts of money on items which cannot be capitalized, such as research and development.

In order to partially offset the advantages that large businesses have in attracting management talent, the tax legislation would also revise the stock option rules for small businesses to provide that an optionee could hold his option for up to eight years prior to exercise against the present five years). Also, he cold hold the stock for a minimum of one year after exercise (against the present three years) and still receive long-term capital gain treatment on his profit.

A persistent problem for small construction firms—particularly affecting minority contractors in inner-city areas—is their inability to obtain adequate surety bonding. Under the proposals, SBA would be authorized to guarantee surety companies against loss resulting from the breaching by small construction firms of bid bonds, payment bonds or performance bonds, on contracts amounting to as much as $500,000. Such a guarantee could cover up to 90 percent of the amount of a surety's loss, and would constitute a strong inducement for him to provide bonding protection to small firms.

SBA will never have sufficient funds to meet the needs of qualifying small concerns, without the help of private financial institutions. Congressional and executive mandates require the participation of private lenders, and authorize SBA to guarantee their loans—sometimes fully, more often up to 90 percent to the loan amount.

Private lenders can provide further help by advising small concerns on the availability of SBA financial assistance in the less well-known programs. Among these, the lease guarantee, federally displaced business, product disaster, and trade adjustment programs deserve the attention of eligible small concerns and their bankers.

These sales, with right ot recourse against SBA, give the private investors a full faith and credit government guarantee as to principal and accrued interest. Nevertheless, the procedure for selling debentures is cumbersome and the direct guarantee authority is infinitely preferable.

Anthony G. Chase is General Counsel of the Small Business Administration. He has a B.A. degree from the University of Washington and a J.D. degree from Georgetown University Law Center. Previously, Mr. Chase was in private law practice, and held the positions of Assistant to the Secretary of Commerce and Assistant to the Comptroller of the Currency.

James M. Proctor is Associate General Counsel for Finance, Small Business Administration. He has an A.B. degree from Princeton University and a J.D. degree from Georgetown Law Center. Before joining SBA, Mr. Proctor was in private law practice in Washington, D.C.

[1] Small Business Act of 1958, as amended, Pub. L. 85-699, July 18, 1958, 72 Stat. 384, 15 U.S.C. §631.
[2] Small Business Investment Act, Pub. L. 85-699, Title I, Aug. 21, 1958, 72 Stat. 689, 15 U.S.C. §§661-696 (1964 ed.), as amended, 15 U.S.C. §671 et seq. (Supp. V 1965-69).
[3] 15 U.S.C. §636(a) (1).
[4] 15 U.S.C. §636(a) (7).
[5] In participation and guaranty loans the individual loan can exceed $350,000 by the amount of the private lender's participation.
[6] When SBA purchases the guaranteed portion, it pays accrued interest to the date of purchase at a rate not in excess of 8% per annum. 13 C.F.R. Part 120, §120.3(b) (2) (iv), 34 F.R. 1945, 2248.
[7] 15 U.S.C. §636(b) (1), (2).
[8] 15 U.S.C. §636(b) (3).
[9] 15 U.S.C. §636(b) (4).
[10] 15 U.S.C. §636(e).
[11] 19 U.S.C. §1912.
[12] See Ascher, "Trade Policy Mechanism . . .", *International Commerce*, April 6, 1970, p. 6.

[13] H.R. 14870.

[14] 15 U.S.C. §636(b) (5).

[15] E.g., S.3528, 91st Cong., 2d Sess.

[16] 42 U.S.C. §2901.

[17] 15 U.S.C. §695.

[18] 15 U.S.C. §696.

[19] The small business concern being assisted may invest up to one-fourth of the required local injection in the LDC and this investment may be either equity or debt. (13 C.F.R. §108.502-1(e).)

[20] 15 U.S.C. §692.

[21] The statute fixes no maximum on the amount of rental that may be guaranteed under a single lease; however, SBA has administratively limited this to $9 million and imposes stricter screening procedures to all guarantees above $2.5 million.

[22] See Sections 243, 542, 1242, and 1243 of Internal Revenue Code, as amended (Title 26 of U.S. Code).

[23] In the fiscal year ended March 31, 1969, the return on invested capital for the SBIC industry was 9.5%; SBIC's with $1-5 million of invested capital and in operation for 5 years or more had a return of 12.1%, and the comparable figure for SBIC's with $5 million or more capital was 15.9%.

[24] Pub. L. 90-104, Oct. 11, 1967, 81 Stat. 268, effective on Jan. 9, 1968.

[25] Senate Report No. 368, 90th Cong., 1st Sess., June 27, 1967, 5-6.

[26] Subparagraph (2) of Section 302(b), added by Section 204 of SBI Act Amendments of 1967, fn. 5, *supra.*

[27] House Report No. 552, House Banking and Currency Committee, 90th Cong., 1st Sess., *Small Business Act Amendments of 1967,* Aug. 14, 1967, at 9-10.

[28] Pub. L. 91-152, 91st Cong., Dec. 23, 1969, 83 Stat. 371, 378.

[29] Compt. Gen. decision B-149685, Mar. 20, 1968.

[30] Fn. 11, *supra.*

[31] Section 201 of S.3699.

[32] SBIC Regulation, 13 C.F.R. Part 107 (Rev. as of Jan.1, 1970), amended by addition of new §107.813, 35 F.R. 11462, July 7, 1970.

[33] See James K. Brown, *"Arcata Investment Company, The Prototype 'MESBIC,'" The Conference Board Record,* Vol. VII, No. 4, Apr. 1970, 57; Burt Schorr, *"New Investment Firms Help Minority Groups Build Stake in Business," The Wall Street Journal,* May 5, 1970; *The MESBIC Consortium: A Chamber Plan for Participation in "Project Enterprise,"* An Urban Affairs Publication of the Chamber of Commerce of the United States, March 1970; Louis L. Allen, *"Making Capitalism Work in the Ghettos," Harvard Business Review,* May-June 1969, 83; "The Role of Banks in the Urban Challenge" (Addresses by David M. Kennedy and Donald M. Graham), Continental Illinois National Bank and Trust Company of Chicago, Dec. 9, 1968; Stanley M. Rubel, *"SBIC's at the Crossroads," Bankers Monthly Magazine,* July 15, 1969, 19; and Proceedings of ABA National Institute, Business in the Ghetto, April 11-12, 1969 (Collection of articles on Private Financing; Public Financing and Assistance; Franchising Problems; Problems of Locally Owned Business; Operations of National Companies; Consumer Credit; and Special Problems), 25 *The Business Lawyer* [Special Issue] Sept. 1969, 13-236.

[34] President Nixon's Message on Small Business (H. Doc. 91-284) was transmitted to the Congress on March 20, 1970. The accompanying legislative proposals, which have since been introduced as S. 3699 in the Senate and H.R. 16644 in the House of Representatives, were transmitted on March 23, 1970, by the Administrator of the Small Business Administration.

"This is a case where I'm going to give you one of these answers 'on one hand and on the other hand.' President Truman said, you know, he wanted one-armed economists so you couldn't do that."
—University of Minnesota Professor Walter W. Heller

by **Dr. Victor J. Danilov**
executive editor
Industrial Research

SOURCES OF VENTURE CAPITAL

Investors are ready to finance good ideas if

NEARLY EVERY scientist and engineer has considered — at one time or another—the feasibility of starting his own company. He is intrigued by the responsibility of running his own business, earning a fortune, and/or developing a successful product or service.

In most instances, however, such thinking rarely goes beyond the dream stage. The individual recognizes his shortcomings as an entrepreneur; does not want to jeopardize his security; fails to develop a marketable idea; or lacks the necessary funds to launch a new company.

The lack of sufficient capital probably is the most common obstacle to the birth and success of new science- and technical-based companies. Without financial resources, it is virtually impossible even for the most daring individual or the best idea to succeed.

Before World War II, there was little hope of obtaining financial assistance from the outside, unless it came from relatives, friends, or an occasional private investor.

Commercial banks were not set up to provide "venture" or "risk" capital. Restricted by banking regulations and tradition, they could make only short-term loans, and then only with ample collateral.

Investment bankers were reluctant to supply the funds or to handle the sale of securities for a new company with limited resources and little or no record of performance.

But things are different today. It is possible to obtain venture capital from a number of sources, including some commercial and investment bankers under certain circumstances.

This change was brought about by the postwar establishment of venture capital investment groups that specialize in funding high-risk enterprises, often based on scientific or technological advances.

As a result, it is much easier for a scientist or engineer to start his own company—providing he is willing to share the ownership.

The venture capital groups are interested primarily in "capital gain," and therefore seek to exchange cash for "equity"—a portion of the ownership. They are not in the loan business, although they occasionally will lend urgently needed funds to companies in their "portfolio."

The amount of equity that an entrepreneur must give up will vary with the size and nature of the investment, the record and worth of the company, and the bargaining abilities of the parties involved.

Sometimes, an investment is stalled because the individual refuses to surrender a portion of the stock in return for the capital. In such cases, venture capital representatives frequently will tell the entrepreneur that he is better off with a share of a well-financed company than with 100% of a failing one. And they generally are right.

It takes more than a willingness to give up equity to obtain venture capital. The venture capital groups are besieged by men and women seeking financing at almost any cost. Perhaps that is why the odds against obtaining venture capital are so high—something like 25 or 50 to 1.

Venture capital groups usually require a detailed report that includes: a brief history of the company; a description of its facilities, products, and services; an analysis of the present and future market; financial statements; a projection of sales, cash flow, and financial needs; biographical sketches of key personnel; personal, business, and technical references; the names of principal suppliers and customers; and other such pertinent information.

It normally takes about six to eight weeks for an investment application to be processed. During this time, the venture capital group checks on the performance and integrity of the principals; reviews the company's products, markets, and competition; studies the firm's organizational structure, facilities, and potential; and considers the financial and other plans.

Some applications are rejected almost upon presentation because insufficient time is allowed for appraisal; the project needs further development before it can be evaluated; the company's growth opportunities appear limited; the proposed valuation of the project or stock is unrealistic; and the company's plans are inconsistent with the venture capital firm's long-range objectives.

Three stages of investment

Venture capital groups ordinarily are interested in investing at three stages in a company's development:

■ "Start-up" or "seed" money to

PRODUCTS DEVELOPED *with the aid of venture capital take many forms. They include: a Cryonetics variable temperature cryostat (left); an Itek image motion stabilization system (upper left); a GCA subsidiary vacuum annealing furnace (upper right); and a Potter Instrument random access memory system (right).*

the entrepreneur is willing to share ownership.

finance launching of an enterprise.

■ "Venture" funds to carry the company to a size where it can secure capital and loans from the public stock market, commercial banks, and other conventional sources.

■ "Growth" capital for major expansion of the company.

Of the three stages, the first appears to have the least appeal to many venture capital people. It is the riskiest type of investment. However, it also promises the greatest gain.

Most venture capital groups prefer to have what they call a "track record" on investment applicants. This means they would like to see the entrepreneur start the business on his own, and then come to them after some years of operation. In this way, they feel they are better able to evaluate the performance and potential of the man and his company.

If an applicant lacks this background, venture capital representatives sometimes will equate experience as a manager or similar position of responsibility in their evaluation.

In preparing this article, *Industrial Research* found that nearly all major venture capital groups gave as much weight — if not more — to "management" as they did to the "idea" in evaluating investment opportunities.

Most venture capital officials said good ideas are plentiful, but that good management people who can exploit ideas are rare. As a result, many promising innovations are bypassed by venture capital groups simply because the principals do not appear to possess the necessary qualities.

Venture capital groups prefer "management teams" rather than "one-man shows." They feel management depth is essential because of the diversity of talents required in a growing company built on scientific or technological know-how. They also regard the team approach as a safeguard on their investment.

The amount of capital that can be raised from venture capital sources ranges from a few thousand to several million dollars. However, most venture capital firms rarely are interested in investments below $100,000 and seldom will go above $1-million. If there is a preference, it is between $200,000 and $300,000. This is a substantial investment that gives the venture capital group a sizeable interest in the typical company—without being a drain on its resources.

If the company's progress is satisfactory and additional financing is required at a later date, the venture capital firm generally will provide the funds or arrange for credit through conventional or other capital sources.

The three most common types of equity investments made by venture capital organizations are:

■ Common stock. The exchange of cash for shares is the most frequently employed investment method.

■ Convertible debentures. In this case, the venture capital firm lends money to the company and receives a debenture (a note of indebtedness). The investment group then either can accept repayment of the loan or convert the debenture into an equivalent amount of the company's common

stock at a pre-arranged price.

■ Loans with warrants. In return for a loan, the company issues warrants that gives the venture capital firm an option to purchase common stock—usually at a favorable price—during a specified period of time.

Venture capital groups often expect to have one or more representatives on the board of directors as a result of their investment. They also believe that serious consideration should be given to their "suggestions."

Among the typical suggestions are: a working board with regular meetings; the hiring of a competent financial officer; and preparation of periodic progress reports and financial statements.

The venture capital firm sometimes will offer so-called "management services," which may include such things as staff assistance, financial planning, and marketing guidance. A nominal fee usually is charged for such services.

In general, venture capital organizations are not interested in having controlling interest in a company. Some believe control discourages management. On the other hand, venture capital groups tend to stay away from investments that give them less than 10% of the stock. They feel they are not able to be effective in such a minority position, and that the returns are not worth the effort. An investment of 20% to 30%, therefore, is more common.

Although goals vary, most venture capital firms hope to double their investments in three years and triple

Management abilities are considered as important—if not more in the evaluation of the venture growth and

their money in five years. But it seldom works out that way. Some companies fail, while others succeed beyond the most optimistic forecasts.

The basic venture capital objective is quite simple—to make the company grow and prosper so that its stock can be traded publicly or that it can be merged with a larger company. In either case, the venture capital firm benefits by receiving a considerably higher price for its investment.

Ideally, the entrepreneur who conceived the company and led it to success also benefits in the process. In most instances, he and his associates gain even more than the venture capital group. Unfortunately, this is not always the case. Sometimes the entrepreneur loses control in his fight for survival, and occasionally he has to be replaced because of his lack of management abilities.

Today, there are at least 11 principal sources of venture capital. Of this number, five can be considered general sources and six can be classified as specialists in venture capital.

The general sources are: relatives and friends, commercial banks, investment bankers, private investors, and large companies. Each has its advantages and drawbacks.

Aside from personal savings, the most common source of new venture funding is the entrepreneur's relatives and friends. However, the financing frequently is insufficient to provide the impetus and the continuing support needed "to make it big."

Although still conservative, some commercial banks have become a source of limited venture capital. In many cases, they will make short-term loans as part of a financing package worked out with a wholly owned or affiliated small business investment company that specializes in long-term equity investments.

The investment banker can assist the entrepreneur in at least three ways—he can invest in the company himself, either personally or as a firm; he can arrange for private placement with wealthy individuals; or he can handle the public offering of the stock. Unfortunately, it usually is necessary for the company to be firmly established and to pay a premium for the service.

Private investors — who generally learn about venture capital opportunities through commercial and investment bankers—quite often are willing to invest large sums in speculative

ventures. However, they sometimes are impatient about the bonanza.

A large corporation occasionally will invest in a smaller company, especially if the former is interested in diversifying and the latter is a supplier. But the arrangement can be unhealthy from a business standpoint.

Six major sources

In addition to the foregoing general investment groups, there are six types that specialize in venture capital funding. It is in this area that most of the high-risk financing is taking place today.

The six major venture capital sources are:

■ The venture capital arms of family fortunes, such as the Phipps, Rosenwalds, Whitneys, and Rockefellers.

■ Publicly held venture capital corporations typified by American Research & Development Corp. of Boston.

■ Private venture capital organizations, such as Payson & Trask in New York and Davis & Rock of San Francisco.

■ Informal investment syndicates, usually made up of Wall Street financiers and arranged by investment bankers and lawyers.

■ Small business investment companies (SBICs) licensed and partially financed by the federal government to assist small businesses.

■ State-licensed business development corporations designed to further the state or regional economy. Unlike the others, the development funds usually are interested in making mortgage loans rather than equity investments.

Perhaps the best way to obtain a better insight into venture capital financing is to take a closer look at some of the organizations that are active in the field.

Although history is filled with instances where individuals—and some companies — made available venture capital "for a share of the action," it was not until after World War II that the concept was formalized with the establishment of a number of private and publicly held venture capital investment groups.

Two of the early entries in the venture capital field were Bessemer Securities Corp., established in 1924 by Henry C. Phipps, co-founder of the Carnegie steel empire, and the Starwood Corp., created in 1929 by Julius Rosenwald, then chairman of Sears, Roebuck, & Co.

Although Bessemer made an occasional venture capital investment in the 1920s and 1930s, it was not until after World War II that a "special situations" office was formed to seek out such investments.

At present, Bessemer has about $20-million in venture capital invested in some 30 companies, with approximately half in the technical field. The companies include firms in such diverse areas as magnetics, cryogenics, electronics, oceanography, testing, instruments, and mining.

The Rosenwald family investment firm was known for many years as the NWL Corp. before it become Starwood Corp. in 1960. It was named after Nathan W. Levin, who directed the investments for more than 30 years.

It was Rosenwald money that helped to establish such companies as Litton Industries Inc., Southern Nitrogen Co., and Fansteel Metallurgical Corp.

Starwood has made 14 major investments and six minor financings in recent years. Among the current investments are Nuclear Materials & Equipment Corp., nuclear materials; Trans-Video Corp., community television antennas; and General Corp. of Ohio, insurance.

One of Starwood's most successful ventures was United Technical Publications, which publishes *Electronics Products*, *Electronic Engineers Master*, and other publications. Starwood and American Research & Development Corp. invested $500,000 in United Technical Publications in 1963 for a 51% interest. Early this year, the stock was sold for $5.5-million.

Prewar ventures pay off

Some of the prewar experiences of John Hay Whitney and Laurance S. Rockefeller convinced them that they could make money while being of assistance to inventive minds.

"Jock" Whitney inherited about a third of his father's $250-million estate in 1927. Upon graduation from college, he joined the Lee, Higginson, & Co. brokerage and investment house in New York. While learning the investment business, he became acquainted with Langbourne Williams, a former Lee, Higginson man, who was fighting to gain control of a sulfur company called Freeport Texas.

Because he liked Williams and was convinced of the merits of the latter's case against the Freeport management, Whitney invested $500,000 in the company's common stock. Williams

so—than the excellence of the idea or product
investment potential of new technically oriented companies.

succeeded in his bid and helped elect Whitney as chairman of Freeport's reorganized board—a position held by Whitney until 1957.

Meanwhile, the company's name was changed to Freeport Sulphur and Whitney's original investment grew to more than $10-million. During this period, Whitney also dabbled in an assortment of other ventures.

He helped to finance the development and introduction of the "Technicolor" film process; backed the production of the most successful motion picture in history, "Gone with the Wind;" and put money into a number of publications, including *Newsweek* and *Scientific American*.

After returning from World War II service, Whitney formed J. H. Whitney & Co. with four partners, most of whom were lawyers or investment bankers. With $10-million in capital, the partnership sought to invest in venture capital opportunities found to be "interesting, attractive, and constructive."

Among the early investments were the Spencer Chemical nitrogen chemical firm, the Minute Maid frozen orange juice idea, and San Jacinto Petroleum, an oil and gas producer. All became highly successful, with the Whitney partnership selling its stock at sizeable profits.

However, there also were failures, such as Standard Perlite wallboard from volcanic ash, Kyptar photographic film, Circuitron printed circuits, and Hodges Research & Development.

Since its founding 20 years ago, J. H. Whitney & Co. has received more than 8,000 investment proposals and made about 80 investments—or approximately 1 out of 100 solicitations. It is difficult to calculate how much of a return the company has received on its initial $10-million in capital, but a safe estimate would be that it has been multiplied at least 12 times. More than four-fifths has come from seven key investments.

Among the recent Whitney investments have been General Signal electronic and electrical appliances, Global Marine Exploration floating oil drilling vessels, Memorex computer and instrumentation, and Peninsular Chemresearch specialty fluoride chemicals.

Laurance S. Rockefeller also became interested in venture capital in the 1930s. He made his first risk capital investment in 1938 when he res-

cued one of his boyhood heroes, Capt. Eddie Rickenbacker, who was about to lose control of the young, struggling Eastern Air Lines.

Rockefeller helped to round up $3.5-million to refinance the airline. He bought 24,400 shares of Eastern at $9. The original $219,000 investment—and subsequent purchases — now are worth millions and Rockefeller is Eastern's largest stockholder.

In 1939, the young Rockefeller helped out another pioneer in the airplane field, J. S. McDonnell, who sought funds to develop an advanced type of fighter that was still on the drawing board. Rockefeller put up $10,000 to help McDonnell Aircraft Corp. get its start. When the holdings became worth $400,000, he sold out to reinvest in another new idea.

Immediately following World War II, Rockefeller resumed his venture capital investments by putting $500,-000 into a sputtering rocket company, Reaction Motors. When the firm—which helped to develop the jet engine—was merged with Thiokol Chemical Corp. in 1958, Rockefeller received Thiokol stock worth more than $4-million for his investment.

During the postwar period, Rockefeller decided to expand his venture capital operations. He added a staff to seek out promising ideas worthy of venture capital support, with the emphasis in two areas—aerospace and electronics.

In 1950, several thousands in Rockefeller money was invested in the Marquardt Aircraft Co., which was working on ramjet propulsion. A few years later, the investment was worth millions when Marquardt began making ramjets for the Bomarc missile.

When the Itek Corp. was organized in 1957 to develop optical information-handling equipment, Rockefeller was asked to provide some of the seed money. He invested $875,000, which became worth approximately $10-million in two years.

Successes—and failures

Among the Rockefeller venture capital investments in recent years have been the GCA Corp. (formerly Geophysics Corp. of America), United Nuclear Corp., Mithras Inc., Scientific-Atlanta, Electronic Specialties, Thermo Electron Engineering Corp., and Cryonetics Corp. (Magnion Inc.).

Some of the investments have been sold off, including Piasecki Helicopter (now Boeing's Vertol Div.), Air-

borne Instruments Laboratory (Cutler-Hammer), Aircraft Radio Corp. (Cessna), and General Applied Science Laboratories (Marquardt).

As with Whitney, a number of Rockefeller's investments fell flat. For example, the Wallace Aviation Corp. was sold at a loss when its cold-metal process for making jet engine compressors proved to be more costly than conventional methods.

Two other ventures that failed were Platt LePage & Co., in the helicopter field, and Island Packers, a canning endeavor that folded from the lack of fish.

Rockefeller's venture capital efforts differ from others in two principal respects:

■ Sometimes the idea for a new company will be conceived within the organization, and then a management team will be recruited to operate the company, as was done with GCA Corp.

■ Investments usually are made on a one-third ratio basis, with management, Rockefeller, and an investment partner sharing equally.

When GCA was founded in 1958, Milton Greenberg, director of the Air Force's Geophysics Research Directorate, was sought out and hired as the person best qualified to run the company. In return, Greenberg and other top scientists and officers in the company were given one-third of the equity.

Rockefeller is an unusual venture capitalist in several other respects. With a personal fortune estimated at around $200-million, he hardly needs high-risk investments. But he believes that the wealthy have a social responsibility to risk their riches, to assist creative minds, and to support constructive projects.

It was the early venture capital exploits of Rosenwald, Whitney, and Rockefeller that called attention to the need for—and opportunities in—high-risk investments based in science and technology.

However, it was not until after World War II that investment firms specializing in venture capital came into being. The technological explosion during and after the war contributed to this development.

The first publicly held venture capital corporation was founded in Boston in 1946. It was established by a group of civic-minded business leaders who recognized the need for providing financial support for new ideas that offer promise of higher production, employment, and living standards.

Today, American Research & Development Corp. is one of the largest and most successful venture capital organizations. It has investments in 44 companies and net assets of approximately $80-million.

ARD was conceived primarily by two men—Ralph E. Flanders, president of the Boston Federal Reserve Board who later represented Vermont in the Senate, and Merrill Griswold, chairman of the Massachusetts Investors Trust.

They were aided by Dr. Karl T. Compton, then president of Massachusetts Institute of Technology; Gen. Georges Doriot, a professor of industrial management at Harvard Business School who served in the Army as director of the Military Planning Div. of the Office of the Quartermaster General during World War II; and a group of financiers who helped to provide the initial capital of nearly $3.4-million.

Included in this latter group were: Paul F. Clark, president of John Hancock Life Insurance Co.; Lessing J. Rosenwald, chairman of Sears, Roebuck, & Co.; David L. Luke, president of West Virginia Pulp & Paper Co.; and Thomas Lamont, chairman of J. P. Morgan & Co.

Flanders served as the first president of ARD, but turned the job over to Doriot in the first year following his election to the Senate. The soft-spoken "General" has headed ARD ever since.

Helps start 80 companies

During its 20 years of operation, American Research & Development Corp. has helped to father more than 80 companies — nearly all based on technological innovations.

One of ARD's first ventures was High Voltage Engineering Corp. It invested $200,000 in MIT Professor Robert J. Van de Graaff's research in supervoltages, which produced the so-called "Van de Graaff" accelerator. While ARD's holdings in the company have decreased from 55% to 6% of the voting securities, the investment has resulted in a gain of more than $16-million over the years.

There are many similar success stories among ARD's diversified investments. For instance, a $403,000 investment in Ionics Inc., which specializes in electrochemical and membrane processes for desalination, is now worth almost $3-million; a $581,-339 investment in Teledyne Inc., a manufacturer of aviation and geo-

physical instruments, has appreciated to $5.6-million; and a $1.2-million interest in Optical Scanning Corp. (formerly Digitek Corp.), a producer of optical mark sensing equipment, grew to over $3-million within six years.

The most recent big winner is Digital Equipment Corp., which makes equipment to gather, store, and process data. ARD helped to establish the company with a $408,125 investment in 1957. Digital Equipment went public last August, and now ARD's interest in the computer upstart is worth more than $40-million.

Among the other companies in ARD's portfolio are: Adage Inc., hybrid computers; Camco Inc., petroleum tools and services; Giannini Controls Corp., electronic instruments and controls; Solid State Products Inc., specialized semiconductors; Cordis Corp., medical instrumentation; Cooper, Tinsley Laboratories Inc., pharmaceuticals, and Tridair Industries, air cargo equipment.

Under Doriot's leadership, American Research & Development Corp. has been instrumental in establishing similar venture capital investment groups in Canada and Europe in the last four years.

ARD has a $464,305 investment (9% of the voting securities) in Canadian Enterprise Development Corp. and a $511,642 interest (8%) in the European Enterprises Development Co.

Thus far, the two foreign groups have made only limited investments, but they show the potential of duplicating ARD's record in this country.

Doriot points out that ARD has no specific formula for financing projects. "Each investment opportunity is considered separately, and the form of participation is tailored to meet the individual requirements of the situation." However, ARD does seek an equity position or its equivalent in all ventures.

The amount of capital invested also is flexible. In general, initial investments are in the $50,000 to $1-million range. "But situations requiring capital in excess of $1-million also are of decided interest, regardless of the field," adds Doriot.

In cases where substantial capital or specialized assistance is needed, ARD sometimes will obtain the support of other groups in the investment.

Despite the care exercised in investments, ARD has had its share of losers. In fact, the very first investment—in a degreasing gun—flopped. Among its other failures have been

companies involved in quick-frozen apple juice, deveined shrimp, audio devices, and tuna processing.

Marriage of money and talent

Another venture capital investment firm that was born following World War II was the partnership of Payson & Trask in New York. In this instance, it was a marriage of the money of Mrs. Charles S. Payson (the former Joan Whitney) and the investment skills of Frederick K. Trask, a commercial banker.

The firm was organized in 1947 by Mrs. Payson, who has used her share of the Whitney fortune to invest in industry, entertainment, and sports and to support worthy projects in medicine, education, fine arts, and charity. She is best known as owner of the New York Mets baseball team.

Mrs. Payson put up several million dollars and gave Trask a free hand in organizing and developing the firm. Since then, the firm has invested in approximately 60 companies. It currently has an interest in 25 companies, with about half being technical.

Unlike many other venture capital firms, Payson & Trask is not interested in financing the launching of new companies. It prefers to wait until the company has existed a year or two before considering investment.

Payson & Trask makes investments ranging from $25,000 to $500,000. Although it does not seek control, the firm wants a "position of consequence" in investments, according to Marshall Rawle, managing partner. This means at least 20% to 60% of the equity and one or two representatives on the board.

'Management' is key

The most significant factor in a company appraisal is "management," states Robert D. Stillman, one of the partners. Although the firm does not have a checklist of desirable management characteristics, it has found that successful managements usually exhibit a combination of "high character and integrity, dedication and energy, solid technical competence, humility in financial and business areas, and the flexibility to meet changing conditions," Stillman explains.

Among the investments of Payson & Trask have been: Hartford Steel Ball Co., Ohio Rubber Co., Trygon Electronics Inc., Hampshire Chemical Corp., Crystalonics Inc., United States Instrument Corp., and Maumee Chemical Co. (recently merged with Sherwin-Williams).

Innovators frequently are told that a share of a

A number of venture capital firms have followed in the footsteps of Payson & Trask. Among the leaders are Davis & Rock of San Francisco; Draper, Gaither, & Anderson of Palo Alto; and Fox, Wells, & Rogers of Stamford, Conn.

Davis & Rock probably has had the fastest growth among all the venture capital investment firms. From a modest beginning several years ago, it has earned more than $30-million.

The man largely responsible for this success is Arthur Rock, a virtually penniless security analyst who became a millionaire through his venture capital investments.

The whole thing started in 1957 when Rock was working on underwriting deals for Hayden, Stone Inc. He learned about a group of Beckman Instruments scientists who wanted to start their own company. Within a few months, Rock helped to arrange financing for the group from Fairchild Camera & Instrument.

The new company was called Fairchild Semiconductor. It flourished so well that two years later Fairchild Camera & Instrument exercised an option and bought control for $3-million in stock.

The coup increased Rock's bankroll and threw the spotlight on a dozen glamour stocks that he had recommended in a series of market letters for Hayden, Stone Inc.

In 1961, he cautioned investors that the stocks had gone too high. Again, Rock proved right, as many of the leaders became victims of the 1961-62 crash in electronic stocks.

It was at this time that Rock left Hayden, Stone (although he remains a limited partner) and joined with Thomas J. Davis Jr., a lawyer and former vice president of Kern County Land, to form the venture capital partnership of Davis & Rock. The initial capital of $3.5-million was provided by some 30 investors.

Then came a series of investments that brought fame and fortune:

■ The first deal was to exchange $200,000 of D&R stock for 13,333 shares of Teledyne Inc., which was started with Rock's aid in 1961 by two Litton Industries vice presidents. Later, D&R paid $460,000 for another 15,932 shares. The investment has nearly tripled in value since then.

■ The second major investment was in Scientific Data Systems, formed by a spinoff group from Packard-Bell's ailing computer division. Davis & Rock invested $280,000 in SDS. In 1965, SDS netted $3-million in profits

from sales of some $45-million. D&R's capital gain amounted to more than $20-million.

■ The third development was Astrodata Inc., a spinoff from Epsco Inc., a producer of data processing equipment. Davis & Rock bought 60,000 shares for $5 per share and earned a profit of $2-million in two years.

One of the newest partnerships in the venture capital field is Greylock & Co., a Boston-headquartered firm backed by a group of six prominent families for the purpose of equity capital investments. It was formed a year ago.

The general partners are William Elfers, a former vice president of American Research & Development Corp., and Daniel S. Gregory, formerly assistant to the president of John P. Chase Inc., investment counselor and mutual fund manager.

Greylock & Co. invests principally in young growth companies having promising records and needing developmental capital, and established small- or medium-sized companies which are beginning new expansion programs or bringing in outside participants for the first time. It is interested in investments in the range of $200,000 to $600,000.

686 SBICs established

The greatest number of venture capital investment firms are SBICs that were spawned by the Small Business Investment Act of 1958. At the last counting, there were 686 licensed small business investment companies. They have made available nearly $1-billion to small businesses in over 20,000 separate transactions since the act was passed eight years ago.

A business is considered "small" and eligible for SBIC financing if its assets do not exceed $5-million; its net assets are not more than $2.5-million; and its average net income after taxes for each of the preceding two years was under $250,000 (without benefit of tax loss carry-forward).

The SBICs come in all sizes and types. Their individual capitalization ranges from $300,000 to $29-million. Some are quite broad and others are highly specialized. Of the 686 small business investment companies, only about two-thirds are active.

Most of the SBICs are owned by relatively small groups of local investors. However, the stock of about 50 is publicly traded; more than 80 SBICs are partially or wholly owned by commercial banks; and some are subsidiaries of other corporations.

An SBIC may borrow up to double its private investment from the federal government, with a maximum government participation of $4.7-million. It may use this money to finance small businesses in three ways — by straight loans, equity-type investments, or a combination of the two. All financings must be for at least five years, except that a borrower may elect to have a prepayment clause included in the financing agreement.

An SBIC may invest up to 20% of its capital in a single small business. For the smallest SBIC, the maximum loan or investment is $60,000; the largest is several million dollars.

SBICs can be found in all but six states (Maine, Nevada, North Dakota, South Dakota, Vermont, and Wyoming). Nearly half (330), however, are located in only four states— California with 118, New York with 102, Texas with 56, and Massachusetts with 54.

Of the 686 small business investment companies, about 30 have scientific or technological implications in their names. To this list could be added another 20 that have extensive investments in the science- or technical-based enterprises.

Among the leading SBICs are the Boston Capital Corp. of Boston, Narragansett Capital Corp. of Providence, Midland Capital Corp. of New York, Greater Washington Industrial Investments Inc. of Washington D.C., First Capital Corp. of Chicago, Continental Capital Corp. of San Francisco, and Electronics Capital Corp. of San Diego (which is the largest).

All have heavy investments in companies based on scientific and technological innovations. They have started or given financial assistance to such companies as Potter Instrument Co., Possis Machine Corp., C-E-I-R Inc., Defense Research Corp., Tyco Laboratories Inc., B & F Instruments Inc., Data Products Inc., Basic Systems Inc., and Alpine Geophysical Associates Inc.

The 686 licensed SBICs currently are undergoing a thorough investigation by the Small Business Administration as a result of a Congressional probe into alleged irregularities in their operations, such as impairment of capital, the making of speculative real estate loans, failure to invest government funds, and disregard for reporting procedures. However, it does not appear that any of the leading SBICs are involved.

The business development corporations licensed by states are compar-

successful firm is better than 100% of nothing.

able—in some respects—to the small business investment companies at the federal level. The principal difference is in their primary purpose—to serve a public need rather than to make a substantial profit. Another difference is the emphasis on long-term mortgage loans.

Although most are designed only to make high-risk, long-term loans as a means of helping industry and the economy to grow, a few also are interested in minority equity investments. The Southeastern Pennsylvania Development Fund, for example, frequently will make loans in which a portion can be converted to equity at a favorable price.

There are 24 business development corporations in 22 states. Only Pennsylvania — with three groups — has more than one business development corporation.

The first state business development corporation was the Development Credit Corp. of Maine, which was formed in 1949. The newest was just established in Colorado. The stockholders in nearly all business development corporations are business and civic leaders in the state.

The venture capital concept has proved so successful in the United States that similar investment groups are being formed in other countries.

In addition to the venture organizations in Canada and Europe that were mentioned earlier, there are comparable investment groups in Great Britain, Sweden, and Japan.

There are two major groups in Great Britain—the government-sponsored National Research Development Corp. and the privately financed Industrial & Commercial Finance Corp., which recently absorbed Technical Development Capital Ltd.

Established in 1948, the NRDC is an independent corporation financed by government loans and the income from licensing. Its primary objective is to promote the adoption by industry of new products and processes invented in government, university, and private laboratories by advancing money where necessary to bring them to a commercial stage.

The privately funded ICFC offers long-term financing in return for an equity interest. It has made investments in more than 1,700 companies since is was founded two decades ago.

Incentive AB was organized in Sweden three years ago and has venture capital investments in about a dozen companies. It is patterned after American Research & Development Corp.

In Japan, three small business investment companies have been organized under a 1963 act based on the American SBIC program. The investment groups—in Tokyo, Nogoya, and Osaka — only invest in "joint-stock companies" with a capital of less than 50-million yen ($139,000) or no more than 300 employes.

There appears to be ample venture capital available in this country—and to some extent abroad—if a scientist or engineer has a good idea, possesses management talents, and wants to start his own business.

There are a variety of sources looking for high-risk investments with promising growth potential. Frequently, these sources also offer invaluable management services in addition to financial aid.

But the aspiring entrepreneur usually must pay a price—the sharing of equity and some degree of control for cash and other assistance. And if business does not develop as anticipated, he even may find his company sold against his wishes.

This may appear to be a cruel world to the person who lacks the funds to exploit his idea. However, it also can be a happy one under the right circumstances.

Venture capital meets a definite need in science, industry, and the economy. But it is not free or without risk — for either the entrepreneur or the investor. ■

■ **Robert E. Marcum**
Booz, Allen & Hamilton
and
Edward O. Boshell, Jr.
H. M. Byllesby & Co.

Financing the Small and
Medium-Size Business

THE DEVELOPMENT of new industries, of new enterprises in older industries, or of new ventures by established firms obviously requires funds—and in many cases the companies involved aren't able to enter national credit markets to get them.

Where, then, can such a company obtain financing for its ventures?

This is a problem that is being faced today by many companies, particularly since the recent stock market decline, which has caused some firms to defer equity issues

---

A MANAGEMENT REVIEW SPECIAL FEATURE

MANAGEMENT REVIEW

and turn to other sources for needed capital. It is being faced by small and medium-size companies that want to expand or diversify their operations, as well as by new enterprises that are just getting set up in business. And, although it's true that no one is beating down their doors to force money on them, there are many sources of funds that such companies can tap to meet their needs. These sources fall logically into two main categories: debt sources and equity sources.

Debt Sources of Funds

The largest volume of funds for small and medium-size businesses does not come directly from conventional lenders and investors, but arises from selling transactions—that is, interbusiness credit. Through trade credit, a firm that is barred access to particular capital markets because of high costs can be financed indirectly by these same capital markets at lower rates because of the interposition of a selling firm with a better credit standing. This is not only the largest volume source, but it is apparently one of the easiest to tap; in fact, trade credit seems to expand in response to tight money policy.

Short-term capital is furnished almost exclusively by commercial banks. Because loans to smaller companies are usually small, the cost of lending becomes a greater proportion of the loan, and these loans are less profitable. Moreover,

smaller concerns are usually poorer credit risks. Why, then, do banks approve such a high percentage of loan applications? There seem to be four reasons: (1) the desire to create an image of progressiveness and civic-mindedness; (2) competitive pressures for new business; (3) personal introductions and pressures from existing customers; and (4) the possibility that smaller businesses will grow and become profitable customers.

Banks do, of course, refuse loan requests—most frequently because of the inadequacy of the owner's equity in the business, poor earnings, and questionable management ability. Moreover, some businesses are simply not profitable enough to pay the charges lenders would be obliged to make if they covered all costs and netted a return on capital.

These problems are accentuated in the case of new businesses. The new business can seldom obtain an unsecured loan, and banks require more collateral of a new business than of other borrowers, the loans often being secured by both company and personal assets. Generally, however, they will lend to new businesses.

Long-Term Credit

A company that has shown some evidence of success can obtain long-term capital for expansion purposes. Although banks prefer short-term credit, they do, in fact, supply about 80 per cent of the long-term capital borrowed by smaller firms for expansion.

Besides the commercial banks, the following are potential suppliers of longer-term debt:

- Life insurance companies
- Commercial credit corporations
- Savings and loan associations
- Trust companies
- Pension plan trusts
- Factors
- Small Business Administration
- State development credit corporations

Although all these are potential suppliers of credit, there is a considerable range of actual participation.

Little information is available about savings and loan associations, but these companies have tended to concentrate on the consumer mortgage market rather than the market for business loans. In so conservative an operation as trust funds are reported to be, venture funds would surely be rare. Commercial credit corporations and factors provide a very small amount of the long-term debt consumed by the smaller business.

There is evidence that conventional financing institutions such as insurance companies and savings institutions of all kinds are endeavoring to tap the small-business sector of the economy as a field for long-term investment. Intermediaries through which they could do so on a substantial scale have only recently been developed in the form of the small business investment companies. However, the SBIC's have yet to prove themselves to insurance and savings institutions and therefore are not yet effective as intermediaries.

Laws and Restrictions

The problems of dealing directly with an insurance company are great. The companies are bound by numerous laws and regulations that vary from state to state, but in general, before they can accept a long-term unsecured obligation, the earning power of the borrowing firm must have been sufficient to cover one and a half times the interest charge for five years on the average, and including the past year. No new venture, no matter how meritorious, can be considered unless the company has enough physical assets to be the subject of a mortgage.

Although the Small Business Administration is organized for the express purpose of making long-term loans to small businesses, certain restrictions in the operation of the SBA prohibit it from meeting all the long-term loan requirements of small business. These restrictions are: (1) The loans must be of sound value, or so secured as reasonably to insure repayment; (2) the loan may not be in excess of $250,000; and (3) the loan may not exceed a ten-year term. Although the last two regulations are not particularly burdensome to small business, the first is restrictive enough to reduce the value of the SBA as a source of funds for many small companies. A recent study indicated that the combined loan and commitment total for the SBA and the Veterans Administration amounted to less than 4 per cent of small business loans outstanding at Federal Reserve member banks.

The function of state development credit corporations is to stimulate a state's economic prosperity. Usually, a business may apply for a credit corporation loan only if it cannot obtain enough credit from conventional sources. In the states where development credit corporations are active, the lending by these institutions was recently found to amount to about 2 per cent of the small business loans of commercial banks.

Both the SBA and state development credit corporations are said to accept greater risks than conventional institutions. Nevertheless, neither of them make loans to new businesses.

Cost of Loans

In general, smaller firms pay higher rates of interest for debt funds of all maturities than do larger firms. This is a reflection of the greater risk involved for the lender and the higher proportional cost of making smaller loans. In addition to paying a higher rate, the small borrower pays a less flexible rate of interest at banks than does the large borrower. The inability of smaller borrowers to turn elsewhere for funds when money is tight apparently restricts their ability to evade high interest rates.

It is interesting to note that some firms—probably companies in which the asset value is almost pure equity—are able to get loans equal to their total asset value, and it is not unusual to find banks willing to match the amount of a small firm's equity with loaned funds.

Credit ratings apparently reflect the credit-worthiness of all sizes of firms equally well. Therefore, companies that establish and preserve a reputation for credit-worthiness should be able to obtain funds to the extent of the amount of the equity, at least for the short term. The general uncertainty of the fortunes of small businesses may stand forever in the way of their ever being substantial users of long-term credit.

Equity Sources of Funds

Excluding the personal savings of individual owners of businesses, their friends and relatives, and retained earnings of the business, the following are the principal sources of equity funds that are actually being tapped with some degree of success:

- Wealthy individuals
- Family estates
- Partners and associates in investment banking houses

- Investment banking firms, for their own account
- Closed-end investment companies
- Venture-capital firms
- Pension funds
- Nonfinancial corporations seeking diversification
- Dissatisfied corporate officers
- Wealthy men seeking active management roles
- Retired or semiretired businessmen
- Previous employees
- Suppliers
- Customers
- Employees
- The security markets

In practice, by far the largest block of equity capital put into a new business comes from the entrepreneur, and relatives and friends seem to be the next most significant source of funds. Local capitalists and business firms have supplied fairly large amounts of capital in financing a relatively few firms.

In ferreting out funds, businessmen often call on middlemen who are in an especially advantageous position to know of possible sources. These middlemen include tax lawyers or accountants with wealthy clients, management consultants, investment banking houses, commercial banks, brokerage firms, and patent attorneys. They usually charge a finder's fee ranging from 3 per cent for amounts near a million dollars to 5 or 10 per cent for lesser amounts.

It is a common practice for several investors to bank together to supply the funds needed. Individual investments are usually in the $5,000-to-$50,000 range; the total sum invested by one group in any firm will often be in the range of $100,000 to $1,000,000. Individual investors usually consider their investment a one-shot affair, and they are not able or willing to provide follow-up shots of capital. On the other hand, venture-capital firms and investment companies are often prepared to provide additional funds if the ultimate expectation continues to be promising.

Wheeling and Dealing

The professional suppliers of equity capital report that there is a widespread demand by small businesses for loan funds, particularly for long terms—but the financial condition of small companies often does not justify long-term loans. When the proprietor of such a business finds he cannot get capital in loan form, his next step is to find the specialized investors who are willing to put money into his venture. Basically, this is a process of negotiating, bargaining, or dealing. A venture-capital firm or an investment company usually screens each application carefully before investing for its own account or recommending the situation to others. The evaluation undertaken by individual investors is usually less formal and less vigorous.

Wealthy individual investors, especially those who band together into an investing group, seem to accept the judgment of friends or of any person who acts as leader of the group.

Venture-capital firms often supply continuing financial and management advice to the firm in which they have acquired an interest. In contrast, few individual investors want to assume managerial responsibility. Most investors, however, feel the need for some kind of ultimate or contingent control in order to protect their interest, and representation on the board of directors is the most common means of satisfying this need.

Once having started, most firms are obliged to depend on retained earnings as the primary source of additional capital. For new or small firms, this is often an unreliable source of funds, and if a firm suffers reverses, outside capital may be essential to continue operations. Unfortunately, outside capital is often quite difficult to obtain under these circumstances.

Cost of Equity Funds

Both individual and professional investors in a new business expect a rate of return of about 20 per cent annually; the majority feel that an investment is not worthwhile unless there is the promise of doubling it within three to five years, with a very strong preference for three years. Growth prospects are important to investors in these special situations, because they are "locked in" until the firm has either grown large enough to have its securities traded publicly or until it can be sold or merged with a larger company. When debt instruments are involved in addition to stock participation, the rate of interest is usually a nominal 5 or 6 per cent.

Most investors demand between 20 and 50 per cent of the equity in the company, the exact proportion depending on the sum of money involved, the amount already invested by the owners, prospective profits, the extent to which successful operations depend on the special talents or abilities of the owners, the bargaining power of the principals, the degree of risk involved, and the returns that are currently available in other investment opportunities.

Some venture funds want no control, other than the right to have a watchdog representative on the board of directors, but investors backing a new invention or a new product often expect to receive a majority interest in the company being formed—usually, between 51 and 67 per cent.

The Security Markets

The security markets are not ordinarily a fruitful source of capital —either debt or equity—for any but well - established companies. About 70 per cent of the private placements of debt, for example, are made by companies with assets of fifty million dollars or more. Private placement of equity issues is similarly concentrated in the large-company end of the corporate spectrum.

An Expensive Method

The cost of flotation for publicly offered issues rises sharply as the size of the offering declines, so it can be an extremely expensive way for smaller companies to raise funds. Businesses attempting to sell securities have usually been in business for some time and have experienced an identifiable measure of success. Most investment bankers feel that the right time for a company to go public is when it is approaching the distribution of dividends and its success is reasonably assured. By that time in a firm's history, however, the pressing need for venture capital is past. There are investment banking houses that have developed specialized techniques of investigative and offering procedure that make small issues economically feasible, but very few investment bankers would consider an issue involving less than a million dollars.

The characteristics that public investors look for in smaller companies — a satisfactory earnings record, a superior product in a known market that offers a unique potential, good management, and strong growth possibilities — are similar to the characteristics sought by private investors. But businesses

making a successful sale through the security markets must have made some kind of a recognized start. Because the market will not accept securities of unknown firms, and because of the high costs resulting from that fact, the securities market is not usually a fruitful source of venture capital for smaller companies.

Recent Developments

The Small Business Investment Act of 1958 is an attempt to establish a formalized structure to bridge the gap between large institutional lenders and small business. To start up, a small business investment corporation (SBIC) needs a minimum of $300,000 in capital. Up to $150,000 of this can be obtained from the Small Business Administration, which will purchase the SBIC's debentures, and the remaining $150,000 comes from the interested investors. In addition, another $150,000 can be obtained from the SBA on loan, and an SBIC is permitted to borrow as much as four times its capital and surplus. Thus, even the smallest SBIC has the theoretical total of some 1.5 million dollars for investment. In practice, however, the SBIC's have not been able to obtain the leverage funds; insurance companies and commercial banks have been hesitant to invest in SBIC's that are not related to their own activities.

In addition to the problem of

raising capital, the SBIC's have run into other troubles. There is a coolness in the rest of the financial community toward the SBIC's as a sound investment risk, and there is a mass of red tape surrounding the program. Moreover, SBIC managers are complaining that most of the small businesses approaching them for funds are not even worth investigating.

To overcome some of these problems, the SBIC's have asked for legislative changes that include: (1) the creation of a federal agency where an SBIC could discount notes and debentures; (2) the right to set up nontaxable reserves to provide for possible future losses; and (3) exempting the SBIC's from the Investment Act of 1940, thus allowing them to offer stock options to attract and retain desirable personnel.

On their own, the SBIC's are attempting two methods of easing their plight. One is joint participation among SBIC's on individual ventures—to pool risks, reduce the strain on funds in short supply, and bypass legal restrictions on lending excessive amounts to any one client. The second method is seeking equity funds by public sale of common stock, although this attempt has not been universally successful.

The Institutional Gap

Among authorities who have spoken out on the issue, there seems to be a consensus that the sources of debt funds are adequate. A Federal Reserve survey of venture-capital suppliers determined that capital is available, but primarily to the relatively more promising businesses—and on rather stiff terms. Of course, from the viewpoint of the smaller businessman, there is a shortage of long-term debt and equity capital—but it is doubtful that this need can ever be filled.

The Wrong Question?

The development of the SBIC's is an attempt to bridge the gap between large institutional investors and smaller businesses that need capital, and although SBIC's may meet some of the demand for venture capital, they can never fill the demand that is created by the sum of all the hopes and dreams of would-be entrepreneurs. The important question may be not, "What institutional structure can fill the institutional gap in our system of money supply?" but rather, "Why does this gap exist?" And the inescapable conclusion is that it exists because it is simply not economically feasible to fill it under the present circumstances of uncertainty surrounding the smaller business—an uncertainty that is caused mainly by the untested value of the managements of new ventures.

What can be done, then, to promote a greater supply of funds on an equitable and practical basis? Any substantial increase in the supply of venture funds will depend, first, on finding a better measure of managerial ability, so that the capable managers can be assisted and funds will not be wasted on those unable to cope with the realities of the business world; and second, on developing adequate records of business failures for causes not directly attributable to management error, so suppliers of funds may know with greater certainty what their loss rate will be.

Today and Tomorrow

Whatever techniques may later be developed by the government or the financial industry, the problem for those seeking venture capital today is to create some tangible evidence of their ability to handle funds profitably. With the continuing diffusion of personal wealth, the only growing source of business venture capital is apparently the funds of large corporations that have more cash than they need for their own operations. Although local capitalists are still the backbone of the venture-capital supply, large corporations, the investing public, and the savings institutions could become great suppliers—if the uncertainties surrounding smaller business ventures could be defined and quantified so feasible ventures could be more easily identified, and if adequate intermediaries can develop to a point where their securities, both debt and equity, can be successfully sold on the public markets. If these intermediaries do not develop successfully, the continuing breakdown of large individual capital pools will make the job of locating venture funds increasingly more costly and time-consuming. ◆

Reprinted from FINANCIAL ANALYSTS JOURNAL, September - October 1968—Copyright 1968

The Pattern of Success in
Venture Capital Financing

by William Rotch

THE GROWTH of the U. S. economy depends to a large extent on the willingness of businessmen to try something new, be it a new product, process, or market. Such new ventures require financing and entail considerable risk. Whereas large corporations can continually underwrite research and development activities, there are many new ventures that spring up independently and require their own financing. For interested investors these new enterprises involve considerable risk, but may also offer a shot at substantial gains. Knowing what pattern of success other venture capitalists have had will help in applying measures to the task. For those who may be concerned with the way public policies affect the availability of risk capital an insight into the problems that confront the venture capitalist should help in developing the kind of legal and tax framework that will stimulate the desired activity. This article will review the actual pattern of results in a way which should be of interest both to investors and to those concerned with the government's regulatory framework.

Since most venture capital financing has customarily been provided by individuals and partnerships, a representative pattern of gains and losses has not been generally available to the public. Recently, however, two sources of public information have provided a comprehensive view of a substantial amount of this type of financing, and a typical pattern of success is beginning

to emerge. One source of information is the record shown by a number of the Small Business Investment Companies which provide venture capital. Only a few of the 600 odd SBIC's are true venture capital firms, but since they are mostly the larger SBIC's, they represent a significant proportion of the total SBIC loans and investments, now amounting to over $500 million. This study will examine the record of seven publicly held, venture capital SBIC's, which have provided loans and investments amounting to around $135 million. In these seven SBIC's we can see the results of 281 investments made over a period of about six years.

The other source of data is the published record of the American Research and Development Corporation. The activities of this venture capital firm cover a span of twenty years, and involve the investment of almost $30 million in 87 different client companies.

In examining the pattern of results achieved by these firms, we shall consider three aspects of their operation which have been crucial to success: the length of time that elapsed before investments were sold, the size of the gain or loss that was realized, and the proportion of losses and gains in the total portfolio.

The Time Required and Rate of Gain Realized

Though venture capital firms have been described in a number of ways, the distinguishing characteristic used in this study is an investment policy aimed at achieving most of the investment company's profits through capital gains. Evidence of such a policy would be the existence of current or deferred equity interest in most client companies through use of financing instruments such as common stock, convertible debentures, or notes with warrants for the purchase of common stock. This is not to say that venture capital firms never use straight debt, for they often combine notes and stock in a financing package. The key indicator remains the firm's reliance

WILLIAM ROTCH *is Professor of Business Administration at the University of Virginia, Graduate School of Business Administration. Some of the initial analysis for this article was done while Visiting Associate Professor at the Amos Tuck School of Business Administration at Dartmouth College.*

Investment Management

on its equity interest as the main source of profit on the investment.

In achieving long run profits through realization of capital gains, a venture capital firm will be concerned with the length of time it must hold the investment before realizing a gain (or loss) in relation to the original investment. The shorter the time and the greater the rate of gain[1] (or smaller the rate of loss) the more successful the financing firm will be. Looking first at the investment record of American Research and Development Corporation we can see what these factors were and how they related to each other.

American Research and Development Corporation was formed in late 1946 to provide equity-type venture capital for the development of new ideas, products and processes. By the end of 1966 its initial paid in capital of just over $5 million had grown to over $19 million from sales of additional stock in 1951, 1959, and 1960. In its twenty years of operation it had committed over $29 million to 87 client companies, for an average of about $330,000 per company. It had never borrowed money, apparently preferring instead to rely on the borrowing capacity of its client companies, enhanced as it was by the equity capital which ARDC provides.

Table I

AMERICAN RESEARCH AND DEVELOPMENT CORPORATION
Record of Realized Capital Gains

Years to Realization	Number of Sales[1]	Total Peak Commitment	Total Realized Gain	Percent Realized Gain
2-3	10	$1,322,000	$ 582,000	44%
4-5	16	3,024,000	3,289,000	109
6-7	4	542,000	935,000	173
8-9	5	1,045,000	798,000	76
10-11	5	419,000	1,128,000	269
12-13	2	112,000	1,138,000	1,030
14-15	1	41,000	909,000	2,220
16-17	1	45,000	1,324,000	2,940
18-20	2	145,000	1,156,000	798

The weighted average years to realization was 5.9 years, weighted by total peak commitment.

1. The number of sales exceeds the number of companies financed since in a few instances two or more partial sales were made in different years.
Source: Company Annual Reports.

Table I shows how long it took ARDC to realize capital gains and what the rate of gain was when realized. The first line of the table says that during the twenty-year period of operation, investments totalling $1,322,000 were concluded in two or three years, and from these investments a $582,000 gain was realized which is 44% of the amount invested. The peak commitment is used as the "cost" since in a number of instances an initial investment was augmented by later additions. Though sometimes debt repayment reduced

_____

1. Footnotes appear at end of article.

the peak amount, the peak figure represents the amount ARDC had at risk.

The table shows that higher rates of gain were realized from investments which were held for longer periods of time. On the average, weighting the period in years by the amount of investment held for that period, ARDC realized its gains about six years after an investment was first made. Not shown in the table since no gain had been realized, is ARDC's best investment: Digital Equipment Corporation. At the end of 1966 this investment showed an 11,000% unrealized gain. The initial investment was made in 1957, so when the gain is realized it will have taken over ten years.

As for capital losses, it is generally accepted that losses appear earlier than gains.[2] The record shown by ARDC does not support this theory when the full twenty years are considered. On the average (as with capital gains, weighting the time period by the amount committed) capital losses were realized after more than eight years of the investment. Table II gives the distribution of losses by length of period.

Table II

AMERICAN RESEARCH AND DEVELOPMENT CORPORATION
Record of Realized Capital Losses

Years to Realization	Number of Sales[1]	Total Peak Commitment	Total Realized Loss	Percent Realized Loss
2-3	5	$1,084,000	$ 856,000	79%
4-5	2	251,000	56,000	22
6-7	3	315,000	282,000	90
8-9	1	205,000	205,000	100
10-11	3	366,000	178,000	49
12-13	1	63,000	34,000	54
14-15	3	2,802,000	1,110,000	40
16-17	1	277,000	267,000	96
18-20		0	0	

The weighted average years to realization was 8.7 years, weighted by total peak commitment.

1. The number of sales exceeds the number of companies financed since in a few instances two or more partial sales were made in different years.
Source: Company Annual Reports.

In attempting to reconcile this 20-year record with that of the venture capital SBIC's, many of which show little realized gains but large amounts of realized losses and unrealized gains, one is tempted to conclude that the SBIC record is as much a result of the time it has taken their managements to learn the intricacies of venture capital financing as it is an indication of the expected long run pattern. Perhaps it is fair to say that experienced venture capitalists can not avoid incurring losses, but fewer of their investments become realized losses in their early years.

Since few SBIC's were started before 1961 (most of the 600-700 firms operating in 1967 were started between September 1960 and March 1962), the oldest were only about seven years old in 1967. Considering

ARDC's six-year average for realizing gains, one can see that the SBIC's had not had sufficient time to complete the investment cycle on many of their investments. To be sure some capital gains had been realized from the acquisition or merger of their client companies, and through the few public offerings which had been made, but on the whole, several more years will be needed before the record is long enough to make a good measure of the average SBIC cycle time.

The Proportion of Gains and Losses

It is difficult, if not impossible, for a venture capital firm to avoid sustaining losses. The nature of the risk capital business results in some successful and some unsuccessful investments. The important thing is to have large enough gains on the winners, and a small enough number of losers, to come out ahead. A review of the record regarding these two aspects will help make clear the problems faced in practice by venture capitalists.

Table III

AMERICAN RESEARCH AND DEVELOPMENT CORPORATION
Summary of Operating Results

Period of Operation	12/46 to 12/66
Percent of Financing Having Equity Position 12/31/66	99.7%
Percent of Financing Showing Debt Only 12/31/66	0.3%
Total Amount Committed Over the Period (000)	$29,000
Number of Companies Financed	87
Average Peak Financing (000)	$330

	Percent of Total Committed*	Amount Committed (000)	Amount Gain or Loss (000)	Present Gain or Loss
Realized Loss	19%	$ 5,380	$ 2,990	56%
Unrealized Loss	7	1,960	380	19
Still Committed, No Gain or Loss	20	5,830		
Financing Concluded, No Gain or Loss	5	1,390		
Unrealized Gain	27	7,730	71,970	930
Realized Gain	23	6,650	11,180	168
		$28,940		

Percent of Financing Concluded	47%
Stockholder Gains from Spin-offs (000) (Included in Realized Gains)	$1,725

*Adds to 101% because of rounding.
Source: Company Annual Reports.

Table III shows an analysis of the American Research and Development Corporation's investment record. The table covers 20 years of operation and shows that ARDC is indeed a true venture capital firm. All but 0.3% of the firm's loans and investments at the end of 1966 were in situations in which ARDC had an equity interest. The total amount committed ($29 million) represents the sum of the peak amount of financing pro-

vided each client company. As before, the peak amount is used since in most cases the peak amount remained committed for most of the period of the investment.

The center part of the table shows a six-way breakdown of the total funds committed. This shows how much of ARDC's funds went to investments that became losers, how much broke even, how much went to winning situations, and how much is thus far unproven. The amount of actual or indicated gain or loss is also shown.

With 47% of the financing concluded, and another 34% showing unrealized gain or loss, a pattern has been fairly well established. Around a quarter of the funds committed have gone to losing situations, on which losses have been around 55%. About half of committed funds have gone to winning situations, on which realized gains have averaged almost 170%. Unrealized gains at the end of 1966 were about 930% of the amount committed in those situations. Over the 20-year period very few investments were terminated with no gain or loss (most of these were the payment of convertible debentures or notes with unexercised options) showing how seldom a venture capitalist comes out even.

The most significant figure is the unrealized gain of $72 million, $53 million of which is the unrealized gain on the stock of Digital Equipment Corporation. This single potential gain is almost ten times the total realized and unrealized gain on High Voltage Engineering, which contributed ARDC's next largest gain to date. Such an excellent outcome with a relatively modest investment (the maximum commitment to Digital Equipment was less than one-half a million dollars) is the venture capitalist's dream.

However, considering the whole 20-year record to December 31, 1966, recognizing income and capital gains dividends when declared and assuming that all unrealized gains were realized and distributed on December 31, 1966, the stockholders' investment would have resulted in approximately a 14% compounded annual return.[3] (Without the unrealized gain from Digital Equipment the compounded rate would have been about 8%.)[4] Thus when the effects of time adjustment are introduced, and the offsetting losses and low returns on some of the investments are considered, we see that this venture capital firm needed several tremendous successes to produce an overall record which to the end of 1966 had been very good but something less than phenomenal.

Though venture capital SBIC's have been operating for a far shorter period of time, a similar pattern is beginning to emerge. Table IV shows an analysis of seven SBIC's with combined assets in March 1967 of about $100 million. The concluded financing already amounts to about 36% of the total commitments, and another 31% shows some unrealized gain or loss.

Investment Management

Table IV — SUMMARY OF

	Business Funds			Boston Capital			Capital Southwest		
Period of Operation	8/61 - 3/67			7/60 - 3/67			3/62 - 3/67		
Percent of Financing Having an Equity Position 3/67	76.5%			99.7%			97.1%		
Percent of Financing Having Debt Only March '67	23.5%			.3%			2.9%		
Total Amount Committed Over Period (000)	$32,800			$29,700			$22,300		
Number of Companies Financed	56			53			45		
Average Peak Financing Per Co. (000)	$585			$560			$500		
	A	B	C	A	B	C	A	B	C
	Percent of Total Committed	Amount (000) Committed	Amount Gain or Loss (000)						
Realized Loss	15%	$ 4,800	$3,530	21%	$ 6,100	$4,420	13%	$ 2,900	$2,730
Unrealized Loss	10%	3,400	270	11%	3,200	1,640	14%	3,200	920
Still Committed, No Gain or Loss	40%	13,300		31%	9,200		42%	9,300	
Financing Concluded, No Gain or Loss	16%	5,100		1%	200		3%	700	
Unrealized Gain	3%	1,000	430	14%	4,300	5,540	21%	4,600	17,380
Realized Gain	16%	5,200	8,090	22%	6,700	1,800	7%	1,600	2,810
	100%	$32,800		100%	$29,700		100%	$22,300	
Percent of Total Financing Concluded	47%			43%			23%		
Stockholder Gains from Spin-offs (000) (Included in Realized Gains Above)	about $5,000			none			$2,400		

Source: Company Annual Reports.

As with ARDC around one quarter of the funds committed have resulted in realized or unrealized losses. However, when realized, losses at 79% have been a bit higher than ARDC's experience. Gaining investments amounted to a bit less than a third of total funds committed, and when realized or spun off the gains have averaged about 112% of the peak commitments. The remaining 43% of funds committed represents unproven investments or those that were concluded without gain or loss.[5]

Rate of Gain Required by Venture Capitalists

The record shows that venture capitalists are confronted with two hurdles. It takes time to develop an equity investment to the point at which it can be sold at a gain, and some of the investments can be expected to turn sour and result in losses. These two factors mean that a fairly large rate of gain will be needed on those investments which turn out to be successful if the overall effort is to return a profit. How much must that gain be?

A hypothetical example, based on the average amounts and percentages taken from the preceding analysis of actual performance, will illustrate the required rate of capital gain.

Suppose a venture capital firm is financed by $5 million in equity and has 33% debt leverage of $2.5 million. Suppose also that its objective is to make 15% return on net worth, or 10% on total assets, after both interest and operating expenses, and including capital gains and losses. Currently this hypothetical firm has net operating income of 2% of assets so that the balance of 8% must be provided by capital gains. It has 90% of its $7.5 million capital invested and expects that about 40% of this will be in losing situations on which it will probably lose 60%. Thus expected losses, when the $6.75 million portfolio has turned over, would be about $1.62 million. It expects 10% of its investments to be concluded with no gain or loss and to realize its gains on half of the $6.75 million invested.[6] How high must these gains be to achieve the overall goal of 15% return on net worth?

As stated above capital gains must provide an 8% compounded annual return on assets if the firm is to achieve its goal of 15% return on net worth. The 8% required annual return on $7.5 million in assets would be satisfied by a one time gain of $3.5 million, realized after five years. Since expected losses of $1.62 million must be recouped, a total capital gain of $5.12 million must be realized at the end of five years. This is a little over 150% of the $3.375 million cost of that half of the portfolio which is expected to result in capital gains. In other words, in five years the firm must be able to make gains averaging over 150% on those of its investments that produce some capital gain.

If, instead of five, it takes six years on the average to realize gains (ARDC's average), then the gain will have to be 175% of the original investment. Table V shows what gains would have to be realized for four different

INVESTMENT RESULTS OF SEVEN SBIC'S

Narragansett Capital	SBIC of New York	Greater Wash. Ind'l Inv.	LaSalle St. Capital	Totals
7/60 - 3/67	11/61 - 3/67	4/60 - 3/67	9/60 - 3/67	
100%	97.2%	99.6%	91.3%	
0	2.8%	.4%	8.7%	
$21,100	$12,650	$9,700	$6,900	$135,150
34	31	41	21	281
$620	$410	$240	$330	$480

A	B	C	A	B	C	A	B	C	A	B	C	A	B	C	C/B
6%	$ 1,200	$ 820	21%	$ 2,640	$1,970	19%	$1,800	$1,720	18%	$1,230	$1,170	15%	$ 20,670	$16,360	79%
0	0	0	33%	4,160	1,310	6%	600	320	0	0	0	11%	14,560	4,460	31%
50%	10,500		14%	1,800		31%	3,000		18%	1,250		36%	48.350		
2%	400		7%	860		12%	1,200		17%	1,140		7%	9,600		
33%	6,900	6,290	18%	2,310	3,690	17%	1,700	2,870	38%	2,670	4,140	17%	23,480	40,340	172%
10%	2,100	1,910	7%	880	2,920	15%	1,400	2,150	9%	610	890	14%	18,490	20,560	112%
101%	$21,100		100%	$12,650		100%	$9,700		100%	$6,900		100%	$135,150		
	17%			35%			46%			44%			36%		
	none			$2,200			$800			$300			$10,700		

investment lives and three objective rates of return. Changes in other variables could also be considered, but however one looks at it, the success of equity oriented venture capitalists depends on obtaining a high rate of capital gain on those investments that turn out to be winners.

Nature of the Venture Capital Business

With the foregoing quantitative analysis of investment results as a background let us now look at some other aspects of the venture capital business. What are some of the important problems which face the manager of a venture capital firm?

The most difficult problems seem to stem not so much from the need to avoid the loss situations, but from the difficulty of developing and capitalizing on the gain situations, particularly with respect to the long term nature of the investments and the high rate of gain which must be made. The long time period reflects two hazardous difficulties. The investment must often be in a non-liquid state for many years. Unlike a mutual fund, a venture capital firm usually can not withdraw from a situation early without great financial sacrifice. The other difficulty reflected by the long time period is the necessity of betting now on a series of events that extend many years in the future. One is betting now on what will happen to an industry, a product, and a firm's management, and such long term projections are filled with opportunities for events to go astray.

Table V

RATE OF CAPITAL GAIN REQUIRED UNDER VARIOUS CONDITIONS

Table shows the rate of capital gain which would be required at the end of the period shown, under the assumed conditions stated below. The rate of capital gain is shown as a percent of the cost of the investments that produce the gain, here assumed to be half of the portfolio. The gain is the amount required to produce the firm's rate of return goal, and includes coverage of expected losses.

Goal	Required Return on the Portfolio	Years Before Losses and Gains Are Realized			
		3 Years	5 Years	7 Years	10 Years
10%	5.2%	80%	134%	136%	178%
15	8.9	106	154	210	316
20	12.6	134	212	308	504

Basic Conditions Assumed:

1. That the venture capital firm's debt leverage is 50% of equity.
2. That net operating profit, after interest and before any reserves for losses and any realized capital gains or losses is 2% of total assets.
3. That the invested portfolio is 90% of total assets.
4. That 50% of the portfolio results in capital gains.
5. That 40% of the portfolio results in losses which average 60% of the investment.
6. That 10% of the portfolio breaks even.

Translation of three possible rate of return goals for the investment firm into required rates of return on the portfolio is as follows:

If the firm's objective rate of return on equity is	10%	15%	20%
then considering debt leverage the rate of return on assets must be	6.7%	10%	13.3%
less net operating profit of 2% leaves	4.7%	8%	11.3%
Since the portfolio equals 90% of assets, the required return from capital gains on the portfolio must be	5.2%	8.9%	12.6%

Investment Management

Table VI

SBIC INVESTMENT POLICY RELATED TO SIZE AND PROFITABILITY
March 31, 1967

	Small SBIC's		Medium SBIC's		Large SBIC's		Largest SBIC's	
	Most Profitable	Other	Most Profitable	Other	Most Profitable	Other	Most Profitable	Other
Net Income as % of Assets ..	3.2%	(2.7%)	3.1%	(2.5%)	6.7%	(.9%)	7.8%	2.3%
Total Gross Loans and Investments (000,000) ...	$15.2	$41.6	$40.8	$102.9	$43.8	$116.8	$48.7	$121.5
% in Loans	79%	73%	74%	57%	61%	44%	28%	41%
% in Debt Securities	16%	16%	22%	30%	25%	39%	41%	32%
% in Capital Stock	5%	11%	4%	13%	14%	17%	31%	27%

Notes:
1. The size grouping is based on the SBIC's statutory capital. The groups are defined as follows: Small: not over $325,000; Medium: $325,000 to $1,000,000; Large: $1 million to $5 million; Largest over $5 million.
2. The "most profitable" SBIC's in each group are those companies in the top quarter as to total return on invested capital for the current year and which did not report losses for the previous year.
3. Net income is after provision for losses and taxes and includes net realized gains or losses.
4. Loans are financing instruments which have no equity interest. Debt securities are convertible debentures, notes with warrants, or some other form of debt with potential equity interest. Capital stock includes common and preferred stock and rights for which a separate value has been stated.

Source: SBA Condensed Financial Statements.

The high rate of gain required also presents acute problems. Discussions with at least a dozen SBIC managers show that many of the most promising companies that seek risk capital are on the brink of major growth. In such situations presidents of small companies often tend to be overly optimistic about their company's prospects. If it is preparing to take an equity position, the investment firm's staff must be able to see through the haze of optimism to discover what the real potential is. Furthermore in a new enterprise the process of growth itself puts new demands on the president. Whereas he may have performed ably at an early stage through direct contact with employees and customers, at double or triple the size he will have to develop the ability to organize and lead subordinates who then become the ones with the direct contacts. He must change from a doer of jobs to a manager of people. The investment firm's staff must be able to recognize their client's ability to grow in administrative skill and his capacity to deal with the radical changes which the sought for growth will bring.

Once an investment is made, it is seldom possible to leave it alone. There will be continuing demands on the time and ability of the venture capital firm's staff as they are called upon to review progress and occasionally to take an active part in the affairs of the client companies.

Size of Venture Capital Firms

The record shown by the whole SBIC industry indicates that it is the larger firms that have chosen to be venture capitalists looking for profits from capital gains. The smaller firms have chosen to be lenders looking to interest as the primary source of income. From the record shown in Table VI we see that not only have

the smaller SBIC's used mainly straight debt, but also the most profitable among the small SBIC's (through March, 1967) were those which used a higher proportion of debt. Only in the largest group, those with capital over $5 million, do we find the most profitable firms tending to be equity oriented. Thus the record indicates that it is more difficult for a small firm to succeed in equity financing, and in fact few of the small SBIC's have attempted to be primarily equity financing firms.

One important reason why an equity oriented venture capital firm needs to be fairly large is the high degree of managerial skill required to evaluate and work with client companies. Income must be sufficient to support a competent staff. With expenditures for salaries and consulting advice typically between 1% and 1.4% of funds invested for all sizes of SBIC's,[7] the smaller firms have little with which to pay competent managers. A firm with over $2 million would seem to be the minimum viable size for an equity oriented venture capital firm.

Size is also important to enable a venture capital firm to sustain losses. The record indicates that it is almost inevitable that a firm will lose on some of its investments. There is also evidence that many investments will require additional funds, either to bail them out of trouble or to capitalize on beginning success. An ability to absorb losses and have reserve funds available also is a reason that equity oriented investment firms need to have an ample supply of capital.

Finally, it must be recognized that capital gains which are the primary source of profit for these firms can only be secured by selling the investment. Sales may come through merger or acquisition by a larger company, or through a public issue. With any of these routes, and particularly with a public issue, the client company must be of sufficient size to make the transaction meaningful and economically worthwhile. A $100,000 company is an unlikely candidate, and a $500,000 company is still rather small. One can see that commitments by a venture capital firm will probably have to exceed $100,000-$200,000 in most cases if a significant position is to be obtained and if the amount of growth needed to reach a saleable size is not to be too great. Since a number of investments are useful for diversification and indeed are required in some cases (an SBIC is not allowed to invest more than 20% of its capital in one enterprise) this approach suggests that a viable size for an equity oriented investment firm is well over $1,000,000 in capital.

Conclusions

This review of the operating practices and results of a number of venture capital firms has suggested several conclusions:

1. It is unreasonable for an equity oriented venture capital firm to expect to avoid losses. It appears that substantial losses on 25% to 40% of the investments should be anticipated.

2. A significant period of time is usually required for investments to mature to a point where they can be sold at a profit. An average of 6-7 years is indicated for a business whose characteristics are similar to those of American Research and Development Corporation.

3. In order to make a reasonable return for the venture capital firm's stockholders, and considering the probability of investment losses and the time required to realize capital gains, a gain (above cost) of 150% to 200% will usually be necessary.

4. For a number of reasons a venture capital firm needs to be above a certain size in order to have a good chance of operating successfully. The minimum viable size is at least $1 million and probably above $2 million in investable funds. The reasons for this derive from the need for competent staff, the need for reserves to cover losses and make additional commitments, and the need to be able to finance enterprises that are large enough to have a good chance of growing to a saleable size.

The pattern of success that emerges is not an easy one to achieve. Venture capital firms by the nature of their business are betting on the development and growth of enterprises over a long period of time. A high degree of risk is inherent in the route they take to financial gain. Persistence, patience, skill, and a measure of courage are requisites for a successful conduct of this business. That there are men with these attributes is fortunate since these enterprises are often the cutting edge of our technological development, and indeed of the economy itself. ◆

Investment Management

FOOTNOTES

1. Rate of gain here refers to the ratio: sales price minus cost all divided by cost, or capital gain as a percent of cost.

2. See for example p. 10 "Encouraging Venture Capital for Small Business" a study prepared for the Small Business and Venture Capital Associates in 1966 and published by Associated Educational Services Corporation, a Division of Simon & Schuster, Inc. The authors state "Venture capital financing . . . is a very risky business. Losses are frequent and tend to occur more quickly than gains."

3. This calculation was made as follows: Stockholder investment was based on the amounts and years in which stock was sold to the public by the company. Sales after 1946 were discounted to year zero. Income and capital gains dividends were discounted from the year declared to year zero. Stockholder gains from distributions of High Voltage Engineering stock were taken at the market value at the time of distribution and discounted to year zero. Total net assets on December 31, 1966 or $93 million, including unrealized gains, were also discounted to year zero. The discount rate at which cash outflows equalled cash inflows when all were discounted to year zero was approximately 14%.

4. For comparison, the Dow Jones Industrial Average increased by a factor of about 4 during this 20-year period, which corresponds to an average annual compounded return of about 7%. Adding to this an average dividend yield of about 4½% over the period, the return from combined dividends and capital gains on the D.J.I. stocks was around 11½%.

5. This pattern of winners and losers resembles the record shown by the venture capital firm of J. H. Whitney Company during the years from 1949 to 1960. In this period 50 investments were made, 38 of them under $500,000. In these 38, the firm lost substantially all its investment in 15, broke even on 6, made a substandard return on 4 and was successful in 13. Overall the net gain on the 38 was apparently not as good as on the 12 larger investments, for it was with the very large investments of over $2 million that the firm achieved its substantial success. (These figures were reported by Wrede Petersmeyer, former partner of J. H. Whitney Company, at the 1966 Annual NASBIC meeting, November 28-December 1, 1966. Proceedings, p. 111.)

6. The 40%-10%-50% split was derived from the record of the seven SBIC's shown in Table IV. The 36% of total investments remaining in unproven investments was allocated to the loss, no change, and gain categories in proportion to the record of these other categories thus far. With similar allocation of unproven investment, American Research and Development Corporation shows a slightly more favorable split: 33% in loss investment; 7% in the no change category and 60% in the gain category.

7. For the year ending March, 1964, the last year for which salary expenses of SBIC's were published by the SBA, salary and consulting costs as a percent of funds being managed were as follows: Small SBIC's, 1.04%; Medium SBIC's, 1.39%; Large SBIC's, 1.41%; Largest SBIC's, 1.23%. For ARDC in the year 1966, considering investments at cost, the percent was .77%.

Assessing Technological Ventures for Bank Loans

ARNOLD M. RUSKIN

In a complex, innovative society, a high percentage of new businesses will be technological in nature. Banks must be prepared to properly evaluate these new customers.

When an engineer or scientist cum entrepreneur approaches a banker for a loan to finance growth and development of his business, how can the banker realistically evaluate the risk inherent in the venture?

Surely the banker wants to classify his loans as accurately as possible. His motive, of course, is to assign interest rates which in the long run will result in a suitable overall rate of return, even when an occasional loss must be written off. But what is the chance of a partial or complete loss on loans to technological entrepreneurs? Can all risks be lumped into a single class? Or, is there a chance the banker will lose preferred business to his competition by not giving it preferred treatment? In short, how can the level of risk resulting from the technological nature of the enterprise be properly evaluated? How can the information necessary to make the evaluation be obtained? A scheme which may assist bankers in answering these questions is outlined here.

USING CONVENTIONAL INDICATORS

A first step in the approach is to decide if, on the average, the conditions which pertain to a technologically based enterprise are different from those which pertain to other forms of enterprise. One may assert that the risk attached to a technological venture is no different from the risk attached to any other kind of venture, but the evidence is to the contrary.

First of all, by its very nature, a technological venture operates in the presence of rapidly changing environmental conditions. Non-technological industries typically do not change quite so fast. Secondly, the rate of business success for at least a major subset of technological ventures is several times better than that of new ventures as a whole: eighty per cent of one group of technological enterprises studied were still in business four to five years after their formation, whereas, among business generally, most new companies formed in the United States fail within the first few years.[1] Clearly the banker who wishes to accurately assess the risks associated with technological ventures must study this group of ventures afresh instead of simply applying criteria developed to serve over a broad range of general business.

Given the fact that technologically based ventures differ from business ventures generally, this does not mean that tools or indicators used by bankers to assess general business cannot be used with technological ventures if the tools are properly calibrated. For example, ratios which indicate solvency, such as the current ratio and the acid test, can and probably should be used in evaluating the ability of a technological venture to carry safely additional debt of various types and terms. Yet, ratio analysis can be applied meaningfully only if appropriate guideline ratios are used, and here "appropriate" means "appropriate in terms of the characteristics of technological ventures."

Appropriate guidelines can be determined best by studying the financial histories of representative technologically based firms. One would examine, for example, correlations between various ratios computed from balance sheets on the one hand, and current and lagged indicators of business success on the other. Business success could be roughly indicated by whether the firm was still in business some years later. Finer indication might be obtained from growth or recession of sales volume and gross earnings, number of employees, payroll (corrected for inflation), capital funds costs (compared with the prime rate), and, of course, net earnings. Regardless of the indicators used, a judgment would first be made about the level of performance which represents a satisfactory outcome; then an examination would be made of the various ratios to see if there are relations between the outcome and the values of the several ratios. This process could be carried out in a straightforward way by the statistical technique of multiple regression with dummy variables.[2]

It is implicit in this analytical approach that there be a sample of technologically based firms which have a range of financial and business histories covering the spectrum represented by the banker's loan applicants. Thus, we have a chicker and-egg affair. If bankers are loath to make loans because they feel unsure of their judgment, then there may exist few example firms which can be analyzed to see how the bankers may have done better.

Fortunately, the situation is not quite this bleak. Not every financier has always waited for the guidelines, and some technological ventures have received medium-term loans from banks or other backing from financial intermediaries.[3] Also, some technologically based firms have apparently received financial backing from non-banking organizations.[4] With appropriate searching, therefore, one should be able to find a sufficient number of examples, say a few hundred, with which to develop ratio analysis guidelines.

EVALUATING GROWTH RATES

The use of ratio analysis will provide an assessment of a firm's creditworthiness at a given point in time, usually the present. But in his consideration of the creditworthiness of a technological venture, the banker must also examine the firm's plans for its development. Typically, success of a technological venture depends upon obtaining a position in a new market before competitors have sewn everything up. Consequently, the banker must assess the loan applicant's plan for developing his venture and predict if the applicant will be able to keep up with, or ahead of, his competition. For this purpose, the banker needs an estimate of the current position of the competition, some notion of how fast the field will develop, and a proposed plan of development for the firm's venture.

Estimating the competition's current position is a most difficult task. The difficulty stems, of course, from the proprietary or secretive way a firm treats its proposed developments. In fact, well-kept secrets make merely identifying the

competition a task of inference rather than deduction, and of qualitative rather than quantitative assessment. The topic is so complex that its discussion is postponed to the next section which is devoted solely to analyzing the competition environment. Here the discussion is confined to a quantitative assessment of growth rates.

Let us presume that the procedures outlined in the next section have borne fruit and that the banker has identified the loan applicant's competitors and estimated their positions. He must then forecast how fast the field will develop and judge whether the loan applicant's projected rate of development is sufficiently competitive to be a good risk. One way to approach this problem is to chart growth curves for the applicant's area of endeavor and compare the applicant's proposed development against them.

The importance of the comparison being made against typical growth or development curves for the industry in which the loan applicant is working cannot be overstressed. Development rates vary considerably from one technologically based area to another, and valid conclusions can be drawn only from relevant comparisons.

The Growth Curve

Technological venture typically grow along a curve like the one shown in Figure 1. In this

FIGURE 1. A TYPICAL CURVE OF EXPENDITURE TO DATE VS. TIME

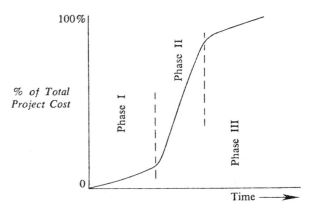

figure, total expenditure to date is plotted versus time elapsed since the beginning of the project. In the early stages of the venture's development, as long as progress depends primarily on the work of a very few inventive individuals, expenditures are at a relatively slow rate (Phase I). When the end of Phase I is reached and the rate of progress can be accelerated by increasing the total effort applied, it is typical for such accelerations actually to occur, along with a higher rate of expenditures. This is shown by the middle, more steeply rising part of the curve (Phase II). Finally, the venture matures and the rate of expenditure slows down, as indicated by the flat, upper right part of the curve (Phase III).

Because the typical growth curve is not linear and because a definite end point is not apparent, it is awkward to characterize in a way which permits meaningful comparisons among separate projects. Refer, for example, to Figure 2, in which there are two growth curves. Which of them will appear to be the better risk if the evaluation point is, say, at ten per cent of the total expenditure? Clearly, if a short time-to-maturation is considered an advantage, the more steeply rising curve is the better risk. Yet, if one were simply to extrapolate

FIGURE 2. TWO EXPENDITURE CURVES
SHOWING DIFFERENT GROWTH RATES

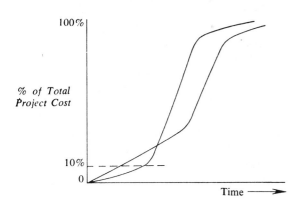

the time required to bring the project to completion on the basis of the time required to expend the first ten per cent, he would conclude that the less steeply rising curve would mature earlier. Alternatively, one can see that it is the change in the rate of progress between Phases I and II which is really the important characteristic of the growth curve. This characterisitc is particularly significant in evaluating the competition, for it is necessary to know their inclination or ability to mount an intense development effort.

The less steeply rising curve represents a less drastic change in the rate at which the project is advanced over the course of the project. Indeed, were the initial rate maintained throughout the project, a linear extrapolation would work satisfactorily. But for our purposes, we are interested in a sudden change in the curve's steepness. We digress somewhat to describe a way of focusing on the rate as it pertains to this crucial aspect of the curve.

We may approximate these typical growth curves by "S" curves, as shown in Figure 3.[6] "S" curves can be characterized by the equation:

$$m = Mi^{(rt)} \tag{1}$$

where M is the total expenditure for the project at maturity, r is the growth rate, m is the amount already expended at time t, and i is the value or cost of the initial development expressed as a fraction of the total development. If it is more convenient to use a straight-line relation instead of an exponential one, equation (1) can be reworked to a linear form by rearranging and taking logarithms.[7] Equation (1) or its alternative forms can be used both to estimate typical rates of growth for endeavors in the area in question and to estimate the time of project completion for the foremost competitor with which the applicant must contend.

FIGURE 3. "s" OR CUMULATIVE
DISTRIBUTION CURVE

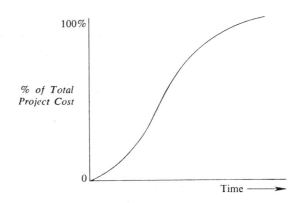

Estimating Growth Rates

To obtain typical or guideline values of the rate of growth, the banker will have to rely on published literature,[8] on company reports, and on expert opinions. What the banker requires are the initial investment expressed as a fraction of the total and the time required for essential completion of the project.[9]

A brief comment is warranted about obtaining values for the initial investment as a fraction of the total investment. Such values are documented rather less well than total expenditures and some inference must be made to obtain a value. For convenience, one may use a value of 0.05 or 0.10 as a figure for the fraction of the total expenditure which is the initial expenditure. These fractions are suggested by the finding that research on a basic invention forms only 5 to 10 per cent of the total cost of successfully launching a new product in the marketplace.[10] After a banker has followed closely the progress of loan applicants in technological categories, he may wish to revise the figure he uses for the cost of the initial investment (i) in light of his experience.

With values for i and t for projects in the applicant's field of endeavor, the banker can calculate the growth rate for each project. It is clear that each example or instance for which the banker can obtain data (in a given field) may yield a value for r slightly different from those derived from other examples. At this point, the banker must decide whether there is a trend over time which is causing r to change. If so, he may extrapolate his values of r to the present time to obtain an estimate of the best value of r to use. If the values of r do not seem to be following a trend, the banker can choose to use an average value or perhaps the fastest growth rate, i.e., the largest r, as a standard in assessing his client's proposed development.

Maturation Time

Having obtained a growth rate to use as a standard for the loan applicant's field of endeavor, the banker can calculate the time by which the applicant's project must mature if it is to develop as quickly as the field generally develops. This calculation is made by reworking the formula for the curve in Figure 3 to show explicitly the relation between the present stage of development and the completion point.[11] With his own estimate of the project's completion date, based on empirical industry data, the banker can assess the loan applicant's estimated completion date. If the two figures are not of the same order, the timeliness of the applicant's project warrants serious review.[12]

So far, the analysis in this section has dwelled on predicting the time a typical firm in the loan applicant's field would take to bring the project to maturity if it were continuing on from the same point the applicant is now. But clearly not all competing firms will be at the same place as the applicant. If the banker knows the positions of the competition, he can of course use equation (7) (Footnote 11) to estimate when these projects will mature. And these dates can be compared with the completion dates in applicant's plan.

Even if the present position of each competitor is unknown, it is useful to estimate how long each rival would require to go from, say, 0.1 per cent completion to 99.9 per cent completion. If the growth rate r is known for the industry, this

period of elapsed time can be computed from equation (7). In this case, m_f would be set at $0.999 M$; m_i would be set at $0.001 M$. The time t_i would be set at zero, and time t_f would be calculated as the elapsed time from the present.

APPRAISING THE ENVIRONMENT

In addition to the quantitative criteria for creditworthiness already discussed, there are two qualitative aspects which must be met satisfactorily before the loan applicant and his project can be termed a good loan risk. One aspect, mentioned at the beginning of the preceding section, concerns the environment in which the firm operates. The second relates to some attributes of the loan applicant and his team and is discussed in the next section.

The environment faced by a firm can be classified into three parts: a climate, a factor or input market, and an output or product market. *Climate* concerns such things as expectations about the future, tax considerations, public awareness of or concern about technological growth, and so forth. From the standpoint of the would-be technological entrepreneur, climate may be an unknown complex of forces or stimuli which make the enterprise attractive. A particularly aware entrepreneur may raise various elements of climate to a level of conscious recognition; he may make an explicit estimate of the yield from the venture as a result of the climate being what it seems to be. On the basis either of this estimate or of a less explicit feeling about the climate, the entrepreneur who becomes an applicant for a loan to extend his enterprise has already decided that a favorable climate exists. What the banker must do is verify whether such a view of the climate is warranted in light of the facts available. Some indicators are capital investment plans of corporations, governmental spending plans, and the bank's experience with its own or its correspondents' customers.

If the applicant's optimism seems justified, then the banker can turn to determining if the entrepreneur's estimate of his factor market situation is reasonable. The key elements in this assessment are the types and amounts of specific factors required and their availability in the market at the prices the entrepreneur has indicated. The banker may require expert technical opinion to assist in reviewing the type and amount of factors required. The market availability of capital equipment and raw material factors can be judged by bids reported in the trade press;[13] the availability of labor can, with a little effort, be learned from such sources as employment agencies.

Output Market

Assuming that the banker has satisfied himself that the loan applicant's favorable view of both the general climate and his factor markets is reasonable, he must now examine the applicant's intended output or product market to determine if it seems sound. An analysis of the output market for a technologically based firm must include consideration of both potential customers and competitors for those customers.

In comparison with some other types of enterprise, say retail selling, technologically based firms typically have a limited potential clientele. This may be an advantage, for it facilitates the loan applicant's providing a good estimate of his potential market if he bothers to study two points: which types of concerns are likely customers and the economics of their using his product. The banker should corroborate the applicant's estimates on these points, and again the services of a knowledgeable consultant may be in order.

More difficult to appraise than the potential customers are the competitors for these customers. There are really two distinct types of competition. One is the competing firm which can produce a substitute for the loan applicant's product. This type of competition can be expected to arise among three types of firms. First, there are obvious, even traditional, competitors such as Procter and Gamble versus Lever Brothers. Second, there are sleeper competitors such as Armour versus Procter and Gamble, still in the toilet soap field. Sleeper competitors can be found in industries which have suitable by-products or marketing outlets which allow entry into the field at less-than-normal costs of entry. And third, a source of competition may be the loan applicant's own potential customers. It takes only mention of the phrase, "make or buy," to point out how important this consideration is.

The banker can ask the loan applicant to survey the intended market for the three sources of competition described above and to estimate the nature, strength, and likelihood of competition. The applicant's study can serve as an information resource in judging his competitive position, if the study is done with apparent thoroughness and reasonableness. If the study seems superficial or if its conclusions seem ill-founded, then these negative aspects will themselves provide the banker with useful insight about the applicant's perceptions of and readiness for the ordeals of operating an enterprise. Also, if a corroborative study is deemed necessary, it is more easily undertaken with the applicant's study at hand than it would be without it. Moreover, requiring the applicant to make such a detailed survey may result in his gaining a better appreciation of his situation so that he can plan his enterprise realistically.

The second type of competttion is linked to obsolescence of the loan applicant's intended market. Here are some examples:

The second type of competition is linked to obsolescence of the loan applicant's intended market. Here are some examples:

- An improved method for manufacturing buggy whips is vitiated by the almost complete replacement of buggies by the automobile.

- An improved coal stoker for household central heating is no longer required in regions which gain access to cheaper or otherwise more desirable natural gas or oil.

- A technique for keeping magnetic recording wire from snarling is obviated by the development of a satisfactory magnetic recording tape.

- A marginal improvement in the life of some types of vacuum tubes is outmoded by the development of cheap, reliable transistors.

It takes only brief reflection to realize that predicting sources of this second type of competition is but a small step removed from crystal ball-gazing. The ease of making accurate predictions can be aided immeasurably, however, by breaking a big unknown into its constituent parts, each of which is of more manageable size. Just as one can improve his estimate of a firm's overall profitability by estimating separately the profitability of each profit-making product line or service, so one can estimate better the competitive environment by examining its constituent elements.

Consider a loan applicant who wants financing to develop a new nozzle for applying spray to potato plants as a way of eliminating crop damage from potato bugs. What potential competition can be foreseen for this venture in the form of obviating the need for a better nozzle?

First of all, we note that the main aim of keeping the bugs out of the potatoes is the preservation of potatoes as an economical source of carbohydrate. This suggests that there is a fundamental problem, namely the provision of nutrients, which gives rise to derived problems, e.g., getting rid of potato bugs. But surely, few people would immediately see potato bugs as a problem if they were asked to envision obstacles associated with providing carbohydrate nutrients. Indeed, most people would first ponder which of several possible paths to take in starting with the main problem. And they may choose alternatives which exclude potatoes and potato bugs.

If we assume, nevertheless, that potatoes will be cultivated as a source of carbohydrate, then there is a second tier of alternatives regarding bugs on potat es. We can conceive, for example, of developing a train of potatoes which would not be susceptible o bugs. This is an alternative to keeping the bugs away from the potatoes.

At a third tier of alternatives, there are the several possible ways of keeping the bugs away from the potato, either eradicating bugs or diverting their attention by providing something else for them to eat which they prefer to potatoes. If eradication is considered, there are several ways of doing this; one way involves spraying. And at the next level of alternatives are various ways of applying a particular spray, one of which involves the nozzle in question.

Hierarchy of Alternatives

A hierarchy of alternatives has thus been created, ranging from whether to use potatoes as a source of carbohydrate to the derived question of how best to apply spray. For virtually any issue, we can trace such a hierarchy. It behooves the banker to identify the hierarchy, for therein lies information regarding sources of competition via obviation: The alternatives of a given tier represent sources of such competition for all schemes which are at lower or more derived levels of the hierarchy.

The banker now has a means of identifying potential sources of competition via obviation. But a formidable task still remains in assessing the likelihood of their having an impact on the loan applicant's venture. To attack this problem, a specific approach is proposed:

Beginning at the immediate or most derived end of the hierarchy, the banker can examine each alternative in the next tier above to determine which of them could be implemented easily. Some factors determining the ease of implementation are new technology required, the amount of new fixed costs which would be incurred in adopting an alternative (including writing off present investments in equipment and training), and the incentive for changing over (including lower costs, better results, or greater flexibility). Alternatives that are obviously difficult to implement do not represent a serious threat to the proposed venture and can be set aside. This type of analysis can be performed at each successively higher tier of the hierarchy until the most fundamental tier is reached and all alternatives are examined.

On the face of it, this procedure described seems to be a Herculean task. While one does not want to understate its demands, neither should the effort be considered more onerous than it really is. In practice the generation of alternatives and a cursory but meaningful estimate of the difficulty of their implementation can be accomplished in a few manhours by flexible thinkers and knowledgeable assessors. The key to obtaining worthwhile results in such a short time is the fact that the procedure is not one of providing workable alternatives which will surmount every hidden and apparent obstacle. Rather, it is merely one of identifying approaches and the obstacles which would have to be overcome if the alternatives were to be made viable. As in the case of identifying competition by direct substitution, the loan applicant can be required to provide an initial analysis of competition by obviation. If financing opportunities are scarce, the applicant should be glad to improve his chances of getting a loan by demonstrating the soundness of his proposal.

APPRAISING THE LOAN APPLICANT AND HIS TEAM

Technological ventures, like other businesses, require people who are talented in the skills required by their roles and who are committed to achieving success in their common venture. The banker can rely on his general business judgment to assess commitment, but a knowledgeable assessment of the skill situation may demand an uncommon appreciation of the workings of a technological venture.

The critical aspect of development work is the ability to synthesize new products and install new procedures. Indeed, the *raison d'etre* for the technological venture is to market its innovation (at a profit, of course). The routine application of known art may be relatively unimportant to the venture; in any case, if it is truly routine, it can be purchased either as semi-finished work or as labor in factor markets.

Determinants of Innovative Productivity

There are many factors which contribute to high productivity in innovative work, and much research and plain conjecture exist on the topic.[14] There are three particular aspects which seem very important determinants of innovative productivity and which are also amenable to assessment by the banker. The presence of these three factors is a source of optimism, and their wholesale absence is a cause for pessimism.

It should, of course, be remembered that talented people are being considered. The question is not whether they are capable of doing the job but rather under what circumstances are they likely to be productive. Clearly, the assumption of talented people must be verified. It is taken for granted that the banker would satisfy himself that this prerequisite is met.

It has been amply demonstrated[15] that, on the average, the more productive personnel maintain a higher level of interpersonal contact with others working in related fields than do less productive personnel. The technical man working in isolation is usually less productive than he would be if he worked in such a way that he would be stimulated by others. While professional dialogue with competent colleagues is usually the best source of stimulation, the use of consultants, attending symposia, and the use of library resources are all effective means of reducing the degree of isolation which technical personnel expdrience. The banker should ascertain what the loan appicant's team is doing to reduce their isolation and thereby enhance their own productivity when he attempts to assess the quality of the loan risk.

Another determinant of productivity, from the banker's view, is the degree to which individual team members are contributing to the overall goal instead of to some personal goal not strictly aligned with the overall goal. Consider the following example: Engineer X is keen to perfect his design to its most reliable, technically optimal configuration. It's a matter of pride or self-image and personal integrity as far as X is concerned. Yet to optimize his design X will require six weeks' more design time than can be accommodated by the marketing program, which is already under way. A wasted marketing program represents not only money lost but also goodwill lost from prospective customers. And this goodwill cannot necessarily be recouped merely by spending more money in marketing promotion; it may be lost for a generation regardless of any new promotion investment. Clearly, X must not optimize his own subtask, for to do so will result in a non-optimal overall result. Yet there may be little anyone other than engineer X can do about the situation. If X holds back on finishing a critical part of the design in order to gain time for working on his pet features, even reassigning X or firing him when the trouble is spotted may not get the design completed without considerable loss of valuable time. So an assessment of the quality of risk must consider the congruence of individual objectives and the overall objectives of the project. The banker should assess the objectives of key technical people directly and not merely accept the statement of the loan applicant.

A third determinant of innovative productivity concerns the familiarity and understanding the team members have regarding each other.[16] Innovative work involves unforeseen problems. Solutions to these problems will at times require complexes of skills not assembled by random assignment of personnel. Indeed, very particular combinations of skills may be required and they can be assembled only by a thorough, even intimate knowledge of each individual's strengths and weaknesses. It is not sufficient for only "the boss" to have an encyclopedic file of his team's human resources; this type of knowledge must exist throughout the team.

The banker can easily determine if the team is composed of people who have worked together, in various combinations, before. A glaring omission of previous common project assignments among various segments of the team is a danger sign.

The Management

In addition to consideration of the productivity of individuals or groups of individuals, there should also be a consideration of the management responsible for guiding the project. Some research indicates that technical management absorbs about 25 percent of the creative technical manpower in development enterprises.[17] Such a high proportion of the available talent represents an important aspect of technological ventures and deserves though about its effectiveness.

Bankers familiar with managing their own operations are familiar with both general and specific requirements for effective management. But in an innovative venture, three aspects of management recur frequently and loom especially important: defining goals, generating alternatives, and identifying hazards. While no technical manager of competent people would try to perform each of these tasks in detail himself, he nevertheless has full responsibility for seeing that they are performed properly. Unless timely attention is paid to these tasks, the whole operation may go awry even when good technical work is performed.

The banker may partially assess management's astuteness in these vital areas by considering the loan proposal with an eye to these factors. In addition, he may pose changes in the market or in technological state-of-the-art to the loan applicant/manager and see if the manager considers these vital aspects when asked to comment. An absence of ability in these areas is a sign that the overall risk is higher than it need be.

A STRATEGY FOR THE APPRAISAL

The four aspects of assessing the extraordinary risk attached to technological ventures—conventional indicators, growth rates, the environment, and the loan applicant and his team—are like links in a chain. All the links must be strong for the chain to hold. Thus, the banker must assure himself that all four aspects are satisfactory if he is to consider the venture a good risk;[18] he needs to arrive at an overall judgment.

Since all four aspects must pass their test, and since the assessment of each aspect is more-or-less independent of the others, the sequence of tests can be arranged to suit the convenience of the banker. When a good data file on growth rates and guidelines for using conventional indicators have been prepared, it will probably be easiest to check the two quantitative aspects first. With properly determined gauge values, these aspects can be assessed quite routinely. If the venture passes its test for the two quantitative aspects, then the qualitative aspects need to be examined. These are less routine and require experienced judgments; as a result they are more expensive and should be made, if possible, only after the more routine tests have been passed.

When the bank first begins an appraisal scheme of the type outlined here, however, data on growth rates and guidelines for conventional indicators may be relatively sketchy. In this circumstance, it will be helpful to begin by assessing the qualitative aspects. This will obviate the necessity for having data for those types of ventures which fail to pass the tests on the qualitative aspects. For those ventures which do pass the tests on qualitative aspects, data can be developed to test the quantitative aspects, or, where this is impractical and there are reasons for having faith in the proposed venture, the risk can be assumed and the venture can be used as a source of data for future cases.

The ultimate success of using the scheme outlined, or any alternative, depends upon learning from experience. Each new technological venture that is finally financed, whether by corporate funds, loans, or customer contracts, e.g., government-financed development, is a potential source of experience for guiding subsequent judgments. It is never too early to begin accumulating records of this experience as a start in applying the scheme. It is even possible for various banks to pool their raw data, as members of a credit bureau pool their data. With an arrangement of this type, it would be only a relatively short time before a significant body of experience was collected to aid participating members in their assessment of technological ventures.

Arnold M. Ruskin is Associate Professor of Engineering at Harvey Mudd College, Claremont, California. He has an M.B.E. degree from the Claremont Graduate School and a Ph.D. in engineering from the University of Michigan. Dr. Ruskin is a registered professional engineer in California and has been a Faculty Fellow at the Pacific Coast Banking School.

[1] Roberts, E. B., "A Basic Study of Innovators: How to Keep and Capitalize on Their Talents," *Research Management*, 11, No. 4 (July, 1968), pp. 249-266.

[2] Multiple regression analysis is a form of curve-fitting for n-dimensional situations. The curious reader is directed to standard texts on the subject, e.g., Lindgren, B. W., *Statistical Theory*, New York: The MacMillan Company (1968), or Voik, Wm., *Applied Statistics for Engineers*, New York: McGraw-Hill Book Co., Inc. (1958).

[3] Morgan, R. F., *Making an Idea Into a Business*, London: Technical Development Capital, Limited (November, 1967); Sheahan, D., "Bankers Don't Savy Electronics," *Defense & Aerospace Systems*, 13 (May 6, 1968), p. 22; Yetman, John, **Private** Communication (Controller, Industrial & Commercial Finance Corp. Ltd., Birmingham, England).

[4] Marathon Securities Corp., *Report for the Six Months Ended July 31, 1966*, New York (1966); Subcommittee on Military Operations, Committee on Government Operations, House of Representatives, 86th Congress, *Organization and Management of Missile Programs*, Washington, D.C., U.S. Government Printing Office (1959), p. 39.

[5] Balog, J., and Moriarty, D. P., "The Use of Technological Information in Investment Decision-Making" *Financial Analysts Journal*, 23 (July, 1967), pp. 76-79; Roberts, E. B., *"A General Theory of Research and Development*, N.Y., Harper & Row (1964).

[6] Peters, C. C., & Van Voorhis, W. R., *Statistical Procedures and Their Mathematical Bases*, New York: McGraw-Hill Book Co., Inc. (1945), pp. 433-437.

[7]

$$\frac{m}{M} = i^{(r^t)} \tag{2}$$

$$\log \frac{m}{M} = r^t \log\ (i) \tag{3}$$

$$\log \left(\log \frac{m}{M}\right) = t\ \log\ (r) + \log\ (\log i) \tag{4}$$

[8] See: Adler, L., "Time-Lag in New Product Development," *Journal of Marketing*, 30 (Jan., 1966), pp. 17-21; Marshall, A. W., & Meckling, W. H., *Predictability of Cost, Time & Success of a Development*, RAND Corp. Report P-1821 (Dec. 11, 1959); National Science Foundation, *Funds for Research and Development in Industry*, Washington, D.C.: U.S. Government Printing Office (issued annually).

[9] "Essential completion" is used instead of actual completion because the latter implies m equal M at the completion point. Putting m equal to M, however, creates a computational difficulty, namely evaluating the logarithm of the logarithm of one. This difficulty can be circumvented as follows: Let $m = 0.995\ M$ and compute r, and let $m = 0.999M$ and compute a second value of r. Clearly, these two calculations will produce different values for r, but they should be relatively close, and they may be extrapolated to give a value corresponding to actual completion, i.e., $m = M$. As an illustration, consider the following situation:

Presume that the "initial investment," i, for a development was 10 per cent of the final investment incurred and that the time for development was five years. Then substituting into equation (3) gives

$$\log \left(\frac{m}{M}\right) = r^5\ \log\ (0.10)$$

If $m = 0.995\ M$, then r_1^5 is

$$r_1{}^5 = \log\ (0.995)/\log\ (0.10) = \frac{-0.00501}{-2.30259} = 0.00217,$$

$5 \log r_1 = \log\ (0.00217)$,
$\log r_1 = -1.243$, and
$\quad r_1 = 0.289.$

Similarly, if $m = 0.999\ M$, then $r_2{}^5$

$$r_2{}^5 = \log\ (0.999)/\log\ (0.10) = \frac{-0.00100}{-2.30259} = 0.00043$$

$5 \log r_2 = \log\ (0.00043)$
$\log r_2 = -1.550$, and
$\quad r_2 = 0.213.$

Extrapolating linearly from r_1 and r_2 to r ($m = M$) gives $r_{m\ =\ M} = 0.194$.

U.S. Department of Commerce, *Technological Innovation: Its Environment and Management* (1967), cited in Matthews, P. A., & Dennison, T., *Technological Innovation in the Steel Industry*, Iron & Steel Institute Centenary Meeting (1969).

[11] Write equation (4), in footnote 7, for two different times, t_1 and t_f, where t_1 represents the present time and t_f represents the completion or final time:

$$\log\left(\log\frac{m_1}{M}\right) = t_1 \log(r) + \log(\log i) \tag{5}$$

and

$$\log\left(\log\frac{m_f}{M}\right) = t_f \log(r) + \log(\log i) \tag{6}$$

Solving equations (5) and (6) for log (log i) and equating, since i is a constant and log (log i) is a constant, one obtains

$$\log\left(\log\frac{m_1}{M}\right) - t_1 \log(r) = \log\left(\log\frac{m_f}{M}\right) - t_f \log(r) \tag{7}$$

Equation (7) relates the present time and final time, t_1 and t_f, respectively, and the present amount of expenditure, m_1, and the final amount of expenditure, m_f. Of course, m_f and M are the same amount, but for the purposes of calculation m_f must be set to a value like 99.5 percent or 99.9 percent of M. By using such figures, one can compute corresponding values for time, e.g., $t(m_f = 0.995M)$ or $t(m_f = 0.999M)$. The following example illustrates the technique.

Consider a case where a given technological field has an r of 0.2, the present stage of a project's development, m_1, is 15 percent M, and one and a half years were required to reach this point. How long will be required to reach 99 percent M? In this case t_1 is 1.5 and the unknown is $t(m_f = 0.99)$. Using equation (7), we write

$$\log(\log 0.15) - 1.5 \log(0.2) = \log(\log 0.99) - t_f \log(0.2) \tag{8}$$

Rearranging and solving for t_f,

$$t_f = \frac{\log(\log 0.99) - \log(\log 0.15)}{\log(0.2)} + 1.5 \tag{9}$$

or

$$t_f = \frac{\log\left(\dfrac{\log 0.99}{\log 0.15}\right)}{\log(0.2)} + 1.5. \tag{10}$$

Thus,

$$t_f = \frac{-5.25}{-1.61} + 1.5 \tag{11}$$

or

$$t_f = 4.8 \text{ years.} \tag{12}$$

Thus, a total of 4.8 years, or 3.3 years from the present, is the time expected to reach 99 percent of the total project duration.

[12] It has been observed, by E. B. Roberts (in *A General Theory of Research and Development*, published by Harper & Row), that original estimates of the effort required to bring a research and development effort to fruition are usually too low. This situation need not alarm the banker if he realizes that his judgment of the applicant's proposed program should be made in light of *actual development experiences*.

[13] A suitable way to identify relevant sources of trade data is via Coman, E. T., Jr., *Sources of Business Information*, Berkeley, California: University of California Press (1964).

[14] See: Cole, R. I., *Improving Effectiveness in R & D*, Washington, D.C.: Thompson Book Co., Inc. (1967); Orth, C. D., III, Bailey, J. C., & Wolek, F. W., *Administering Research & Development*, Homewood, Ill.: Richard D. Irwin, Inc. (1964); Pelz, D. C., & Andrews, F. M., *Scientists in Organizations*, New York: John Wiley & Son, Inc. (1966) Chap. 3; Roberts, E. B., *A General Theory of Research & Development*, New York: Harper & Row (1964).

[15] Pelz, D. C. & Andrews, F. M., *op. cit.*; Roberts, E. B., *op. cit.*

[16] Roberts, E. B., *op. cit.*

[17] Hirsch, Q., Melwitt, W., Oakes, W. J. & Patton, R. A., "The Relation of Utilization to the Shortage of Scientists," IRE *Transactions on Engineering Management*, EM-5, No. 3 (September, 1958), p. 88.

[18] Alternatively, the banker can use a probabilistic approach.

In this approach he first estimates the probabilities (either statistically or intuitively) associated with the desired outcomes for each independent dimension or assessment. He then obtains an estimate of the probability of the desired overall outcome by multiplying the independent probabilities. Clearly, one low independent probability will cause the overall probability product to be low.

HOW A BUSINESS PLAN IS READ

by Joseph Mancuso

It is not the critic who counts, nor the man who points out how the strong man stumbled, or where the doer of deeds could have done better. The credit belongs to the man who is actually in the arena; whose face is marred by dust and sweat and blood; who strives valiantly, who errs and comes short again and again; who knows great enthusiasms, the great devotions, and spends himself in a worthy cause; and who, at the worst, if he fails, at least fails while daring greatly, so that his place shall never be with those cold and timid souls who know neither victory nor defeat.

Source unknown

INTRODUCTION

A document written to raise money for a growing company is called a business plan. The most popular types are written for entrepreneurial companies seeking a private placement of funds from venture capital sources. Internal venture management teams of larger companies are also writing business plans.[1] While these newer types seldom circulate to external private placement sources, they do progress upward within the organization for approval by corporate managements.

Differences certainly exist between the entrepreneurial and the internal venture group's business plans but they are quite small. The major difference rests in the risk and rewards structure of the enterprise, and not in the reading or writing of the document. The objectives of both types of plans are the same, launching a new business or expanding a promising small business. The ultimate responsibility for success or failure in one case rests with an entrepreneur/venture capitalist and in the other with a manager/vice president. However, the document used to consummate the financing is called the business plan, no matter where it originates. In both cases, the document needs to be thorough and well done to be successful.

The vast majority of business plans are prepared by entrepreneurs seeking to secure venture capital. Although the new venture groups within large companies are expanding their activities, they do not approach the number of existing small companies seeking the same goal. In addition, start-up companies are a special breed; their entrepreneurial business plans continue despite the depressed economic conditions of the country.

The term "business plan" is the more formal name for the **document**, whereas the financial community prefers the nickname "deal." While it is crude and a bit harsh, it has a shock value which makes it realistic and more descriptive. "Business plan" is the formal way of saying "deal." Some financiers carry this attempted realism one step farther and describe the fund-raising process as an imitation of the T.V. program "Let's Make a Deal." In my opinion, this too has shock value, but a little too much. Consequently, it's not in popular usage.

THE VENTURE CAPITALIST

Venture capitalists are sent hundreds of business plans annually, yet each year they invest in only a handful of businesses. The number of deals reviewed by a venture capitalist depends on their reputation, which, in turn, depends on their past successes. There are currently about 500 venture capital firms in the U.S.A. The number of successes contained within a venture capital portfolio seldom exceeds one in ten. Or, in baseball language, a batting average of .100 is typical. A typical venture portfolio might be invested in ten companies. While only one winner is the average, the typical portfolio would have five businesses that are essentially bankrupt. Two or three of the remainder are marginal firms with little real potential while one or two firms may still have a spark of hope to become a big winner. Understanding this pattern highlights the dangers of the venture business and demonstrates the crucial nature of a single winner.[2]

One of the reasons for the hundreds of deals arriving at a single venture capitalist's office is the multiple exposures given a single business plan. An unknowing entrepreneur in dire need of funds often will mail his business plan to a large list of venture capitalists. Such lists of venture capital are available from several sources. This multiple exposure, or the more popular phrase of "shopping the deal," has a reverse effect. Instead of improving it often seriously weakens the chances of raising the needed capital. On the other hand, not showing it to anyone assures an unsuccessful placement. A thin line exists between too few and too many potential investors. Incidentally, the Security Exchange Commission (SEC) frowns on showing a deal to more than 25 potential investors. However, this rule is seldom enforced but it should be discussed in detail with your lawyer before writing a business plan.

THE BUSINESS PLAN

Most articles on business plans focus on how to write them.[3] Checklists, blank forms, and sample plans are the substance for the how-to-write articles. As a guide, they help catch items which might be overlooked. They force a full and balanced consideration of the many intertwined issues. To be helpful they must be broad in scope but this also decreases their effectiveness for a single reader. These articles often contain excerpts of business plans or a table of contents from a typical business plan.

Below is such a table of contents:

1) Introduction
2) Use of Proceeds and Terms of Placement
3) The Product Area
4) The Market and Competition
5) The Company Management Team
6) Plant Facilities
7) Financial Data and Pro-forma Statements
8) Appendices

A central message in all the how-to-write advice is to tailor the document to meet the needs and desires of the potential investors. And, in my opinion, that's sound advice. This doesn't mean to exaggerate, lie, or inflate the sales projections, however. Not at all. It does mean to place emphasis on the items of special interest for a specific potential investor. Each investor group has its own set of characteristics, and tailoring a plan to suit its ob-

jectives makes good common sense. In some cases, a business plan is written in modular form. Various module combinations are used for different investors depending upon the characteristics of the firm. A single plan often will not suffice for all its possible uses.

The definition of a "good" business plan is one which raises money. A "bad" plan doesn't attract investors. It's that simple. But don't be confused. A "good" plan may raise the money but the business may still fail. A "good" business plan does not assure business success. However, a "bad" business plan almost always means business failure. To succeed at the more crucial objectives of a profitable business requires a "good" business plan plus a good business. They are not one and the same.

Business plans are comprehensive documents which often require several months to compile. Although they do vary in length and complexity, the process of writing it forces coordination of external legal, financial and accounting assistance. In addition, internal analysis of manufacturing, finance and marketing must coincide with the external activities. This coordination adds time to the preparation. Between $1,000 and $10,000 for outside services to prepare a business plan is fairly typical. The company management intuitively believes their plans thoroughness and sophistication reflect on the company's likelihood of success. Consequently, there is a tendency to do it well and sometimes to do it and re-do it.

Yet, most business plans are not read in detail from cover to cover. While it may have taken five weeks to compile, the potential investors will typically invest only five minutes in reading it. A venture capitalist who receives a dozen plans a day, just doesn't have the time to read every plan which is sent to him. In fact, a leading venture capitalist at a large Boston bank, claims he never reads the plan. "They all say the same thing and it's never true," is his comment, "so I never read them."

Don't take this to mean you don't need to write a business plan. It's necessary and essential to raising new money. This is true for internal or external entrepreneurs. If you don't have one it will immediately be conspicuous by its absence. And you will be turned away by everyone until you do have one. It's a paradox but it's true. And I doubt that this fact of financial life will change. You must write one if for no other reason than to prove you can do it. It may never be read, but that doesn't matter.

HOW TO WRITE A BUSINESS PLAN

My notion, to be developed in this article, is to write a plan to meet the requirements of the plan's reader, not your own. My opinion has been formulated during the past ten years as I wrote or read about 300 individual business plans. Based upon field research with several dozen venture capitalists and several hundred entrepreneurs, I concluded that knowledgeable investors all spend the precious five minutes in about the same manner. The purpose of this article is to describe how business plans are interpreted.

Before I do, I shall highlight several additional sources of how-to-write a business plan. You may find these helpful as well.

1) Ch. 12, p. 137 of "Up Your Own Organization" by Donald Dible, The Entrepreneur Press, Mission Station, Drawer 27591, Santa Clara, CA 95051.

2) "The Business Plan," a spiral bound booklet written by Winfred Brown and Leroy Sinclair, Technimetrics, Inc., 919 3rd Ave., N.Y., NY 10022.

3) "Business Plans for Small Manufacturers," Management Aid #218, Small Business Administration, Washington, D.C. 20416, 24 page booklet.

4) In addition, two of my reading books, THE ENTREPRENEUR'S HANDBOOK (Artech House, 610 Washington St., Dedham, MA 02026) and ENTREPRENEURSHIP AND VENTURE MANAGEMENT (co-authored with Prof. Cliff Baumback, published by Prentice-Hall, Englewood Cliffs, NJ 07632) offer numerous articles on this and related subjects.

HOW A BUSINESS PLAN IS READ

Little, if anything, has been written on how a business plan is actually analyzed. To gain insight into this procedure, I conducted in-depth interviews with about two dozen venture capitalists and about twice as many others in the financial community. These others included bankers, lawyers, accountants, and consultants. This research was done intermittently over the past three years. Besides asking how it was read, I actually spent several days at several locations to observe and verify what I was told. Moreover, as an investor in several entrepreneurial companies, I have also read several hundred business plans. To my surprise, almost all of us analyzed the plans in identical manners. The five minutes is a good average if all the plans which are never read are excluded. Here, from my research is how it's done, on a step by step basis. Remember, a maximum of one minute is all that's invested in each of these steps.

Step 1 - Determine the characteristics of company and industry.
Step 2 - Determine the terms of the deal.
Step 3 - Read the latest balance sheet.
Step 4 - Determine the caliber of the people in the deal.
Step 5 - Determine what's different about this deal.
Step 6 - A once over lightly.

Step 1 - Determine the characteristics of company and industry

Each venture capitalist has preferred areas for investment. Some like high technology, some like low technology. Some like computers, while others like consumer goods and still others prefer publishing. A single venture capitalist is seldom at ease in every industry, just as a single entrepreneur could not manage an enterprise in varied industries with equal skill.

Their area of expertise is developed over the years based upon the venture capitalist's past successes. In short, if they were successful once in one industry, they are more receptive to deals involving the same industry. This is fundamental. Consequently, many venture capitalists never read a business plan beyond Step #1. They have little interest in the industry, regardless of the terms of the deal. They only read the cover page before they say, "no."

Beyond this consideration, the potential investor considers the glamour of the industry. Are there any larger publicly traded companies in the same industry? If so, how high is the stock price earning multiple (P/E ratio) for these firms. Or, better yet, is there another larger company who is extremely successful in this industry? In the computer industry, the Data General Corporation in Southboro, Massachusetts could point to Digital Equipment Corporation in Maynard, Massachusetts.

In the consumer goods industry, many small companies point to Avon Products. A company which eventually failed, Lanewood Laboratories, Inc. (Boston, Massachusetts) raised $500,000 in a business plan which pointed to Lestoil (Adell Chemical Company, Holyoke, Massachusetts). Lanewood had little of substance in their business plan other than the parallel of another successful company. Not so with Data General. However, both the successful and unsuccessful companies find it easier to raise funds when another company has pioneered a success.

Industry glamour rises and falls much like the length of women's skirts. Ten years ago it was electronics, followed by franchising, followed by computers. Next year it will probably be energy. Despite the obvious problems with glamour fads, we must also accept them as a reality. They exist and they make a difference. Consequently, if your industry is momentarily considered "glamorous," your chances of securing funds suddenly increase.

After the potential investor examines and evaluates the industry, he will quickly categorize the company within the industry. He'll quickly determine the following facts about the company:

1) Past 12 months' annual sales
2) Profit or loss for last year
3) Number of employees
4) Share of market
5) Degree of technology
6) Geographic location of facilities

Depending upon the interpretation of the above, he'll be able to quickly determine if the company matches the venture capitalist's visions of an ideal investment. Is it too large or small? Is it too far away? There are numerous, acceptable reasons for not making the investment, Seldom, if ever, is a venture capitalist faulted for the investments he didn't make. More often and more intense is the criticism for the investments he actually selected. The sequence in step one is check the industry and then check the company.

Step 2 - The terms of the deal

How much of a company is being sold at what price represents the substance of the terms of the deal. The peripheral issue is in what form (debt or equity) is the deal being offered. Many venture firms strongly prefer convertible debt or debt with warrants rather than a straight equity deal. Their structure as a profit-making enterprise may require the venture firm to generate income to pay salaries and overhead. This is in addition to the capital gains expected from the capital portfolio. Naturally, these firms would prefer interest bearing debt to help cover this overhead and a few of them will reject deals which don't satisfy this basic requirement. In these cases this is not a peripheral issue, but in the majority of cases the more substantive issue of "how much for how much" is of more concern.

Consequently, a well done business plan informs the reader of the following items on the first page:

1) Percentage of company being sold (after dilution)
2) The total price of this percentage of the company (per share figures also included)
3) The minimum investment (number of investors sought)
4) The total valuation (after the placement) being placed on the company
5) The terms of the investment
   a) common stock
   b) preferred stock
   c) convertible debentures
   d) stock with warrants
   e) straight equity

Unfortunately, many "deals" do not spell these issues out plainly. Consequently, the little time which is invested in looking over the plan is extended digging out these details. If they were clearly stated at the beginning of the plan, the potential investors could spend more time analyzing the more positive selling features (like the product literature) of the plan. A summary sheet in a business plan saves everyone's time and increases an interested reader's enthusiasm.

Finally, after the terms are known, the follow-up analysis focuses on these related issues.
   A) How does this price per share of this placement compare with the founder's price per share. Are the founders re-investing again in this placement?
   B) What was the value of the company at the last placement and why has it changed?
   C) The use of funds and more specifically, will the new money be used to repay old debts or to undertake new activities which, in turn, will increase profitability?

Step 3 - Read the balance sheet

A current balance sheet is usually located just prior to the appendix and pro-forma cash flow and income statements. It's often the first page of the financial exhibits. It's the only financial page ever glanced at during an initial reading of a business plan.

Here's the one minute process used by potential investors while interpreting the balance sheet (and income statement). Incidentally, Merrill, Lynch,Pierce, Fenner & Smith, One Liberty Plaza, 16 Broadway, N.Y., N.Y. 10006 offers a free 24-page brochure entitled "How to Read A Financial Report," 3rd edition which contains greater detail on the same subject. It's worth acquiring before writing a business plan.

Below is all the financial information needed to make a quick evaluation of the deal. It's much preferred to any pro-forma analysis. What I shall describe is the actual process used to read a balance sheet from the top down. It's a four step process. Here are the four steps.

Step A - Determine liquidity
Step B - Determine debt/equity structure
Step C - Examine net worth
Step D - Examine assets and liabilities

Step A - Check working capital or current ratio, each of which measures about the same thing.
    A) Working Capital = Current Assets minus Current Liabilities
    B) Current Ratio = Current Assets divided by Current Liabilities
Below is a typical balance sheet.

Cash	$ 50,000
Accounts Receivable	$ 200,000
Inventories	$ 250,000
TOTAL current assets	$ 500,000
Accounts Payable	$ 250,000
Notes Payable (one year)	$ 75,000
Accrued Expenses Payable	$ 100,000
Federal Income Tax Payable	$ 25,000
TOTAL current liabilities	$ 450,000

Working Capital = $50,000
Current Ratio = 1.1

A firm's working capital should be positive while the current ratio should be greater than one. These two statements say the same thing in different words. A current ratio closer to two indicates a more average company. A company with a positive $100,000 of working capital is liquid but may be tight on cash.

Step B - Examine the debt to equity ratio.

$$\text{Debt equity ratio} = \frac{\text{Total Debt}}{\text{Total Equity}} \quad \text{divided by}$$

This ratio reveals how much credit a debt source (bank) has already extended to the company. In addition, it offers insight into the remaining borrowing power of the company. A 50% debt to equity ratio, where a lender advances 50 cents for every equity dollar is a ballpark upper limit for this ratio. Seldom will debt sources advance one debt dollar for every equity dollar. Consequently, a debt to equity ratio of one is rare. While a debt to equity ratio of 10% indicates the company has borrowing power remaining.

Step C - Examines the net worth. The potential investor will extract from the balance sheet the amount of money initially invested in the firm, which is the initial capitalization provided by the founders. The cumulative profits (or losses) to date which are contained within retained earnings offer another benchmark of the company's success (or lack of it) to date. Below is a typical balance sheet.

Long term debt (current portion due this year shown under current liabilities)	$100,000
Capital stock (initial capitalization)	250,000
Retained earnings (profit or loss to date)	(100,000)
Owners equity (combines capitalization and retained earnings)	$150,000

$$\frac{\text{Debt}}{\text{Equity}} = \frac{100,000}{150,000} = .75$$

A prospective investor interprets this information as follows. The founders began the company with $250,000 and have lost $100,000 since its inception. The company has a long term interest bearing note which was probably awarded to the company because of the initial capital of $250,000. However, due to the losses to date, the company has little remaining borrowing power.

A quick check will be made to determine if any or all assets (receivable, inventory, fixed assets) are pledged to secure any of the debt. If they are free and unincumbered, this would indicate more borrowing power.

As a rule of thumb, a debt source (band) will allow the following debt to be secured against assets.

Asset	Percentage of balance sheet value which can be borrowed against
Cash or Marketable securities	100%
Accounts Receivable	75%-85%
Inventory	20%-30%
Fixed Assets	Percentage will depend on market value, not on book value.

Step D - Examine the assets and liabilities. A quick check of the assets and liabilities is the next step. First, check to be sure all assets are real (tangible) and check liabilities to verify that any debt is to bonafide outsiders not to insiders (such as notes to stockholders).

By examining the asset categories investors check to be sure soft assets such as good will, patents, or capitalized Research & Development are not large or unreasonable. For some unexplained reason, small companies often choose to capitalize R & D or organizational expenses rather than writing off these expenses in the period they occur. This practice is frowned upon by all potential investors because it distorts the balance sheet and impairs future earnings. The slang term for it is "capitalized crap" and it's a sure sign of danger. If it's large, it can dampen an investor's interest.

Furthermore, entrepreneurs and friends and relatives of entrepreneurs often choose to make their initial investment in a small company as debt rather than equity. It makes these founders feel more secure because it offers some protection in the event of bankruptcy. So, in a quick check, a potential investor determines who is owed how much by the company.

This four step process (A through D) usually takes less than one minute from beginning to end. In the initial reading of the business plan, potential investors are not necessarily probing the balance sheet in depth but rather searching for red flags.[4] Before an investment is consummated, the balance sheet, income statement, and pro-formas will be analyzed in considerable detail. However, during the first glance, the above analysis plus a quick look to determine the magnitude of last year's sales from the profit & loss statement is the extent of the financial investigation. The balance sheet, along with a magnitude of sales, provides sufficient data to judge whether or not a more detailed financial investigation is warranted.

Step 4 - Management's Capabilities

This step is focused on the single most crucial aspect of the business plan. Potential investors begin by examining the founders, board of directors, current investors, outside professional services (accountants, lawyers, bankers, consultants) in hopes of uncovering a familiar name. The reputations and "quality" of the team are issues in this measure. Unfortunately, this is a subjective area and, as such, is open to a wide range of individual interpretations. What is "good" to some is not so good for others. Because it is subjective, opinions and assessments fluctuate dramatically.

If they know someone, and they usually do, (at least they will know someone who knows someone) this person will set the tone for the whole deal, regardless of his affiliations with the company. Even if he's only a small investor, the company loses its identity and the business plan becomes known as "John Smith's deal" around the office. These known insiders become the links for further information by the potential investors.

Consequently, the reputation of all the individuals surrounding the business is of serious impact in securing additional funds. For start-up deals or for situations where the company is unknown to the potential investors, here's what they look at in analyzing management's abilities. This format is about the same for both internal and external businesses. However, internal venture teams are greatly assisted when the project directors are considered highly by top management. Many times this "golden boy" syndrome becomes the single crucial variable in approving new corporate funds.

1) Track record of founders and managers including where they worked and how well they performed in the past. Without a doubt, this is the single most crucial ingredient when assessing "management's abilities."

2) Balance and experience of the inner management team — How long have they worked together and the degree of balance between marketing, finance, and manufacturing represented by the operating managers.

3) Who is the financial man (or bank or accountant) and what are his credentials? Potential investors much prefer a "deal" with one strong full time financial type. He speaks this language and is more at home with money than products. Potential investors like to envision this financial type as a caretaker for the newly arrived funds.

Step 5 - The Unique Selling Proposition

What's different about this deal is the eventual pivotal issue of whether or not a specific venture capital firm chooses to invest. The same holds true for internal venture management teams in larger companies.

Is there an unusual feature in the product, do they have a patent, an unusual technology, or a significant lead over competition? Is this a company whose critical skill rests in marketing, manufacturing or finance? Does the company's strength match the skills needed to succeed in this industry? Or is there an imbalance? What's different about this company and how significantly different or better is their product, is the investor's most central concern.

Does this company have the potential to open up a whole new industry like Polaroid, Xerox, IBM, Digital Equipment Corporation, McDonald's or Hewlett-Packard? Or, on the other hand, is this a modest idea with limited future growth? A venture capitalist needs a return of greater than ten times on his investment just to stay even (1 in 10 succeed) and he is seldom intrigued with companies which hold a marginal advantage over competing firms or products. In essence, this is what Rosser Reaves has called the Unique Selling Proposition (U.S.P.). Good ideas or products which are both unique and better attract capital. Marginal improvements do not possess enough up side potential to offset the risks inherent in a new business venture. The U.S.P. must be truly exciting to attract funds.

Step 6 - A Once Over Lightly

After the above analysis, the final minute is usually spent thumbing through the business plan. A casual look-see at product literature, graphs, unusual exhibits, samples, letters of recommendation, letters of intent, is the purpose of this last double check. Here, for some unexplained reason, the venture capitalist is double checking that the prior 5-minutes invested digesting the plan hasn't missed some crucial aspects.

Seldom, if ever, are any new opinions formed during this final minute. Yet, everyone engages in this leafing process. It has little substance and I've wondered if they'd catch a playboy-centerfold if it were inconspicuously placed among all the exhibits. This inevitable activity certainly supports the arguments for unusual enclosures. A product sample pasted on a page, or a letter with a meaningful letterhead will be given a quick glance. Consequently, an unusual chart or two can be crucial in maintaining interest. While it will not make the big difference in the final analysis, it will extend the readership of a business plan.

After this final step, the analysis is over and the decision to obtain more information or to say "No" is made. Ninety-nine times out of a hundred the decision is to return the plan with no interest. The "deal" is turned down.

A few make a phone call or two beyond this stage and then turn down the deal after a detail or two is confirmed. However, even these deals are actually rejected during the first reading; the act of saying "No" is merely postponed a few additional days.

How to become the one in one hundred, how to write a successful "deal", as I have said earlier, is the subject of many authors. My intent in this article is not to address that issue, but to offer insight into what happens to your plan when it finally reaches the top of the pile. While these findings are not specifically "how to write" solutions, they should be considered before a business plan is written. Understanding the reading process may alter your final writing of a business plan.

Actually writing and reading a business plan is a circular process. My question is "Why not accept the inevitable fact that you'll only get five minutes and address your plan to this process?" This article is not intended to give birth to a new format or table of contents for a business plan because changes in form are not needed. However, it should offer insight and thereby alter the writing style and the focus of a deal.

Most entrepreneurs assume a positive relationship between time invested in reading the plan and the likelihood of obtaining capital, "If they'd only read my plan," mumbles the unsuccessful entrepreneur, "they'd be chasing me instead of vice versa." To highlight this feeling, business plans are often dressed in their Sunday best leather bound jackets. Some covers or jackets cost over $10.00 each. The product is only as good as the package is the foundation behind this assumption. Entrepreneurs are insulted when they discover the potential investors neglect the detail of the business plan. Like the author of any manuscript, they seek readership and, in their view, anyone who reads it will be more likely to invest.

THE PLAN PACKAGE

In my research with several dozen venture capitalists, I conducted some small sample tests to determine the method used to select a single business plan from a grouping of five or ten. In my little tests, I placed several "deals" on a table and asked venture capitalists in the Northeast to examine only the covers of the business plans before selecting which of the half dozen plans they would select to read first.

In observing which plans received the most initial attention, it was obviously not the ones with pretty covers. Rather, the company name was the more crucial variable. Next in importance was the geographical location of the company. The third element was the thickness of the plan. The shorter plans received more attention.

In this little test nothing else was revealed about any of the business plans other than what appeared on the cover. The position of the "deals" on the tables was random and I observed each venture capitalist as he glanced over the deals. To conclude, I have ranked the variables as below with No. 1 being most important.

1) Company name
2) Company geographic location
3) Length of business plan
4) Quality of cover

The next question I explored was, "How can an entrepreneur increase the likelihood that a venture capitalist will read his business plan once he's past the cover?" Should he send it along in installments with the final chapter arriving first? Or should he send the first chapter first, or should he send along a summary?

In my research, I concluded summaries and mini-plans were not effective documents. Once it's written a teaser summary only adds delay to the eventual readership of a plan. The sunk cost of having it done is not used to the entrepreneur's advantage. Many times a summary conveys a less substantial understanding of a business. I much prefer to use the document as a whole to increase impact and readership.

I uncovered two additional variables in determining a plan's eventual readership and, to a lesser extent, the likelihood of a venture capitalist making an investment. The first is the method of receiving the plan and second is the success of the "pre-sell" efforts. Like any other product, the degree and quality of the "pre-sell" is vital.

The naive entrepreneur follows the suicidal path of a blind mass mailing. Armed with a directory and a secretary, he mails his plan with a "form letter" to a sampling from the directory. This wastes everyone's time and your money. It never works.

Another bad approach is to make personal visits with the business plan tucked under your arm. This humble, straight-forward approach is like going to a doctor as an unreferred patient. Everyone asks, "Who sent you?" You begin to feel like an intruder. You seldom find the key man in his office or able to see you. This wastes your time and your money.

The best method of delivering a business plan is through a third party. Without a doubt, unless you're already an established and successful entrepreneur, a third party referral adds credence to your plan. It adds more readability than any other variable. Yet, while months are spent preparing the plan, only a few minutes are spent deciding how to deliver it. Like all newly created manuscripts, it's believed to be done only after it's off your desk. Consequently, I suggest optimizing the delivery by using a third party. Any of the group below are acceptable as long as their reputation and liaison with the venture capitalist is positive. It need not be the same person for each potential investor.

1) Consultants
2) Bankers
3) Lawyers
4) Accountants
5) Other entrepreneurs

The second level of improvement, a good job on pre-selling is invaluable and intertwined with the liaison person. If the potential investors were told six months before it arrived about the exciting company and then once a month for the next six months about current developments, they'd be more receptive to reading the plan. After all, the best time to raise money is when you don't need it. The same holds for arousing potential investor interest. A well managed company planning to expand will invest time in such pre-selling often and early. It has a large payoff in the long run.

To recap, have the same person both pre-sell and eventually deliver your plan. Have the company name and location clearly spelled out on the cover page and have it hand-carried by a mutual friend to a select group of venture capitalists.

During the process remember that the two most successful venture capital deals in the Northeast were turned down a number of times before receiving a "yes." In 1958, Digital Equipment Corporation (D.E.C.) finally convinced American Research & Development (A.R.D.) to invest $70,000 which is rumored today to be worth about $250,000,000. In 1968, Mr. Fred Adler made a modest investment in a struggling new company known as Data General Corporation. It's rumored that the four principals each made in excess of $10,000,000 within four years of launching this venture. So, the rewards are high for those that play and win. Unfortunately, however those that play usually lose and plans of this type significantly outnumber the winners. However, winning at the business and raising funds are two separate issues.

The message of this article is to understand the process which will inevitably be used to read and interpret your plan. Once your business is underway it's the entrepreneur's (inside and outside) responsibility to put the company's best foot forward. The sequence and the rationale behind why everyone examines a plan in the same manner should be helpful to both internal and external entrepreneurs.

[1] Donald A. Kunstler, "Corporate Venture Groups" — The need, the responsibility, the organization, the leadership; in Robert E. King, ed. Marketing and the New Science of Planning (Chicago: American Marketing Assoc.) 1968, pp 449-454.
Richard M. Hill, James D. Hlavacket, "Product Development Through Venture Teams" in Fred C. Allvine, ed. Marketing in Motion/Relevance in Marketing (Chicago, American Marketing Assoc.), 1972, pp 138-142.

Peterson, R., New Venture Management In a Large Company, Harvard Business Review, May/June 1967.

Intracorporate Entrepreneurship by Jeffrey C. Susbauer, Bureau of Business Research, Cleveland State University, Cleveland, Ohio 44115.

[2] Albert Kelly, "Venture Capital," Ch. 5, published by the Management Institute, School of Management, Boston College, Chestnut Hill, Mass., 1971.

[3] Adams, Robert M., "An Approach to New Business Ventures," Research Management, Vol. XII, No. 4, 1969, pp 255-261.
Hauser, Stuart and Brichner, William H., "Business Plans for the Scientific Entrepreneur," Research/Development, May 1971, pp 14-17.

What a Venture Capitalist

by Sam Adams

When a Company Isn't a Company

Alan Patricof's office is flooded with late spring sunlight. Its walls are covered with some of the brightly colored hard-edge paintings he began collecting before that school became faddish. His glass-topped desk is a study in transluscence—clear of everything but a thick glass container of rock candy, pieces of which he crunches as he talks. Patricof reaches behind him and pulls out a small plastic cylinder with slits in its walls. "This is used instead of a toggle bolt," says Patricof. "Very strong, good product. Very interesting. But does the man who brought me this have a product or a company? We think he has a product. We don't think he has a company."

To Patricof, the distinction is crucial. Every day he and his associates listen to new business proposals, and by Patricof's count the product-company mistake is one of the common-est committed by budding entrepreneurs. In three years as the head of his own venture capital firm, Patricof has seen a lot of mistakes. He got a taste for the risk capital business in 1969 when he successfully lined up a wad of money to save a then tottering *New York* magazine. Then he went on to establish the Alan Patricof Organization with a pool of about $5 million. Today it owns more than half of the common stock of ASG Industries (formerly American Saint Gobain), the fourth largest glass producer in the U.S.; Childcraft Education, Inc. and RSR, Inc., a $100-million secondary smelter. It owns nearly half of publisher E. P. Dutton and has substantial investments in such companies as Wells National Service, a lessor of television sets to hospitals (its stock is traded on the American Stock Exchange), a consumer periodical called

Shopper's Voice, and a bunch of high-technology companies.

But for every company in his portfolio, Patricof has turned down dozens. Many of their creators might have saved themselves some time had they gone through the obvious but often overlooked exercise of simply thinking their project through. Before an entrepreneur begins to write a business proposal, says Patricof, he should thoroughly analyze the potential market for his product and its feasibility in the current economic environment. He should submit his idea to friends and defy them to find loopholes in it. He should assure himself that there are no legal or trade secret conflicts with his present employer and that his patents are solid.

Next, the entrepreneur should take up the amount of money he needs to raise. "I am a great believer in properly capitalizing," says Patricof. "On the one hand you don't want to start an ambitious project without sufficient capital. On the other, you don't have to raise all your capital on the first day—because, if you are successful, there is no question that the

Looks For

initial money is the most expensive money."

Patricof's advice: Go as far as you can with close-in money—that is money of your own or money raised from friends and relatives. "I give a lot of credit to the guy who puts up his own money, persuades others to work with him evenings and weekends, and maybe lives hand to mouth until he gets to the point where his project makes sense.

"A guy from a huge diversified corporation came here with an impeccable list of credentials," says Patricof, "every one of them a national business name. I looked at his blue-ribbon list, and then I asked him: 'How is it you haven't gotten money from these guys? Why do you come to a stranger? If you could show me that a couple of these guys were investors, I would have to stand up and grab this deal. But you come in and tell me that all of these guys think you're terrific but none of them thinks you're terrific enough to back you.' "

In other words, financial support is the best reference of all. But in most

cases perseverence will be more important than cash in getting a business off the ground. Patricof likes to tell the story of the entrepreneur who came to him with a new medical instrument. The instrument looked very interesting, Patricof relates. It had already been brought through design and prototype stages and a few of the units had been sold. "But he still couldn't prove to my satisfaction that the product had a sufficiently broad market. So I told him: 'Go out and develop $500,000 of backlog and I will finance that backlog.' His face dropped and he said to me, 'I was here a year ago [I didn't know this] and one of your associates told me to come back after I had my initial sales. So here I am and now you're telling me to come back after I've got my backlog.' " Patricof laughs. "Every venture capitalist wants a little more proof, and I am just as guilty of this as anyone else. But look how far he got without us."

Only after he has dealt with the concept and the financial needs should an entrepreneur proceed to a business plan. Any MBA who has

taken a small business course is familiar with the contents of this document—the description of the business, cash flow, additional capital needs and so forth. But to Patricof, the most important element of the business plan is the section describing the credentials of the men who are starting the business.

Patricof looks for people with experience in the field of his new venture. "There are a lot of big problems for the guy who has been an electronics engineer and wants to start a company in the consumer product field," he says.

Next, he looks for marketing ability. "I have just about come to the point, through hard experience, that I will not back a venture unless it involves a man who is fully aware of the marketing environment—the competition, pricing, fit—and can sell the product. You can have the greatest product in the world, the greatest managerial story, the greatest financial story, but if you don't have people who know how to sell that product at a profit, I think you have a risky situation. You see a lot of production guys, engineers who design a product and assume it will fly but who really don't know what the market out there is like."

Let's say the entrepreneur has brought the company as far as it can, has determined his financial needs, and has a succinct, specific business plan. How does he deal with a venture capitalist? "You've got to appreciate the fact that these people are professionals," says Patricof. "There is going to be a lot of nit-picking. Negotiations are going to be protracted. So the worst thing you can do is to come in and say you need the money quickly.

In fact, in Patricof's opinion, the scenario should be staged as casually as possible. The ideal approach goes

Venture capitalist Alan Patricof

something like this: Make an appointment with a venture capitalist and tell him that while you are not ready to take his money yet, you've been working on something you think he might be interested in. Then keep a casual—but active—dialogue going. Let him know when you've sold an order or hired an assistant, and send him your press releases. "Very seldom is a venture capitalist going to push you because he wants your deal so badly," says Patricof. "On the other hand, you don't want to push him so hard you make him feel

threatened. When the day comes that you're ready for financing, the venture capitalist will have made an investment of time, and he is going to want to see something come of it. It takes time to get a guy focused, and that venture capitalist is now focused. If on the day of the closing the deal breaks down, he'll be more disappointed than you."

Another mistake in the presentation is for the partners in a business (Patricof would much prefer to back a team rather than a single individual) to treat each other as equals. Re-

cently three men who had been working together in a billion-dollar corporation came to Patricof with a business proposition, and he asked which of them was the president. They said that none of them was, they were equal partners. "So I said, 'If you are going to run yourselves by committee, it won't work.' Later they returned and I asked again who they had appointed as president. Their answer was still wrong: 'John is the general manager.' That was a big-company answer. They were still in the corporate world." Needless to say, they went elsewhere for their financing.

Another gambit that will help the presentation is to come in with a good lawyer and a good accountant. A "Big-Eight" accountant (one of the eight largest public accountants in the U. S.) will probably be worth the 10% premium that such a firm charges because it will help identify the entrepreneur as a professional. "You reach for anything you can that will give you recognition," says Patricof.

In negotiating the financing, Patricof advises, the start-up businessman should not be afraid of performance deals; *i.e.,* contracts that link the amount of stock to be retained by the owner to the performance of the new company. "Performance deals give the investor confidence that you really believe in the proposal," says

Patricof. But shouldn't the entrepreneur hang onto at least 51% of his company? No, says Patricof. "If you are really as good as you say you are, you can control your company with 1% of the stock. In the first few years, control rests with the guy who is running the company. I would be much more concerned with getting the money to do the job than getting the percentage." As the company progresses, a performance deal will make it possible for the entrepreneur to increase his ownership of his company.

One last piece of advice: Try not to live dangerously. Don't, for instance, stake everything on capturing one big account and then have to fold up shop when that account doesn't come through. "Make sure you have a survival plan," says Patricof. "Funny as it seems, sheer survival works."

Passing a Business Through the Eye of a Banker

Recently an MBA now serving in the venture capital section of a large commercial bank was asked if it was difficult for MBAs to obtain seed money for new businesses. "Yes," he answered, "because other MBAs are the ones who are passing it out."

The jest is at least half true. While no one has made a strict count, there is general agreement that a disproportionate number of MBAs gravitate to the venture capital field. But contrary to the implication that MBA venture capitalists are harder on members of their own fraternity, at

least one of them indicates that the MBA should have a leg up in his battle for seed money. He is University of California MBA Rick Roesch, who, as president of Citicorp Venture Capital Ltd., handles the risk money investments for First National City Corp. Citicorp Venture, a Small Business Investment Corp. with a pool of some $50 million, has investments in about 70 companies, 15 of them outside the U.S.

What would give MBAs a better than even break with Roesch? Adherence to his cardinal rule for a new business proposal: a well thought out, persuasive, *written* business plan. This, of course, is standard fare in the small business course of every business school that has one. "The most successful entrepreneurs have thought through their business plans," says Roesch. "They know their strengths and weaknesses. They know what the competition is offering." And they ought to be able to put all this on paper. Says Roesch: "The entrepreneur is doing himself a disservice to think he can go in eye-to-eye with a prospective investor and simply sell his company. It's safe to say that if it is not on paper, it is not well enough thought out for a venture capitalist to consider it."

Roesch, who with his staff looks at upwards of 2,000 business proposals a

year, finds that their commonest failings are products that are not properly positioned. Frequently, they are aimed at either too well developed a market or one that is too specialized. "We're interested in the man who is determined to build a big company, one with sufficient growth to make it an attractive new issue." What sort of growth would be "sufficient"? "We don't have any hard and fast rules," says Roesch. "Of course, there is an industry rule of thumb that a new venture should be making $1 million after taxes within five to seven years after startup."

To Roesch, the industries that would offer the best crack at achieving that objective include some of the old favorites of the late 1960s: computer hardware, particularly peripherals, computer-related service industries and the medical electronics field. Another interesting area: industries that could receive an assist from the dollar devaluation—for example, textiles.

Finally, Roesch looks for an entrepreneur who has done his apprenticeship at a large corporation. "There is no question," he says, "but what people who have had experience in big business, especially in those companies that have a rapid growth pattern, are better prepared to set up a business." ☐

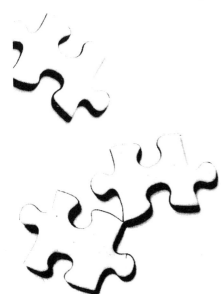

92d Congress \} 2d Session \}	**COMMITTEE PRINT**

VENTURE CAPITAL

A Guidebook for New Enterprises

PREPARED FOR THE

NEW ENGLAND REGIONAL COMMISSION

BY THE

Management Institute

School of Management

Boston College

MARCH 22, 1972

Printed for the use of the Committee on Agriculture and Forestry

---

U.S. GOVERNMENT PRINTING OFFICE

75-292   WASHINGTON : 1972

GUIDE FOR NEW ENTERPRISES

Chapter 5—Venture Capital

The term "venture capital" has no commonly accepted definition but conventional usage, in the United States at least, implies invesment in a business enterprise where the uncertainties have yet to be reduced to risks which are subject to the rational criteria of security analysts.

The concept of venture capital is quite simple. An investor or group of investors, contributes capital money to the new or small corporation in return for an equity position in that corporation. The object is that, as the business grows and prospers, the value of that equity position will increase. Furthermore, at some favorable time in the not too distant future (usually 3–6 years) it will be possible for the investor to convert the value of that equity position into cash or other liquid assets. Thus the appreciation of his investment will be in the form of capital gains.

What distinguishes the true venture capitalist from any other investor is the techniques he employs to achieve his goals, and the degree of

22

risk associated with this type of investment. However, even these char-acteristics are changing as more and more types of investors seek to become "venture capitalists." Two schools of thought are emerging on the investment of venture capital. One is the traditional concept which will be discussed shortly. The second has resulted from institutional investors becoming more adventuresome in their investing policies. These institutional investors have noticed that while their investment in a listed stock might, if they were lucky, double or triple, they were missing out on the stock's more significant gains. By the time the insti-tutions had decided to buy, the firm's original investors had perhaps multiplied their money 50 to 100 times, and even more. However, be-cause the institutions deal in venture capital as a secondary rather than primary interest, they are unable to devote as much time and effort to their venture investments as the traditionalists. Therefore, the new venture capitalists view the field rather differently than the tradition-alists. Generally, they are unencumbered by the same philosophical and altruistic motivations, and they tend to regard a venture invest-ment as just another investment with, of course, greater risks and potential rewards. This outlook is manifested most clearly in what might be called the "one-in-ten" idea of some of the public venture capital and letter stock funds. The theory is that nine out of every ten venture investments will probably be losers, break-evens or only mediocre gainers. But the tenth will hopefully be such a splendid winner that it will more than make up for the other nine.

While these institutions investigate and keep track of a venture in-vestment more closely than they would a listed company, they do not see it as part of their job to assist the corporation in any but the most cursory way. Such assistance would be impractical anyway, because of the large number of companies in which these investors hold a posi-tion. They feel if a company becomes sick, that is the company's problem—a recognized hazard of entrepreneuring.

The head of the securities division of one large insurance company put it this way, "While venture capital is a lot of fun and everyone likes to spend time on it, we have a half billon dollars' worth of marketable securities, much of which is in funds that are competitive/ performance oriented, and we just don't have a lot of time for a few little venture investments. I mean, recently, we spent two man months on a single venture capital deal, and we just can't afford that sort of thing."

In contrast to the non-traditionalists, the traditional venture capi-talist emphasizes the creation of value and a willingess to expend the effort to create that value. This means more than just dollars. And, it means more than just monitoring investments.

One active traditional venture capitalist says: "Too many people today just let companies go adrift and down the tubes. You can't see when the yellow lights are going on unless you are intimately involved with a company. Reviewing quarterly financials of a new company is insufficient, because a small company in one quarter can go from being profitable to bankruptcy."

The traditional venture capitalists also scorn the non-traditionalists for what they term their lottery or "crap-shooting" approach. "Big institutions usually get cold feet when a company comes back for more money. They think this means the company doesn't know what it is

23

doing, and so they figure they ought to write that one off. Hell, some
good companies need four or five financings before they get into the
black and start to go."

THE VENTURE CAPITAL INDUSTRY

Who makes up the venture capital "industry"? In addition to the
traditional venture capital groups and families, some brokerage firms,
pension funds, profit sharing funds, trust companies, insurance companies, hedge funds, specialized mutual funds, investment advisors,
wealthy families and investors are all playing the venture capital
game. However, these latter sources rarely provide initial financing
This remains the task of the traditional venture capitalist.

The traditional organizations consist of both privately and publicly
held companies. Their objectives, motives and methods vary considerably from one to the other. Some are interested primarily in
"frontier" research, others are interested in high technology that has
marketability now or in the very near future. Other venture capitalists
are strong in fields such as marketing, and tend to stay away from
high technology areas.

Some of the more famous of these traditional organizations include: Privately owned—Rockefeller, Whitney, and Payson and
Trask; Publicly owned—American Research and Development,
Greater Washington Investors, and Diebold Venture Capital Corporation.

Several new publicly held venture capital companies have been
established within the past few years. Also, several new partnerships
which specialize in venture capital have spun-off from older, well-
known partnerships in the investment banking field. Many of the new
venture capital partnerships were started because sophisticated investors got tired of the dowdy performance of stocks.

The non-traditional participants consist of wealthy individuals who
for tax and various other reasons want to put their money into higher
risk situations that may provide substantial returns. This group also
includes those institutional investors who wish to direct only a relatively small portion of their funds into venture capital situations
because of the risk involved and their fiduciary responsibilities for
the funds they manage.

The non-traditional participants also include most of the sources
of funds previously mentioned, such as the insurance companies, trust
companies, mutual funds, etc. These participants, however, play a far
different role than do the organized venture capital sources. Whereas,
the traditional group plays an aggressive, involved role, the other participants must play a more passive role. This is easily understood
when one recalls that for the second, non-traditional group a venture
capital investment is a sort of sideline activity; while for the traditional groups, it is their raison d'etre.

To put it another way, the traditional venture capitalist is investing
not only money, but also his time, energy and experience, invaluable
assets to a new company. Furthermore, the investor's appraisal of the
opportunities to capitalize on his varied assets may often be the determining factor in his decision to participate in a venture.

At the far end of the spectrum, of course, is the investor who wants
to take such an active role that he will preempt the prerogatives of

24

the entrepreneur. At the other end is the investor who participates primarily for tax reasons. He will usually offer nothing except dollars to the new company and may even obstruct it when such a movement would be advantageous to his tax situation.

The second part of this book discusses 100 sources of venture capital. It includes both traditional and non-traditional sources and provides considerable information about each firm. The aspiring entrepreneur should study these data carefully and select his potential partner with utmost care.

FORCES MOTIVATING THE VENTURE CAPITALIST

At this point it is appropriate to discuss the reasons why individuals or groups of individuals would want to pool their resources solely for investment in high risk ventures. What motivates the venture capitalist? The answer is simply and directly: the prospect of significant financial gain, i.e., financial gain which goes beyond what is possible in conventional investments in stocks and bonds.

A recent study conducted at the University of Chicago Center for Research in Security Prices described the annual rates of return on a portfolio consisting of equal investments in the common stocks listed on the New York Stock Exchange.[2] The median return on investment over various time intervals was 8.6 percent. The typical venture capitalist, however, expects to increase his investment by a factor of 5 in five years. This requires an annual return of nearly 40 percent, almost five times greater than that attainable on the average NYSE stocks over the 1955–1965 decade.

It might be argued that the wealthy investor would not purchase a portfolio made up of all New York Stock Exchange common stock but would improve his rate of return through an investigation and selection process. This procedure, perhaps the traditional means of capital enhancement for the wealthy individual, however, is becoming less and less attractive. With the institutionalization of the capital markets, with the hordes of security analysts unleashed on common stock (one estimate suggests there are five analysts for each listed stock), and with the impact of the recent Securities and Exchange Commission and court decisions broadening the definition of "insider," thus effectively restricting the dissemination and use of inside information, there is scant opportunity to discover securities that are grossly undervalued. Some recent studies even suggest that the costs of identifying such situations exceed the potential reward attainable. Couple this with the inescapable market-risk inherent in the often nonrational vagaries of the stock market, and some of the forces that have effected the shift of pools of private capital out of traditional investment outlets and made them available for venture situations become apparent.[3]

Contrasted with these historical modes of investment, ventures, even given a greater degree of uncertainty, provide certain attractive

---

[2] Lawrence Fisher and James H. Lorie. "Rates of Return on Investments in Common Stock." The Journal of Business of the University of Chicago, no. 3 (July, 1968), p.p. 1–26.

[3] While these exact circumstances do not inhibit the investment in over-the-counter securities, we believe that the number of security analysts, the lack of continuous information about companies in many instances, the imperfect nature of the O-T-C markets themselves and again the complete lack of control over the market-risk, as well as a greater degree of business-risk involved in such investments, all provide sufficient deterrents from considering even these as viable investment alternatives for many wealthy investors.

25

options which allow the venture capitalist to control and reduce his risk exposure. The first and most apparent involves the screening process. Of the many proposals submitted to the venture capitalist only those with the greatest probability of success are selected. Later in designing the financing package for the selected venture, the venture capitalist can provide some means for effective control of the new enterprise. And, of course, the venture capitalist will also receive continuous information about the progress of the company and may reduce the risk of managerial error by participating in the policy-making decisions of the enterprise.

The venture investor can further reduce his risk through diversification, i.e., investing his resources in a portfolio of risky ventures rather than in just one or a few. The finance literature of the last decade is replete with examples of portfolio theory and elaborate models describing or proving the advantages of a diversified portfolio.

Perhaps the chief advantage of the traditional stock market investment which is denied to the venture capitalist, is liquidity. This is the opportunity to turn the investment into cash in a short period of time with minimum transaction cost, and without depressing the security's price by affecting the supply-demand balance. The venture capitalist clearly holds an illiquid investment, given these criteria of liquidity.

In summary, the venture capitalist is motivated by the reward he can attain. He has weighed the differential of an expected 9 percent to an outside 15 percent return in a traditional investment outlet against an expected 25 to 40 percent (or greater) return in a venture investment. He has considered the illiquidity of the latter, balanced the risks involved under both alternatives and the relative extent to which these risks can be controlled or reduced, and concluded that the expected reward differential is sufficient or, more likely, more than sufficient to warrant providing capital for these new enterprises.

Attaining the Reward

The formula used by the venture capitalist for attaining the desired return on investment is simple and well-understood. After the initial investment, the new company is nurtured and developed until it has an established place in its market, a viable organizational structure, a record of sales and earnings growth and bright prospects for a successful future. At this point the venture capitalist and the entrepreneur sell portions of their ownership in the company to the public at prices comparable to those of other publicly-held companies with similiar prospects. These prices are usually several orders of magnitude greater than the initial investment required to start the company.

The process can perhaps be put in context, if we examine the stages of development of a new successful venture. If the time frame in which the innovative idea is still not a full-time business is considered to be "Stage-Zero," four stages of growth can be described.

Stage-Zero.—Usually at Stage-Zero some monies (usually the principal's own) have been invested, a great deal of effort (on a part-time basis) has been expended, a prototype may have been developed. Or, on the other hand, it is possible that only the time and effort required to organize and plan for the new enterprise have been expended prior to entering Stage-I.

26

Stage-I is the start-up phase. This is the period in which the operation is formalized and the product or service is developed and produced. This start is made with seed capital which can come from a number of diverse sources. The company's initial financing will be largely from selling ownership shares to the financial bankers. This is the classic venture capital step. Here the venture capital company participates with relatively small amounts of funding but, of course, the opportunities for growth are great.

Stage-II occurs when the company has built up a bit of a track record. It has moved through the initial growth phase and some of the conventional techniques of investment analysis can be applied to it. At this point also, the company has developed capital equipment and can begin to plan for long-term growth.

It is in Stage-II that other institutional sources of capital also begin to participate in the financings of the new company.

Stage III.—Further expansion is warranted due to favorable indications regarding the company's potential. The quantities of funds required are much greater than those raised in the earlier stages and the early investors are seeking both realized gains and liquidity. It is at this point that the public equity offering is usually made for the dual purpose of raising additional funds for the company (primary offering) and enabling the initial investors to realize a gain by selling a portion of their shares (secondary offering).

Stage-IV.—The mature company has established itself and become a viable corporation.

In understanding the whole venture capital phenomenon, it is vital to recognize the importance of strong secondary markets. Without highly developed, liquid and organized secondary markets such as the New York Stock Exchange, the American Exchange and, in particular, the Over-the-Counter Market, without a system that provides for many investors with a broad range of investment objectives and varying levels of risk tolerance, the intial investors would find it next to impossible to liquidate their investments and realize a gain. And the opportunities to attain substantial rewards over any short or intermediate time period would just not be available. Moreover, to the extent that venture capital thus became "locked-in," there would be a rapid shrinkage in the number of ventures that could be financed. A pool of venture capital turning over every six years can finance more ventures than a pool of like size turning over every twenty or forty years.

THE ROLE OF HISTORICAL SOURCES OF FINANCING

The historical sources of financing in this context refer to direct public financing utilizing the services of an investment banker, as well as to the varied financial institutions that service our capital markets such as:

      Commercial banks;
      Mortgage institutions;
      Insurance companies;
      Commercial credit companies and factors;
      Pension funds; and
      Mutual funds.

The means of raising funds are seldom available prior to Stage-I in the development of a new venture.

27

During periods of extremely speculative market activity, however, it is often possible to bring a company public soon after "Stage-Zero." While the rewards appear great at the time, the risks of following this procedure may be even greater. A number of new ventures followed this route during the height of the speculative excesses of the 1966–1968 era. The newly offered stock was in great demand and usually rose to a substantial premium in a short time perhaps doubling or tripling in price in three or four weeks. Soon the shareholders realized that the company had yet to achieve Stage-I and Stage-II growth, and consequently, when the speculative fever subsided most of these "hot issues" were selling far below their initial offering price.

Even under normal market conditions there is danger in bringing the company public too early. Although the company may do well, if it should miss an earnings or growth projection (not an unlikely event for a Stage-I or Stage-II company), it will be subject to the criticism from Wall Street analysts. In either situation it is unlikely that these companies will be warmly received when they next attempt a public offering; meaning that a greater ownership share must be sacrificed in order to raise a given amount of new capital.

The financial institutions listed above are seldom available to the new enterprises as sources of funds for two simple reasons. First, most are sources of debt financing. The traditional protection of capital and income afforded the creditor is just not available in the early stages of a new venture. There is no basis for granting credit for the commercial banker, no building for the mortgage institutions and no accounts receivable for the factor. These are the trappings of a Stage-II and Stage-III company. And it is only in these later stages that the institutions will finance a venture. Secondly, even if an institution is allowed to provide equity capital, it is often restricted by law or charter (a) on the portion of its assets it may invest in equity, e.g., life insurance companies, or (b) in the types of equity risks it may take by "prudent-man rules" or "legal lists," e.g., insurance companies and pension funds.

Conventional mutual funds (vs. venture capital funds) are usually restricted in the types of risks the funds may assume, either by their charter or stated investment objective. Some high-growth oriented mutual funds may invest in the early stages of a new venture but this is not a natural outlet for the resources of a mutual fund, unless it participates in the new enterprise with a venture capitalist; then it may participate only if the investment is a small fraction of the mutual fund's total portfolio, for the portfolio manager is usually concerned with forty to eighty separate investments. There is no way he can realistically exercise the desired control over his venture investment nor can he spend great amounts of time screening potential venture opportunities. Secondly, and of most importance, the keystone of a mutual fund is liquidity. The fund stands ready to sell and redeem its shares on demand. As noted, the early investment in a venture situation is illiquid, so that the fraction of the portfolio that the manager can risk investing in ventures is small.

The Venture Capital Process

How does the whole process of securing venture capital work? To begin, it is appropriate to look at the background against which the new technically-oriented company must approach the capital market.

28

Some unique features of the new technically-oriented company are:
1. That it is generally trying to do something which no one has done before; or
2. That it is frequently headed by technical people with little or no previous business experience.

The usual objectives of the technical people starting the new business include:
1. The exploitation of a new product, process or service developed in the laboratory which has not yet been utilized commercially; or
2. The expectation that new products, processes, or services will be developed by their laboratories once they are in business; or
3. Joining in the further development of a new scientific or technological field which is still in the early stages of exploitation.

To put the whole problem in perspective, what are the chances of getting a venture capitalist, either an individual or a firm, to back any given entrepreneurial endeavor? A reputable venture capital firm will, on the average, reject out of hand about 97% of the proposals submitted to it, take a first look at 3%, and in-depth look at probably 1%, and will actually fund less than ½ of 1%.

This may seem to be an extremely high attrition rate from the viewpoint of the entrepreneur. What is the venture capitalist looking for in a venture that causes him to reject over 99.5% of the situations that come to his attention?

The venture investor's motives include both economic and non-economic factors. While the traditional venture capital groups are primarily motivated by the economics of the situation, the individual venture capitalist may often be motivated by additional factors as well. Such reasons as tax advantages available to the wealthy investors have already been discussed. Some additional motivating factors include the desire to build a viable business, the desire for recognition, and the desire to bring technological ideas, goods and services into the service of mankind.

Analysis of a Venture Proposal.—What specifics will the venture capitalist look for in an investment proposal?

1. The People Involved.—It is virtually a unanimous consensus among venture capitalists that people are the most important aspect of a venture situation. A first-rate man with a second-rate idea is preferred to a second-rate man with a first-rate idea. Most new technically based enterprises are the expressions of the personalities, technical competence, and aspirations of their founders.

The management team is the keystone of the new technically oriented business. Most venture capitalists feel that a major weakness on the part of the management team is grounds for the rejection of the proposal. Some investors say that if an idea is particularly outstanding they sometimes assist the initial group in finding additional team members with the necessary skills. The usual criterion for the management team appears to be "balance"—the presence of both technical and managerial skills in complementary proportions.

The potential investors will probe the entrepreneur's mind to find out what kind of person he is; what makes him tick; what are his goals. The best entrepreneurs are people who fundamentally like to run things, organize them and grow them—as well as to have financial rewards.

29

2. The Technology.—In judging the venture against this criterion, the potential investor reveals his character more clearly than in any other part of the decision process. The investors' attitudes toward technology will range from considering only exciting new technological developments to anything that promises capital growth, technological or not.

A standard used by some investors is that the technology be in the area in which they already have some experience either as an investor or an operator. Still another factor might be that the technology must have some promise to civilian (vs. space and military) applications. Some investors may require that the technology have the possibility of attracting some government research and development contracts that would help support the firm in its early years.

Most researchers have reported the ultimate criterion used by investors for selecting a technology appeared to be its general excitement. A dramatic and slightly mysterious technology seemed to have a good deal of attraction even among the sophisticated investors—although not so much now as a very few years ago. For some investors an exciting technology in itself seemed to provide sufficient reason to invest.

3. The Product.—It is virtually impossible today to attract backing for an entrepreneur with nothing but an idea. Even the most sanguine and patient of investors insist that a substanial amount of product and/or process be developed at the expense of the entrepreneur or someone else.

What constitutes an acceptable level of development to attract financing varies widely among investors. In the research conducted, it was found that some investors felt the existence of a working prototype was sufficient, while others felt the product should be essentially ready for manufacture and marketing. A few investors stated they would not even consider a proposal unless the first sale had already been made.

Thus, even when talking about initial equity financing, it is frequently necessary that a substantial investment have already been made by the entrepreneur, if not in money then at least in time and energy.

The product should have a natural product line or follow-on products. If the basis for the new venture is just a new and better way to make widgets, it is inevitable that a year or so later someone else will discover an even better way to make widgets.

4. The Market.—One area most investors in new companies carefully examine prior to investment is market growth. Naturally, this makes it more difficult to find financing for ventures which depend upon markets which do not yet exist, or are not yet developed. Some such ventures are financed, but even here almost all investors demand some substantive indication of commercial promise in the near future.

Of course, of even greater importance than the size and growth characteristics of the market, is the question of competition. If the entrepreneur proposes to sell light bulbs in competition with G.E. or Sylvania, he had better have a very unique light bulb.

In short, the investor must look at the ground rules, the competition, the pricing structure, the distribution patterns, and the industry averages for the market the company proposes to enter.

30

5. Size of Investment.—While many investors do in fact have a "minimum economic investment," the range is enormous. Several investors have put as little as one to two thousand dollars initial capital into tiny new companies. At the other end of the spectrum, one group asserted that they would not consider any investment under one million dollars. It is estimated that most initial capitalization of technology based companies (perhaps as much as 75 percent) falls between $100,000 and $300,000.

One vice-president and general partner of a well-known venture capital firm put it this way: "We aren't interested in making a $25,-000 investment that may some day be worth $50,000 in a small success. We would much rather be prepared to lose all of our money. But, if we are right about the people and everything else, we will create a major success in the corporate sense and fiscally for ourselves." What the true venture capitalists aspire to, at least dream of, is to duplicate something like the Digital Equipment experience.

6. Procedures.—Venture capital investors have a strong sense of risk, and usually employ methods designed to avoid unnecessary quantities of risk. Such practices normally center about the investigation of the proposal in depth, so that some set of highly individual standards may be applied to the situation.

The attempt to apply standards to a company requires some knowledge about it. The amount known about a venture by its backers ranges from 0 to 100 percent. Therefore, the investigation of a proposal by the formalized venture capital groups in particular, has evolved into a highly developed art. This process is very similar for both the publicly and privately held venture capital groups.

Typically, three levels of screening exist through which a proposal must pass before it is considered for investment. For convenience these levels will be referred to as initial, secondary and final.

Initial Screening.—Much of the initial screening is done on a highly informal basis. The reading of a proposal or a brief telephone conversation is usually sufficient to disqualify 80–90 percent of the possible ventures. Though some deserving projects may get rejected by this initial screening, it appears to be, on the whole, an effective and efficient process.

Secondary Screening.—The real scrutiny begins in the secondary screening. Some groups require the applicant to complete an extensive set of questionnaires which cover in detail such things as the technology, the product, market, fiscal and personal histories of the principals. This information is then verified and supplemented by conversations with the entrepreneur's legal counsel and auditors, suppliers, customers, dealers, competitors and the competitors' customers, present and former associates and employers of the principals, etc. In short, the secondary screening encompasses nearly any means which can produce usable information in a rather short-time span. Perhaps 25–50 percent of the projects that are subjected to the secondary screening survive it. These are then subjected to the typically longer process of the final screening.

Final Screening.—The usual reason given for the time delay (6–12 weeks) encountered in the final screening is to conduct a "Market Survey." Such a survey may or may not actually occur. The actual

31

reason for the delay seems to be to provide the venture capital group an opportunity to watch the management team perform under a variety of circumstances.

While the traditional venture capital groups conduct such a vigorous and professional investigation before making a commitment, the non-traditional venture investors are not generally inclined to go to those lengths. The traditional venture capital investors rely heavily on their contacts in business and technical areas in assessing the prospects of a technology, a market, or a group of entrepreneurs. In appraising a potential market, they may also enlist the aid of a professional consulting group to do a limited study. The informal group, or individual, is more likely to simply ask his friends what they think of the prospects, or who they know that might be able to judge. This is especially true in relation to the technology since the informal investors are rarely technically trained.

In spite of all that has been said above, a great deal of irrationality runs through the investment policies of many individuals. Such things as personality conflict can cause the rejection of a very good venture. Similarly, if an investor likes the entrepreneur, he may overlook much that would ordinarily call for the rejection of a proposal.

STRUCTURE OF THE DEAL

The final structure of the venture financing is determined by the circumstances and situation in which the deal is made, and by the relative negotiating power of the two parties. Most venture capitalists prefer to utilize the convertible debenture as their investment vehicle. However, if the particular situation calls for some other instument such as straight common stock so that the company can raise additional debt from commercial banks, the venture capitalist will usually adapt to the situation. Likewise, the percentage of equity sought by the venture capitalist is flexible. For example, situations are not uncommon where the financial partners take 70% of the equity at the time of the financing and then agree to turn over portions of this equity to the entrepreneur (provided he meet certain pre-established goals over the next few years) until the enterpreneur owns 70% and the financial partners 30% of the equity.

The terms of the deal are, for the most part, limited only by the imagination of the parties involved. As a result, all types of innovative arrangements can result.

Most venture capitalists seek a minority position in the companies in which they invest. Some operating corporations have venture capital subsidiaries and utilize venture capital as a technique for diversification. Such firms seek a majority position, or an agreement for future purchase of the company, but these suppliers of venture capital are relatively few.

General Georges F. Doriot of A.R.D. has stated the position of most venture capitalists when he said: "We do not want to manage companies. We do not want to control companies. The SEC deems us to be in control of a company if we have more than 10 percent of the stock. But, what is control? Suppose I finance Mr. X and I hold 99.9 percent of the stock. Then suppose that after six months Mr. X decides to leave. What do I have left? What do I have control over?"

One common thread in most deals seems to be the affinity for participation in management by investors in new companies. But, even

32

this is not universal. The traditional venture capital groups who are more often motivated by the economics of the situation, almost always want representation in management. The individual investor usually does also, but may be much less demanding in this respect because he is somewhat like the institutional investor, in that venture capital is usually a secondary rather than primary occupation for him.

It might be said that there are two reasons for participating in management. One is defensive, that is, to protect an investment. The second is for the satisfaction of involvement, being part of something new and growing.

As for the participative techniques employed, the most customary vehicle is a directorship in the company. Occasionally, a venture capital group will even give a staff member a leave of absence from one to several months, to fill a vacant management role in the new company.

In another common arrangement, the investor wants to be considered as a consultant by management. Such a situation is often written in as a condition in the financing agreement. In a less usual, but not uncommon arrangement, the investor desires a role as a full-time officer of the firm. This situation demands a great caution. Even though the investor may be well qualified for the role, it often causes future problems such as personality conflicts in what has been a smooth running organization.

In general, the venture capital groups expect to participate to some degree in the management of nearly every venture they back. During the first year or two (often called the "handholding period"), the venture groups' representatives may meet with company management as often as twice a week to discuss problems of operation, finance, and planning. Even more frequent contact by telephone is not unusual in periods involving many decisions of some importance. The amount of participation by the venture capital group gradually tapers off, however, to the point where the new enterprise can stand unassisted.

In describing this "hand-holding," one venture capitalist says of his portfolio companies: "We're their mother and father. We wet-nurse them, act as their crying towel, or their whipping boy or scapegoat."

The importance of the venture capitalist's participation in management has been stated by General Doriot: "Because of faster evolution of technical and commercial ideas and developments, because of keener, stronger competition, there is no time to waste. A company cannot be started slowly as it could be in the past. Shortly after it is started, a new compay must obtain and avail itself of some of the good characteristics of a larger company. It must do so early in life so as to be able to survive and grow profitably. It must soon structure itself and become competitively adequate and able in all lines and in all factors of management. It must learn to foresee—to plan. It must learn how to survive accidents in spite of low momentum and lack of resources. As counselors, A.R. & D.'s staff, directors and friends try to help its portfolio companies during their growth and development period."

Financing the Deal

The techniques employed by the traditional venture capitalists for creating value vary widely from one source to another. Some firms prefer to enter the deal on an equal footing with management by taking their equity position in common stock. Others prefer to put up

33

capital in the form of convertible debentures, or as loans with warrants for the purchase of common stock. Some venture capitalists seek a controlling interest, others do not.

In financing the new enterprise, the venture capitalist faces a part of the debt-equity dilemma. The rewards to the financier of a successful venture enterprise are dependent on participation in ownership. The supplier of debt capital, because he is granted a prior claim on income and assets, is rewarded only to the extent that he receives interest payments on the capital provided. And yet, in venture enterprises, this traditional superior claim on assets and income afforded the creditor has little real meaning, since all capital is exposed to the same high degree of uncertainty surrounding the fledgling enterprise's future. If the enterprise is not a success, there will be a precious few assets remaining to be liquidated for the benefit of these creditors. If it is a success, the reward to the creditor is limited to the contractual interest rate. To the provider of debt vis-a-vis equity financing the risk differential is small while the expected reward differential is great. There is, therefore, little incentive for the venture capitalist to provide debt capital.

On the other hand, the responsible venture capitalist must maintain some control over his investments. While control, in this sense, most often conjures up visions of 51 percent ownership, frequently it is not desirable or possible to attain this portion of ownership in the new enterprise. However, with debt capital the venture capitalist can often gain effective or sufficient control of key areas in the company's operations by specifying certain restrictions in a contractual agreement with the new company. For example, the venture capitalist might insist on an acceleration clause which would make the full loan due and payable within one month of default on any one of the following restrictions:

A minimum net working capital limit;
A maximum limit on bank loans and long-term-debt;
A restriction on the creation of senior long-term debt;
A restriction on dividend payments;
A restriction on the acquisition of fixed assets;
A restriction on major changes in the nature of the business;
A restriction on merger with another company;
A restriction on changes in the management of the company;
A restriction on salaries and benefits paid top management.

The prohibition of these actions makes them subject to the consent of the venture capitalist. The penalty for breaking any of the restrictions is the automatic acceleration of the maturity of the loan. Thus, real control can be acquired in many areas vital to the management of the new company through the use of debt.

With debt's major advantages (control) and disadvantages (risk-reward imbalance), venture capitalists frequently employ a hybrid financial instrument which combines the best of both worlds. It allows the full participation in the rewards of ownership while also permitting effective control. It even provides for a superior claim on assets and income, and returns the venture capitalist regular interest payments. The instrument is a convertible debenture, "convertible" because it can be exchanged into a specified number of shares of common

34

stock at the option of the holder, and "debenture" because it is a debt instrument secured by the general credit of the company.[4]

If the venture capitalist wants to participate in potential rewards and also exercise control over his investments, there must exist acceptable and marketable financial instruments flexible enough to accomplish these goals. While many combinations of debt, equity, warrants and other options are used to effect these purposes, the convertible debenture is an example of an increasingly popular financial instrument employed to achieve these somewhat diverse objectives.

THE VENTURE CAPITAL INDUSTRY TODAY

In the United States, the supply of venture capital is believed to be adequate. Although adequate, however, it is not optimally distributed among geographical areas. The distribution problem is manifested in the strong direct correlation between the supply of capital for technologically oriented ventures and the ease of access to such capital in a given area.

There are several areas across the nation which are the centers for venture capital, namely: San Francisco and Los Angeles, Houston and Dallas, Minneapolis, Chicago, New York and Boston. Over the past few years, the opportunity for an entrepreneur with a good idea to raise venture capital and, as more successful venture captial deals have become publicized, more financial sources have sought involvement in venture capital. Likewise, the availability of capital encouraged entrepreneurs to form new businesses. While the bases for these businesses provided sufficient raw materials for careful screening by an increasing number of venture capital sources. The preponderance of technical work being done in New England, particularly in the aerospace industry, has further increased the number of good ideas, which could be financed as new businesses.

From a geographic standpoint, most venture capitalists profess to have no restrictive preferences today. However, because a true venture capitalist provides more than dollars to his portfolio companies, he is faced with the difficulty of monitoring these investments. Since this often involves personal visits to the portfolio company, the venture capitalist then is less likely to participate in a financing that would be difficult to monitor unless he has considerable faith in the ability and willingness of one of the other participants to provide the necessary "hand-holding." So, the proximity of venture capital sources becomes important in assessing the ease or difficulty of starting new businesses in given area.

---

[4] The same goals can be achieved with a combination of debentures and warrants. For an excellent treatment of the differences between these alternatives, see Samuel Hayes and Henry B. Reiling, "Sophisticated Financing Tool: The Warrant," Harvard Business Review (Jan.–Feb., 1969), 137–150.

Appendices

SMALL BUSINESS INVESTMENT COMPANIES

ALABAMA

Associated Business Investment Corp.
Bank for Savings Building, Suite 735
Birmingham, Alabama 35203

Investment Capital Corp.
57 Adams Ave.
Montgomery, Alabama 36103

ALASKA

Alaska Business Investment Corp.
5th Ave. & E. St., Box 600
Anchorage, Alaska 99501

Alaska-Pacific Capital Corp.
425 G. Street, Suite 710
Anchorage, Alaska 99501

Alyeska Investment Co.
1815 South Bragaw
Anchorage, Alaska 99504

ARIZONA

First Southeast SBIC
1611 East Camelback Rd.
Phoenix, Arizona 85016

La Raza Investment Corp.
132 So. Central Ave., Suite C
Phoenix, Arizona 85004 ₍

ARKANSAS

MESBIC of Arkansas, Inc.
300 Spring Bldg., Suite 620
Little Rock, Arkansas 72201

CALIFORNIA

ABCO Equity Funds, Inc.
8929 Wilshire Blvd., Suite 218
Beverly Hills, California 90211

Bancal Capital Corp.
550 South Flower St.
Los Angeles, California 90017

Bankers SBIC
301 20th St.
Oakland, California 94612

Brentwood Associates, Inc.
11661 San Vicente Blvd.
Los Angeles, California 90049

Bryan Capital, Inc.
235 Montgomery St.
San Francisco, California 94104

C S & W Investment Co.
385 Grand Ave.
Oakland, California 94610

Capital City Equity Co.
811 No. Broadway, Suite 444
Santa Ana, California 92701

City Capital Corporation
9255 Sunset Blvd.
Los Angeles, California 90068

City of Commerce Investment Co.
1117-B So. Goodrich Blvd.
Los Angeles, California 90022

Continental Capital Corp.
555 California St., 26th Fl.
San Francisco, California 94104

Crocker Capital Corp.
2 Palo Alto Sq., Suite 334
Palo Alto, California 94304

Appendices

Developers Equity Capital Corp.
9349 Santa Monica Blvd.
Beverly Hills, California 90210

Diversified Equities Corp.
2401 Merced St.
San Leandro, California 94577

Edvestco, Inc.
150 Isabella Ave.
Atherton, California 94025

Equilease Capital Corp.
4340 Redwood Highway
San Rafael, California 94903
Branch of: Equilease Capital Corp.
New York, New York

Equilease Capital Corp.
315 South Beverly Drive
Beverly HIlls, California 90212
Branch of: Equilease Capital Corp.
New York, New York

First SBIC of California
621 So. Spring St., Suite 505
Los Angeles, California 90014

Foothill Venture Corp.
8383 Wilshire Blvd., Suite 528
Beverly Hills, California 90211

H&R Investment Capital Co.
801 American St.
San Carlos, California 94070

Investcal SBIC
1400 Fifth Ave., Suite 305
San Diego, California 92101

Krasne Fund For Small Business
9350 Wilshire Blvd., Suite 416
Beverly Hills, California 90212

North American Capital Corp.
55 River St., Suite 105
Santa Cruz, California 95060

Opportunity Capital Corp. of California
235 Montgomery St.
San Francisco, California 94104

Palo Alto Capital Co.
611 Hansen Way, Bldg. 6
Palo Alto, California 94303

Pioneer Enterprises, Inc.
11255 West Olympic Blvd.
Los Angeles, California 90064

Professional SBIC
5979 West Third St.
Los Angeles, California 90036

Roe Financial Corp.
6100 Kester Ave.
Van Nuys, California 91401

San Joaquin SBI Corp.
P.O. Box 248
Dana Point, California 92629

Small Business Enterprises Co.
555 California St.
San Francisco, California 94104

Southern California Minority Capital Corp.
2651 So. Western Ave.
Los Angeles, California 90018

Space Age SBIC
1368 Lincoln Ave., Suite 111
San Rafael, California 94901

Sutter Hill Capital Corp.
2 Palo Alto Sq., Suite 700
Palo Alto, California 94304

Technology Capital
601 California St.
San Francisco, California 94108

Union America Capital Corp.
445 South Figueroa St.
Los Angeles, California 90017

Warde Capital Corp.
8929 Wilshire Blvd., Suite 500
Beverly Hills, California 90211
Branch of: Warde Capital Corp.
Beverly Hills, California

Wells Fargo Investment Co.
475 Sansome St.
San Francisco, California 94111

West Coast Capital Co.
4800 Southland Park Drive
Sacramento, California 95822

Westamco Investment Co.
8929 Wilshire Blvd., Suite 400
Beverly Hills, California 90211

Western Business Funds
235 Montgomery St., Rm. 2200
San Francisco, California 94104

COLORADO

Central Investment Corp.
811 Central Bank Building
Denver, Colorado 80217

Colorado SBIC, Inc.
P.O. Box 5168
Denver, Colorado 80217

Equilease Capital Corp.
120 Bryant St.
Denver, Colorado 80219
Branch of: Equilease Capital Corp.
New York, New York

CONNECTICUT

All State Venture Capital Corp.
855 Main St.
Bridgeport Connecticut 06601

Anderson Investment Co.
125 Elm St.
New Canaan, Connecticut 06840
Direct Inquiry to: Harlan E. Anderson

Business Ventures Inc.
152 Temple St.
New Haven, Connecticut 06510

Capital for Technology Corp.
799 Main St.
Hartford, Connecticut 06115

Cominvest of Hartford, Inc.
18 Asylum St.
Hartford, Connecticut 06103

Connecticut Capital Corp.
419 Whalley Ave.
New Haven, Connecticut 06511

Conresco Corp.
10 River St.
Stamford, Connecticut 06901
Direct Inquiry to: L.C. Widdoes

Dewey Investment Corp.
101 Middle Turnpike, West
Manchester, Connecticut 06040

Equitronics Capital Corp.
1492 Highridge Rd.
Stamford, Connecticut 06903

First Connecticut SBIC
177 State St.
Bridgeport, Connecticut 06603
Direct Inquiry to:
David Engelson, James M. Breiner

First Miami SBIC
293 Post Rd.
Orange, Connecticut 06477
Branch of: First Miami SBIC
Miami Beach, Florida

First of Orange County Corp.
P.O. Box 1268, Rt. 207
Stamford, Connecticut 12550

Fox, Wells & Rogers
733 Summer St.
Stamford, Connecticut 06902
Direct Inquiry to: Anton H. Rice

Hartford Community Capital Corp.
70 Farmington Ave.
Hartford, Connecticut 06101

Investors Capital Corp.
144 Golden Hill St.
Bridgeport, Connecticut 06603

Investors Capital Corp.
955 Main St.
Bridgeport, Connecticut 06603
Direct Inquiry to: Edward F. Helfer

Manufacturers SBIC, Inc.
1488 Chapel St.
New Haven, Connecticut 06511

Marwit Capital Corp.
111 Prospect St.
Stamford, Connecticut 06901

Nationwide Funding Corp.
10 A Ambassador Drive
Manchester, Connecticut 06040

Northern Business Capital Corp.
7-9 Isaac St.
Norwalk, Connecticut 06850

Nutmeg Capital Corp.
35 Elm St.
New Haven, Connecticut 06510

Appendices

SBIC of Connecticut
1115 Main St.
Bridgeport, Connecticut 06603

Transamerica Capital Corp.
111 Prospect St.
Stamford, Connecticut 06905

DELAWARE

Delaware Investment Co.
P.O. Box 188
Wilmington, Delaware 19899

DISTRICT OF COLUMBIA

Tec-Mod Capital Corp.
1801 K. Street N.W., Suite 823
Washington, D.C. 20006

Allied Capital Corp.
1625 Eye St.
Washington, D.C. 20006
Direct Inquiry to:
George C. Williams, President

Broad Arrow Investment Corp.
1701 Pennsylvania Ave. S.W., Suite 1200
Washington, D.C. 20006
Branch of: Broad Arrow Investment Corp.
Amsterdam, New York

Capital Investment Co. of Washington
1001 Connecticut Ave., N.W.
Washington, D.C. 20036

Greater Washington Industrial Investments
1015 18th St., N.W., Suite 300
Washington, D.C. 20036

Greater Washington Investors, Inc.
1015 18th St.
Washington D.C. 20036
Direct Inquiry to:
Don A. Christenson, President
Mark Rollinson, Vice President

Minority Investments, Inc.
1211 Connecticut Ave., N.W.
Washington, D.C. 20036

Modedco Investment Co.
325 Mass Ave., N.W., Suite 110
Washington, D.C. 20005

SBIC of New York, Inc.
1701 Pennsylvania Ave., N.W.
Washington, D.C. 20006

Venbank, Inc.
4310 Georgia Ave.
Washington, D.C. 20011
Direct Inquiry to:
Edward D. Irons, President

FLORIDA

Atlantic Investment Fund, Inc.
150 S.E. Third Ave.
Miami, Florida 33131

Burger King MESBIC Inc.
7360 No. Kendell Drive
Miami, Florida 33156

First Miami SBIC
420 Lincoln Rd., Suite 379
Miami Beach, Florida 33139

First North Florida SBIC
107 North Madison St.
Quincy, Florida 32351

Florida Crown Minority Enterprise SBIC
604 Hogan St.
Jacksonville, Florida 32203

Gold Coast Capital Corp.
1451 No. Bayshore Drive
Miami, Florida 33132

Growth Business Funds, Inc.
2100 E. Hallandale Beach Blvd.
Hallandale, Florida 33009

Gulf States Capital Corp.
3605 North Davis St.
Pensacola, Florida 32502

Market Capital Corp.
P.O. Box 22667
Tampa, Florida 33622

SB Assist Corp. of Panama City
West Highway 98
Panama City, Florida 32401

Southeast SBIC, Inc.
100 So. Biscayne Blvd.
Miami, Florida 33131

Space Coast SBIC
101 S. Courtenay Parkway
Merritt Island, Florida 32952

Urban Ventures, Inc.
825 So. Bayshore Drive
Miami, Florida 33131

GEORGIA

The Citizens & Southern Capital Corp.
P.O. Box 4899
Atlanta, Georgia 30303

CSRA Capital Corp.
914 Georgia R.R. Bank Bldg.
Augusta, Georgia 30903

Dixie Capital Corp.
2210 Gas Light Tower
Atlanta, Georgia 30303

ECCO MESBIC, Inc.
Central Administration Bldg.
Mayfield, Georgia 31059

Enterprises Now, Inc.
898 Beckwith St., S.W.
Atlanta, Georgia 30314

Equilease Capital Corp.
1720 Peachtree Street, N.W.
Atlanta, Georgia 30309
Branch of: Equilease Capital Corp.
New York, New York

Fidelity Capital Corp.
300 Interstate North
Atlanta, Georgia 30339

Investors Equity, Inc.
2 Peachtree St.
Atlanta, Georgia 30303

Mome Capital Corp.
234 Main St.
Thomson, Georgia 30824

SBI Corp. of Georgia
3510 First National Bank
Atlanta, Georgia 30303

Southeastern Capital SBIC
3715 Northside Parkway, N.W.
Atlanta, Georgia 30327

HAWAII

SBIC of Hawaii, Inc.
1575 South Beretania St.
Honolulu, Hawaii 96814

IDAHO

Industrial Investment Corp.
413 West Idaho St.
Boise, Idaho 83316

Industrial Investment Corp.
1020 Main St.
Buhl, Idaho 83316
Branch of: Industrial Investment Corp.
Boise, Idaho

Utah Capital Corp.
589 North Water Ave.
Idaho Falls, Idaho 83401
Branch of: Utah Capital Corp.
Granger, Utah

ILLINOIS

Abbott Capital Corp.
120 S. Lasalle St., Suite 1148
Chicago, Illinois 60603

Adams Street Capital, Inc.
69 West Washington St.
Chicago, Illinois 60602

Advance Growth Capital Corp.
401 Madison St.
Maywood, Illinois 60153

Alcott Corp.
Box 523
Chicago, Illinois 60690
Direct Inquiry to:
Conrad J. Tuerk, President

Amoco Venture Capital Co.
910 So. Michigan Ave.
Chicago, Illinois 60605

Androck Capital Corp.
1309 Samuelson Rd.
Rockford, Illinois 61101

Appendices

Ascending Citizens Investment Co.
2000 State St.
East St. Louis, Illinois 62205

Atlanta La Salle Capital Corp.
150 So. Wacker Drive
Chicago, Illinois 60606

Baker, Fentress & Co., Inc.
208 South LaSalle St.
Chicago, Ill. 60604
Direct Inquiry to: Robert Spicer

William Blair Co.
135 South LaSalle St.
Chicago, Illinois 60603
Direct Inquiry to: William Hodgson II,
Bruce Thorne, Wallace Flower

Cedco Capital Corp.
162 North State St.
Chicago, Illinois 60601

Chicago Comm. Ventures Inc.
19 So. LaSalle St., Rm. 1114
Chicago, Illinois 60603

Chicago Equity Corp.
188 West Randolph St.
Chicago, Illinois 60601

Combined Opportunities, Inc.
5050 North Broadway
Chicago, Illinois 60640

Conill Venture Corp.
231 South LaSalle St.
Chicago, Illinois 60604
Direct Inquiry to:
John L. Hines, President
Paul Dorfman, Vice President

Cont. Illinois Venture Corp.
231 South La Salle St.
Chicago, Illinois 60604

Doyle, O'Connor & Co., Inc.
150 South Wacker Drive
Chicago, Illinois 60606
Direct Inquiry to: Richard J. Stephenson

Equilease Capital Corp.
2400 East Devon
Des Plaines, Illinois 60018
Branch of: Equilease Capital Corp.
New York, New York

First Capital Corporation of Chicago
1 First National Plaza
Chicago, Illinois 60670
Direct Inquiry to:
Stanley C. Golder, President
Eugene F. Garth, Assistant Vice President

Frontenac Co.
208 South La Sasse St.
Chicago, Illinois 60604
Direct Inquiry to:
Martin J. Koldyke, General Partner
George K. Hendrick, Jr., General Partner
Peter Coladarci, General Partner

Greenebaum & Associates
185 South La Salle St.
Chicago, Illinois 60603
Direct Inquiry to: Edgar N. Greenebaum, Jr.

Heizer Corp.
20 North Wacker Drive
Chicago, Illinois 60606
Direct Inquiry to:
Charles L. Palmer (Non-technology businesses)
William N. Stirlen (Technology businesses)

High Technology Investments, Inc.
2 First National Plaza
Chicago, Illinois 60670
Direct Inquiry to:
Mort N. Miller
William Penner

LaSalle Street Capital Corp.
150 South Wacker Drive
Chicago, Illinois 60606
Direct Inquiry to:
Daniel J. Donahue
David T. Allen

North Central Capital Corp.
203 Mulberry St., P.O. Box 998
Rockford, Illinois 61105

Republic Capital Corp
33 North LaSalle St.
Chicago, Illinois 60602

SB Management Investors Inc.
612 North Michigan Ave.
Chicago, Illinois 60611

The Urban Fund, Inc.
1525 East 53rd St.
Chicago, Illinois 60615

Vanguard Venture Capital Corp.
120 South LaSalle St.
Chicago, Illinois 60603
Direct Inquiry to:
Kenneth M. Arenberg, President

Vencap Fund Ltd.
10 South LaSalle St.
Chicago, Illinois 60603
Direct Inquiry to:
Stanley M. Rubel, General Partner

Woolard & Co., Inc.
135 South LaSalle St.
Chicago, Illinois 60603
Direct Inquiry to:
Francis Wilson, Richard C. G'sell

INDIANA

Indianapolis Business Investment Corp.
1241 North Pennsylvania St.
Indianapolis, Indiana 46202

Interscan Capital Corp.
Box 285
Tipton, Indiana 46072

Waterfield SBIC, Inc.
123 West Berry St.
Fort Wayne, Indiana 46802

Waterfield SBIC, Inc.
45 North Penn St.
Indianapolis, Indiana 46204
Branch of: Waterfield SBIC, Inc.
Fort Wayne, Indiana

IOWA

Moramerica Capital Corp.
American Building
Cedar Rapids, Iowa 52401

KENTUCKY

Equal Opportunity Finance, Inc.
224 East Broadway, Federal Land Building
Louisville, Kentucky 40202

LOUISIANA

Commercial Capital, Inc.
P.O. Box 939
Covington, Louisiana 70433

Delta Capital, Inc.
P.O. Box 708
Slidell, Louisiana 70458

Delta Capital, Inc.
837 Gravier St., Room 1410
New Orleans, Louisiana 70112
Branch of: Delta Capital, Inc.
Slidell, Louisiana

First SBIC of Lafourche, Inc.
1614 South Bayou Drive
Golden Meadow, Louisiana 70357

First SBIC of Louisiana, Inc.
736 Poydras St.
New Orleans, Louisiana 70130

First Southern Capital, Inc.
1208 Commerce Building
New Orleans, Louisiana 70112

Gulf South Venture Corp.
837 Gravier St., Suite 2102
New Orleans, Louisiana 70112

Mid-South Capital Corp.
312 Polk St.
Mansfield, Louisiana 71052

Royal Street Investment Corp.
520 Royal St.
New Orleans, Louisiana 70130

Southern SBIC, Inc.
8137 Oleander St.
New Orleans, Louisiana 70118

MAINE

Massachusetts Capital Corp.
57 Exchange St.
Portland, Maine 04111
Branch of: Massachusetts Capital Corp.
Boston, Massachusetts

MARYLAND

Allied Capital Corp.
4801 Montgomery Lane
Bethesda, Maryland 20014
Branch of: Allied Capital Corp.
Washington, D.C.

Aviation Growth Investments
7315 Wisconsin Ave.
Bethesda, Maryland 20014

Baltimore Community Investment Co.
1925 Eutaw Place
Baltimore, Maryland 21217

Capitol Area Investors, Inc.
101 Light St.
Baltimore, Maryland 21202
Branch of: Capitol Area Investors, Inc.
Fairfax, Virginia

Equilease Capital Corp.
56-04 Baltimore National Pike
Baltimore, Maryland 21228

MASSACHUSETTS

Advent Co.
74 State St.
Boston, Massachusetts 02109

Direct Inquiry to:
Peter A. Brooke, John O. Peterson,
Thomas M. Claflin

American Research & Development Corp.
200 Berkeley St.
Boston, Massachusetts 02110

Direct Inquiry to:
William H. Congleton, Senior Vice President
John A. Shane, Senior Vice President
James F. Morgan, Vice President
Charles J. Coulter, Vice President
Daniel J. Holland, Assistant Vice President

Arrow Investment Corp.
1051 Beacon St.
Brookline, Massachusetts 02146

Atlas Capital Corp.
55 Court St., Suite 200
Boston, Massachusetts 02215

Beacon Capital Corp.
587 Beacon St.
Boston, Massachusetts 02215

Burgess & Leith
53 State St.
Boston, Massachusetts 02109
Direct Inquiry to:
William R. Kitchel, General Partner
Albert W. Moore, General Partner

Business Achievement Corp.
93 Union St.
Newton Center, Massachusetts 02159

The Charles River Partnership
575 Technology Square
Cambridge, Massachusetts 02139
Direct Inquiry to:
Richard M. Burnes, Jr., General Partner
John H. Carter, General Partner
John T. Neises, General Partner

Creative Resources, Inc.
20 Walnut St.
Wellesley Hills, Massachusetts 02181
Direct Inquiry to:
Robert T. Larsen, President
Stanley E. Pratt, Vice President and Treasurer
John J. Murphy, President, DCS Management, Inc.
Robert G. Clark, Chairman of Investment Comm.

Eastern Seaboard Investment Corp.
73 State St., Suite 208
Springfield, Massachusetts 01103

Endowment Management and Capital Corp.
77 Franklin St.
Boston, Massachusetts 02110
Direct Inquiry to:
Joseph McNay, Vice President

Equilease Capital Corp
393 Totten Pond Road, Suite 651
Waltham, Massachusetts 02154
Branch of: Equilease Capital Corp.
New York, New York

Explorer Fund, Inc.
28 State St.
Boston, Massachusetts 02109
Direct Inquiry to:
Stephen D. Paine, President
Judith P. Lawrie

Federal Street Capital Corp.
75 Federal St.
Boston, Massachusetts 02110
Direct Inquiry to:
John H. Lamothe, President
F. Jeffrey Williams

Fidelity Management & Research Co.
35 Congress St.
Boston, Massachusetts 02109
Direct Inquiry to:
Henry W. Hoagland
Dr. Samuel Bodman

Appendices

Financial Investors of Boston, Inc.
185 Devonshire St.
Boston, Massachusetts 02110
Direct Inquiry to:
Stephen Lewinstein

First Capital Corporation of Boston
100 Federal St.
Boston, Massachusetts 02110

First Capital Corporation of Boston
1 Federal St.
Boston, Massachusetts 02110
Direct Inquiry to:
Richard A. Farrell, Vice President
Harry J. Healer, Jr., Treasurer

Foster Dykema Cabot & Co., Inc.
53 State St.
Boston, Massachusetts 02109
Direct Inquiry to:
Hugh K. Foster, President
Jere H. Dykema, Vice President

Gardner and Preston Moss, Inc.
225 Franklin St.
Boston, Mass. 02110
Direct Inquiry to:
Charles C. Cunningham, Jr.
Sholly Kagan

Greater Springfield Investment Corp.
121 Chestnut St., Room 208
Springfield, Massachusetts 01103

Greylock Management Corp.
225 Franklin St.
Boston, Massachusetts 02110
Direct Inquiry to:
Henry F. McCance

GROCO, Inc.
1295 State St.
Springfield, Massachusetts 01101
Direct Inquiry to:
Richard T. Schotte, John H. Lippincott

Inventure Capital Corp.
155 Berkeley St.
Boston, Massachusetts 02116
Direct Inquiry to:
Vincent J. Ryan, Jr., President

Kendall Square Associates
238 Kendall St.
Cambridge, Massachusetts 02142
Direct Inquiry to:
Walt Winshall, General Partnership

Kidder, Peabody & Co., Inc.
75 Federal St.
Boston, Massachusetts 02101
Direct Inquiry to: Nearest Regional Office

Koch Venture Capital, Inc.
45 Hancock St.
Cambridge, Massachusetts 02139
Direct Inquiry to:
William I. Koch, President
Stuart D. Pompian, Vice President

Massachusetts Capital Corp.
1 Boston Place
Boston, Massachusetts 02108
Direct Inquiry to:
Arthur P. Contas, President

Millicap Corp.
Wiggins Ave.
Bedford, Massachusetts 01730
Direct Inquiry to:
John H. Bush, President

National Research Corp.
70 Memorial Drive.
Cambridge, Massachusetts 02142
Direct Inquiry to:
Charles S. Shoup, Jr., Vice President and Gen. Mgr.
Kenneth L. Coleman, Dir. Marketing and Contracts

New England Enterprise Capital Corp.
28 State St.
Boston, Massachusetts 02109

Direct Inquiry to:
Arthur F. Snyder, Treasurer
Richard W. Swett, Assistant Treasurer
Roderick A. MacLeod, Assistant Secretary

Paine Venture Fund
24 Federal St.
Boston, Massachusetts 02110

Direct Inquiry to:
Walter Aikman, General Partner

Pilgrim Capital Corp.
842A Beacon St.
Boston, Massachusetts 02215

Resources and Technology Management Co.
Box 100
Chestnut Hill, Massachusetts 02167

Direct Inquiry to:
Lee M. Holmes, President
Frank A. Horgos, Vice President

Schooner Capital Corp.
141 Milk St.
Boston, Massachusetts 02109

Technology Search Associates
1268 Main St.
Waltham, Massachusetts 02154
Direct Inquiry to:
Hoyt Ecker, Managing General Partner

UST Capital Corp.
40 Court St.
Boston, Massachusetts 02108

W.C.C.I. Capital Corp.
791 Main St.
Worcester, Massachusetts 01610

Worcester Capital Corp.
446 Main St.
Worcester, Massachusetts 01608

Yankee Capital Corp.
77 Franklin St.
Boston, Massachusetts 02110
Direct Inquiry to:
J. Christopher Clifford, Assistant Treasurer

MICHIGAN

Equilease Capital Corp.
1200 Sixth Ave., 502 Executive Plaza
Detroit, Michigan 48226
Branch of:
Equilease Capital Corp.
New York, New York

Michigan Capital & Service, Inc.
410 Wolverine Building
Ann Arbor, Michigan 48108

Midwest SBIC
1921 First National Building
Detroit, Michigan 48202

Motor Enterprises, Inc.
3044 West Grand Blvd., Suite 7-166
Detroit, Michigan 48202

Pooled Resources Investment Min. Ent., Inc.
2990 West Brand Blvd., Room M-15
Detroit, Michigan 48202

MINNESOTA

First Midwest Capital Corp.
80 South Eighth St.
Minneapolis, Minnesota 55402

Minnesota SBIC
2338 Central Ave., N.E.
Minneapolis, Minnesota 55418

Northland Capital Corp.
402 West First St.
Duluth, Minnesota 55802

Northwest Growth Fund, Inc.
960 Northwestern Bank Building
Minneapolis, Minnesota 55402

Retailers Growth Fund, Inc.
5100 Gamble Drive
Minneapolis, Minnesota 55416

Westland Capital Corp.
4014 I.D.S. Center
Minneapolis, Minnesota 55402

MISSISSIPPI

Sunflower Investment Corp.
U.S. Highway 49 West & 2nd St. Ext.
Indianola, Mississippi 38751

Vicksburg SBIC
304 First National Bank Building
Vicksburg, Mississippi 39180

MISSOURI

Atlas SBI Corp.
1808 Main St.
Kansas City, Missouri 64108

Capital for Business, Inc.
P.O. Box 13184
Kansas City, Missouri 64199

Equilease Capital Corp.
7700 Clayton Road
St. Louis, Missouri 63117
Branch of: Equilease Capital Corp.
New York, New York

MONTANA

Capital Investors Corp.
Capitol Building Suite-C
Missoula, Montana 59801

Small Business Improvement Co.
711 Central Ave., P.O. Box 1175
Billings, Montana 59103

NEBRASKA

Moramerica Capital Corp.
1 First National Center, Room 1420
Omaha, Nebraska 68103

Branch of: Moramerica Capital Corp.
Cedar Rapids, Iowa

NEVADA

J & M Investment Corp.
647 West 3rd St.
Reno, Nevada 89502

NEW HAMPSHIRE

Massachusetts Capital Corp.
1838 Elm St.
Manchester, New Hampshire 03104

Branch of: Massachusetts Capital Corp.
Boston, Massachusetts

SCI-tronics Fund, Inc.
43 Spring St.
Nashua, New Hampshire 03060

NEW JERSEY

Broad Arrow Investment Corp.
40 Whippang Road
Morristown, New Jersey 07960

Capital SBIC
143 East State St.
Trenton, New Jersey 08608

Engle Investment Co.
35 Essex St.
Hackensack, New Jersey 07601

Gunwyn Ventures
14 Nassau St.
Princeton, New Jersey 08540

Direct Inquiry to: Gordon Gund,
Peter Danforth, Stephen W. Fillo

Main Capital Investment Corp.
818 Main St.
Hackensach, New Jersey 07601

Monmouth Capital Corp.
1st State Bank Building, P.O. Box 480
Toms River, New Jersey 08753
Branch of: Monmouth Capital Corp.
Toms River, New Jersey

New York Enterprise Capital Corp.
Park 80 Plaza West-One
Saddle Brook, New Jersey 07662

Prudential Minority Enterprises, Inc.
213 Washington St., Box 594
Newark, New Jersey 07101

Rutgers Minority Investment Co.
18 Washington Place
Newark, New Jersey 07101

SBIC of Eastern States
1438 U.S. Route 130
Cinaminson, New Jersey 08077
Branch of: SBIC of Eastern States
Philadelphia, Pennsylvania

NEW MEXICO

New Mexico Capital Corp.
1420 Carlisle N.E.
Albuquerque, New Mexico 87110

NEW YORK

Frederick R. Adler, Esq.
1 Chase Manhattan Plaza
New York, New York 10005
Direct Inquiry to: Frederick R. Adler

American Science Associates
1345 Avenue of the Americas
New York, New York 10019
Direct Inquiry to:
S.L. Lubliner, Partner
Robert Simon, Partner
Gerson Pakula, Partner
Milton Schwartz, Partner
Carl W. Stursberg, Jr., Partner

John A. Andresen
140 Broadway
New York, New York 10005
Direct Inquiry to: John A. Andresen

Bandcap Corp.
420 Lexington Ave., Room 2352
New York, New York, 10017

The Hanover Capital Corp.
485 Madison Ave.
New York, New York 10022

Intercoastal Capital Corp.
18 East 48th St.
New York, New York 10017

Inverness Capital Corp.
345 Park Ave.
New York, New York 10022
Direct Inquiry to:
John Trunk, President

Jersey Enterprises, Inc.
30 Rockefeller Plaza
New York, New York 10020
Direct Inquiry to: H. Ben Sykes

Laird, Inc.
140 Broadway
New York, New York 10005
Direct Inquiry to:
W. Murray Buttner, Harry H. Lynch

Lake Success Capital Corp.
100 Garden City Plaza 516
Garden City, New York 11530

The Loud Venture Capital Corp.
630 Fifth Ave.
New York, New York 10020

M & T Capital Corp.
1 M & T Plaza
Buffalo, New York 14240

Carl Marks & Co.
77 Water St.
New York, New York 10004
Direct Inquiry to: Joseph Steinberg

Mid-Atlantic Fund, Inc.
270 Madison Ave.
New York, New York 10016

Midland Capital Corp.
110 Williams St.
New York, New York 10038
Direct Inquiry to:
Michael desVallieres,
Wayne Williams
Jack Hughes

Minority Equity Capital Co., Inc.
470 Park Ave., South
New York, New York 10016

Multi-Purpose Capital Corp.
31 South Broadway
Yonkers, New York 10701

Neuwirth Financial
1 Battery Park Plaza
New York, New York 10004
Direct Inquiry to: Henry Neuwirth,
Martin D. Sass, Fred Lang

New York Business Assist Corp.
98 Cutter Mill Road, Suite 255
Great Neck, New York 11021

New Court Securities Corp.
70 Pine St.
New York, New York 10013
Direct Inquiry to: Charles L. Lea, Jr.

NL Industries, Inc. (National Lead Company)
111 Broadway
New York, New York 10006
Direct Inquiry to: S. Whitfield Lee

North Street Capital Corp.
250 North St.
White Plains, New York 10625

Alan Patricof Associates, Inc.
1 East 53rd St.
New York, New York 10022
Direct Inquiry to: Alan Patricof

Payson & Trask
748 Madison Ave.
New York, New York 10021
Direct Inquiry to:
Robert D. Stillman, Loring Catlin

Pioneer Capital Corp.
1440 Broadway, Room 1967
New York, New York 10625

Pioneer Venture Corp.
22 East 40th St.
New York, New York 10016

Preferred Capital for Small Businesses, Inc.
16 Court St.
Brooklyn, New York 11201

Printers Capital Corp.
1 World Trade Center, Suite 1927
New York, New York 10048

R&R Financial Corp.
1451 Broadway
New York, New York 10036

Real Estate Capital Corp.
111 West 40th St.
New York, New York 10018

Realty Growth Capital Corp.
156 East 52nd St.
New York, New York 10022

Research and Science Investors, Inc.
405 Lexington Ave.
New York, New York 10017
Direct Inquiry to:
J.H. French, President
H. Wertheim, Vice President

L.M. Rosenthal & Co., Inc.
666 Fifth Ave.
New York, New York 10019
Direct Inquiry to: Stephen E. Kaufman
Thomas Pulling, Furman L. Templeton, Jr.

Royal Business Funds Corp.
250 Park Ave.
New York, New York 10017
Direct Inquiry to:
Stephens M. Pollan, President

SB Electronics Investment Corp.
120 Broadway
Lynbrook, New York 11563

SBIC of New York, Inc.
64 Wall St.
New York, New York 10005

Direct Inquiry to:
Edward J. Bermingham, Jr.
William D. Nolte, Jr.

Schroder Capital Corp.
1 State St.
New York, New York 10006

Direct Inquiry to: Robert C. Heim

Securus Corp. of America
32 East 57th St.
New York, New York 10022

S.I. Industries, Inc.
122 East 42nd St.
New York, New York 10017
Direct Inquiry to: Henry M. Margolis

Southern Tier Capital Corp.
219 Broadway
Monticello, New York 12701

The Sperry & Hutchinson Co.
330 Madison Ave.
New York, New York 10017
Direct Inquiry to: Joseph J. Dans

Sprout Capital Group
140 Broadway
New York, New York 10006
Direct Inquiry to: Lee Halfpenny

Struthers Capital Corp.
630 Fifth Ave.
New York, New York 10020
Direct Inquiry to: Victor Harz

Talcott Ventures Co.
1290 Avenue of the Americas
New York, New York 10019
Direct Inquiry to:
Martin Eisenstadt, Vice President

Tappan Zee SBI Corp.
120 North Main St.
New York, New York 10020

Technical Investors Management Corp.
600 Third Ave.
New York, New York 10022
Direct Inquiry to:
Raymond Frankel, President

Ungersmith Securities Co.
1 Battery Park Plaza
New York, New York 10004
Direct Inquiry to:
William T. Hack, New York
Francis D. Everett, New York
Richard L. Shanaman, West Coast

Union SBIC, Inc.
420 Lexington Ave., Room 2720
New York, New York 10017

C.E. Unterberg, Towbin Co.
61 Broadway
New York, New York 10016
Direct Inquiry to:
Belmont Towbin, Thomas Unterberg

Venrock Associates
30 Rockefeller Plaza
New York, New York 10020
Direct Inquiry to:
Cornelius H. Borman, Jr.

Basic Capital Corp.
40 West 37th St.
New York, New York 10018

Becker Technological Associates
60 Broad St.
New York, New York 10004
Direct Inquiry to: T.V. Schiavoni

Beneficial Capital Corp.
10 East 40th St.
New York, New York 10016

Bessemer Securities Corp.
245 Park Ave.
New York, New York 10017
Direct Inquiry to: Robert H. Buescher

Bonan Equity Corp.
60 East 42nd St., Suite 2530
New York, New York 10017

15 Broad Street Resources Corp.
15 Broad St.
New York, New York 10015

BT Capital Corp.
600 Third Ave.
New York, New York 10017

Burham & Co.
60 Broad St.
New York, New York 10004
Direct Inquiry to:
Robert E. Linton, Partner

Business Development Services, Inc.
570 Lexington Ave.
New York, New York 10022
Direct Inquiry to: T. Walton Storm

Canaveral Capital Corp.
26 Court St., Suite 902
Brooklyn, New York 11201

Capital For Future, Inc.
635 Madison Ave.
New York, New York 10022

Capital Formation MESBIC, Inc.
5 Beekman St.
New York, New York 10038

Carr Management Co.
445 Park Ave.
New York, New York 10022
Direct Inquiry to:
Dayton T. Carr, General Partner

CEDC MESBIC, Inc.
106 Main St.
Hemstead, New York 11550

The Central New York SBIC
738 Erie Blvd., East
Syracuse, New York 13210

Central New York SBIC
1231 Main St.
Buffalo, New York
Branch of: Central New York SIBC
Syracuse, New York

Central New York SBIC
56 North Main St.
Rochester, New York 14604
Branch of: Central New York SBIC
Syracuse, New York

Central New York SBIC
1056 Broadway
Albany, New York 12204
Branch of: Central New York SBIC
Syracuse, New York

Charter New York Corp.
1 Wall St.
New York, New York 10015
Direct Inquiry to:
Allen R. Freedman, Asst. Vice President

Chase Manhattan Capital Corp.
1 Chase Manhattan Plaza
New York, New York 10005
Direct Inquiry to:
Louis L. Allen, President
Arthur Wages, Vice President
Robert D. Hubbard, Vice President
Albert Dykes, Assistant Treasurer

CMNY Capital Co., Inc.
77 Water St.
New York, New York 10005

Coalition SBIC Corp.
55 Fifth Ave.
New York, New York 10003

Communications Fund, Inc.
1271 Avenue of the Americas
New York, New York 10020

Conresco Corp.
444 Madison Ave., Room 3701
New York, New York 10022
Branch of: Conresco Corp.
Stamford, Connecticut

Creative Capital Corp.
99 Park Ave.
New York, New York 10016

Direct Inquiry to:
Milton D. Stewart, John F. Alteio

Cressant Management International, Inc.
61 Rockledge Road, North
Bronxville, New York 10708

Direct Inquiry to:
Walter A. Forbes, President
Garretson W. Chinn, Vice President

Criterion Capital Corp.
10 Fiske Place
Mount Vernon, New York 10550

Cumberland Ventures
200 Park Ave.
New York, New York 10017

Direct Inquiry to:
A. Michael Victory, Kurt L. Kamm

Diebold Venture Capital Corp.
430 Park Ave.
New York, New York 10022

Direct Inquiry to:
George Pratt, Dominic Fitzpatrick

Diversified Technology, Inc.
30 Rockefeller Plaza
New York, New York 10020

Direct Inquiry to:
Gilbert Kennedy

Empire SBI Corp.
57 West 57th St.
New York, New York 10019

Equilease Capital Corp.
387 Park Ave., South
New York, New York 10016

Equity Life Comm. Enterprise Corp.
1285 Avenue of the Americas
New York, New York 10019

Equitable SBI Corp.
350 Fifth Ave.
New York, New York 10001

ESIC Capital, Inc.
420 Lexington Ave.
New York, New York 10006

Excelsior Capital Corp.
115 Broadway
New York, New York 10006

Fairfield Equity Corp.
295 Madison Ave.
New York, New York 10017

The First Connecticut SBIC
60 Wall St.
New York, New York 10005
Branch of: First Connecticut SBIC
Bridgeport, Connecticut

FNCB Capital Corp.
399 Park Ave.
New York, New York 10022
Direct Inquiry:
Russel L. Carson, Assistant Vice President
David G. Arscott, Assistant Vice President
Ronald Millican, Assistant Treasurer
William J. Reilly, Assistant Treasurer

Forum Equity Corp.
214 Mercer St.
New York, New York 10012

The Franklin Corp.
1400 Broadway
New York, New York 10018
Direct Inquiry to: Martin L. Orland

Geiger and Fialkov
15 Columbus Circle
New York, New York 10020
Direct Inquiry to: Herman Fialkov

Globe Capital Corp.
Room 1, N.W. One Old Country Road
Long Island, New York 11514

Great Eastern SBI Corp.
230 Park Ave.
New York, New York 10017

Halle & Stieglitz, Inc.
52 Wall St.
New York, New York 10005
Direct Inquiry to:
Robert A.W. Brauns, Martin B. Freedland

The Hamilton Capital Fund
660 Madison Ave.
New York, New York 10021

White, Weld & Co.
20 Broad St.
New York, New York 10005
Direct Inquiry to:
George G. Montgomery, Jr.

J. H. Whitney & Co.
630 Fifth Ave.
New York, New York 10020
Direct Inquiry to:
Benno C. Schmidt, Managing Partner

Winfield Capital Corp.
237 Mamaroneck Ave.
White Plains, New York 10605

Cameron Brown Capital Corp.
4300 Six Forks Road
Raleigh, North Carolina 27609

Delta Capital, Inc.
320 South Tryon St.
Charlotte, North Carolina 28202
Branch of: Delta Capital, Inc.
Slidell, Louisiana

Equilease Capital Corp.
2915 Providence Road
Charlotte, North Carolina 28211
Branch of: Equilease Capital Corp.
New York, New York

NORTH CAROLINA

First Carolina Capital Corp.
48 Patton Ave.
Asheville, North Carolina 28801

Forsyth County Investment Corp.
4th and Liberty Sts., Pepper Building
Winston-Salem, North Carolina 27101

Hanover SBIC
5710 Old Concord Road
Charlotte, North Carolina 28201

Lowcountry Investment Corp.
West Vernon Ave.
Kinston, North Carolina 28501
Branch of: Lowcountry Investment Corp.
Charleston Hts., South Carolina

Northwestern Capital Corp.
924 B St.
North Wilkesboro, North Carolina 28659

OHIO

Capital Funds Corp.
127 Public Square
Cleveland, Ohio 44114

Columbus Capital Corp.
100 East Broad St., 3rd Fl.
Columbus, Ohio 43215

Commerce Capital Corp.
11 West Sharon Road
Cincinnati, Ohio 45246
Branch of: Commerce Capital Corp.
Milwaukee, Wisconsin

Community Venture Corporation
88 East Broad St.
Columbus, Ohio 43215

Dycap, Inc.
88 East Broad St., Suite 2020
Columbus, Ohio 43215

Gries Investment Co.
922 National City Bank Building
Cleveland, Ohio 44114

OKLAHOMA

Alliance Business Investment Co.
500 McFarlin Building
Tulsa, Oklahoma 74103

American Indian Investment Opportunity, Inc.
555 Constitution St.
Norman, Oklahoma 73069

Bartlesville Investment Corp.
827 Madison Blvd., Box 548
Bartlesville, Oklahoma 74003

Capital, Inc.
City National Bank Tower 2106
Oklahoma City, Oklahoma 73118

First Growth Capital, Inc.
5900 Mosteller Drive
Oklahoma City, Oklahoma 73112

Henderson Funding Corp.
2410 Plaza Prom-Sheperd Mall
Oklahoma City, Oklahoma 73107

Investment Capital, Inc.
1301 Main St.
Duncan, Oklahoma 73533

Oklahoma Small Business Investment
P.O. Box 18897
Oklahoma City, Oklahoma 73118

Phillips Industrial Finance Corp.
Frank Phillips Building, Suite 112
Bartlesville, Oklahoma 74004

OREGON

Capital Investors Corp.
610 S.W. Alder, Suite 1221
Portland, Oregon 97205
Branch of: Capital Investors Corp.
Missoula, Montana

Cascade Capital Corp.
421 S.W. Sixth Ave.
Portland, Oregon 97204

Endeavour Capital Corp.
310 N.E. Oregon St.
Portland, Oregon 97214

Northern Pacific Capital Corp.
2300 S.W. First Ave.
Portland, Oregon 97201

Oregon SBIC
661 High St., N.E.
Salem, Oregon 97301

Trans-Pac Capital Fund, Inc.
1900 S.W. First Ave., Harrison Square
Portland, Oregon 97201

PENNSYLVANIA

Alliance Enterprise Corp.
1616 Walnut St., Suite 802
Philadelphia, Pennsylvania 19103

Capital Corporation of America
1521 Walnut St.
Philadelphia, Pennsylvania 19102

Delaware Valley SBIC
Wolf Building, Market Square
Chester, Pennsylvania 19013

Delaware Valley SBIC
1604 Walnut St.
Philadelphia, Pennsylvania 19103
Branch of: Delaware Valley SBIC
Chester, Pennsylvania

Equilease Capital Corp.
1 Parkway Center, Room 213
Pittsburgh, Pennsylvania 15220
Branch of: Equilease Capital Corp.
New York, New York

Fidelity America SBIC
112 South 21st St.
Philadelphia, Pennsylvania 19103

Frankford Grocery SBIC, Inc.
G St. & Erie Ave.
Philadelphia, Pennsylvania 19124

Greater Philadelphia Venture Capital Corp.
225 South 15th St., Room 920
Philadelphia, Pennsylvania 19102

Osher Capital Corp.
Twnsp. Line Road and Washington Lane
Wyncote, Pennsylvania 19095

Pennsylvania Crowth Investment Corp.
Two Gateway Center
Pittsburgh, Pennsylvania 15222

Philadelphia Venture, Inc.
1712 Locust St.
Philadelphia, Pennsylvania 19103

Progress Venture Capital Corp.
1501 North Broad St.
Philadelphia, Pennsylvania 16146

Sharon SBIC
385 Shenango Ave.
Sharon, Pennsylvania 16146

Sun Capital Corp.
55 Sub. Sav. Center Old Clairton
Pittsburgh, Pennsylvania 15236

PUERTO RICO

Credito Investment Co., Inc.
Recinto Sur & San Justo Sts.
San Juan, Puerto Rico

Popular Investment Co.
Banco Popular Center Building
Hato Rey, Puerto Rico 00909

RHODE ISLAND

Industrial Capital Corp.
111 Westminster St.
Providence, Rhode Island 02903

Direct Inquiry to:
Kenneth Boudrie, Peter Deaux

Narragansett Capital Corp.
40 Westminster St.
Providence, Rhode Island 02903

Narragansett Capital Corp.
10 Dorrance St.
Providence, Rhode Island 02903

Direct Inquiry to:
Arthur D. Little, Vice President
Robert L. Cummings, Treasurer

SOUTH CAROLINA

Charleston Capital Corp.
134 Meeting St., P.O. Box 696
Charleston, South Carolina 29402

Falcon Capital Corp.
89 Broad St.
Charleston, South Carolina 29402

Floco Investment Co.
Highway 52 North
Scranton, South Carolina 29560

Lowcountry Investment Corp.
4444 Daley St.
Charleston Hts., South Carolina 29405

SOUTH DAKOTA

Berkshire Capital, Inc.
405 Eighth Ave., N.W.
Aberdeen, South Dakota 57401

TENNESSEE

C&C Capital Corp.
2643 Kingston Pike
Knoxville, Tennessee 37919

Financial Resources, Inc.
1909 Sterick Building
Memphis, Tennessee 38103

First Cumberland Investments, Inc.
19 South Jefferson, Room 204
Cookeville, Tennessee 38501

The Thirds SBIC
Third National Bank Building, 3rd Fl.
Nashville, Tennessee 37219

TEXAS

Admiral Investment Co., Inc.
5806 S.W. Freeway
Houston, Texas 77027

Alliance Business Investment Co.
4850 One Shell Plaza
Houston, Texas 77002

Branch of: Alliance Business Investment Co.
Tulsa, Oklahoma

Brittany Capital Corp.
1600 Republic Band Building
Dallas, Texas 75201

Business Capital Corp.
5646 Milton St.
Dallas, Texas 75206

Capital Marketing Corp.
9001 Ambassador Row
Dallas, Texas 75247

Central Texas SBI Corp.
P.O. Box 829
Waco, Texas 76703

CSC Capital Corp.
750 Hartford Building
Dallas, Texas 75201

Equilease Capital Corp.
6400 Westpark, Suite 238
Houston, Texas 77027

Branch of: Equilease Capital Corp.
New York, New York

First Business Investment Corp.
Davis Building, Room 1320
Dallas, Texas 75202

First Capital Corp.
821 Washington
Waco, Texas 76703

First Dallas Capital Corp.
1401 Elm St.
Dallas, Texas 75202

First Texas Investment Co.
506 Nebraska St., P.O. Box 495
South Houston, Texas 77587

First Texas Investment Co.
120 Jefferson St., P.O. Box 341
Sulphur Springs, Texas 75482
Branch of: First Texas Investment Co.
South Houston, Texas

Gulf Investment Corp.
115 East Van Buren St.
Harlingen, Texas 78530

MESBIC Fin. Corporation of Dallas
7220 N. Stemmons Freeway-1008
Dallas, Texas 75222

Permian Basic Capital Corp.
P.O. Box 1599
Midland, Texas 79701

Republic SBIC
Republic National Bank Building
Dallas, Texas 75201

Rice Investment Co.
3200 Produce Row
Houston, Texas 77023

The SBIC of Houston
640 West Building
Houston, Texas 77002

South Texas SBIC
P.O. Box 1698
Victoria, Texas 77901

Texas Capital Corp.
2424 Houston National Gas Building
Houston, Texas 77002

Trammell Crow Investment Co.
2720 Stemmons Freeway
Dallas, Texas 75207

United Business Capital, Inc.
1102 South Broadway
La Porte, Texas 77571

West Central Corp.
P.O. Box 412
Dumas, Texas 79029

Western Capital Corp.
2123 First National Bank Tower
Dallas, Texas 75202

UTAH

Intermountain Capital Corporation of Utah
10 West Third South
Salt Lake City, Utah 84101

Utah Capital Corporation
3600 Market St.
Granger, Utah 84119

VERMONT

Vermont Investment Capital, Inc.
Route 14
South Royalton, Vermont 05068

VIRGINIA

Capitol Area Investors, Inc.
3701 Chain Bridge Rd.
Fairfax, Virginia 22030

Capitol Area Investors, Inc.
4023 Chain Bridge Rd.
Fairfax, Virginia 22030
Branch of: Capitol Area Investors, Inc.
Fairfax, Virginia

Investment Funds, Inc.
P.O. Box 12300
Norfolk, Virginia 23502

Metropolitan Capital Corp.
2550 Huntington Ave.
Alexandria, Virginia 22303

Reba Investment Co.
147 Granby St., Room 338
Norfolk, Virginia 23510

SBI Corp. of Norfolk
1216 Granby St.
Norfolk, Virginia 23510

Tidewater Industrial Capital Corp.
Un. Virginia Bank Building, Suite 820
Norfolk, Virginia 23510

Tidewater Industrial Capital Corp.
Un. Virginia Bank Building Suite 820
Norfolk, Virginia 23510

Tidewater Industrial Capital Corp.
T.F. 22 Mil. Cir. Shop Center
Norfolk, Virginia 23502
Branch of:
Tidewater Industrial Capital Corp.
Norfolk, Virginia

Virginia Capital Corp.
808 West United Virginia Bank Building
Richmond, Virginia 23219

WASHINGTON

Capital Investors Corp.
Old National Bank Building, Suite 1005
Spokane, Washington 99201
Branch of: Capital Investors Corp.
Missoula, Montana

Capital Investors Corp.
Dexter Horton Building, Suite 1041
Seattle, Washington 99201

Branch of: Capital Investors Corp.
Missoula, Montana

Cascade Capital Corp.
1100 Second Ave.
Seattle, Washington 98101
Branch of: Cascade Capital Corp.
Portland, Oregon

Futura Capital Corp.
4218 Rooseveltway N.E.
Seattle, Washington 98105

MESBIC of Washington, Inc.
330 Rainier Ave., South
Seattle, Washington 98144

Model Capital Corp.
1106 East Spring St.
Seattle, Washington 98122

N.W. Capital Investment Corp.
1111 West Spruce, P.O. Box 2425
Yakima, Washington 98902

Northwest Business Investment Corp.
929 West Sprague Ave.
Spokane, Washington 99204

SBIC of America
1910 Fairview Ave. East
Seattle, Washington 98102

Washington Capital Corp.
1417 Fourth Ave., P.O. Box 1770
Seattle, Washington 98111

WISCONSIN

Capital Investments, Inc.
735 North Fifth St.
Milwaukee, Wisconsin 53203

Commerce Capital Corp.
6001 North 91st St.
Milwaukee, Wisconsin 53225

Commerce Capital Corp.
106 West Second St.
Ashland, Wisconsin 53225
Branch of: Commerce Capital Corp.
Milwaukee, Wisconsin

Commerce Capital Corp.
9 South Main
Fond Du Lac, Wisconsin 54937
Branch of: Commerce Capital Corp.
Milwaukee, Wisconsin

First Wisconsin Investment Corp.
735 North Water St.
Milwaukee, Wisconsin 53202

Growth SBIC
811 East Wisconsin Ave., Suite 940
Milwaukee, Wisconsin 53202

Moramerica Capital Corp.
123 West Washington Ave.
Madison, Wisconsin 53701
Branch of: Moramerica Capital Corp.
Cedar Rapids, Iowa

Rec. Business Opportunities Corp.
316 Fifth St.
Racine, Wisconsin 53403

Wisconsin Capital Corp.
840 North Third St.
ilwaukee, Wisconsin 53203

PERIODICALS OF VALUE TO SMALL BUSINESS

Administrative Science Quarterly
Cornell University
Graduate School of Business
  and Public Administration
Ithaca, New York

Advanced Management Journal
Society for Advancement of Management
135 West 50th Street
New York, New York 10020

American Legion Magazine
P.O. Box 1954
Indianapolis, Indiana 46206

The Banker's Magazine
89 Beach Street
Boston, Massachusetts 02111

British Journal of Marketing
Business Publication Ltd.
Mercury House
Waterloo Road
London SE1 England

Business Horizons
Indiana University
Graduate School of Business
Bloomington, Indiana 47401

Business Topics
Michigan State University
Bureau of Business
  and Economic Research
East Lansing, Michigan 48823

Business Week
330 West 42nd Street
New York, New York 10036

California Management Review
University of California
Berkeley, California 94720

Chemical and Engineering News
American Chemical Society
1155 16th Street
Washington, D.C. 20030

Doubleday & Company, Inc.
Garden City
New York 11530

Dun's
Dun and Bradstreet Publications Corp.
466 Lexington Avenue
New York, New York 10017

Electronics News
Fairchild Publications, Inc.
7 East 12th Street
New York, New York 10003

Financial Analysts' Journal
Financial Analysts Federation
219 East 42nd Street
New York, New York 10016

Forbes
Forbes, Incorporated
60 Fifth Avenue
New York, New York 10011

Fortune
Rockerfeller Center
New York, New York 10020

Harvard Business Review
Harvard University
Graduate School of Business Administration
Soldiers Field Road
Boston, Massachusetts 02163

Industrial Management
Industrial Management Society
2217 Tribune Tower
Chicago, Illinois 60611

Industrial Marketing
Crain Communications, Inc.
740 Rush Street
Chicago, Illinois 60611

Industrial Research
Industrial Research Boulevard
Beverly Shores, Indiana 46301

Industrial Research and Development
UNIDO
United Nations Publications
New York, New York 10017

International Management
330 West 42nd Street
New York, New York 10036

Journal of Advertising Research
Advertising Research Foundation
3 East 54th Street
New York, New York 10022

Journal of Applied Psychology
American Psychological Association, Inc.
1200 17th Street, Northwest
Washington, D.C. 20036

Journal of Business
Seton Hall University
School of Business Administration
Bureau of Business Research
East Orange, New Jersey 07079

Journal of Business
University of Chicago
5801 Ellis Avenue
Chicago, Illinois 60637

Journal of Marketing
American Marketing Association
230 Michigan Avenue
Chicago, Illinois 60601

Journal of Small Business Management
Editor: Stanley J. Kloc, Jr.
Bureau of Business Research
West Virginia University
Morgantown, West Virginia 20506

Lybrand Journal
c/o Lybrand, Ross and Montgomery
Bowling Green, New York 10004

Machine Design
Penton Publishing Company
Penton Building
Cleveland, Ohio 44113

Management Accounting
National Association of Accountants
919 Third Avenue
New York, New York 10022

Management of Personnel Quarterly
University of Michigan
Bureau of Industrial Relations
Graduate School of Business Administration
Ann Arbor, Michigan 48104

Management Review
American Management Association, Inc.
135 West 50th Street
New York, New York 10020

Management Today
Management Publications Ltd.
Gellow House
5 Winsley Street
London W1N 8AP England

Marketing Communications
Decker Communications, Inc.
106 Boston Post Road
Waterford, Connecticut 06385

Marquette Business Review
Marquette University
College of Business Administration
Milwaukee, Wisconsin 53233

The MBA
MBA Communications
555 Madison Avenue
New York, New York 10022

MSU Business Topics
Michigan State University
Bureau of Business and Economic Research
East Lansing, Michigan 48823

Monthly Review of Management and Research
formerly: *Management Research*
Box 4
Dolton, Illinois 60419

Nations Business
Chamber of Commerce of U.S.
1615 First Street, Northwest
Washington, D.C. 20006

Personnel Psychology
Box 6565, College Station
Durham, North Carolina 27708

Research and Development Management
108 Crowley Road
Oxford, OX4, IJF England

Research Management
Box 51
Red Bank, New Jersey 07701

Sales Management
Sales Management, Inc.
630 Third Avenue
New York, New York 10017

Taxes
Commerce Clearing House, Inc.
4025 West Pederson Avenue
Chicago, Illinois 60646

THINK
IBM Corporation
Armonk, New York 10504

Wall Street Journal
30 Broad Street
New York, New York 10004

BOOKS ABOUT SMALL BUSINESS

American Small Businessman
by John M. Bunzel
Alfred A. Knopf, Inc.
New York, 1962 $5.95

Business Policy in Growing Firms
by Robert B. Buchele
Intext/Chandler Publishing Co.
New York, 1967

The Enterprising Man
by O. Collins and D. Moore
University of Michigan
Ann Arbor, Michigan, 1964

Entrepreneurial Dimensions of Management
by G. Jay Anyon
Livingston Publishing Co.
18 Hampstead Circle
Wynnewood, Pennsylvania 19096

Entrepreneurship & Venture Management
by J. Mancuso and C.M. Baumback
Prentice-Hall
Englewood Cliffs, New Jersey, 1974

The Future of Small Business
by Edward D. Hollander
Frederick A. Praeger, Inc.
New York, 1967 $15.00

*How to Organize and Operate
 A Small Business*
by P.C. Kelley, K. Lawyer and
 C.M. Baumback
Prentice-Hall
Englewood Cliffs, New Jersey

How to Run A Small Business
by J.K. Lasser
McGraw-Hill Book Co.
New York, 1963

The Organization Makers
by O. Collins and D. Moore
University of Michigan
Ann Arbor, Michigan, 1970

The R & D Game
MIT Press
Cambridge, Massachusetts, 1969

*Management of Small Enterprises
 Cases and Readings*
by William Rotch
University Press of Virginia
Charlottesville, Virginia, 1967 $6.00

Managing the Small Business
by L.L. Steinmetz, John B. Kline and
 D.P. Stegall
Richard D. Irwin, Inc.
Homewood, Illinois, 1968

Managing the Smaller Company
Ed. by Russell Banks
Management Association, Inc.
New York, 1969 $13.00

Small Business Management
by H.N. Broom and J.G. Longenecker
South-Western Publishing Co.
Burlingame, California, 1971

Small Business Management
by Hosmer, Tucker and Cooper
Richard D. Irwin, Inc.
Homewood, Illinois, 1966

Small Business Management: A Casebook
by Windsor A. Hosmer
Richard D. Irwin, Inc.
Homewood, Illinois, 1966 $14.60

*Starting and Succeeding
in Your Own Small Business*
by Louis L. Allen
Grosset & Dunlap
New York, 1968

Technology and Change
by D. Schon
Dell
New York, 1967

SOURCES OF HELP AND VENTURE CAPITAL LISTS

1. The SBA publishes on a quarterly basis a complete listing of SBIC's — (Small Business Investment Companies) listing name, address, and size category. Write:

    SBA Investments Divisions
    1441 2nd Street, N.W.
    Washington, D.C. 20416

2. Stanley M. Rubel publishes "A Guide to Venture Capital" — plus newsletters and other material on venture capital (SBIC/Venture Capital monthly newsletter). Write:

    Capital Publishing Company
    10 South LaSalle Street
    Chicago, Illinois 60603

3. A 134 page study by the Management Department at Boston College entitled "Venture Capital — A guidebook for New Enterprise" published in March, 1972 is especially good for Northeastern U.S.A. businesses. Write:

    U.S. Government Printing Office
    Re: Committee Print No. 75-292
    Washington, D.C. 20416

4. Leroy W. Sinclair publishes a hard cover book entitled "Venture Capital" which offers details on all venture capital firms across the U.S.A. In addition, he also publishes a spiral bound book entitled "The Business Plan" which is a practical guide on "how to" write a business plan. Write:

    Technimetrics, Inc.
    919 3rd Avenue
    New York, New York 10022

5. Donald Dible has written a 300 page how-to-do-it book entitled "Up your own organization." Especially helpful are the appendixes which offer reviews of many forms of help including excellent bibliographies and venture capital lists. Write:

    The Entrepreneur Press
    Mission Station Drawer 2759T
    Santa Clara, California 95051

6. Mr. John Komives, The director of the not-for-profit Center for Venture Management offers many valuable services for entrepreneurs, not the least of which is a bibliography of articles and a monthly newsletter. Write:

    Center for Venture Management
    811 East Wisconsin Avenue
    Milwaukee, Wisconsin 53202

7. D & B produces an excellent booklet of 50 pages which identifies many of the good articles and books on small business. This is especially valuable for specific industries as reports on special opportunities are numerous. Write:

    Dun & Bradstreet
    99 Church Street
    New York, New York 10007

8. List of Publications and Committee memberships of the select committee on Small Business of the House of Representatives. Write:

    Government Printing Office
    No. 87-842 Pamphlet
    Washington, D.C.
    77th-92d Congress, Jan. 1973

9. Pamphlets & books published by the U.S. Government agencies, such as the Small Business Administration, should be purchased from the Superintendent of Docu-

ments, Government Printing Office, Washington, D.C. 20401
Free SBA pamphlets (and they are numerous) may be obtained from the SBA, Washington, D.C. 20416 or from local SBA branch office.

10. Journal of small business is published quarterly for the National Council for Small Business Management Development. This is an academic journal which publishes excellent articles for small businessmen. Write:

    Lillian B. Dreyer
    Secretary
    NCSBMD
    351 California Street
    San Francisco, California 94104

11. A newsletter is published for small businessmen which offers items of interest to all small businessmen and especially relevant to small business and the government. Write:

    Newsletter Small Business
    1225 19th Street, N.W.
    Washington, D.C. 20036

12. A group of New England small businessmen have formed an organization for their mutual benefit known as Smaller Business Association of New England (SBANE). They hold seminars and offer a newsletter. Write:

    Mr. Lew Shattuck
    SBANE
    69 Hickory Drive
    Waltham, Massachusetts 02154

13. An excellent monthly brochure is offered free by the Bank of America entitled "The Small Business Reporter." Write:

    Small Business Reporter
    Bank of America
    Box 37000
    San Francisco, California 94137

14. I have written an easy-reader entitled "Fun 'n' Guts" — the entrepreneur's philosophy (Addison-Wesley 1973). A combination of telling it like it is, humor, and advice along with a good bibliography is available in this book.

15. Besides the low cost pamphlets offered by the Small Business Administration, they also offer numerous services and seminars. Inquire about Service Case of Retired Executives (SCORE) and the student team of the Small Business Institute (SBI). Each may be of value to you.

16. An interesting book of readings is available in a book "Managing the Dynamic Small Firm" by Lawrence A. Klatt. Write:

    Wadsworth Publishing Co., Inc.
    Belmont
    California 94002

17. A book of readings in paperback form is available:

    Mancuso and Baumback
    Entrepreneurship & Venture
    Management
    Prentice-Hall
    Englewood Cliffs, New Jersey

PROFESSIONAL ASSOCIATIONS OF VALUE TO SMALL BUSINESS

American Management Association
135 W. 50th Street
New York, N.Y. 10020

Association of Management Consultants
811 E. Wisconsin Avenue
Milwaukee, Wisconsin 53202

Presidents Association
135 West 50th Street
New York, N.Y. 10020

Society of Professional Management Consultants
Western Regional Group
III Sutter St., Suite 620
San Francisco, CA 94104
